EVERYMAN, I will go with thee,
and be thy guide,
In thy most need to go by thy side.

SIR THOMAS WYATT

Born in 1503 at Allington Castle, Kent. Courtier, poet and musician. Travelled in France and Italy. Died 6 October 1542.

HENRY HOWARD: EARL OF SURREY

Born c. 1517. Soldier and poet. Earl marshal of England. Executed by Henry VIII in 1547.

SIR PHILIP SIDNEY

Born 30 November 1554 at Penshurst, Kent. Soldier, poet and diplomat. Died of battle wounds at Arnheim, 17 October 1586.

SIR WALTER RALEGH

Born in 1552 at Budleigh, Devonshire. Soldier, courtier, explorer and writer. Executed after long imprisonment, 29 October 1618.

SIR JOHN DAVIES

Born April 1569 at Tisbury, Wiltshire. Lawyer and poet. Called to the Bar in 1595. Lord chief justice. Died 8 December 1626.

Silver Poets of the Sixteenth Century

Edited with an introduction by
Gerald Bullett

Dent: London and Melbourne
EVERYMAN'S LIBRARY

No 985 Hardback ISBN 0 460 00985 0
No 1985 Paperback ISBN 0 460 11985 0

INTRODUCTION

THE word *silver* in the title of this volume, where *minor* might perhaps have been expected, marks its editor's resolve to distinguish without disparagement and to admire without extravagance. It acknowledges a distinction between this particular assembly of poets and their more eminent contemporaries and near-contemporaries, while implying that the least we can claim for them is a silver-tongued eloquence. Nor will the judicious reader complain if he finds, as he will, some golden verses here. The critical survey of English poetry is an activity different in principle, as well as in kind, from marking examination-papers; and the terms *major* and *minor*, convenient enough for broad generalizing judgments, are apt to become meaningless or worse when applied to particular poems. More than one 'minor' poet lives for us today by virtue of a poem or poems which no sensible person, if the question were put, could regard as anything but 'major' in quality. Take Ralegh's seven lines:

> Even such is Time, that takes in trust
> Our youth, our joys, our all we have,
> And pays us but with earth and dust:
> Who in the dark and silent grave,
> When we have wandered all our ways,
> Shuts up the story of our days.
> But from this earth, this grave, this dust,
> My God shall raise me up, I trust.

Or Sidney's, perennially fresh, exquisitely artificial, *My true love hath my heart*. Or the best of Wyatt's lyrics. Or that early anonymous carol, *I sing of a maiden*. Minor poems, or major? The question makes no sense. These things are poetry, and leave nothing more to be said.

Our *Silver Poets of the Sixteenth Century* range in time from the virtual beginning of the English Renaissance to beyond the end of the Elizabethan Age. Renaissance, rebirth, of what? The question cannot be answered in a word. We may use the term, if we will, to denote that process of transition between the mediaeval and the modern world which gave tumult and colour to the sixteenth century, that intellectual and spiritual ferment by which the mind of man, first on the shores of the Mediterranean and much later in this island, was quickened and enlarged with a sense of old freedoms regained and of new regions to be explored. But we have to be on our guard against two assumptions that are apt to creep in unobserved: (i) that a process is necessarily a progress, or in other words that the 'mind of the age' (that useful, simplifying fiction) moves consistently in one direction, and (ii) that history consists of a number of quite distinct 'periods' or 'ages' laid end to end. The life of man is not logical: it is merely chronological. And the infinitely complex continuum we call history knows nothing of our arbitrary time-divisions. We cannot say that the Middle Ages came to an end in any particular year: some of the institutions we most cherish today are mediaeval in origin. Nor can we with any precision determine when and how the Renaissance began. That it was not unconnected with the excited rediscovery of ancient classical literature (Greek and Latin) is evident; but the revival of learning was a symptom rather than a cause, for there was certainly an inward urge independent of any external stimulus, an urge to escape into rebirth from the cramping safety, the too narrow confinement, of that mediaeval certitude which had a final answer to every question. And an inward urge can hardly be dated. History, moreover, rebuts all attempts to impose on it the pattern of a consistent ideological development: it insists on confronting us with paradox and contradiction. The classical revival itself, so conspicuous a feature of the Renaissance, produced consequences which in Italy, the country of its origin, actually retarded that movement. Petrarch, who lived and died in fourteenth-century Italy, on the one hand gave immense impetus to the study of the ancients, and on the other, by writing the *Canzoniere*, provided an inspiration and a model for Englishmen a century after his death. He lived to deprecate the fame of his Italian poems ('my juvenile sillinesses' he called them): a passion for antiquity, a veneration for the virtues and graces of ancient Rome, made him look with contempt on vernacular writing, and both he and his friend Boccaccio wrote what they mistakenly considered to be their more important works in Latin. Their example was widely followed: with the result that Italian as a literary medium fell into long neglect. The greatest of all Italian poets, who died when Petrarch was a boy of seventeen, had taken the opposite view; for Dante, extolling the literary potentialities of the mother-tongue, 'which we receive from our nurses and use without rules', looked eagerly for that revival of vernacular literature which Petrarch, the brilliant 'precursor of the Renaissance', did his best to prevent. A parallel though smaller example of indiscriminate classicism is found in England, a century later, when Gabriel Harvey, fighting a forlorn battle against the very grain of the English language, succeeded for a while in infecting English poets, Sidney among them, with a disdain of rhyme and an ambition to write English verse in classical quantitative metres.

The two earliest of our silver poets, though the gap is not a wide one, lived and died before the other three were born. They need neither trumpeting nor apology: their poems will speak for them. But we can hardly arrive at a just estimate of their comparative worth unless we remember, while reading them, that they had not, as later poets had, the example of such work as Spenser's and Shakespeare's to guide them. Their task was, not to carry on the tradition of English verse, for (except in the lighter, singing measures) that had been virtually lost, but to create a new one. Chaucer had been dead for well over a century, his language had undergone much change, the key to his scansion (the occasional sounding of an ordinarily mute *e*) had almost certainly been lost, when Sir Thomas Wyatt (1503–42) and his friend Henry Howard Earl of Surrey (1517–47) began writing the 'songes and sonettes' which Tottel first printed in 1557. These two, both in bulk and quality, were the chief contributors to that famous miscellany. For this reason, and because they did much by their example to 'reform the English numbers', they are linked together in the literary histories; but their work differs much in style and poetic value. Both men were courtiers, employed in various diplomatic missions by Henry VIII. Wyatt, the son of a man who by long and faithful service had endeared himself to Henry VII both before and after his accession, had a firmer footing at court than the young Earl of Surrey, who at the age of twenty-nine was executed on a trumped-up charge a few days before the death of his bloodthirsty sovereign. Wyatt visited France

and Italy and was influenced by the literatures of those coun-
tries, as Chaucer had been long before him. He introduced
into English an adaptation of the Petrarchan sonnet and wrote
three satires in *terza rima*. From Italy, too, he borrowed
conventional themes and 'conceits', of love unrequited and love
forsaken; and his verse, like Surrey's, includes many direct
translations. But many of his lyrics, some of which are ex-
quisite in their blend of haunting cadence with a direct personal
utterance, show clearly and unmistakably the influence of the
English song-books then so much in fashion. His best work
was done in these native measures.

In reading Wyatt's sonnets it is necessary to remember that
he was doing something new and difficult, laying the first
foundations of a form which it was left for later poets to perfect.
Similar allowances have to be made, throughout, for Surrey.
Surrey is rightly honoured for having, in Gilfillan's phrase
(1856), 'improved the mechanical part of our poetry'. He did
much to restore to use the five-foot iambic line of Chaucer.
But, though the lyrics *Give place, ye lovers* and *When raging love*
are outstandingly successful in their kind, Surrey's distinctive
and historically most important achievement was the invention
of English blank verse, the medium in which Shakespeare's
and Milton's masterpieces were to be written. The judgment
that held Surrey to be a better poet than Wyatt has been reversed
in recent times, but no one would wish to belittle this great
service. Frederick Morgan Padelford, in 1920, produced for
the University of Washington a scholarly edition of Surrey's
works, with full textual notes and an elaborate critical apparatus
for which we must be grateful. But Padelford's remarks on
prosody should be received with great caution. 'Surrey's
outstanding contribution to prosody,' he writes, 'was his
insistence that metrical accent should be coincident with
sentence stress and word accent. . . . The prevailing disregard
of this principle may be illustrated by the following sonnet,
one of Wyatt's earlier compositions:

'The lónge love thát in mý thought dóeth hárbár
And ín my hért doeth képe his résidénce
I'nto my fáce preséth with bólde preténce
And thérein cámpeth spréding hís banér.
Shé that me lérneth tó love ánd suffré,
And wílles that mý trust ánd lustes négligénce

> Be ráyn'd by réason, sháme and réverénce,
> With hís hardíness táketh displeasúre.
> Where with áll untó the hértes forrést he fléith,
> Léving his énterpríse with páyn and crý,
> And thér him hídeth ánd not ápperéth.
> Whát may I dó where mý maistér feréth,
> Bút in the féld with hím to lýve and dýe?
> For goóde is thé liff énding faithfullý.'

Now no one contends that Wyatt's sonnets are models of correct versification; admittedly his rhythms are often awkward and blundering. But Padelford's pointing of this particular specimen is quite fantastically wrong. That a learned editor who is also a specialist in the period can go so wide of the mark in reading a piece of verse suggests that some remarks on the subject will not be out of place here. For it will be fatal to his enjoyment if a reader approaches Wyatt and Surrey with the resolve to scan them by a mechanical syllabic rule that is alien to the best English practice. Let us try a more reasonable style of pointing:

> The lóng lóve that ín my thóught doeth hárbar
> And ín my hért doeth képe his résidénce
> I'nto my fáce préseth with bóld preténce
> And thérein cámpeth spréding his banér.
> Shé that mé lérneth to lóve and súffre,
> And wílles that my trúst and lústès néglighénce
> Be ráyn'd by réason, sháme and réverénce,
> With hís hardíness táketh displeasúre.
> Wherewitháll únto the hértes fórrest he fléith,
> Léving his énterpríse with páyn and crý,
> And thére hím hídeth and nót appéreth.
> Whát may I dó whére my maíster féreth,
> Bút in the féld with hím to lýve and dýe?
> For góode is the liff énding faithfullý.

Each line has, after all, five stresses. They are not all of equal weight; they do not (nor need they) fall on alternate syllables; the eighth line with its French accentuations (as in *hardiesse* and *déplaisir*) is awkward to English ears; and the versification in general is loose. But at least the thing is readable, whereas 'The lóng | love thát | in mý | thought dóeth | harbár' is mere gibberish, which Wyatt could not have intended. The same editor, remarking that in Surrey 'the accent occasionally falls on the weak syllable of a noun', quotes as examples:

> Whose moist poisón dissolved hath my hate

> The wylde forést, the clothed holtes with grene

But I am confident that Surrey did not intend us to say 'poisón' or 'forést'; and in fact the lines present no metrical difficulty at all. True, each has an irregular second foot, trochee instead of iamb. But why not? This talk of trochees and iambs belongs rather to the grammar books than to literary criticism. The jargon of (a classical and so largely irrelevant) prosody is no necessary part of an English poet's equipment, useful though it may be to a student of Greek verse. Many of the loveliest of English lyrics have been written by men to whom such terms were Greek in more senses than one.

The *t'rum-t'tum* method of scanning blank verse is derived presumably from the fundamental error that syllable-counting is the basis of English metre. It is a method that can be applied with consistent success only to the worst examples. Surrey may or may not have aimed at strict uniformity of stress in his blank verse, but mercifully he did not achieve it. Either inexpertness or native sense—most probably an alternation of the two—saved him from the flat pedestrianism of the lesser Elizabethans and their undistinguished successors. He can be clumsy, and he can be metrically tedious; but he escapes the consistent tedium which must result, in English, from an exact undeviating identity between the basic metre and the actual tempo: in the best blank verse one is conscious or half-conscious of both, and much of the energy of the verse is generated by the tension between them, or, in other words, by the variety of the patterns woven on a basic metrical structure. Try *t'rum-t'túm* on Milton,

> Of mán's first dís-obédience, ánd the frúit

and the result is merely ludicrous: whereas let the stresses fall where they naturally incline (the fourth falls on silence, at the comma),

> Of mán's first disobédience,' and the frúit

and you have a line boldly irregular but none the less firmly based on the five-foot structure, a structure which becomes plain enough in the sequence as a whole:

> Of man's first disobedience and the fruit
> Of that forbidden tree whose mortal taste
> Brought death into the world, and all our woe,
> With loss of Eden, till one greater man
> Restore us, and regain the blissful seat,
> Sing, heavenly Muse!

Both Wyatt and Surrey aimed, with some success, at restoring to English numbers not so much 'correctness' as fluency, a fluency frustrated by the metrical disorder prevailing in their day. But like all true poets they wrote by ear, not by counting syllables. If the opposite could be maintained of them, one would be forced to conclude that their arithmetic was surprisingly weak. The pursuit of 'correctness' for its own sake was the error of a later century, the eighteenth: the least fruitful period in our poetic history. Sixteenth-century poets pursued —and overtook—a livelier quarry.

The first published of Wyatt's poems were published (in Tottel) fifteen years after his death and possibly twenty years or more after the best of them were written. It is to be supposed that during that interval the reform of numbers had proceeded to a point at which smoothness of versification was regarded as a prime essential. Some such idea is certainly behind the numerous alterations which Tottel or his editor is now known to have made in the poems of Wyatt. It is probable, but not certain, that he did the same with Surrey's: of Wyatt's the assertion can be made with confidence. Tottel was the only printed source of Wyatt's poems till 1816, when G. F. Nott produced an edition from two British Museum manuscripts, bringing to light many hitherto unprinted poems, noting borrowings from foreign literatures, and presenting Wyatt's prose as well as his verse. About a hundred years later Miss A. K. Foxwell's minute examination of the manuscript sources established an overwhelming probability that the poet himself had no hand or voice in Tottel's alterations, and led to the publication, in 1913, of her edition of Wyatt's poems, in which, for the first time, the true texts were made generally available. They often differ significantly from Tottel's versions, and the smoothness of Tottel is seen to have been got at the expense of Wyatt's very individual, and often moving, musical cadences. Wyatt was an accomplished musician as well as a poet: he knew the value, as Tottel's editor did not, of an unexpected pause, a surprising change of beat. When Tottel came upon:

> They flee from me that sometime did me seek,
> With naked foot stalking in my chamber:
> I have seen them gentle, tame, and meek,
> That now are wild and do not remember
> That some time they put themselves in danger
> To take bread at my hand . . .

he exclaimed, we may suppose, 'This will never do!'—and proceeded to 'correct' these lines to read as follows:

> They flee from me that sometime did me seek,
> With naked foot stalking within my chamber:
> Once have I seen them gentle, tame, and meek,
> That now are wild and do not once remember
> That sometime they have put themselves in danger
> To take bread at my hand . . .

So, by writing 'within' for 'in' he hurries past 'stalking' instead of lingering on it as Wyatt does; by writing 'Once have I seen' instead of '*I* have seen' he turns a stark forceful line into something conventional and tame; the fourth line he weakens by the insertion of 'once', which steals the emphasis from the potent word 'remember'; and by adding a syllable to the fifth line he disastrously shifts the balance of stresses and makes us say 'sometime they' instead of the more simple, natural, double-stressed 'some time'. It is the imposition of a mechanical prosodic theory upon a poem that has, in its true form, a subtle cadence and a beautiful directness. This does not imply that we shall find no metrical uncertainty or clumsiness in Wyatt: he did not master the new trick all at once. But we should beware lest in making allowance for faults we miss the metrical subtlety that occurs in his maturer work. Let us be still and listen, and if we have ears we shall easily detect the difference between them.

Our five poets here collected have many qualities in common, but each has his individual style, his personal difference. Each

sings, or sighs, in his own voice. All were men of breeding
and culture. All were courtiers (unless we except John Davies,
the lawyer) and men of the world as well as poets, and in this
as in much else they are typical of their times. Three of them
died young, three were tried for their lives on charges of treason,
and two (unoffending victims of malice) were beheaded. Here
again they present a true picture of their brilliant, violent,
highminded, treacherous times. As for the content of their
work, until we reach Ralegh we have little but variations,
though in different styles, upon the same everlasting theme:
romantic love. The spirit of the Renaissance, its idealization
of the beloved (despite or because of her almost monotonous
'cruelty', often a synonym, it would seem, for 'virtue'), its
frank delight in bodily beauty, its blend of soaring fancy with
touches of homely realism, and through all its eager ingenuous
curiosity: these are clearly visible in the 'exuberant specimens
of genuine though young poetry' (to borrow a phrase of Leigh
Hunt's) to be found in Wyatt, in Surrey, and pre-eminently in
Sidney. Sir Philip Sidney (1554–86) stands out for us, as for
his contemporaries, as the very embodiment of grace, courtesy,
and heroic virtue, the fine flower and noble ornament of his
time. He was scholar, poet, man of action, and man of
letters. He wrote a spirited, scholarly, engaging defence of
poetry, in answer to the Puritan pamphleteer Stephen Gosson,
and a long prose romance, which his sister the Countess of
Pembroke had the courage and good sense to preserve, against
his express wish. He died at Arnhem, after days of suffering,
at the age of thirty-two, from wounds received in battle against
the Spaniards at Zutphen, 'a tournament' (says his most recent
biographer, Miss Mona Wilson) 'as splendid and as futile as
Chevy Chace'. Historians have nothing to urge against him
except the crime of being in love (at a distance) with another
man's wife, Penelope Rich (née Devereux), whom he first met
when she was twelve and he some eight years older. She is sup-
posed to have been the Stella of the sonnets, just as Elizabeth
Fitzgerald is supposed to have been the fair Geraldine celebrated
in Surrey's poems. Wyatt's heartless or faithless ladies, on the
other hand, remain anonymous, though Anne Boleyn has been
suggested as a radiant possibility. These are trivial conjec-
tures and have no bearing on the much-debated question of
the poets' sincerity. All three were influenced by a literary

convention, and borrowed something, both of theme and style, from earlier poets: Wyatt and Surrey from the Italian sonneteers, and Sidney (it cannot be doubted) from Wyatt and Surrey: which latter fact, by the way, gives the measure of our debt to that gallant pair of pioneers. But all were normal men, exceptional only in their genius; they can hardly have needed to pretend to an acquaintance with the agonies and ecstasies of romantic love; and whether their Stellas and Geraldines—or for that matter Petrarch's Laura either—were fictitious or actual persons is of no consequence at all, since they had evidently a very real existence in the imagination of the poets. The only sincerity we are legitimately concerned with is poetic sincerity: by that, not by factual truth, a poem stands or falls.

Among the admiring friends of Sidney, and as generously admired by him, were Spenser and Ralegh: Spenser the 'poets' poet', in his day second only to Shakespeare himself, and Ralegh the adventurer, a complex personality rich in contradictions, a man proud, vain, arrogant, self-willed, magnanimous, and at the last, with gain not loss of dignity, humble. The poetry of Sir Walter Ralegh (1552–1618) takes us, as his story does, into a twilit region shot through with the steel-cold gleam of impending tragedy. I call him proud because so his contemporaries called him: his 'naeve of pride' when he was the Queen's first favourite made him 'the best-hated man in England'. And I call him humble because only a man who had learnt true humility, the first and last virtue, could have written *Even such is Time* and the superb invocation to Death: 'O eloquent, just, and mighty Death! whom none could advise, thou hast persuaded; what none hath dared, thou hast done; and whom all the world hath flattered, thou only hast cast out of the world and despised. Thou hast drawn together all the far-stretched greatness, all the pride, cruelty, and ambition of man, and covered it all over with these two narrow words: *Hic iacet*.' Pride, cruelty, and ambition: he had his share of all three, unless for the word cruelty we substitute the more negative ruthlessness. He was also a man of vision and high courage, fine clothes and fine flourishes, elaborate courtesy and unbridled ostentation. In fine he was outstandingly Elizabethan. For we have to remember that the Elizabethan Age, both in England and on the continent of Europe, is at once a splendid and a squalid story. In manners and morals it is infinitely remote from us: as remote as the Chinese Empire of Kubla Khan. Its great adventurers, combining a ferocious virility with habits which to us seem oddly effeminate, paraded in gorgeous colours and adorned themselves with rings and jewels. Its mob was regaled with a substantial diet of bear-baitings, executions, floggings, and the harrying of religious dissenters both Catholic and Protestant. And its literature is unsurpassed. Ralegh was a great captain of men. He wrote poetry because poetry was in him to write, left his manuscripts for anyone to find or lose, and withheld his name from the anthologies; for to set up as a poet, the example of Spenser notwithstanding, was no part of a gentleman's ambition. Yet, typical Elizabethan though he was, his best things, perhaps the only ones we can be quite sure are his, have an accent, a spirit, a probing melancholy wit, that seems sometimes to anticipate the mind of a later generation: a something seldom found (outside Shakespeare) in the poetry of his time. There are indeed a few conventional pieces, which any competent Elizabethan poet might have written; but

> Give me my scallop-shell of quiet,
> My staff of faith to walk upon,
> My scrip of joy, immortal diet,
> My bottle of salvation . . .

such poems as this, with its noble blend of passion and curious artifice, bear Ralegh's own mark, the mark of a man and a visionary who did everything with a fine flourish and in almost everything failed magnificently. He was condemned to death on a transparently false charge, reprieved at the last moment, and executed without further trial fifteen years later, some twelve of which had been spent in prison. He had ample time in which to savour the vanity of human ambition.

If Ralegh is typical of his age, so too is the lawyer-poet Sir John Davies (1569–1626), not to be confused with his namesake of Hereford, also a poet. Since the publication in 1943 of Dr Tillyard's *The Elizabethan World Picture* the notion that the Elizabethans lived in a new mental world, completely or almost completely emancipated from mediaevalism, has been untenable. The best minds of the age, for all their delight in decorative word-play and airy speculation, were profoundly thoughtful, their thought being dominated by the two related ideas of *order* and *degree*. Any rebellion against authority was in their eyes a deadly sin, and the proposition that all men are in any sense equal would have seemed to them the craziest heresy: the 16th-century *Book of Common Prayer*, still in use, is crystal clear on the point. The mediaeval conception of a rigidly ordered universe not only survived into Elizabethan times but was taken utterly for granted, as we take for granted the rotation of the earth. It was expressed in three figures or metaphors: as a chain of being linking all created things to the Creator (hence degree), as a cosmic dance (hence order, harmony), and as a set of correspondences between higher and lower, outer and inner, macrocosm and microcosm. Tillyard's view is that we have been too much dazzled by the brilliant externals of the age to give due attention to its seriousness, its concern with theology, its unquestioning fidelity to ideas which to us may seem ingenuous or arbitrary or merely fantastic but to the Elizabethans were familiar and even commonplace. In the light of this new knowledge the didacticism of Sir John Davies is seen to be as truly and typically Elizabethan as are the entrancingly ingenious love-lyrics of the period. Of his two, his only two, substantial poems *Orchestra* is the richer in poetical quality, though its theme, the universal dance, is less attractive and important to us of today than to the poet's contemporaries. His hundred and thirty-six stanzas carry lightly their burden of allegorical symbolism and rise at moments to an almost Spenserian grace of expression:

> For of her barons brave and ladies fair,
> Who had they been elsewhere most fair had been,
> Many an incomparable lovely pair
> With hand in hand were interlinked seen,
> Making fair honour to their sovereign Queen:
> Forward they paced and did their pace apply
> To a most sweet and solemn melody.

So subtle and curious was the measure, the poet continues, that Penelope

> Ween'd she beheld the true proportion plain
> Of her own web, weaved and unweaved again,
> But that her art was somewhat less, she thought,
> And on a mere ignoble subject wrought.

For here, like to the silkworm's industry,
Beauty itself out of itself did weave
So rare a work and of such subtilty
As did all eyes entangle and deceive
And in all minds a strange impression leave:
In this sweet labyrinth did Cupid stray,
And never had the power to pass away.

As when the Indians, neighbours of the morning,
In honour of the cheerful rising sun
With pearl and painted plumes themselves adorning
A solemn stately measure have begun,
The god, well-pleas'd with that fair honour done,
Sheds forth his beams, and doth their faces kiss
With that immortal glorious face of his.

A. B. Grosart, for whose devoted service as an editor of
sixteenth-century poets we must always be grateful, however
sharply we may dissent from some of his judgments, praises
Orchestra indeed, but is misled into accepting it at its face-value
as a 'mere sport of wit', and reserves his highest commendations
for *Nosce Teipsum*, which in a series of admirably smooth and
charmingly sententious quatrains sets out to establish the im-
mortality of the soul. As a clergyman Grosart may be sup-
posed to have had a special sympathy with the poet's intention
and to have been fondly uncritical of his ingenuous logic. He
values the poem first of all for the 'deep and original thinking'
in which a reader today will find it deficient, and has severe
things to say of those who would 'exalt the workmanship at
the expense of the material'. But if by 'material' he means the
abstract argument, and if he implies that the proof of any poem
is in the detachable 'thought' of it and not in the poetry, he
surely misconceives the situation. *Nosce Teipsum* is a piece of
attractively clear and luminous argumentation in verse. It is
not, and could not be, continuously or predominantly poetical,
and frankly accepting that limitation it has the great virtue of
not pretending to be more or other than it is. Clarity and
directness, aptness of imagery and grace of diction and move-
ment, these and the spirit of benign self-persuasion that informs
the whole are what we enjoy in the reading. It matters nothing

to our enjoyment whether or not the poet convincingly expounds a proof of immortality: it is enough that he is exposing to us, whether he knows it or not, his gentle, eager, curious, learned, childlike, half mediaeval and wholly Elizabethan mind.

GERALD BULLETT

CONTENTS

SIR THOMAS WYATT

1503–42

THOUGH Wyatt is a poet who shows to best advantage in selection, for the sake of completeness our edition includes all the songs and lyrical pieces that are unquestionably and distinctively his, as well as the three satires in *terza rima* and one of the two *canzoni* translated from Petrarch. For the rest, his verse includes some sonnets, rondeaux, and epigrams, of which only the best examples are given here, two or three short moralizing pieces of small intrinsic interest, and metrical paraphrases of a number of Psalms, which present-day readers will certainly prefer to read in the Bible versions. Wyatt's poems were not printed during his life. They were first brought together, from Tottel (1557) and subsequently discovered manuscript sources, by G. F. Nott in 1816. Of the three manuscripts among which they are distributed not one can with certainty be claimed as the author's final text, though there are strong reasons for preferring at least two of them to Tottel, and one (the D manuscript) contains sixty-three pieces not found either in Tottel or elsewhere. The textual problems implicit in this situation were exhaustively studied by A. K. Foxwell, whose invaluable two volumes (1913), edited 'from the MSS and early editions', remain the last word in the scholarship of the subject; but for a full critical appraisal see Tillyard, *The Poetry of Sir Thomas Wyatt*. In the present volume the spelling (except of archaic words) has been modernized and the poems repunctuated throughout, both for ease in reading and to remove that air of 'quaintness' which, since it did not exist for Wyatt's contemporaries, does not truly belong to them. In other respects our text represents its editor's choice between Nott and Foxwell, with a strong leaning towards the latter. Tottel's elaborate titling of the individual poems has been discarded, both for Wyatt and for Surrey, who follows him in this volume.

TEN SONNETS

i

WHOSO list to hunt, I know where is an hind,
But as for me, helas, I may no more.
The vain travail hath wearied me so sore,
I am of them that farthest come behind.
Yet may I by no means my wearied mind
Draw from the Deer, but as she fleeth afore
Fainting I follow.   I leave off therefore,
Since in a net I seek to hold the wind.
Who list her hunt (I put him out of doubt)
As well as I may spend his time in vain.
And graven with diamonds in letters plain
There is written her fair neck round about:
'Noli me tangere, for Caesar's I am,
And wild for to hold, though I seem tame.'

ii

EACH man me telleth I change most my devise,
And on my faith me think it good reason
To change propose like after the season,
For in every case to keep still one guise
Is meet for them that would be taken wise,
And I am not of such manner condition
But treated after a diverse fashion,
And thereupon my diverseness doth rise.
But you that blame this diverseness most,
Change you no more, but still after one rate
Treat ye me well, and keep ye in the same state,
And while with me doth dwell this wearied ghost
My word nor I shall not be variable,
But always one your own both firm and stable.

iii

FAREWELL, Love, and all thy laws for ever:
Thy baited hooks shall tangle me no more.
Senec and Plato call me from thy lore,
To perfect wealth my wit for to endeavour.
In blind error when I did persever,
Thy sharp repulse, that pricketh aye so sore,
Hath taught me to set in trifles no store,

And scape forth, since liberty is liever.
Therefore farewell, go trouble younger hearts,
And in me claim no more authority:
With idle youth go use thy property,
And thereon spend thy many brittle darts.
For, hitherto tho' I 've lost all my time,
Me lusteth no longer rotten boughs to climb.

iv

I FIND no peace, and all my war is done,
I fear, and hope.   I burn, and freeze like ice.
I fly above the wind, yet can I not arise.
And naught I have, and all the world I season.
That loseth nor locketh holdeth me in prison,
And holdeth me not, yet can I scape nowise:
Nor letteth me live nor die at my devise,
And yet of death it giveth me occasion.
Without eyen I see, and without tongue I plain:
I desire to perish, and yet I ask health:
I love another, and thus I hate myself:
I feed me in sorrow, and laugh at all my pain.
Likewise displeaseth me both death and life,
And my delight is causer of this strife.

v

MY galley chargèd with forgetfulness
Through sharp seas in winter nights doth pass
Tween rock and rock, and eke mine enemy alas,
That is my lord, steereth with cruelness.
And every oar a thought in readiness,
As though that death were light in such a case,
An endless wind doth tear the sail apace
Of forced sighs and trusty fearfulness.
A rain of tears, a cloud of dark disdain,
Hath done the wearied cords great hinderaunce:
Wreathed with error and eke with ignoraunce
The stars be hid that led me to this pain.
Drowned is reason that should me comfort,
And I remain despairing of the port.

vi

I ABIDE and abide and better abide,
And after the old proverb the happy day.
And ever my lady to me doth say
'Let me alone and I will provide.'

I abide and abide and tarry the tide,
And with abiding speed well ye may.
Thus do I abide, I wot, alway,
Nother obtaining nor yet denied.
Ay me, this long abiding
Seemeth to me as who sayeth
A prolonging of a dying death
Or a refusing of a desired thing.
Much were it better for to be plain
Than to say abide, and yet shall not obtain.

vii

DIVERS doth use (as I have heard and know),
When that to change their ladies do begin,
To moan and wail and never for to lynn,
Hoping thereby to pease their painful woe.
And some there be that when it chanceth so
That women change, and hate where love hath been,
They call them false and think with words to win
The hearts of them that otherwhere doth go.
But as for me, though that by chance indeed
Change hath outworn the favour that I had,
I will not wail, lament, nor yet be sad,
Nor call her false that falsely did me feed:
But let it pass, and think it is of kind
That often change doth please a woman's mind.

viii

MY love took scorn my service to retain:
Wherein me thought she usèd cruelty,
Since with good will I lost my liberty
To follow her which causeth all my pain.
Might never care cause me for to refrain,
But only this, which is extremity,
Giving me naught, alas, nor to agree
That, as I was, her man I might remain.
But since that thus ye list to order me
That would have been your servant true and fast,
Displease thee not my doting days be past
And with my loss to live I must agree.
For, as there is a certain time to rage,
So is there time such madness to assuage.

ix

TO rail or jest, ye know I use it not,
Though that such cause sometime in folks I find:
And though to change ye list to set your mind,
Love it who list, in faith I like it not.
And if ye were to me as ye are not,
I would be loth to see you so unkind.
But since your faith must needs be so, be kind:
Though I hate it, I pray you love it not.
Things of great weight I never thought to crave:
Thus is but small: of right deny it not.
Your feigning ways, as yet forget them not,
But like reward let other lovers have:
That is to say, for service true and fast,
Too long delays, and changing at the last.

x

YOU that in love find luck and abundaunce,
And live in lust and joyful jollity,
Arise, for shame, do away your sluggardy!
Arise, I say, do May some observaunce!
Let me in bed lie dreaming in mischaunce,
Let me remember the haps most unhappy
That me betide in May most commonly,
As one whom Love list little to advaunce.
Sephan said true that my nativity
Mischaunced was with the ruler of the May:
He guess'd, I prove, of that the verity.
In May my wealth and eke my life, I say,
Have stond so oft in such perplexity.
Rejoice! Let me dream of your felicity.

FIVE EPIGRAMS

i

WHO hath heard of such cruelty before?
That when my plaint remembered her my woe
That caused it, she, cruel more and more,
Wished each stitch, as she did sit and sew,
Had prickt mine heart for to increase my sore.
And, as I think, she thought it had been so,
For as she thought 'This is his heart indeed'
She pricked hard, and made herself to bleed.

FIVE EPIGRAMS

ii

THE enemy of life, decayer of all kind,
That with his cold withers away the green,
This other night me in my bed did find
And offered me to rid my fever clean.
And I did grant, so did despair me blind.
He drew his bow with arrow sharp and keen
And strake the place where love had hit before,
And drave the first dart deeper more and more.

iii

THE fruit of all the service that I serve
Despair doth reap, such hapless hap have I.
But though he have no power to make me swerve,
Yet, by the fire, for cold I feel I die.
In paradise, for hunger still I sterve;
And, in the flood, for thirst to death I dry.
So Tantalus am I, and in worse pain
Amids my help, and helpless doth remain.

iv

LUX my fair falcon, and your fellows all,
How well pleasant it were, your liberty!
Ye not forsake me that fair might ye befall;
But they that sometime liked my company,
Like lice away from dead bodies they crawl.
Lo, what a proof in light adversity!
But ye my birds, I swear by all your bells,
Ye be my friends, so be but few else.

v

[WRITTEN IN PRISON]

SIGHS are my food, drink are my tears;
Clinking of fetters such music would crave;
Stink and close air away my life wears;
Innocency is all the hope I have.
Rain, wind or weather I judge by mine ears.
Malice assaulted that righteousness should have.
Sure I am, Brian, this wound shall heal again,
But yet, alas, the scar shall still remain.

RONDEAU

HELP me to seek, for I lost it there,
And if that ye have found it, ye that be here,
And seek to convey it secretly,
Handle it soft and treat it tenderly,
Or else it will plain and then appear:

But rather restore it mannerly,
Since that I do ask it thus honestly:
For to lose it, it sitteth me too near.
　　　　Help me to seek.

Alas, and is there no remedy?
But have I thus lost it wilfully?
Iwis it was a thing all too dear
To be bestowed and wist not where:
It was my heart, I pray you heartily
　　　　Help me to seek.

TRANSLATION

From the Italian of Petrarch

MINE old dear enemy, my froward master,
Afore that Queen I caused to be acited
Which holdeth the divine part of nature:
That like as gold in fire he mought be tried.
Charged with dolour, there I me presented
With horrible fear, as one that greatly dreadeth
A wrongful death, and justice alway seeketh.

And thus I said: 'Once my left foot, madame,
When I was young I set within his reign:
Whereby other than fiery burning flame
I never felt, but many a grievous pain.
Torment I suff'red, anger and disdain,
That mine oppressed patience was past
And I mine own life hated at the last.

'Thus hitherto have I my time passed
In pain and smart.   What ways profitable,
How many pleasant days, have me escaped
In serving this false liar so deceivable?
What wit have words so prest and forcible
That may contain my great mishappiness
And just complaints of his ungentleness?

'O small honey, much aloes and gall,
In bitterness have my blind life tasted:
His false sweetness, that turneth as a ball
With the amorous dance, have made me traced:
And where I had my thought and mind ataced
From all earthly frailness and vain pleasur,
He took me from rest and set me in error.

'He hath made me regard God much less than ought,
And to myself to take right little heed,
And for a woman have I set at nought
All other thoughts, in this only to speed:
And he was only counsellor of this deed,
Always whetting my youthely desire
On the cruel whetstone tempered with fire.

'But alas, where now had I ever wit,
Or else any other gift given me of nature,
That sooner shall change my wearied sprite
Than the obstinate will that is my ruler?
So robbed my liberty with displeasure
This wicked traitor whom I thus accuse
That bitter life have turned me in pleasant use.

'He hath chased me through divers regions,
Through desert woods and sharp high mountains,
Through froward people and strait pressions,
Through rocky seas, over hills and plains,
With weary travail and labourous pains:
Always in trouble and in tediousness,
In all error and dangerous distress.

'But neither he nor she my other foe
For all my flight did ever me forsake,
That though timely death hath been too slow
That as yet it hath me not overtake,
The heavenly goodness of pity do it slake.
And note this, his cruel extreme tyranny,
That feedeth him with my care and misery.

'Since I was his, hour rested I never,
Nor look for to do, and eke the waky nights
The banisht sleep may no wise recover.
By deceit and by force, over my sprites
He is ruler, and since [then] never bell strikes
Where I am that I hear not, my plaints to renew.
And he himself he knoweth that I say is true.

'For never worms have an old stock eaten
As he my heart, where he is alway resident
And doth the same with death daily threaten.
Thence come the tears and the bitter torment,
The sighs, the words, and eke the languishment
That annoy both me and peradventure other:
Judge thou, that knowest the one and the other.'

Mine adversary, with grievous reproof,
Thus he began: 'Hear, Lady, the other part,
That the plain truth, from which he draweth aloof,
This unkind man shall show ere that I part.
In young age I took him from that art
That selleth words and maketh a clattering knight
And of my wealth I gave him the delight.

'Now, shameth he not on me for to complain
That held him evermore in pleasant game
From his desire that might have been his pain.
Yet only thereby I brought him to some frame,
Which, as wretchedness, he doth greatly blame;
And toward honour I quickened his wit,
Where else as a daskard he might have sit.

'He knoweth that Atrides, that made Troy fret,
And Hannibal, to Rome so troublous,
Whom Homer honoured, Achilles that great,
And the African, Scipion the famous,
And many other by much virtue glorious
Whose fame and honour did bring them above,
I did let fall in base dishonest love.

'And unto him, though he no dele worthy were,
I chose right the best of many a million,
That under the moon was never her peer
Of wisdom, womanhood, and discretion:
And of my grace I gave her such a façon
And eke such a way I taught her for to teach,
That never base thought his heart might have reach.

'Evermore thus to content his maistress,
That was his only frame of honesty,
I stirred him still toward gentleness
And caused him to regard fidelity.
Patience I taught him in adversity.
Such virtues he learned in my great school:
Whereof he repenteth, the ignorant fool.

'These were the deceits and the bitter gall
That I have used, the torment and the anger,
Sweeter than for to enjoy any other in all.
Of right good seed ill fruit I gather,
And so hath he that the unkind doth further.
I nourish a serpent under my wing,
And of his nature now 'ginneth he to sting.

'And, for to tell at last my great service,
From thousand dishonesties I have him drawn,
That by my means in no manner of wise
Never vile pleasure him hath overthrown.
Where in his deed shame hath him always gnawen,
Doubting report that should come to her ear,
Whom now he accuseth he wonted to fere.

'Whatsoever he hath of any honest custom,
Of her and me holdeth he every whit;
But lo, there was never nightly phantom
So far in error as he is from his wit.
To plain on us, he striveth with the bit
Which may rule him and do him pleasure and pain
And in one hour make all his grief remain.

'But one thing there is above all other:
I gave him winges wherewith for to fly
To honour and fame, and if he would farther
Than mortal things, above the starry sky:
Considering the pleasure that an eye
Might give in earth by reason of his love,
What should that be that lasteth still above?

'And he the same himself hath said ere this,
But now forgotten is both that and I
That gave her him, his only wealth and bliss.'
And at this word, with deadly shright and cry,
'Thou gave her me,' quoth I, 'but by and by
Thou took her straight from me, that woe worth thee!'
'Not I,' quoth he, 'but price, that is well worth.'

At last both, each for himself, concluded,
I trembling, but he with small reverence:
'Lo, thus as we have now each other accusèd,
Dear Lady, we wait only thy sentence.'
She, smiling: 'After this said audience
It liketh me,' quoth she, 'to have heard your question.
But longer time doth ask resolution.'

SONGS AND LYRICS

I

MY lute awake! perform the last
Labour that thou and I shall waste,
And end that I have now begun:
And when this song is sung and past,
My lute be still, for I have done.

As to be heard where ear is none,
As lead to grave in marble stone,
My song may pierce her heart as soon.
Should we then sigh, or sing, or moan?
No, no, my lute, for I have done.

The rocks do not so cruelly
Repulse the waves continually
As she my suit and affection,
So that I am past remedy;
Whereby my lute and I have done.

Proud of the spoil that thou hast got
Of simple hearts through Love's shot,
By whom, unkind, thou hast them won:
Think not he hath his bow forgot,
Although my lute and I have done.

Vengeance shall fall on thy disdain
That makest but game on earnest pain:
Think not alone under the sun
Unquit to cause thy lovers plain;
Although my lute and I have done.

May chance thee lie withered and old
In winter nights that are so cold,
Plaining in vain unto the moon;
Thy wishes then dare not be told:
Care then who list, for I have done.

And then may chance thee to repent
The time that thou hast lost and spent
To cause thy lovers sigh and swoon:
Then shalt thou know beauty but lent,
And wish and want as I have done.

Now cease, my lute: this is the last
Labour that thou and I shall waste,
And ended is that we begun.
Now is this song both sung and past:
My lute be still, for I have done.

II

ONCE, as methought, Fortune me kiss'd,
And bade me ask what I thought best,
And I should have it as me list,
Therewith to set my heart in rest.

I askèd but my dear heart
To have for evermore mine own;
Then at an end were all my smart;
Then should I need no more to moan.

Yet, for all that, a stormy blast
Had overturn'd this goodly day,
And Fortune seemèd at the last
That to her promise she said nay.

But like as one out of despair
To sudden hope revivèd I:
Now Fortune showeth herself so fair
That I content me wonderly.

My most desire my hand may reach,
My will is alway at my hand;
Me need not long for to beseech
Her that hath power me to command.

What earthly thing more can I crave?
What would I wish more at my will?
Nothing on earth more would I have?
Save that I have, to have it still.

For Fortune now hath kept her promess,
In granting me my most desire:
Of my sufferance I have redress,
And I content me with my hire.

III

THEY flee from me that sometime did me seek,
With naked foot stalking in my chamber:
I have seen them gentle, tame, and meek,
That now are wild, and do not remember
That some time they put themselves in danger
To take bread at my hand; and now they range
Busily seeking with a continual change.

Thankt be Fortune, it hath been otherwise
Twenty times better; but once in speciall,
In thin array, after a pleasant guise,
When her loose gown from her shoulders did fall,
And she me caught in her arms long and small,
Therewith all sweetly did me kiss,
And softly said, 'Dear heart, how like you this?'

It was no dream; I lay broad waking:
But all is turn'd, thorough my gentleness,
Into a strange fashion of forsaking;
And I have leave to go of her goodness;
And she also to use new-fangleness.
But since that I so kindely am servèd,
I would fain know what *she* hath deservèd.

IV

THE restful place, reviver of my smart,
The labours' salve, increasing my sorrow;
The body's ease, and troubler of my heart;
Quieter of mind, and my unquiet foe;
Forgetter of pain, remembering my woe;
The place of sleep wherein I do but wake,
Besprent with tears, my bed, I thee forsake!

The frosty snows may not redress my heat,
Nor yet no heat abate my fervent cold.
I know nothing to ease my pains mete:
Each cure causeth increase by twenty fold,
Renewing cares upon my sorrows old.
Such overthwart effects they do me make
Besprent with tears my bed for to forsake.

Yet helpeth it not: I find no better ease
In bed or out: this most causeth my pain.
Where I do seek how best that I may please,
My lost labour, alas, is all in vain.
Yet that I gave I cannot call again;
No place from me my grief away can take;
Wherefore with tears, my bed, I thee forsake.

V

RESOUND my voice, ye woods that hear me plain,
Both hills and vales causing reflexion;
And rivers eke, record ye of my pain,
Which have ye oft forced by compassion,
As judges, lo, to hear my exclamation:
Among whom pity, I find, doth remain;
Where I it seek, alas, there is disdain.

Oft ye rivers, to hear my woeful sound
Have stopt your course, and plainly to express
Many a tear by moisture of the ground
The earth hath wept to hear my heaviness,
Which causeless to suffer without redress,
The hugy oaks have roarèd in the wind,
Each thing methought complaining in their kind.

Why then, alas, doth not she on me rue?
Or is her heart so hard that no pity
May in it sink, my joy for to renew?
O tigress heart, who hath so cloakèd thee,
That art so cruel, covered with beauty?
There is no grace from thee that may proceed,
But, as reward, death for to be my meed?

VI

WHERE shall I have at mine own will,
Tears to complain? where shall I fet
Such sighs that I may sigh my fill,
And then again my plaints repeat?

For, though my plaint shall have none end,
My tears cannot suffice my woe:
To moan my harm have I no friend;
For Fortune's friend is mishap's foe.

Comfort, God wot, else ha ve I none
But in the wind to waste my wordes;
Nought moveth you my deadly moan,
But all you turn it into bordes.

I speak not now to move your heart,
That you should rue upon my pain.
The sentence given may not revert:
I know such labour were but vain.

But since that I for you, my dear,
Have lost that thing that was my best,
A right small loss it must appear
To lose these words and all the rest.

But though they sparkle in the wind,
Yet shall they show your falsèd faith,
Which is return'd unto his kind:
For like to like, the proverb saith.

Fortune and you did me avance;
Methought I swam and could not drown,
Happiest of all: but my mischance
Did lift me up to throw me down.

And you with your own cruelness
Did set your foot upon my neck,
Me and my welfare to oppress,
Without offence your heart to wreak.

Where are your pleasant words, alas?
Where is your faith, your steadfastness?
There is no more, but all doth pass,
And I am left all comfortless.

But for because it doth you grieve,
And also me my wretched life,
Have here my truth: shall nought relieve,
But death alone, my very strife.

Therefore farewell, my life my death,
My gain my loss, my salve my sore!
Farewell also with you my breath!
For I am gone for evermore.

VII

FAREWELL the reign of cruelty:
Though that with pain my liberty
Dear have I bought, and wofully
Finish'd my fearful tragedy.

Of force I must forsake pleasure;
A good cause just, since I endure
Thereby my woe, which be ye sure
Shall therewith go me to recure.

I fare as one escap'd that fleeth,
Glad he is gone yet still feareth,
Spied to be caught and so dreadeth
That he for nought his pain leseth.

In joyful pain rejoice my heart,
Thus to sustain of each a part.
Let not this song from thee astart,
Welcome among my pleasant smart.

VIII

IT may be good, like it who list,
But I do doubt who can me blame:
For oft assured, yet have I mist,
And now again I fear the same.
The windy words, the eyes' quaint game,
Of sudden change make me aghast:
For dread to fall I stand not fast.

Alas, I tread an endless maze
That seek to accord two contraries:
And hope still and nothing hase
Imprison'd in liberties.
As one unheard, and still that cries;
Always thirsty, and yet nothing I taste;
For dread to fall I stand not fast.

Assured, I doubt I be not sure;
And should I trust to such surety,
That oft hath put the proof in ure
And never hath found it trusty?
Nay, sir, in faith it were great folly.
And yet my life thus I do waste:
For dread to fall I stand not fast.

IX

IN faith I wot not what to say,
Thy chances been so wonderous,
Thou Fortune, with thy divers play
That makest the joyful dolorous,
And eke the same right joyous.
Yet though thy chain hath me enwrapt,
Spite of thy hap, hap hath well hapt.

Though thou me set for a wonder,
And seekest thy change to do me pain,
Men's mind yet may thou not order;
And honesty, an it remain,
Shall shine for all thy cloudy rain.
In vain thou seekst to have trapp'd:
Spite of thy hap, hap hath well hapt.

In hindering thou didst me further,
And made a gap where was a stile:
Cruel wills been oft put under;
Weening to lour, thou didst smile.
Lord, how thyself thou didst beguile,
That in thy cares wouldst me have lapp'd!
But spite of hap, hap hath well hapt.

X

MARVEL no more although
The songs I sing do moan,
For other life than woe
I never provèd none.
And in my heart also
Is graven with letters deep,
A thousand sighs and mo,
A flood of tears to weep.

How many a man in smart
Find matter to rejoice?
How many a mourning heart
Set forth a pleasant voice?
Play whoso can that part,
Needs must in me appear
How fortune overthwart
Doth cause my mourning cheer.

Perdie there is no man,
If he never saw sight,
That perfectly tell can
The nature of the light.
Alas, how should I than,
That never taste but sour,
But do as I began,
Continually to lour?

But yet perchance some chance
May chance to change my tune,
And when such chance doth chance,
Then shall I thank Fortune.
And if I have chance,
Perchance ere it be long,
For such a pleasant chance,
To sing some pleasant song.

XI

PASS forth, my wonted cries,
Those cruel ears to pierce,
Which in most hateful wise
Do still my plaints reverse.
Do you, my tears, also
So wet her barren heart,
That pity there may grow,
And cruelty depart.

For though hard rocks among
She seems to have been bred,
And of the tiger long
Been nourishèd and fed,
Yet shall not nature change
If pity once win place,
When as unknown and strange
She now away doth chase.

And as the water soft,
Without forcing or strength,
Where that it falleth oft
Hard stones doth pierce at length:
So in her stony heart
My plaints at last shall grave,
And, rigour set apart,
Win grant of that I crave.

Wherefore, my plaints, present
Still so to her my suit
As ye, through her assent,
May bring to me some fruit.
And as she shall me prove,
So bid her me regard,
And render love for love,
Which is a just reward.

XII

YOUR looks so often cast,
Your eyes so friendly roll'd,
Your sight fixèd so fast,
Always one to behold:
Though hide it fain ye would,
It plainly doth declare
Who hath your heart in hold,
And where good-will ye bear.

Fain would ye find a cloak
Your brenning fire to hide,
Yet both the flame and smoke
Breaks out on every side.
Ye cannot love so guide
That it no issue win:
Abroad needs must it glide
That brens so hot within.

For cause yourself do wink
Ye judge all other blind,
And secret it you think
Which every man doth find.
In waste oft spend ye wind
Yourself in love to quit:
For agues of that kind
Will show who hath the fit.

Your sighs you fet from far,
And all to wry your woe;
Yet are ye ne'er the narre:
Men are not blinded so.
Deeply oft swear ye no,
But all those oaths are vain,
So well your eye doth show
Who puts your heart to pain.

Think not therefore to hide
That still itself betrays,
Nor seek means to provide
To dark the sunny days.
Forget those wonted ways;
Leave off such frowning cheer;
There will be found no stays
To stop a thing so clear.

XIII

DISDAIN me not without desert,
Nor leave me not so suddenly,
Since well ye wot that in my heart
I mean ye not but honestly.
     Disdain me not.

Refuse me not without cause why,
For think me not to be unjust,
Since that by lot of fantasy
The careful knot needs knit I must.
     Refuse me not.

Mistrust me not, though some there be,
That fain would spot my steadfastness:
Believe them not, seeing that ye see
The proof is not as they express.
     Mistrust me not.

Forsake me not, till I deserve,
Nor hate me not till I offend;
Destroy me not till that I swerve:
But since ye know what I intend,
     Forsake me not.

Disdain me not that am your own,
Refuse me not that am so true,
Mistrust me not till all be known,
Forsake me not now for no new.
        Disdain me not.

XIV

FOR want I will in woe I plain,
Under colour of soberness;
Renewing with my suit my pain,
My wanhope with your steadfastness.
Awake therefore of gentleness;
Regard, at length, I you require,
The swelting pains of my desire.

Betimes who giveth willingly,
Redoubled thanks aye doth deserve;
And I, that sue unfeignedly
In fruitless hope, alas, do sterve.
How great my cause is for to swerve,
And yet how steadfast is my suit,
Lo, here ye see: where is the fruit?

As hound that hath his keeper lost,
Seek I your presence to obtain,
In which my heart delighteth most,
And shall delight though I be slain.
You may release my band of pain;
Loose then the care that makes me cry
For want of help, or else I die.

I die, though not incontinent,
By process yet consumingly
As waste of fire which doth relent,
If you as wilful will deny.
Wherefore cease of such cruelty,
And take me wholly in your grace,
Which lacketh will to change his place.

XV

IF ever man might him avaunt
Of Fortune's friendly cheer,
It was myself, I must it grant,
For I have bought it dear.
And dearly have I held also
The glory of her name,
In yielding her such tribute, lo,
As did set forth her fame.

Sometime I stood so in her grace
That, as I would require,
Each joy I thought did me embrace
That furthered my desire.
And all those pleasures, lo, had I
That fancy might support;
And nothing she did me deny
That was unto my comfort.

I had, what would you more, perdie?
Each grace that I did crave:
Thus Fortune's will was unto me
All thing that I would have.
But all too rathe, alas the while,
She built on such a ground:
In little space, too great a guile
In her now have I found.

For she hath turnèd so her wheel
That I, unhappy man,
May wail the time that I did feel
Wherewith she fed me than.
For broken now are her behests,
And pleasant looks she gave,
And therefore now all my requests
From peril cannot save.

Yet would I well it might appear
To her my chief regard:
Though my deserts have been too dear
To merit such reward.
Sith Fortune's will is now so bent
To plague me thus, poor man,
I must myself therewith content,
And bear it as I can.

XVI

THE answer that ye made to me, my dear,
When I did sue for my poor heart's redress,
Hath so appall'd my countenance and my cheer
That in this case I am all comfortless,
Since I of blame no cause can well express.

I have no wrong where I can claim no right,
Nought ta'en me fro where I have nothing had,
Yet of my woe I cannot so be quite:
Namely, since that another may be glad,
With that that thus in sorrow makes me sad.

Nor none can claim, I say, by former grant
That knoweth not of any grant`at all;
And by desert, I dare well make avaunt,
Of faithful will there is nowhere that shall
Bear you more truth, more ready at your call.

Now good then call again that bitter word
That touch'd your friend so near with pangs of pain,
And say, my dear, that it was said in bourd:
Late, or too soon, let it not rule the gain
Wherewith free will doth true desert retain.

XVII

SO unwarely was never no man caught
With steadfast look upon a goodly face,
As I of late: for suddenly, methought,
My heart was torn out of his place.

Thorough mine eye the stroke from hers did slide,
Directly down unto my heart it ran:
In help whereof the blood thereto did glide,
And left my face both pale and wan.

Then was I like a man for woe amazed,
Or like the bird that flyeth into the fire;
For while that I upon her beauty gazed,
The more I burn'd in my desire.

Anon the blood start in my face again,
Inflam'd with heat that it had at my heart,
And brought therewith thereout in every vein
A quaking heat with pleasant smart.

Then was I like the straw when that the flame
Is driven therein by force and rage of wind;
I cannot tell, alas, what I shall blame,
Nor what to seek, nor what to find.

But well I wot the grief holds me so sore
In heat and cold, betwixt hope and dread,
That, but her help to health doth me restore,
This restless life I may not lead.

XVIII

PERDIE, I said it not,
Nor never thought to do:
As well as I ye wot
I have no power thereto.
And if I did, the lot
That first did me enchain
Do never slack the knot,
But strait it to my pain.

And if I did, each thing
That may do harm or woe
Continually may wring
My heart whereso I go:
Report may always ring
Of shame on me for aye
If in my heart did spring
The words that you do say.

And if I did, each star
That is in heaven above
May frown on me to mar
The hope I have in love!
And if I did, such war
As they brought out of Troy,
Bring all my life afar
From all this lust and joy!

And if I did so say,
The beauty that me bound,
Increase from day to day
More cruel to my wound,
With all the moan that may
To plaint may turn my song;
My life may soon decay
Without redress, by wrong.

If I be clear fro thought,
Why do you then complain?
Then is this thing but sought
To turn me to more pain.
Then that that ye have wrought
You must it now redress;
Of right therefore you ought
Such rigour to repress.

And as I have deserved,
So grant me now my hire;
Ye know I never swerved,
Ye never found me liar.
For Rachel have I served
(For Leah cared I never),
And her I have reserved
Within my heart for ever.

XIX

WHEN first mine eyes did view and mark
Thy fairè beauty to behold,
And when mine ears listened to hark
The pleasant words that thou me told,
I would as then I had been free
From ears to hear, and eyes to see.

And when my lips first gan to move,
Whereby my heart to thee was known,
And when my tongue did talk of love
To thee that hast true love down thrown,
I would my lips and tongue also
Had then been dumb, no deal to go.

And when my hands have handled aught
That thee hath kept in memory,
And when my feet have gone and sought
To find and get thee company,
I would each hand a foot had been,
And I each foot a hand had seen.

And when in mind I did consent
To follow this my fancy's will,
And when my heart did first relent
To taste such bait, my life to spill,
I would my heart had been as thine,
Or else thy heart had been as mine.

XX

SINCE Love will needs that I shall love,
Of very force I must agree:
And since no chance may it remove.
In wealth and in adversity
I shall alway myself apply
To serve, and suffer patiently.

Though for goodwill I find but hate,
And cruelly my life to waste,
And though that still a wretched state
Should pine my days unto the last,
Yet I profess it willingly
To serve, and suffer patiently.

For since my heart is bound to serve,
And I not ruler of mine own,
Whatso befall, till that I sterve
By proof full well it shall be known
That I shall still myself apply
To serve, and suffer patiently.

Yea though my grief find no redress,
But still increase before mine eyes,
Though my reward be cruelness,
With all the harm hap can devise,
Yet I profess it willingly
To serve, and suffer patiently.

Yea though Fortune her pleasant face
Should show, to set me up aloft,
And straight my wealth for to deface,
Should writhe away, as she doth oft,
Yet would I still myself apply
To serve, and suffer patiently.

There is no grief, no smart, no woe,
That yet I feel, or after shall,
That from this mind they make me go:
And, whatsoever me befall,
I do profess it willingly
To serve, and suffer patiently.

XXI

WHAT rage is this? what furor of what kind?
What power, what plague doth weary thus my mind?
Within my bones to rankle is assigned,
      What poison, pleasant sweet?

Lo, see, mine eyes swell with continual tears;
The body still away sleepless it wears;
My food nothing my fainting strength repairs,
      Nor doth my limbs sustain.

In deep wide wound the deadly stroke doth turn
To curèd scar that never shall return.
Go to, triumph, rejoice thy goodly turn,
      Thy friend thou dost oppress.

Oppress thou dost, and hast of him no cure;
Nor yet my plaint no pity can procure,
Fierce tiger fell, hard rock without recure,
      Cruel rebel to love!

Once may thou love, never beloved again;
So love thou still, and not thy love obtain;
So wrathful love with spites of just disdain
      May threat thy cruel heart!

XXII

I SEE that chance hath chosen me
Thus secretly to live in pain,
And to another given the fee
Of all my loss to have the gain:
By chance assign'd thus do I serve,
And other have that I deserve.

Unto myself sometime alone
I do lament my woful case,
But what availeth me to moan
Since truth and pity hath no place
In them to whom I sue and serve,
And other have that I deserve?

To seek by mean to change this mind,
Alas, I prove it will not be;
For in my heart I cannot find
Once to refrain, but still agree,
As bound by force, alway to serve,
And other have that I deserve.

Such is the fortune that I have,
To love them most that love me least;
And, to my pain, to seek and crave
The thing that other have possest:
So thus in vain alway I serve,
And other have that I deserve.

And till I may appease the heat,
If that my hap will hap so well,
To wail my woe my heart shall frete,
Whose pensive pain my tongue can tell.
Yet thus unhappy must I serve,
And other have that I deserve.

XXIII

LIKE as the bird in the cage enclosed,
The door unsparrèd and the hawk without,
'Twixt death and prison piteously oppressed,
Whether for to choose standeth in doubt:
Certes, so do I, which do seek to bring about
Which should be best by determination,
By loss of life liberty, or life by prison.

O mischief by mischief to be redressed,
Where pain is best there lieth little pleasure,
By short death out of danger yet to be delivered,
Rather than with painful life, thraldom, and dolour,
For small pleasure, much pain to suffer,
Sooner therefore to choose, me thinketh it wisdom,
By loss of life liberty, than life by prison.

By length of life yet should I suffer,
Awaiting time and fortune's chance.
Many things happen within an hour:
That which me opprest may me advance.
In time is trust which by death's grievance
Is utterly lost.   Then were it not reason
By death to choose liberty, and not life by prison?

But death were deliverance, in life length of pain.
Of two ills let see now choose the best.
This bird to deliver, you that hear her plain,
Your advice, you lovers, which shall be best:
In cage in thraldom, or by hawk to be opprest?
And which for to choose make plain conclusion:
By loss of life liberty, or life by prison?

XXIV

IF thou wilt mighty be, flee from the rage
Of cruel will; and see thou keep thee free
From the foul yoke of sensual bondage:
For though thine empire stretch to Indian sea
And for thy fear trembleth the farthest Thule,
If thy desire have over thee the power,
Subject then art thou, and no governor.

If to be noble and high thy mind be movèd,
Consider well thy ground and thy beginning;
For he that hath each star in heaven fixèd,
And gives the moon her horns and her eclipsing,
Alike hath made thee noble in his working;
So that wretched no way may thou be,
Except foul lust and vice do conquer thee.

All were it so thou had a flood of gold
Unto thy thirst, yet should it not suffice;
And though with Indian stones, a thousandfold
More precious than can thyself devise,
Ychargèd were thy back, thy covetise
And busy biting yet should never let
Thy wretched life, ne do thy death profet.

XXV

TO seek each where where man doth live,
The sea, the land, the rock, the clive,
France, Spain, and Ind, and everywhere;
Is none a greater gift to give,
Less set by oft, and is so lief and dear,
Dare I well say, than that I give to year.

I cannot give brooches nor rings,
These goldsmith's work, and goodly things,
Pierrie nor pearl, orient and clear;
But for all that can no man bring
Liefer jewel unto his lady dear,
Dare I well say, than that I give to year.

Nor I seek not to fetch it far;
Worse is it not tho' it be narr;
And as it is it doth appear
Uncounterfeit, mistrust to bar,
Left whole and pure withouten peer,
Dare I will say, the gift I give to year.

To thee therefore the same retain;
The like of thee to have again
France would I give, if mine it were.
Is none alive in whom doth reign
Lesser disdain; freely therefore, lo here
Dare I well give, I say, my heart to year.

XXVI

THERE was never nothing more me pained,
Nor nothing more me moved,
As when my sweetheart her complained
That ever she me loved.
   Alas the while!

With piteous look she said, and sigh'd:
'Alas what aileth me,
To love and set my wealth so light
On him that loveth not me?'
   Alas the while!

'Was I not well void of all pain,
When that nothing me grieved?
And now with sorrows I must complain,
And cannot be relieved.'
   Alas the while!

'My restful nights and joyful days
Since I began to love
Be take from me; all thing decays,
Yet can I not remove.'
   Alas the while!

She wept and wrung her hands withal,
The tears fell in my neck.
She turned her face and let it fall,
Scarcely therewith could speak.
   Alas the while!

Her pains tormented me so sore
That comfort had I none,
But cursed my fortune more and more
To see her sob and groan
   Alas the while!

XXVII

HEAVEN and earth, and all that hear me plain,
Do well perceive what care doth make me cry,
Save you alone, to whom I cry in vain:
Mercy, madame!   Alas I die, I die!

If that you sleep, I humbly you require
Forbear a while, and let your rigour slake,
Since that by you I burn thus in this fire;
To hear my plaint, dear heart, awake! awake!

Since that so oft ye have made me to wake
In plaint, and tears, and in right piteous case,
Displease you not if force do now me make
To break your sleep, crying alas! alas!

It is the last trouble that ye shall have
Of me, madame, to hear my last complaint;
Pity at least your poor unhappy slave,
For in despair, alas, I faint, I faint.

It is not now but long and long ago
I have you served as to my power and might
As faithfully as any man might do,
Claiming of you nothing of right, of right,

Save of your grace only to stay my life
That fleeth as fast as cloud before the wind;
For since that first I entered in this strife,
An inward death hath fret my mind, my mind.

If I had suffered this to you unware,
Mine were the fault, and you nothing to blame;
But since you know my woe and all my care,
Why do I die, alas, for shame, for shame!

I know right well my face, my look, my tears,
Mine eyes, my words, and eke my dreary chere
Have cried my death full oft unto your ears;
Hard of belief it doth appear, appear.

A better proof I see that ye would have
How I am dead, therefore, when ye hear tell,
Believe it not, although ye see my grave.
Cruel! unkind! I say farewell! farewell!

XXVIII

AFTER great storms the calm returns,
And pleasanter it is thereby;
Fortune likewise that often turns
Hath made me now the most happy.

The Heaven that pitied my distress,
My just desire, and my cry,
Hath made my languor to cesse,
And me also the most happy.

Whereto despairèd ye, my friends?
My trust alway in her did lie
That knoweth what my thought intends:
Whereby I live the most happy.

Lo, what can take hope from that heart
That is assurèd steadfastly?
Hope therefore ye that live in smart,
Whereby I am the most happy.

And I that have felt of your pain
Shall pray to God continually
To make your hope your health retain,
And me also the most happy.

XXIX

THOUGH this the port, and I thy servant true,
And thou thyself dost cast thy beams from high
From thy chief house, promising to renew
Both joy and eke delight, behold yet how that I,
Banished from my bliss, carefully do cry,
Help now, Cytherea, my lady dear,
My fearful trust, en vogant la galere.

Alas, the doubt that dreadful absence giveth!
Without thine aid assurance is there none:
The firm faith that in the water fleteth
Succour thou therefore: in thee it is alone.
Stay that with faith that faithfully doth moan,
And thou also givest me both hope and fear.
Remember thou me, en vogant galere.

By seas and hills elongèd from thy sight,
Thy wonted grace reducing to my mind,
Instead of sleep thus I occupy the night:
A thousand thoughts and many doubts I find.
And still I trust thou canst not be unkind,
Or else despair my comfort and my chere,
Would she forthwith, en vogant la galere.

Yet, on my faith, full little doth remain
Of any hope whereby I may myself uphold,
For since that only words do me retain
I may well think the affection is but cold.
But since my will is nothing as I would,
And in thy hands it resteth whole and clear,
Forget me not, en vogant la galere.

XXX

O GOODLY hand
Wherein doth stand
My heart distrast in pain:
Fair hand, alas,
In little space
My life that dost restrain.

O fingers slight,
Departed right,
So long, so small, so round:
Goodly begone,
And yet alone
Most cruel in my wound.

With lilies white
And roses bright
Doth strive thy colour fair:
Nature did lend
Each finger's end
A pearl for to repair.

Consent at last,
Since that thou hast
My heart in thy demesne,
For service true
On me to rue
And reach me love again.

And if not so,
Then with more woe
Enforce thyself to strain
This simple heart,
That suffered smart,
And rid it out of pain.

XXXI

AND if an eye may save or slay,
And strike more deep than weapon long,
And if an eye by subtle play
May move one more than any tongue,
How can ye say that I do wrong
Thus to suspect without desert?
For the eye is traitor of the heart.

To frame all well, I am content
That it were done unweetingly;
But yet I say, who will assent
To do but well, do no thing why
That men should deem the contrary?
For it is said, by men expert,
That the eye is traitor of the heart.

But yet, alas, that look, all soul,
That I do claim of right to have
Should not methinks go seek the school
To please all folk, for who can crave
Friendlier thing than heart withsave
By look to give in friendly part?
For the eye is traitor of the heart.

And my suspect is without blame,
For, as ye say, not only I
But other mo have deem'd the same.
Then is it not [my] jealousy,
But subtle look of reckless eye
Did range too far, to make me smart,
For the eye is traitor of the heart.

But I your Friend shall take it thus,
Since you will so, as stroke of chance,
And leave further for to discuss
Whether the stroke did stick or glance.
But 'scuse who can, let him advance
Dissembled looks, but for my part,
My eye must still betray my heart.

And of this grief ye shall be quit,
In helping Truth steadfast to go:
The time is long that [he] doth sit
Feeble and weak, and suff'reth woe.
Cherish him well, continue so:
Let him not fro your heart ascart:
Then fears not the eye to show the heart.

XXXII

IF Fancy would favour,
As my deserving shall,
My love, my paramour,
Should love me best of all.

But if I cannot attain
The grace that I desire,
Then may I well complain
My service, and my hire.

Fancy doth know how
To further my true heart,
If Fancy might avow
With Faith to take part.

But Fancy is so frail,
And flitting still so fast,
That Faith may not prevail
To help me, first nor last.

For Fancy at his lust
Doth rule all but by guess:
Whereto should I then trust
In truth or steadfastness?

Yet gladly would I please
The fancy of her heart,
That may me only ease
And cure my careful smart.

Therefore, my lady dear,
Set once your fantasy
To make some hope appear
Of steadfast remedy.

For if he be my friend,
And undertake my woe,
My grief is at an end
If he continue so.

Else Fancy doth not right,
As I deserve and shall,
To have you day and night,
To love me best of all.

XXXIII

MY hope, alas, hath me abused,
And vain rejoicing hath me fed:
Lust and joy have me refused,
And careful plaint is in their stead.
Too much advancing slaked my speed,
Mirth hath caused my heaviness,
And I remain all comfortless.

Whereto did I assure my thought
Without displeasure steadfastly:
In Fortune's forge my joy was wrought,
And is revolted readily.
I am mistaken wonderly,
For I thought nought but faithfulness,
Yet I remain all comfortless.

In gladsome cheer I did delight,
Till that delight did cause my smart,
And all was wrong where I thought right.
For right it was that my true heart
Should not from truth be set apart,
Since truth did cause my hardiness:
Yet I remain all comfortless.

Sometime delight did tune my song,
And led my heart full pleasantly,
And to myself I said among:
'My hap is coming hastily'—
But it hath happèd contrary.
Assurance causeth my distress,
And I remain all comfortless.

Then if my note now do vary,
And leave his wonted pleasantness,
The heavy burden that I carry
Hath alter'd all my joyfulness.
No pleasure hath still steadfastness,
But haste hath hurt my happiness.
And I remain all comfortless.

XXXIV

ALL heavy minds
Do seek to ease their charge,
And that that most them binds
    To let at large.

Then why should I
Hold pain within my heart,
And may my tune apply,
    To ease my smart?

My faithful lute
Alone shall hear me plain;
For else all other suit
    Is clean in vain.

For where I sue
Redress of all my grief,
Lo, they do most eschew
    My heart's relief.

Alas, my dear,
Have I deservèd so?
That no help may appear
    Of all my woe?

Whom speak I to,
Unkind and deaf of ear?
Alas, lo, I go,
    And wot not where.

Where is my thought?
Where wanders my desire?
Where may the thing be sought
    That I require?

Light in the wind
Doth flee all my delight;
Where truth and faithful mind
    Are put to flight.

Who shall me give
Feath'red wings for to flee,
The thing that doth me grieve
    That I may see?

Who would go seek
The cause whereby to pain?
Who could his foe beseek
    For ease of pain?

My chance doth so
My woful case procure,
To offer to my foe
My heart to cure.

What hope I then
To have any redress?
Of whom or where or when
    Who can express?

No since despair
Hath set me in this case,
In vain oft in the air
    To say Alas!

I seek no thing
But thus for to discharge
My heart of sore sighing,
    To plain at large,

And with my lute
Sometime to ease my pain;
For else all other suit
Is clean in vain.

XXXV

COMFORT thyself, my woful heart,
Or shortly on thyself thee wreak;
For length redoubleth deadly smart;
Why sigh'st thou, heart, and wilt not break?

To waste in sighs were piteous death;
Alas, I find thee faint and weak.
Enforce thyself to lose thy breath;
Why sigh'st thou, heart, and wilt not break?

Thou know'st right well that no redress
Is thus to pine; and for to speak,
Perdie, it is remediless.
Why sigh'st thou then, and wilt not break?

It is too late for to refuse
The yoke, when it is on thy neck:
To shake it off, vaileth not to muse:
Why sigh'st thou then, and wilt not break?

To sob and sigh it were but vain,
Since there is none that doth it reck.
Alas, thou dost prolong thy pain:
Why sigh'st thou then, and wilt not break?

Then in her sight, to move her heart,
Seek on thyself thyself to wreak:
That she may know thou suffered'st smart,
Sigh there thy last, and therewith break.

XXXVI

ALAS the grief, and deadly woful smart,
The carefull chance shapen afore my shert,
The sorrowful tears, the sighs hot as fire,
That cruel love hath long soked from my heart!
And for reward of over great desire
Disdainful doubleness have I for my hire.

O lost service, O pain ill rewarded,
O pitiful heart with pain enlargèd,
O faithful mind too suddenly assented,
Return alas, sithens thou art not regarded.
Too great a proof of true faith presented
Causeth by right such faith to be repented.

O cruel causer of undeservèd change,
By great desire unconstantly to range,
Is this your way for proof of steadfastness?
Perdie you know (the thing was not so strange)
By former proof too much my faithfulness!
What needeth then such coloured doubleness?

I have wailed thus, weeping in nightly pain,
In sobs and sighs, alas, and all in vain,
In inward plaint and heart's woful torment.
And yet, alas, lo, cruelty and disdain
Have set at nought a faithful true intent,
And price hath privilege truth to prevent.

But though I starve, and to my death still mourn,
And piecemeal in pieces though I be torn,
And though I die, yielding my wearied ghost,
Shall never thing again make me return.
I quit [pursuit] of that that I have lost,
To whomsoever lust for to proffer most.

XXXVII

SINCE ye delight to know
That my torment and woe
Should still increase
Without release,
I shall enforce me so
That life and all shall go,
For to content your cruelness.

And so this grievous train
That I too long sustain
Shall sometime cesse,
And have redress,
And you also remain
Full pleasèd with my pain,
For to content your cruelness.

Unless that be too light,
And that ye would ye might
See the distress
And heaviness
Of one slain outright,
Therewith to please your sight,
And to content your cruelness.

Then in your cruel mood
Would God forthwith ye would
With force express
My heart oppress,
To do your heart such good
To see me bathe in blood,
For to content your cruelness.

Then could ye ask no more:
Then should ye ease my sore,
And the excess
Of my distress:
And you should evermore
Defamèd be therefor,
For to repent your cruelness.

XXXVIII

SUCH hap as I am happèd in
Had never man of truth I ween.
At me Fortune list to begin
To show that never hath been seen,
A new kind of unhappiness;
Nor I cannot the thing I mean
    Myself express.

Myself express my deadly pain
That can I well, if that might serve;
But when I have not help again,
That know I not, unless I sterve,
For hunger still amiddes my food,
[Lacking the thing] that I deserve
    To do me good.

To do me good what may prevail,
For I deserve, and not desire,
And still of cold I me bewail,
And rakèd am in burning fire;
For though I have, such is my lot,
In hand to help that I require,
   It helpeth not.

It helpeth not but to increase
That that by proof can be no more;
That is, the heat that cannot cease;
And that I have, to crave so sore.
What wonder is this greedy lust
To ask and have, and yet therefore
   Refrain I must!

Refrain I must. What is the cause?
Sure as they say 'So hawks be taught.'
But in my case layeth no such clause,
For with such craft I am not caught.
Wherefore I say, and good cause why,
With hapless hand no man hath raught
   Such hap as I.

XXXIX

I HAVE sought long with steadfastness
To have had some ease of my great smart;
But nought availeth faithfulness
To grave within your stony heart.
But hap, and hit, or else hit not,
As uncertain as is the wind;
Right so it fareth by the shot
Of Love, alas, that is so blind.

Therefore I play'd the fool in vain,
With pity when I first began
Your cruel heart for to constrain,
Since love regardeth no doubtful man.
But of your goodness all your mind
Is that I should complain in vain.
This is the favour that I find:
Ye list to hear how I can plain!

But tho' I plain to please your heart,
Trust me I trust to temper it so,
Not for to care which do revert;
All shall be one, or wealth, or woe.
For Fancy ruleth, though Right say nay,
Even as the goodman kist his cow:
None other reason can ye lay
But as who saith: 'I reck not how.'

XL

TO wish, and want, and not obtain,
To seek and sue ease of my pain,
Since all that ever I do is vain,
    What may it avail me?

Although I strive both day and hour
Against the stream, of all my power,
If Fortune list yet for to lower,
    What may it avail me?

If willingly I suffer woe,
If from the fire me list not go,
If then I burn to plain me so,
    What may it avail me?

And if the harm that I suffer,
Be run too far out of measure,
To seek for help any further,
    What may it avail me?

What tho' each heart that heareth me plain
Pitieth and plaineth for my pain:
If I no less in grief remain,
    What may it avail me?

Yea though the want of my relief
Displease the causer of my grief,
Since I remain still in mischief,
    What may it avail me?

Such cruel chance doth so me threat
Continually inward to freat,
Then of release for to treat
    What may it avail me?

Fortune is deaf unto my call;
My torment moveth her not at all;
And though she turn as doth a ball,
      What may it avail me?

For in despair there is no rede;
To want of ear, speech is no speed;
To linger still alive as dead,
      What may it avail me?

XLI

      IF chance assign'd
      Were to my mind
      By very kind
      Of destiny,
      Yet would I crave
      Nought else to have
      But life and liberty.

      Then were I sure
      I might endure
      The displeasure
      Of cruelty:
      Where now I plain,
      Alas, in vain,
      Lacking my life for liberty.

      For without the one
      The other is gone,
      And there can none
      It remedy:
      If the one be past
      The other doth waste,
      And all for lack of liberty.

      And so I drive,
      As yet alive,
      Although I strive
      With misery:
      Drawing my breath,
      Looking for death,
      And loss of life for liberty.

But thou that still
Mayst at thy will
Turn all this ill
Adversity:
For the repair
Of my welfare
Grant me but life and liberty.

And if not so,
Then let all go
To wretched woe,
And let me die:
For the one or the other,
There is none other:
My death, or life with liberty.

XLII

AT most mischief
I suffer grief;
For of relief
Since I have none,
My lute and I
Continually
Shall us apply
To sigh and moan.

Nought may prevail
To weep or wail;
Pity doth fail
In you, alas!
Mourning or moan,
Complaint or none,
It is all one,
As in this case.

For cruelty
That most can be
Hath sovereignty
Within your heart;
Which maketh bare
All my welfare:
Nought do ye care
How sore I smart.

No tiger's heart
Is so pervert,
Without desert
To wreak his ire;
And you me kill
For my goodwill:
Lo, how I spill
For my desire!

There is no love
That can ye move,
And I can prove
None other way;
Therefore I must
Restrain my lust,
Banish my trust
And wealth away.

Thus in mischief
I suffer grief,
For of relief
Since I have none,
My lute and I
Continually
Shall us apply
To sigh and moan.

XLIII

TO cause accord or to agree
Two contraries in one degree,
And in one point, as seemeth me,
To all man's wit it cannot be:
  It is impossible.

Of heat and cold when I complain,
And say that heat doth cause my pain,
When cold doth shake me every vein,
And both at once, I say again
  It is impossible.

That man that hath his heart away,
If life liveth there, as men do say,
That he heartless should last one day
Alive, and not to turn to clay,
  It is impossible.

'Twixt life and death, say what who saith,
There liveth no life that draweth breath;
They join so near, and eke i' faith,
To seek for life by wish of death,
    It is impossible.

Yet Love, that all things doth subdue,
Whose power there may no life eschew,
Hath wrought in me that I may rue
These miracles to be so true
    That are impossible.

XLIV

WHAT death is worse than this
    When my delight,
My weal, my joy, my bliss,
    Is from my sight?
    Both day and night
My life, alas, I miss.

For though I seem alive
    My heart is hence:
Thus bootless for to strive
    Out of presence
    Of my defence
Toward my death I drive.

Heartless, alas, what man
    May long endure?
Alas, how live I than?
    Since no recure
    May me assure,
My life I may well ban.

Thus doth my torment grow
    In deadly dread.
Alas, who might live so
    Alive as dead?
    Alive to lead
A deadly life in woe?

XLV

PATIENCE for my device,
Impatience for your part:
Of contraries the guise
Is ever the overthwart.
Patience: for I am true.
The contrary for you.

Patience: a good cause why.
You have no cause at all.
Therefore you stand awry,
Perchance sometime to fall.
Patience then, take him up,
And drink of patience' cup.

Patience! no force for that
But brush your gown again.
Patience, spurn not thereat;
Let no man know your pain.
Patience, even at my pleasure,
When yours is out of measure.

The other was for me,
This patience is for you.
Change when ye list let see,
For I have ta'en a new.
Patience, with a good will,
Is easy to fulfil.

XLVI

PATIENCE though I have not,
The thing that I require,
I must of force, God wot,
Forbear my most desire:
For no ways can I find
To sail against the wind.

Patience, do what they will
To work me woe or spite,
I shall content me still
To think both day and night:
To think, and hold my peace,
Since there is no redress.

Patience withouten blame,
For I offended nought:
I know they know the same,
Though they have changed their thought.
Was ever thought so moved,
To hate that it hath loved?

Patience of all my harm,
For Fortune is my foe;
Patience must be the charm
To heal me of my woe.
Patience without offence
Is a painful patience.

XLVII

PATIENCE of all my smart!
For Fortune is turn'd awry:
Patience must ease my heart
That mourns continually.
Patience to suffer wrong
Is a patience too long.

Patience to have a nay
Of that I most desire,
Patience to have alway
And ever burn like fire.
Patience without desart
Is grounder of my smart.

Who can with merry heart
Set forth some pleasant song
That always feels but smart
And never hath but wrong?
Yet patience evermore
Must heal the wound and sore.

Patience to be content
With froward Fortune's train,
Patience to the intent
Somewhat to slake my pain.
I see no remedy,
But suffer patiently.

To plain where is none ear
My chance is chancèd so,
For it doth well appear
My friend is turn'd my foe:
But since there is no defence,
I must take patience.

Who would have ever thought
A heart that was so set
To have such wrong me wrought
Or to be so counterfeit?
But who that trusteth most
Is like to pay the cost.

I must of force, God wot,
This painful life sustain,
And yet I know not
The chief cause of my pain.
This is a strange disease,
To serve and never please.

I must of force endure
This drawght drawn awry,
For I am fast and sure
To have the mate thereby.
But note I will this text:
To draw better the next.

XLVIII

THO' I can not your cruelty constrain
For my goodwill to favour me again,
Though my true and faithful love
Have no power your heart to move—
    Yet rue upon my pain.

Tho' I your thrall must evermore remain,
And for your sake my liberty restrain,
The greatest grace that I do crave
Is that ye would vouchsave
    To rue upon my pain.

Though I have not deservèd to obtain
So high reward, but thus to serve in vain,
Though I shall have no redress,
Yet of right ye can no less
      But rue upon my pain.

But I see well that your high disdain
Will no wise grant that I shall more attain;
Yet ye must grant at the least
This my poor and small request:
      Rejoice not at my pain.

XLIX

PROCESS of time worketh such wonder
That water, which is of kind so soft,
Doth pierce the marble stone asunder
By little drops falling from aloft.

And yet a heart that seems so tender
Receiveth no drop of the stilling tears
That always still cause me to render,
The vain plaint that sounds not in her ears.

So cruel, alas, is nought alive,
So fierce, so froward, so out of frame:
But some way, some time, may so contrive
By means the wild to temper and tame.

And I that always have sought, and seek
Each place, each time for some lucky day,
This fierce tiger, less I find her meek,
And more denied the longer I pray.

The lion in his raging furour
Forbears that sueth, meekness for his [boot;]
And thou, alas, in extreme dolour
The heart so low thou treads under thy foot.

Each fierce thing, lo, how thou dost exceed,
And hides it under so humble a face!
And yet the humble to help at need
Nought helpeth time, humbleness, nor place.

L

IF in the world there be more woe
Than I have in my heart;
Whereso it is, it doth come fro,
And in my breast there doth it grow,
For to increase my smart.
Alas, I am receipt of every care,
And of my life each sorrow claims his part.
Who list to live in quietness
By me let him beware,
For I by high disdain
Am made without redress,
And unkindness, alas, hath slain
My poor true heart all comfortless.

LI

LIKE as the swan towards her death
Doth strain her voice with doleful note,
Right so sing I with waste of breath
I die! I die! and you regard it not.

I shall enforce my fainting breath,
That all that hears this deadly note
Shall know that you doth cause my death.
I die! I die! and you regard it not.

Your unkindness hath sworn my death,
And changèd hath my pleasant note
To painful sighs that stop my breath.
I die! I die! and you regard it not.

Consumeth my life, faileth my breath:
Your fault is forger of this note.
Melting in tears a cruel death
I die, I die, and you regard it not.

My faith with me after my death
Buried shall be, and to this note
I do bequeath my weary breath
To cry: 'I die!—and you regard it not.'

LII

'AH Robin,
Jolly Robin,
Tell me how thy leman doth?
And thou shalt know of mine.'

'My lady is unkind, perdie!'
'Alack, why is she so!
'She loveth another better than me,
And yet she will say, no.'

'I find no such doubleness:
I find women true.
My lady loveth me doubtless,
And will change for no new.'

'Thou art happy while that doth last,
But I say as I find,
That woman's love is but a blast
And turneth like the wind.'

'If that be true yet as thou sayest
That women turn their heart,
Then speak better of them thou mayest
In hope to have thy part.'

Such folks shall take no harm by love
That can abide their turn;
But I, alas, can no way prove
In love but lack and mourn.

'But if thou wilt avoid thy harm,
Learn this lesson of me:
At others' fires thyself to warm,
And let them warm with thee.'

LIII

IN eternum I was once determed,
For to have loved and my mind affirmed,
That with my heart it should be confirmed,
      In eternum.

Forthwith I found the thing that I might like,
And sought with love to warm her heart alike,
For, as methought, I should not see the like
     In eternum.

To trace this dance I put myself in prese;
Vain hope did lead, and bade I should not cease,
To serve to suffer, and still to hold my peace
     In eternum.

With this first rule I fordered me apace,
That, as methought, my truth had taken place
With full assurance to stand in her grace
     In eternum.

It was not long ere I by proof had found
That feeble building is on feeble ground:
For in her heart this word did never sound,
     'In eternum.'

In eternum then from my heart I kest
That I had first determed for the best:
Now in the place another thought doth rest
     In eternum.

LIV

MOST wretched heart, most miserable,
Since thy comfort is from thee fled,
Since all thy truth is turned to fable,
Most wretched heart, why art thou not dead?
    'No! no! I live, and must do still:
    Whereof I thank God, and no mo.
    For I myself have at my will,
    And he is wretched that weens him so.'

But yet thou hast both had and lost
The hope so long that hath thee fed,
And all thy travail and thy cost!
Most wretched heart, why art thou not dead?
    'Some other hope must feed me new:
    If I have lost, I say what tho?
    Despair shall not therewith ensue,
    For he is wretched that weens him so.'

The sun, the moon doth frown on thee,
Thou hast darkness in daylight's stead:
As good in grave, as so to be!
Most wretched heart, why art thou not dead?
   'Some pleasant star may show me light,
   But though the heaven would work me woe,
   Who hath himself shall stand upright,
   And he is wretched that weens him so.'

Hath he himself that is not sure?
His trust is like as he hath sped.
Against the stream thou mayst not dure:
Most wretched heart, why art thou not dead?
   'The last is worst: who fears not that
   He hath himself whereso he go.
   And he that knoweth what is what,
   Saith he is wretched that weens him so.'

Seest thou not how they whet their teeth
Which to touch thee sometime did dread?
They find comfort for thy mischief:
Most wretched heart, why art thou not dead?
   'What though that curs do fall by kind
   On him that hath the overthrow?
   All that cannot oppress my mind,
   For he is wretched that weens him so.'

Yet can it not be then denied,
It is as certain as thy creed,
Thy great unhap thou canst not hide.
Unhappy then, why art thou not dead?
   'Unhappy, but no wretch therefore!
   For hap doth come again, and go,
   For which I keep myself in store,
   Since unhap cannot kill me so.'

LV

BLAME not my lute, for he must sound
Of this or that as liketh me;
For lack of wit the lute is bound
To give such tunes as pleaseth me;
Though my songs be somewhat strange,
And speak such words as touch thy change,
     Blame not my lute.

My lute, alas, doth not offend,
Though that perforce he must agree
To sound such tunes as I intend,
To sing to them that heareth me; ·
Then though my songs be somewhat plain,
And toucheth some that use to feign,
   Blame not my lute.

My lute and strings may not deny,
But as I strike they must obey;
Break not them then so wrongfully,
But wreak thyself some other way;
And though the songs which I indite
Do quit thy change with rightful spite,
   Blame not my lute.

Spite asketh spite and changing change,
And falsèd faith must needs be known;
The faults so great, the case so strange,
Of right it must abroad be blown:
Then since that by thine own desart
My songs do tell how true thou art,
   Blame not my lute.

Blame but thyself that hast misdone,
And well deservèd to have blame;
Change thou thy way so evil begone,
And then my lute shall sound that same:
But if till then my fingers play
By thy desert their wonted way,
   Blame not my lute.

Farewell, unknown, for though thou break
My strings in spite with great disdain,
Yet have I found out for thy sake,
Strings for to string my lute again.
And if perchance this sely rhyme
Do make thee blush at any time,
   Blame not my lute.

LVI

MY pen, take pain a little space
To follow that which doth me chase,
And hath in hold my heart so sore;
But when thou hast this brought to pass,
My pen, I prithee write no more.

Remember oft thou hast me eased,
And all my pains full well appeased,
But now I know, unknown before,
For where I trust I am deceived;
And yet, my pen, thou canst no more.

A time thou hadst as other have
To write which way my hope to crave.
That time is past, withdraw, therefore:
Since we do lose that other have,
As good leave off and write no more.

In worth to use another way,
Not as we would but as we may,
For once my loss is past restore,
And my desire is my decay.
My pen, yet write a little more.

To love in vain who ever shall,
Of worldly pain it passeth all,
As in like case I find wherefore
To hold so fast and yet to fall!
Alas, my pen, now write no more.

Since thou hast taken pain this space
To follow that which doth me chase
And hath in hold my heart so sore,
Now hast thou brought my mind to pass.
My pen, I prithee write no more.

LVII

TAKE heed betime, lest ye be spied;
Your loving eyes cannot hide;
At last the truth will sure be tried.
    Therefore take heed.

For some there be of crafty kind,
Though you show no part of your mind,
Surely their eyes ye cannot blind.
    Therefore take heed.

For in like case themselves hath been
And thought right sure none had them seen:
But it was not as they did ween.
    Therefore take heed.

Although they be of divers schools
And well can use all crafty tools,
At length they prove themselves but fools.
    Therefore take heed.

If they might take you in that trap,
They would soon leave it in your lap.
To love unspied is but a hap.
    Therefore take heed.

LVIII

AT last withdraw your cruelty,
Or let me die at once.
It is too much extremity,
Devisèd for the nonce,
To hold me thus alive,
In pain still for to drive.
What may I more sustain,
Alas, that die would fain,
And cannot die for pain?

For to the flame wherewith ye burn,
My thought and my desire,
When into ashes it should turn
My heart by fervent fire,
Ye send a stormy rain
That doth it quench again,
And make mine eyes express
The tears that do redress
My life in wretchedness.

Then when these should have drown'd
And overwhelm'd my heart,
The heart doth them confound,
Renewing all my smart.
Then doth flame increase,
My torment cannot cease,
My woe doth then revive,
And I remain alive,
With death still for to strive.

But if that ye would have my death,
And that ye would none other,
Shortly then for to spare my breath,
Withdraw the one or tother.
For thus your cruelness
Doth lett itself doubtless,
And it is reason why
No man alive, nor I,
Of double death can die.

LIX

TO wet your eye withouten tear,
And in good health to feign disease,
That you thereby mine eye might blear,
Therewith your other friends to please:
And though ye think ye need not fear,
Yet so ye can not me appease,
But (as ye list) fawn, flatter, or glose,
Ye shall not win if I do lose.

Prate, and paint, and spare not,
Ye know I can me wreak;
And if so be ye care not,
Be sure I do not reck.
And though ye swear it were not,
I can both swear and speak
By God and by this cross,
If I have the mock ye shall have the loss.

LX

I LOVE, lovèd, and so doth she,
And yet in love we suffer still;
The cause is strange, as seemeth me,
To love so well and want our will.

O deadly yea! O grievous smart!
Worse than refuse, unhappy gain!
I love: who ever play'd this part,
To love so well, and live in pain?

Were ever hearts so well agreed,
Since love was love as I do trow,
That in their love so well did speed,
To love so well, and live in woe?

Thus mourn we both and hath done long,
With woful plaint and carefull voice.
Alas, it is a grievous wrong
To love so well and not rejoice!

And here an end of all our moan,
With sighing oft my breath is scant;
Since of mishap ours is alone
To love so well and yet to want.

But they that causers be of this,
Of all our cares God send them part,
That they may know what grief it is
To love so well and live in smart.

LXI

FAREWELL, all my welfare!
My shoe is trod awry.
Now may I cark and care,
To sing lullay-by-by.
Alas, what shall I do thereto?
There is no shift to help me now.

Who made it such offence
To love for love again?
God wot that my pretence
Was but to ease his pain,
For I had ruth to see his woe!
Alas, more fool, why did I so?

For he from me is gone,
And makes thereat a game;
And hath left me alone
To suffer sorrow and shame.
Alas, he is unkind doubtless
To leave me thus all comfortless.

It is a grievous smart
To suffer pain and sorrow,
But most grieved my heart
He laid his faith to borrow,
And falsèd hath his faith and troth,
And he forsworn by many an oath.

All ye lovers, perdie,
Hath cause to blame his deed,
Which shall example be
To lett you of your speed;
Let never woman again
Trust to such words as man can sayn.

For I unto my cost
Am warning to you all
That they whom you trust most
Soonest deceive you shall.
But complaint cannot redress
Of my great grief the great excess.

LXII

THE heart and service to you proffer'd
With right good will full honestly,
Refuse it not since it is offer'd,
But take it to you gentilly.

And though it be a small present,
Yet good, consider graciously
The thought, the mind, and the intent
Of him that loves you faithfully.

It were a thing of small effect
To work my woe thus cruelly,
For my goodwill to be object:
Therefore accept it lovingly.

Pain or travail, to run or ride,
I undertake it pleasantly:
Bid ye me go and straight I glide
At your commandment humbly.

Pain or pleasure now may you plant,
Even which it please you steadfastly;
Do which you list, I shall not want
To be your servant secretly.

And since so much I do desire
To be your own assuredly,
For all my service and my hire
Reward your servant liberally.

LXIII

WHAT meaneth this?   When I lie alone
I toss, I turn, I sigh, I groan:
My bed me seems as hard as stone.
        What meaneth this?

I sigh, I plain continually:
The clothes that on my bed do lie,
Always methink they lie awry.
        What meaneth this?

In slumbers oft for fear I quake;
For heat and cold I burn and shake;
For lack of sleep my head doth ake.
        What meaneth this?

A mornings then when I do rise,
I turn unto my wonted guise,
All day after muse and devise:
        What meaneth this?

And if perchance by me there pass
She unto whom I sue for grace,
The cold blood forsaketh my face.
        What meaneth this?

But if I sit near her by,
With loud voice my heart doth cry,
And yet my mouth is dumb and dry.
   What meaneth this?

To ask for help no heart I have;
My tongue doth fail what I should crave;
Yet inwardly I rage and rave.
   What meaneth this?

Thus have I passèd many a year,
And many a day, though nought appear
But most of that that most I fear.
   What meaneth this?

LXIV

IS it possible that so high debate,
So sharp, so sore, and of such rate,
Should end so soon, and was begun so late?
   Is it possible?

Is it possible so cruel intent,
So hasty heat, and so soon spent,
From love to hate, and thence for to relent?
   Is it possible?

Is it possible that any may find
Within one heart so diverse mind,
To change or turn as weather and wind?
   Is it possible?

Is it possible to spy it in an eye
That turns as oft as chance on die,
The truth whereof can any try?
   Is it possible?

It is possible for to turn so oft
To bring that lowest that was most aloft,
And to fall highest yet to light soft.
   It is possible!

All is possible, whoso list believe,
Trust therefore first and after preve,
As men wed ladies by licence and leave.
   All is possible.

LXV

ALAS, poor man, what hap have I
That must forbear that I love best!
I trow it be my destiny,
Never to live in quiet rest.

No wonder is though I complain,
Not without cause ye may be sure:
I seek for that I cannot attain,
Which is my mortal displeasure.

Alas, poor heart, as in this case
With pensive plaint thou art opprest,
Unwise thou were to desire place
Whereas another is possest.

Do what I can to ease thy smart,
Thou wilt not lett to love her still.
Hers and not mine I see thou art:
Let her do by thee as she will.

A carefull carcass full of pain
Now hast thou left to mourn for thee.
The heart once gone, the body is slain:
That ever I saw her, woe is me!

Mine eye, alas, was cause of this,
Which her to see had never his fill;
To me that sight full bitter is,
In recompense of my goodwill.

She that I serve all other above
Hath paid my hire, as ye may see.
I was unhappy, and that I prove,
To love above my poor degree.

LXVI

AND wilt thou leave me thus?
Say nay, say nay, for shame,
To save thee from the blame
Of all my grief and grame.
And wilt thou leave me thus?
Say nay, say nay!

And wilt thou leave me thus
That hath loved thee so long
In wealth and woe among?
And is thy heart so strong
As for to leave me thus?
Say nay, say nay!

And wilt thou leave me thus,
That hath given thee my heart
Never for to depart
Neither for pain nor smart:
And wilt thou leave me thus?
Say nay, say nay!

And wilt thou leave me thus
And have no more pity
Of him that loveth thee?
Helas thy cruelty!
And wilt thou leave me thus?
Say nay, say nay!

LXVII

THAT time that mirth did steer my ship
Which now is fraught with heaviness,
And Fortune beat not then the lip
But was defence of my distress,
Then in my book wrote my mistress:
'I am yours, you may well be sure,
And shall be while my life doth dure.'

But she herself which then wrote that
Is now mine extreme enemy.
Above all men she doth me hate,
Rejoicing of my misery.
But though that for her sake I die,
I shall be hers, she may be sure,
As long as my life doth endure.

It is not time that can wear out
With me that once is firmly set:
While Nature keeps her course about
My love from her no man can lett.
Though never so sore they me threat,
Yet am I hers, she may be sure,
And shall be while that life doth dure.

And once I trust to see that day,
Renewer of my joy and wealth,
That she to me these words shall say:
'In faith, welcome!' to me myself,
'Welcome my joy, welcome my health,
For I am thine, thou mayest be sure,
And shall be while that life doth dure.'

Lo me, alas, what words were these!
Incontinent I might find them so!
I reck not what smart or disease
I suffered, so that I might know
[After my passèd pain and woe]
That she were mine, and might be sure
She should be while that life doth dure.

LXVIII

AS power and wit will me assist,
My will shall will even as ye list.

For as ye list my will is bent
In everything to be content,
To serve in love till life be spent;
So you reward my love thus meant,
    Even as ye list.

To feign or fable is not my mind,
Nor to refuse such as I find,
But as a lamb of humble kind
Or bird in cage, to be assign'd
    Even as ye list.

When all the flock is come and gone,
Mine eye and heart, agreeth in one,
Hath chosen you, only, alone,
To be my joy, or else my moan.
    Even as ye list.

Joy if pity appear in place,
Moan if disdain do show his face,
Yet crave I not, as in this case,
But as ye lead to follow the trace
    Even as ye list.

Some in words much love can feign,
And some for words give words again:
Thus words for words in words remain,
And yet at last words do obtain
    Even as ye list.

To crave in words I will eschew,
And love in deed I will ensue;
It is my mind both whole and true,
And for my truth I pray you rue
    Even as ye list.

Dear heart, I bid your heart farewell,
With better heart than tongue can tell;
Yet take this tale, as true as gospel,
Ye may my life save or expel
    Even as ye list.

LXIX

SOMETIME I sigh, sometime I sing;
Sometime I laugh, sometime mourning
As one in doubt, this is my saying;
Have I displeas'd you in anything?

Alack, what aileth you to be grieved?
Right sorry am I that ye be moved.
I am your own, if truth be proved;
And by your displeasure as one mischieved.

When ye be merry then am I glad;
When ye be sorry then am I sad;
Such grace or fortune I would I had
You for to please howe'er I were bestad.

When ye be merry why should I care?
Ye are my joy and my welfare.
I will you love, I will not spare,
Into your presence as far as I dare.

All my poor heart and my love true
While life doth last I give it you,
And you to serve with service due,
And never to change you for no new.

LXX

THE knot which first my heart did strain,
When that your servant I became,
Doth bind me still for to remain
Always your own as now I am.
And if you find that I do feign,
With just judgment myself I damn,
   To have disdain.

If other thought in me do grow
But still to love you steadfastly,
If that the proof do not well show
That I am yours assuredly,
Let every wealth turn me to woe
And you to be continually
   My chiefest foe.

If other love or new request
Do seize my heart but only this,
Or if within my wearied breast
Be hid one thought that means amiss,
I do desire that mine unrest
May still increase, and I to miss
   That I love best.

If in my love there be one spot
Of false deceit or doubleness,
Or if I mind to slip this knot
By want of faith or steadfastness,
Let all my service be forgot
And when I would have chief redress
   Esteem me not.

But if that I consume in pain
Of burning sighs and fervent love
And daily seek none other gain
But with my deed these words to prove,
Methink of right I should obtain
That ye would mind for to remove
   Your great disdain.

And for the end of this my song,
Unto your hands I do submit
My deadly grief and pains so strong
Which in my heart be firmly shut,
And when ye list, redress my wrong,
Since well ye know this painful fit
        Hath last too long.

LXXI

IT was my choice, it was no chance,
That brought my heart in other's hold,
Whereby it hath had sufferance
Longer, perdie, than reason would.
Since I it bound where it was free
Methinks iwis of right it should
        Accepted be.

Accepted be without refuse,
Unless that Fortune have the power
All right of love for to abuse.
For, as they say, one happy hour
May more prevail than right or might.
If Fortune then list for to lower,
        What vaileth right?

What vaileth right if this be true?
Then trust to chance and go by guess:
Then whoso loveth may well go sue
Uncertain Hope for his redress.
Yet some would say assuredly
Thou mayst appeal for thy release
        To Fantasy.

To Fantasy pertains to choose.
All this I know, for Fantasy
First unto love did me induce,
But yet I know as steadfastly
That if love have no faster knot,
So nice a choice slips suddenly:
        It lasteth not.

It lasteth not that stands by change;
Fancy doth change, Fortune is frail;
Both these to please the way is strange.
Therefore methinks best to prevail,
There is no way that is so just,
As troth to lead though tother fail,
   And thereto trust.

LXXII

HEART oppress'd with desperate thought
Is forcèd ever to lament:
Which now in me so far hath wrought
That needs to it I must consent.
Wherefore all joy I do refuse,
And cruel will thereof accuse.

If cruel will had not been guide,
Despair in me had [found] no place;
For my true meaning she well espied,
Yet for all that would give no grace.
Wherefore all joy I do refuse,
And cruel will thereof accuse.

She might well see and yet would not,
And may daily, if that she will,
How painful is my hapless lot,
Joined with despair me for to spill.
Wherefore all joy I do refuse,
And cruel will thereof accuse.

LXXIII

FULL well it may be seen
To such as understand,
How some there be that ween
They have their wealth at hand:
Through love's abusèd band
But little do they see
The abuse wherein they be.

Of love there is a kind
Which kindleth by abuse,
As in a feeble mind
Whom fancy may induce
By love's deceitful use
To follow the fond lust
And proof of a vain trust.

As I myself may say,
By trial of the same,
No wight can well bewray
The falsehood love can frame.
I say, twixt grief and game,
There is no living man
That knows the craft love can.

For love so well can feign
To favour for the while
That such as seeks the gain
Are servèd with the guile,
And some can this concile
To give the simple leave
Themselves for to deceive.

What thing may more declare
Of love the crafty kind,
Than see the wise, so ware,
In love to be so blind?
If so it be assign'd,
Let them enjoy the gain
That thinks it worth the pain.

LXXIV

SINCE love is such that as ye wot
Cannot always be wisely used,
I say therefore then blame me not
Though I therein have been abused.
For as with cause I am accused,
Guilty I grant such was my lot,
And though it cannot be excused
Yet let such folly be forgot.

For in my years of reckless youth
Methought the power of love so great
That to his laws I bound my truth
And to my will there was no lett.
Me list no more so far to fet
Such fruit, lo, as of love ensu'th:
The gain was small that was to get,
And of the loss the less the ruth.

And few there is but, first or last,
A time in love once shall they have;
And glad I am my time is past,
Henceforth my freedom to withsave.
Now in my heart there shall I grave
The granted grace that now I taste:
Thankèd be fortune that me gave
So fair a gift, so sure and fast.

Now such as have me seen ere this,
When youth in me set forth his kind
And folly framed my thought amiss,
The fault whereof now well I find,
Lo, since that so it is assign'd
That unto each a time there is,
Then blame the lot that led my mind
Some time to live in love's bliss.

But from henceforth I do protest,
By proof of that that I have passed,
Shall never cease within my breast
The power of Love so late outcast:
The knot thereof is knit full fast,
And I thereto so sure profess'd
For evermore with me to last
The power wherein I am possess'd.

LXXV

LO, how I seek and sue to have
That no man hath, and may be had!
There is [no] more but sink or save,
And bring this doubt to good or bad.
To live in sorrows always sad,
I like not so to linger forth:
Hap evil or good I shall be glad
To take that comes, as well in worth.

Should I sustain this great distress,
Still wandering forth thus to and fro
In dreadful hope to hold my peace
And feed myself with secret woe?
Nay, nay, certain, I will not so!
But sure I shall myself apply
To put in proof this doubt to know,
And rid this danger readily.

I shall assay by secret suit
To show the mind of mine intent,
And my deserts shall give such fruit
As with my heart my words be meant.
So by the proof of this consent
Soon out of doubt I shall be sure,
For to rejoice or to repent,
In joy or pain for to endure.

LXXVI

SINCE so ye please to hear me plain,
And that ye do rejoice my smart,
Me list no longer to remain
To such as be so overthwart:

But cursèd be that cruel heart
Which hath procured a careless mind
For me and mine unfeignèd smart,
And forceth me such faults to find.

More than too much I am assured
Of thine intent, whereto to trust;
A speedless proof I have endured;
And now I leave it to them that lust.

LXXVII

NOW must I learn to live at rest,
And wean me of my will;
For I repent where I was prest
My fancy to fulfil.

I may no longer more endure
My wonted life to lead,
But I must learn to put in ure
The change of womanhed.

I may not see my service long
Rewarded in such wise,
Nor I may not sustain such wrong
That ye my love despise.

I may not sigh in sorrow deep,
Nor wail the want of love,
Nor I may neither crouch nor creep
Where it doth not behove.

But I of force must needs forsake
My faith so fondly set,
And from henceforth must undertake
Such folly to forget.

Now must I seek some other ways
Myself for to withsave,
And as I trust by mine essays
Some remedy to have.

I ask none other remedy
To recompense my wrong
But once to have the liberty
That I have lack'd so long.

LXXVIII

FORGET not yet the tried intent
Of such a truth as I have meant:
My great travail so gladly spent
    Forget not yet.

Forget not yet when first began
The weary life ye know, since whan
The suit, the service none tell can.
    Forget not yet.

Forget not yet the great assays,
The cruel wrong, the scornful ways,
The painful patience in denays.
    Forget not yet.

Forget not yet, forget not this,
How long ago hath been, and is,
The mind that never meant amiss.
    Forget not yet.

Forget not then thine own approved,
The which so long hath thee so loved,
Whose steadfast faith yet never moved:
　　Forget not this.

LXXIX

O MISERABLE sorrow, withouten cure,
If it please thee, lo, to have me thus suffer,
At least yet let her know what I endure,
And this my last voice carry thou thither
Where lived my hope, now dead for ever:
For as ill grievous is my banishment,
As was my pleasure when she was present.

LXXX

IF with complaint the pain might be express'd
That inwardly doth cause me sigh and groan,
Your hard heart and your cruel breast
Should sigh and plain for my unrest
And, though it were of stone,
Yet should remorse cause it relent and moan.

But since it is so far out of measure
That with my words I can it not contain,
My only trust, my heart's treasure,
Alas, why do I still endure
This restless smart and pain?
Since if ye list ye may my woe restrain.

LXXXI

YE know, my heart, my lady dear,
That since the time I was your thrall
I have been yours both whole and clear,
Though my reward hath been but small:
So am I yet, and more than all.
And ye know well how I have serv'd,
As if ye prove it shall appear,
　　　　How well, how long,
　　　　　　How faithfully,
　　　　And suffered wrong
　　　　　　How patiently.
Then since that I have never swerved,
Let not my pains be undeserved.

Ye know also, though ye say nay,
That you alone are my desire,
And you alone it is that may
Assuage my fervent flaming fire.
Succour me then I you require!
Ye know it were a just request,
Since ye do cause my heat, I say.
    If that I burn,
    It will ye warm,
    And not to turn,
    All to my harm,
Sending such flame from frozen breast
Against all right for my unrest.

And I know well how scornfully
Ye have mistaken my true intent,
And hitherto how wrongfully
I have found cause for to repent.
But if your heart doth not relent,
Since I do know that this ye know,
Ye shall slay me all wilfully.
    For me and mine
    And all I have,
    Ye may assign
    To spill or save.
Why are ye then so cruel foe
Unto your own that loves you so?

LXXXII

SINCE you will needs that I shall sing,
Take it in worth such as I have:
Plenty of plaint, moan, and mourning,
In deep despair and deadly pain.
Bootless for boot, crying to crave
    To crave in vain.

Such hammers work within my head
That sound nought else unto my ears
But fast at board and wake a-bed:
Such tune the temper to my song
To wail my wrong, that I want tears
    To wail my wrong.

Death and despair afore my face,
My days decay, my grief doth grow;
The cause thereof is in this place,
Whom cruelty doth still constrain
For to rejoice, though I be woe,
       To hear me plain.

A broken lute, untunèd strings,
With such a song may well bear part,
That neither pleaseth him that sings
Nor them that hear, but her alone
That with her heart would strain my heart
       To hear it groan.

If it grieve you to hear this same
That you do feel but in my voice,
Consider then what pleasant game
I do sustain in every part
To cause me sing or to rejoice
       Within my heart.

LXXXIII

ME list no more to sing
Of love nor of such thing,
How sore that it me wring;
For what I sung or spake,
Men did my songs mistake.

My songs were too diffuse;
They made folk to muse.
Therefore me to excuse,
They shall be sung more plain,
Neither of joy nor pain.

What vaileth then to skip
At fruit over the lip?

    .   .   .   .

For fruit withouten taste
Doth nought but rot and waste.

What vaileth under kay
To keep treasure alway
That never shall see day?
If it be not used,
It is but abused.

What vaileth the flower
To stand still and wither;
If no man it savour
It serves only for sight,
And fadeth towards night.

Therefore fear not to assay
To gather, ye that may,
The flower that this day
Is fresher than the next.
Mark well, I say, this text.

Let not the fruit be lost
That is desirèd most:
Delight shall quite the cost.
If it be ta'en in time,
Small labour is to climb.

And as for such treasure
That maketh thee the richer,
And no deal the poorer,
When it is given or lent,
Methinks it were well spent.

If this be under mist,
And not well plainly wist,
Understand me who list.
For I reck not a bean:
I wot what I do mean.

LXXXIV

THE joy so short alas, the pain so near,
The way so long, the departure so smart,
The first sight, alas, I bought too dear
That so suddenly now from hence must part.
The body gone yet remain shall the heart
With her, the which for me salt tears doth rain,
And shall not change till that we meet again.

The time doth pass, yet shall not my love;
Though I be far, always my heart is near.
Though other change, yet will not I remove;
Though other care not, yet love I will and fear;
Though other hate, yet will I love my dear;
Though other will of lightness say adieu,
Yet will I be found steadfast and true.

When other laugh, alas then do I weep;
When other sing, then do I wail and cry;
When other run, perforced I am to creep;
When other dance, in sorrow I do lie;
When other joy, for pain well near I die;
Thus brought from wealth, alas, to endless pain,
That undeservèd, causeless to remain.

LXXXV

'HOW should I
Be so pleasant,
In my semblant,
As my fellows be?'

Not long ago,
It chancèd so,
As I did walk alone,
I heard a man
That now and than
Himself did thus bemoan:

'Alas,' he said,
'I am betray'd,
And utterly undone;
Whom I did trust
And think so just,
Another man hath won.

'My service due
And heart so true
On her I did bestow:
I never meant
For to repent,
In wealth nor yet in woe.

'Each western wind
Hath turned her mind
And blown it clean away:
Thereby my wealth
My mirth and health
Are driven to great decay.

'Fortune did smile
A right short while
And never said me nay,
With pleasant plays
And joyful days
My time to pass away.

'Alas! alas!
The time so was,
So never shall it be,
Since she is gone
And I alone
Am left as you may see.

'Where is the oath,
Where is the troth
That she to me did give?
Such feignèd words
With sely bourds
Let no wise man believe.

'For even as I
Thus wofully
Unto myself complain,
If ye then trust
Needs learn ye must
To sing my song in vain.

'How should I
Be so pleasant,
In my semblant,
As my fellows be?'

LXXXVI

WHAT should I say,
Since faith is dead
And truth away
From you is fled?
Should I be led
With doubleness?
Nay, nay, mistress.

I promised you
And you promised me
To be as true
As I would be.
But since I see
Your double heart,
Farewell my part!

Thought for to take
It is not my mind,
But to forsake
[One so unkind]
And as I find,
So will I trust.
Farewell, unjust!

Can ye say nay
But you said
That I alway
Should be obey'd?
And thus betray'd
Or that I wist!
Farewell, unkist!

LXXXVII

GIVE place all ye that doth rejoice,
And love's pangs hath clean forgot.
Let them draw near and hear my voice
Whom Love doth force in pains to fret,
For all of plaint my song is set,
Which long hath served and nought can get.

A faithful heart so truly meant
Rewarded is full slenderly;
A steadfast faith with good intent
Is recompensèd craftily;
Such hap doth hap unhappily
To them that mean but honestly.

With humble suit I have assay'd
To turn her cruel-hearted mind,
But for reward I am delay'd,
And to my wealth [1] her eyes be blind.
Lo, thus by chance I am assign'd
With steadfast love to serve the unkind.

What vaileth truth, or steadfastness,
Or still to serve without repreef? [2]
What vaileth faith or gentleness
Where cruelty doth reign as chief?
Alas, there is no greater grief
Than for to love and lack relief.

Care doth constrain me to complain
Of love, and her uncertainty
Which granteth nought but great disdain
For loss of all my liberty.
Alas, this is extremity
For love to find such cruelty.

For love to find such cruelty,
Alas, it is a careful lot;
And for to void such mockery
There is no way but slip the knot.
The gain so cold, the pain so hot,
Praise it who list, I like it not.

LXXXVIII

SPITE hath no power to make me sad,
Nor scornfulness to make me plain.
It doth suffice that once I had,
And so to leave it is no pain.

_____
[1] *well being*   [2] *reprieve*

Let them frown on that least doth gain,
Who did rejoice must needs be glad;
And though with words thou ween'st to reign,
It doth suffice that once I had.

Since that in checks thus overthwart
And coyly looks thou dost delight,
It doth suffice that mine thou wert,
Though change hath put thy faith to flight.

Alas, it is a peevish spite
To yield thyself and then to part,
But since thou seest thy faith so light,
It doth suffice that mine thou wert.

And since thy love doth thus decline,
And in thy heart such hate doth grow,
It doth suffice that thou wert mine,
And with good will I quite it so.

Sometime my friend, farewell my foe,
Since thou change I am not thine:
But for relief of all my woe
It doth suffice that thou wert mine.

Praying you all that hear this song
To judge no wight, nor none to blame,
It doth suffice she doth me wrong,
And that herself doth know the same.

And though she change it is no shame,
Their kind it is, and hath been long.
Yet I protest she hath no name:
It doth suffice she doth me wrong.

LXXXIX

AH my heart, ah, what aileth thee?
To set so light my liberty,
Making me bond when I was free?
    Ah my heart, ah, what aileth thee?

When thou were rid from all distress,
Void of all pain and pensiveness,
To choose again a new mistress!
    Ah my heart, ah, what aileth thee?

When thou were well thou could not hold:
To turn again, that were too bold;
Thus to renew my sorrows old,
   Ah my heart, ah, what aileth thee?

Thou knowest full well that but of late
I was turn'd out of Love's gate.
And now to guide me to this mate!
   Ah my heart, ah, what aileth thee?

I hoped full well all had been done,
But now my hope is ta'en and won.
To my torment to yield so soon—
   Ah my heart, ah, what aileth thee?

XC

HATE whom ye list, for I care not.
Love whom ye list, and spare not.
Do what ye list, and dread not.
Think what ye list, I fear not.
For as for me I am not
But even as one that recks not
Whether ye hate or hate not,
For in your love I dote not.
Wherefore I pray you forget not,
But love whom ye list, for I care not.

XCI

TANGLED I was in love's snare,
Oppress'd with pain, torment with care:
Of grief right sure, of joy full bare,
Clean in despair by cruelty.
But ha! ha! ha! full well is me,
For I am now at liberty.

The woful days so full of pain,
The weary night all spent in vain,
The labour lost for so small gain,
To write them all it will not be.
But ha! ha! ha! full well is me,
For I am now at liberty.

Every thing that fair doth show,
When proof is made it proveth not so,
But turneth mirth to bitter woe,
Which in this case full well I see.
But ha! ha! ha! full well is me,
For I am now at liberty.

Too great desire was my guide,
And wanton will went by my side,
Hope rulèd still and made me bide,
Of love's craft the extremity.
But ha! ha! ha! full well is me,
For I am now at liberty.

With feignèd words, which were but wind,
To long delays I was assign'd;
Her wily looks my wits did blind;
Thus as she would I did agree.
But ha! ha! ha! full well is me,
For I am now at liberty.

Was never bird tangled in lime*
That brake away in better time
Than I that rotten boughs did climb
And had no hurt but scapèd free.
Now ha! ha! ha! full well is me,
For I am now at liberty.

XCII

LONGER to muse
On this refuse
I will not use,
But study to forget.
Let my all go,
Since well I know
To be my foe
Her heart is firmly set.

Since my intent,
So truly meant,
Cannot content
Her mind, as I do see
To tell you plain,
It were in vain
For so small gain
To lose my liberty.

For if he thrive
That will go strive
A ship to drive
Against the stream and wind,
Undoubtedly
Then thrive should I
To love trulye
A cruel-hearted mind.

But sith that so
The world doth go
That every woe
By yielding doth increase,
As I have told
I will be bold
Thereby my pains to cease.

Praying you all
That after shall
By fortune fall
Into this foolish trade,
Have in your mind
(As I do find)
That oft by kind
All women's love do fade.

Wherefore apace
Come take my place
Some man that has
A lust to burn the feet:
For since that she
Refuseth me
I must agree,
And perdie to forget.

XCIII

LOVE doth again
Put me to pain,
And yet all is but lost.
I serve in vain
And am certain
Of all mislikèd most.

Both heat and cold
Doth so me hold
And comber so my mind
That when I should
Speak and behold,
It driveth me still behind.

My wits be past,
My life doth waste,
My comfort is exiled;
And I in haste
Am like to taste
How love hath me beguiled.

Unless that right
May in her sight
Obtain pity and grace,
Why should a wight
Have beauty bright
If mercy have no place?

Yet I, alas,
Am in such case
That back I cannot go,
But still forth trace
A patient pace
And suffer secret woe.

For with the wind
My fir èd mind
Doth still inflame,
And she unkind,
That did me bind,
Doth turn it all to game.

Yet can no pain
Make me refrain,
Nor here and there to range:
I shall retain
Hope to obtain
Her heart that is so strange.

But I require
The painful fire
That oft doth make me sweat,
For all my ire
With like desire
To give her heart a heat.

Then she shall prove
How I her love,
And what I have offer'd:
Which should her move
For to remove
The pains that I have suffer'd.

And better fee
Than she gave me
She shall of me attain,
For whereas she
Show'd cruelty,
She shall my heart obtain.

XCIV

WITH serving still
    This have I won,
For my goodwill
    To be undone.

And for redress
    Of all my pain,
Disdainfulness
    I have again.

And for reward
    Of all my smart,
Lo, thus unheard
    I must depart!

Wherefore all ye
    That after shall
By fortune be,
    As I am, thrall,

Example take
    What I have won,
Thus for her sake
    To be undone!

XCV

NOW all of change
Must be my song,
And from my bond now must I break,
Since she so strange
Unto my wrong
Doth stop her ears to hear me speak.

Yet none doth know
So well as she
My grief, which can have no restraint,
That fain would follow
Now needs must flee,
For fault of ear unto my plaint.

I am not he
By false assays
Nor feignèd faith can bear in hand,
Though most I see
That such always
Are best for to be understand.

But I that truth
Hath always meant
Doth still proceed to serve in vain:
Desire pursu'th
My time misspent,
And doth not pass upon my pain.

Of Fortune's might
That each compels,
And me the most, it doth suffice
Now for my right
To ask nought else
But to withdraw this enterprise.

And for the gain
Of that good hour
Which of my woe shall be relief,
I shall refrain
By painful power
The thing that most hath been my grief.

I shall not miss
To exercise
The help thereof that doth me teach.
That after this
In any wise
To keep right within my reach.

And she unjust
Which feareth not
In this her fame to be defiled,
Yet once I trust
Shall be my lot
To 'quite the craft that me beguiled.

XCVI

ABSENCE absenting causeth me to complain,
My sorrowful complaints abiding in distress,
And departing most privy increaseth my pain,
Thus live I uncomforted wrappèd all in heaviness.

In heaviness I am wrappèd, devoid of all solace,
Neither pastime nor pleasure can revive my dull wit,
My spirits be all taken, and death doth me menace,
With his fatal knife the thread for to kit.

For to cut the thread of this wretched life,
And shortly bring me out of this case:
I see it availeth not, yet must I be pensive,
Since fortune from me hath turnèd her face.

Her face she hath turnèd with countenance contrarious,
And clean from her presence she hath exiled me,
In sorrow remaining as a man most dolorous,
Exempt from all pleasure and worldly felicity.

All worldly felicity now am I private,
And left in desert most solitarily,
Wandering all about as one without mate;
My death approacheth; what remedy?

What remedy, alas, to rejoice my woful heart,
With sighs suspiring most ruefully?
Now welcome! I am ready to depart.
Farewell all pleasure! welcome pain and smart!

XCVII

PATIENCE, for I have wrong
And dare not show wherein,
Patience shall be my song,
Since Truth can nothing win.
Patience then for this fit:
Hereafter comes not yet.

XCVIII

WILL ye see what wonders love hath wrought,
 Then come and look at me.
There need no where else to be sought,
 In me ye may them see.

For unto that that men may see
 Most monstrous thing of kind
Myself may best comparèd be:
 Love hath me so assign'd.

There is a rock in the salt flood,
 A rock of such nature
That draweth the iron from the wood
 And leaveth the ship unsure.

She is the rock, the ship am I,
 That rock my deadly foe
That draweth me there where I must die
 And robbeth my heart me fro.

A bird there fleeth, and that but one,
 Of her this thing ensueth,
That when her days be spent and gone,
 With fire she reneweth.

And I with her may well compare
 My love that is alone
The flame whereof doth aye repair
 My life when it is gone.

XCIX

DEEM as ye list, upon good cause
I may or think of this or that:
But what or why myself best knows
Whereby I think and fear not.
But thereunto I may well think
The doubtful sentence of this clause:
I would it were not as I think,
I would I thought it were not.

For if I thought it were not so,
Though it were so it griev'd me not:
Unto my thought it were as though
I hearkened though I hear not.
At that I see I cannot wink,
Nor from my thought so let it go.
I would it were not as I think,
I would I thought it were not.

Lo, how my thought might make me free,
Of that perchance that needeth not.
Perchance no doubt the dread I see,
I shrink at that I bear not.
But in my heart this word shall sink,
Until the proof may better be:
I would it were not as I think,
I would I thought it were not.

If it be not, show no cause why
I should so think, then care I not;
For I shall so myself apply
To be that I appear not:
That is, as one that shall not shrink
To be your own until I die.
And if that be not as I think,
Likewise to think it is not.

C

I AM as I am and so will I be,
But how that I am none knoweth truly.
Be it evil, be it well, be I bond, be I free,
I am as I am and so will I be.

I lead my life indifferently,
I mean nothing but honesty,
And though folks judge full diversly,
I am as I am and so will I die.

I do not rejoice nor yet complain,
Both mirth and sadness I do refrain,
And use the mean since folks will feign:
Yet I am as I am, be it pleasure or pain.

Divers do judge as they do trow,
Some of pleasure and some of woe,
Yet for all that nothing they know:
But I am as I am, wheresoever I go.

But since judgers do thus decay,
Let every man his judgment say.
I will it take in sport and play,
For I am as I am, whosoever say nay.

Who judgeth well, well God him send;
Who judgeth evil, God them amend;
To judge the best therefore intend,
For I am as I am and so will I end.

Yet some there be that take delight
To judge folks' thought for envy and spite.
But, whether they judge me wrong or right,
I am as I am, and so do I write.

Praying you all that this do read
To trust it as you do your creed,
And not to think I change my weed,
For I am as I am however I speed.

But how that is I leave to you;
Judge as ye list, false or true;
Ye know no more than afore ye knew,
Yet I am as I am, whatever ensue.

And from this mind I will not flee,
But to you all that misjudge me
I do protest, as ye may see,
That I am as I am and so will be.

CI

STAND, whoso list, upon the slipper top
Of court's estate, and let me here rejoice
And use my quiet without lett or stop,
Unknown in court, that hath such brackish joys.

In hidden place so let my days forth pass
That, when my years be done, withouten noise
I may die aged after the common trace.

For him death grippeth right hard by the crop
That is much known of other, and of himself, alas,
Doth die unknown, dazed, with dreadful face.

CII

ACCUSÈD though I be without desert,
Sith none can prove believe it not for true:
For never yet, since that you had my heart,
Intended I to false or be untrue.
Sooner I would of death sustain the smart
Than break one word of that I promised you.
Accept therefore my service in good part:
None is alive that can ill tongues eschew.
Hold them as false, and let not us depart
Our friendship old in hope of any new.
Put not thy trust in such as use to feign,
Except thou mind to put thy friend to pain.

CIII

MADAME, withouten many words,
Once, I am sure, ye will, or no:
And if ye will, then leave your bourds,
And use your wit, and show it so:

And with a beck you shall me call,
And if of one that burneth alway
Ye have any pity at all,
Answer him fair with yea or nay.

If it be yea, I shall be fain;
If it be nay, friends as before;
Ye shall another man obtain,
And I mine own and yours no more.

Answer to the Foregoing

[ANONYMOUS]

OF few words, Sir, you seem to be,
And where I doubted what I would do
Your quick request hath causèd me
Quickly to tell you what you shall trust to.

For he that will be callèd with a beck
Makes hasty suit on light desire,
Is ever ready to the check,
And burneth in no wasting fire.

Therefore, whether you be lief or loth,
And whether it grieve you light or sore,
I am at a point, I have made an oath:
Content you with Nay, for you get no more.

CIV

SUFFICÈD not, madame, that you did tear
My woful heart, but thus also to rent
The weeping paper that to you I sent,
Whereof each letter was written with a tear?
Could not my present pains, alas, suffice
Your greedy heart? and that my heart doth feel
Torments that prick more sharper than the steel,
But new and new must to my lot arise?
Use then my death.   So shall your cruelty,
Spite of your spite, rid me from all my smart,
And I no more such torments of the heart
Feel as I do.   This shall you gain thereby.

CV

MISTRUSTFUL minds be movèd
To have me in suspect,
The truth it shall be provèd,
Which time shall once detect.

Though falsehood go about
Of crime me to accuse,
At length I do not doubt
But truth shall me excuse.

Such sauce as they have servèd
To me without desart,
Even as they have deservèd,
Thereof God send them part.

An Epitaph of Sir Thomas Gravener, Knight

UNDER this stone there lieth at rest
A friendly man, a worthy knight,
Whose heart and mind was ever prest
To favour truth, to further right.

The poor's defence, his neighbour's aid,
Most kind always unto his kin;
That stint all strife, that might be stay'd;
Whose gentle grace great love did win.

A man that was full earnest set
To serve his prince at all assays:
No sickness could him from that lett:
Which was the shortening of his days.

His life was good, he died full well.
The body here, the soul in bliss.
With length of words why should I tell
Or farther show that well known is?
Since that the tears of more and less
Right well declare his worthiness.

VIVIT POST FUNERA VIRTUS

SATIRES

I

MINE own John Poynz, since ye delight to know
The cause why that homeward I me draw,
And flee the press of courts whereso they go

Rather than to live thrall, under the awe
Of lordly looks, wrapped within my cloak,
To will and lust learning to set a law:

It is not for because I scorn and moke
The power of them to whom fortune hath lent
Charge over us, of right, to strike the stroke:

But true it is that I have always meant
Less to esteem them than the common sort
Of outward things that judge in their intent

Without regard what doth inward resort.
I grant some time that of glory the fire
Doth touch my heart.   Me list not to report

Blame by honour and honour to desire,
But how may I this honour now attain
That cannot dye the colour black a liar?

My Poynz, I cannot frame my tune to feign,
To cloak the truth for praise without desert
Of them that list all vice for to retain.

I cannot honour them that sets their part
With Venus and Bacchus all their life long,
Nor hold my peace of them, although I smart.

I cannot crouch nor kneel to do so great a wrong
To worship them, like God, on earth alone
That are as wolves these sely lambs among.

I cannot with words complain and moan,
Nor suffer nought nor smart without complaint,
Nor turn the word that from my mouth is gone:

I cannot speak and look like a saint,
Use wiles for wit or make deceit a pleasure,
And call craft counsel, for profit still to paint;

I cannot wrest the law to fill the coffer,
With innocent blood to feed myself fat,
And do most hurt where most help I offer.

I am not he that can allow the state
Of high Caesar, and damn Cato to die
That with his death did scape out of the gate

From Caesar's hands (if Livy do not lie)
And would not live when liberty was lost,
So did his heart the common weal apply.

I am not he such eloquence to boast
To make the crow singing as the swan,
Nor call the lion of coward beasts the most

That cannot take a mouse as the cat can,
And he that dieth for hunger of the gold
Call him Alexander, and say that Pan

Passeth Apollo in music manifold,
Praise Sir Topas for a noble tale
And scorn the story that the knight told,

Praise him for counsel that is drunk of ale,
Grin when he laugheth that beareth all the sway,
Frown when he frowneth and groan when he is pale,

On others' lust to hang both night and day.
None of these points would ever frame in me;
My wit is nought: I cannot learn the way.

And much the less of things that greater be,
That asken help of colours of devise
To join the mean with each extremity,

With the nearest virtue to cloak always the vice;
And as to purpose likewise it shall fall
To press the virtue that it may not rise.

As drunkenness good fellowship to call,
The friendly foe with his double face
Say he is gentle and courteous therewithal,

And say that favel hath a goodly grace
In eloquence, and cruelty to name
Zeal of justice, and change in time and place,

And he that suffereth offence without blame
Call him pitiful, and him true and plain
That raileth reckless to every man's shame:

Say he is rude that cannot lie and feign,
The lecher a lover, and tyranny
To be the right of a prince's reign.

I cannot I, no no it will not be!
This is the cause that I could never yet
Hang on their sleeves that weigh, as thou mayst see,

A chip of chance more than a pound of wit.
This maketh me at home to hunt and hawk,
And in foul weather at my book to sit,

In frost and snow then with my bow to stalk:
No man doth mark whereso I ride or go,
In lusty leas at liberty I walk,

And of these news I feel nor weal nor woe,
Save that a clog doth hang yet at my heel.
No force for that, for it is ordered so

That I may leap both hedge and dyke full well:
I am not now in France to judge the wine,
With savoury sauce the delicates to feel,

Nor yet in Spain where one must him incline
(Rather than to be) outwardly to seem:
I meddle not with wits that be so fine.

Nor Flanders cheer letteth not my sight to deem
Of black and white, nor taketh my wit away
With beastliness: they beasts do so esteem.

Nor I am not where Christ is given in prey
For money, poison, and traïson at Rome:
A common practice uséd night and day.

But here I am in Kent and Christendom,
Among the Muses, where I read and rime:
Where if thou list, my Poynz, for to come,
Thou shalt be judge how I do spend my time.

II

MY mother's maids, when they did sew and spin,
They sang sometime a song of the field mouse,
That for because her livelood was but thin

Would needs go seek her townish sister's house.
She thought herself endured to much pain:
The stormy blasts her cave so sore did souse

That when the furrows swimmed with the rain
She must lie cold and wet in sorry plight,
And, worse than that, bare meat there did remain

To comfort her when she her house had dight:
Sometime a barleycorn, sometime a bean,
For which she laboured hard both day and night

In harvest time, whilst she might go and glean.
And when her store was stroyéd with the flood,
Then well away! for she undone was clean.

Then was she fain to take, instead of food,
Sleep if she might, her hunger to beguile.
'My sister' quoth she 'hath a living good,

'And hence from me she dwelleth not a mile.
In cold and storm she lieth warm and dry
In bed of down, and dirt doth not defile

'Her tender foot, she laboureth not as I.
Richly she feedeth and at the rich man's cost,
And for her meat she needs not crave nor cry.

'By sea, by land, of the delicates the most
Her cater seeks and spareth for no peril.
She feedeth on boiled, baken meat, and roast,

'And hath thereof neither charge nor travail.
And, when she list, the liquor of the grape
Doth goad her heart till that her belly swell.'

And at this journey she maketh but a jape:
So forth she goeth, trusting of all this wealth
With her sister her part so for to shape

That, if she might keep herself in health,
To live a lady while her life doth last.
And to the door now is she come by stealth,

And with her foot anon she scrapeth full fast.
The other for fear durst not well scarce appear,
Of every noise so was the wretch aghast.

At last she asked softly who was there,
And in her language, as well as she could,
'Peep,' quoth the other.　'Sister, I am here.'

'Peace,' quoth the town mouse, 'why speakest thou
And by the hand she took her fair and well.　　[so loud?
'Welcome,' quoth she, 'my sister, by the rood.'

She feasted her that joy it was to tell
The fare they had; they drank the wine so clear;
And as to purpose now and then it fell

She cheered her with: 'How, sister, what cheer?'
Amids this joy there fell a sorry chance,
That, wellaway! the stranger bought full dear

The fare she had.　For as she looks, askance,
Under a stool she spied two steaming eyes
In a round head with sharp ears.　In France

Was never mouse so feared, for though the unwise
Had not yseen such a beast before,
Yet had nature taught her after her guise

To know her foe and dread him evermore.
The town mouse fled; she knew whither to go.
The other had no shift, but wondrous sore

Feared of her life at home she wished her tho.
And to the door, alas, as she did skip
(Th' heaven it would, lo, and eke her chance was so)

At the threshold her sely foot did trip,
And ere she might recover it again
The traitor cat had caught her by the hip

And made her there against her will remain
That had forgotten her poor surety, and rest,
For seeming wealth wherein she thought to reign.

Alas, my Poynz, how men do seek the best
And find the worst, by error as they stray!
And no marvail, when sight is so opprest

And blind the guide.   Anon out of the way
Goeth guide and all in seeking quiet life.
O wretched minds! there is no gold that may

Grant that ye seek, no war, no peace, no strife.
No, no, although thy head were hoopt with gold,
Sergeant with mace, hawbert, sword, nor knife

Cannot repulse the care that follow should.
Each kind of life hath with him his disease:
Live in delight even as thy lust would,

And thou shalt find when lust doth most thee please
It irketh strait and by itself doth fade.
A small thing it is that may thy mind appease.

None of ye all there is that is so mad
To seek grapes upon brambles or breers,
Nor none I trow that hath his wit so bad

To set his hay for conies over rivers,
Ne ye set not a drag net for an hare.
And yet the thing that most is your desire

Ye do misseek with more travail and care.
Make plain thine heart, that it be not knotted
With hope or dread, and see thy will be bare

From all affects whom vice hath ever spotted.
Thyself content with that is thee assigned,
And use it well that is to thee allotted,

Then seek no more out of thyself to find
The thing that thou hast sought so long before,
For thou shalt find it sitting in thy mind.

Mad, if ye list to continue your sore,
Let present pass, and gape on time to come,
And deep yourself in travail more and more.

Henceforth, my Poynz, this shall be all and some:
These wretched fools shall have nought else of me.
But to the great God and to his high doom

None other pain pray I for them to be
But, when the rage doth lead them from the right,
That, looking backward, virtue they may see

Even as she is, so goodly fair and bright.
And whilst they clasp their lusts in arms across
Grant them, good Lord, as thou mayst of thy might,
To fret inward for losing such a loss.

III

[TO SIR FRANCIS BRIAN]

A SPENDING hand that alway poureth out
Had need to have a bringer in as fast,
And on the stone that still doth turn about

There groweth no moss.   These proverbs yet do last.
Reason hath set them in so sure a place
That length of years their force can never waste.

When I remember this, and eke the case
Wherein thou stands, I thought forthwith to write,
Brian, to thee who knows how great a grace

In writing is to counsel man the right:
To thee, therefore, that trots still up and down
And never rests, but running day and night

From realm to realm, from city, street, and town.
Why dost thou wear thy body to the bones
And mightst at home sleep in thy bed of down

And drink good ale so nappy for the nones,
Feed thyself fat and heap up pound by pound?
Likest thou not this? No, why? For swine so groans

In sty, and chaw the tords moulded on the ground,
And drivel on pearls, the head still in the manger,
Then of the harp the ass to hear the sound.

So sacks of dust be filled up in the cloister
That serves for less than do these fatted swine.
Though I seem lean and cry, without moister,

Yet will I serve my prince, my lord and thine;
And let them live to feed the paunch that list,
So I may live to feed both me and mine.

By God, well said! But what and if thou wist
How to bring in as fast as thou dost spend,
That I would learn. And it shall not be missed

To tell thee how. Now hark what I intend.
Thou knowest well first whoso can seek to please
Shall purchase friends where truth shall but offend:

Flee therefore truth: it is both wealth and ease.
For though that truth of every man hath praise,
Full near that wind goeth truth in great misease.

Use virtue as it goeth nowadays,
In word alone to make thy language sweet,
And of the deed yet do not as thou says,

Else be thou sure thou shalt be far unmeet
To get thy bread, each thing is now so scant.
Seek still thy profit upon thy bare feet,

Lend in nowise, for fear that thou do want,
Unless it be as to a dog a cheese,
By which return be sure to win a cant

Of half at least: it is not good to lese.
Learn at Kittson, that in a long white coat
From under the stall without lands or fees

Hath leapt into the shop, who knoweth by rote
This rule that I have told thee here before.
Sometime, also, rich age beginneth to dote:

See thou when there thy gain may be the more,
Stay him by the arm whereso he walk or go,
Be near alway and, if he cough too sore,

When he hath spit tread out and please him so.
A diligent knave that picks his master's purse
May please him so that he withouten mo

Executor is, and what is he the worse?
And, if so chance you get nought of the man,
The widow may for all thy charge deburse

A rivell'd skin, a stinking breath.   What then?
A toothless mouth shall do thy lips no harm.
The gold is good, and though she curse or ban

Yet where thee list thou mayst lie good and warm.
Let the old mule bite upon the bridle
Whilst there do lie a sweeter in thine arm.

In this also see you be not idle:
Thy niece, thy cousin, thy sister or thy daughter,
If she be fair, if handsome be her middle,

If thy better hath her love besought her,
Avance his cause and he shall help thy need:
It is but love, turn it to a laughter.

But ware I say, so gold thee help and speed,
That in this case thou be not so unwise
As Pandar was in such a like deed:

For he, the fool of conscience, was so nice
That he no gain would have all for his pain.
Be next thyself, for friendship bears no price.

Laughst thou at me? Why, do I speak in vain?
No, not at thee, but at thy thrifty gest?
Wouldst thou I should, for any loss or gain,

Change that for gold that I have ta'en for best
Next godly things, to have an honest name?
Should I leave that, then take me for a beast.

Nay then farewell, and if thou care for shame
Content thee then with honest poverty,
With free tongue what thee mislikes to blame,

And for thy truth sometime adversity,
And therewithal this gift I shall thee give:
In this world now, little prosperity,
And coin to keep as water in a sieve.

HENRY HOWARD: EARL OF SURREY

1517–47

TEXTUALLY, the Surrey situation is similar to that of Wyatt. In both cases manuscripts exist which are often at variance with Tottel. But since Surrey's verse in general is metrically smoother (which is not to say better) than Wyatt's, the changes assumed to have been made by Tottel are apt to be less disastrous, affecting diction rather than cadence. In preparing the present text the editor has consulted both Tottel and Nott, with frequent and grateful resort to the manuscript versions printed by Padelford. As throughout this volume, the spelling has been discreetly modernized and the poems re-punctuated. All Surrey's lyrics and sonnets are included; and to these are added, because it is the earliest example of English blank verse, his translation of the Second Book of Virgil's *Aeneid*. In fine, everything of Surrey's is here except the Fourth Book of the *Aeneid* and the Old Testament paraphrases (*Ecclesiastes* and *Psalms*).

I

THE sun hath twice brought forth the tender green
And clad the earth in lively lustiness,
Once have the winds the trees despoilèd clean,
And once again begins their cruelness,
Since I have hid under my breast the harm
That never shall recover healthfulness.
The winter's hurt recovers with the warm;
The parchèd green restorèd is with shade;
What warmth, alas, may serve for to disarm
The frozen heart, that mine inflame hath made?
What cold again is able to restore
My fresh green years, that wither thus and fade?
Alas, I see nothing hath hurt so sore
But Time, in time, reduceth a return:
Yet Time my harm increaseth more and more,
And seems to have my cure always in scorn.
Strange kind of death in life that I do try,
At hand to melt, far off in flame to burn,
And like as time list to my cure apply,
So doth each place my comfort clean refuse.
Each thing alive that sees the heaven with eye
With cloak of night may cover and excuse
Himself from travail of the day's unrest,
Save I, alas! against all others use,
That then stir up the torment of my breast
To curse each star as causer of my fate.
And when the sun hath eke the dark represt,
And brought the day, it doth nothing abate
The travail of mine endless smart and pain;
For then, as one that hath the light in hate,
I wish for night, more covertly to plain;
And me withdraw from every haunted place,
Lest in my chere my chance appear too plain.
And in my mind I measure, pace by páce,
To seek the place where I myself had lost,
That day that I was tangled in that lace,
In seeming slack, that knitteth ever most.
But never yet the travail of my thought

Of better state could catch a cause to boast,
For if I found, some time that I have sought,
Those stars by whom I trusted of the port,
My sails do fall, and I advance right nought;
As anchor'd fast my spirits do all resort
To stand at gaze, and sink in more and more
The deadly harm which she doth take in sport.
Lo, if I seek, how I do find my sore!
And if I fly, I carry with me still
The venomed shaft, which doth his force restore
By haste of flight.   And I may plain my fill
Unto myself, unless this careful song
Print in your heart some parcel of my tene:
For I, alas, in silence all too long,
Of mine old hurt yet feel the wound but green.
Rue on my life; or else your cruel wrong
Shall well appear and by my death be seen.

II

THE soote season, that bud and bloom forth brings,
With green hath clad the hill, and eke the vale.
The nightingale with feathers new she sings;
The turtle to her make hath told her tale.
Summer is come, for every spray now springs,
The hart hath hung his old head on the pale;
The buck in brake his winter coat he flings;
The fishes flete with new repairèd scale;
The adder all her slough away she slings;
The swift swallow pursueth the flies smale;
The busy bee her honey now she mings;
Winter is worn that was the flowers' bale.
And thus I see among these pleasant things
Each care decays, and yet my sorrow springs!

III

WHEN youth had led me half the race
That Cupid's scourge had made me run,
I lookèd back to mete the place
From whence my weary course begun.

And then I saw how my desire
By guiding ill had lett the way:
Where, too greedy of their hire,
Had eyes lost me many a noble prey.

For when in sighs I spent the day,
And could not cloak my grief with game,
The boiling smoke did still bewray
The persant heat of hidden flame.

And when salt tears did bain my breast,
Where Love his pleasant trains hath sown,
The bruit thereof the fruits opprest,
Ere that the blooms were sprung and blown.

And when mine eyes did still pursue
The flying chase that was their quest,
Their greedy looks did oft renew
The hidden wound within my breast.

When every look these cheeks might stain,
From deadly pale to glowing red;
By outward signs appearèd plain
The woe wherewith my heart was fed.

But all too late Love learneth me
To paint all kind of colours new,
To blind their eyes that else should see
My sparkled cheeks with Cupid's hue.

And now the covert breast I claim
That worships Cupid secretly
And nourisheth his sacred flame
From whence no blazing sparks do fly.

IV

SUCH wayward ways hath Love, that most part in discord
Our wills do stand, whereby our hearts but seldom do accord.
Deceit is his delight, and to beguile and mock
The simple hearts, which he doth strike with froward diverse stroke.
He causeth the one to rage with golden burning dart,
And doth allay with leaden cold again the other's heart.
Hot gleams of burning fire, and easy sparks of flame,
In balance of unequal weight he pondereth by aim.
From easy ford, where I might wade, and pass full well,
He me withdraws, and doth me drive into a deep dark hell;
And me withholds where I am called, and offered place,
And wills me that my mortal foe I do beseech of grace.

He letts me to pursue a conquest well near won,
To follow where my pains were lost ere that my suit begun.
So by these rules I know how soon a heart may turn
From war to peace, from truce to strife, and so again return.
I know how to convert my will in others' lust,
Of little stuff unto myself to weave a web of trust,
And how to hide my harm with soft dissembled chere
When in my face the painted thoughts would outwardly appear.
I know how that the blood forsakes the face for dread,
And how by shame it stains again the cheek with flaming red.
I know under the green, the serpent how he lurks;
The hammer of the restless forge I know eke how it works;
I know, and can by rote, the tale that I would tell;
But oft the words come forth awry of him that loveth well.
I know in heat and cold the lover how he shakes;
In singing how he can complain, in sleeping how he wakes,
To languish without ache, sickless for to consume,
A thousand things for to devise, resolving all in fume.
And though he list to see his lady's face full sore,
Such pleasure as delights his eye doth not his health restore.
I know to seek the track of my desirèd foe,
And fear to find that I do seek.   But chiefly this I know:
That lovers must transform into the thing beloved,
And live (alas, who could believe?) with sprite from life removed.
I know in hearty sighs, and laughters of the spleen,
At once to change my state, my will, and eke my colour clean.
I know how to deceive myself withouten help;
And how the lion chastisèd is by beating of the whelp.
In standing near my fire, I know how that I freeze;
Far off I burn; in both I waste, and so my life I lese.
I know how love doth rage upon a yielding mind,
How small a net may take and mesh a heart of gentle kind,
Or else, with seldom sweet to season heaps of gall,
Revivèd with a glimpse of grace, old sorrows to let fall.
The hidden trains I know, and secret snares of love;
How soon a look may print a thought, that never will remove.
That slipper state I know, those sudden turns from wealth;
That doubtful hope, that certain woe, and sure despair of health.

V

WHEN Summer took in hand the winter to assail
With force of might and virtue great, his stormy blasts to quail,
And when he clothèd fair the earth about with green,
And every tree new garmented, that pleasure was to seen,

Mine heart gan new revive, and changèd blood did stir
Me to withdraw my winter woes, that kept within my dore.
'Abroad,' quoth my desire, 'assay to set thy foot
Where thou shalt find the savour sweet, for sprung is every root,
And to thy health, if thou were sick in any case,
Nothing more good than in the spring the air to feel a space.
There shalt thou hear and see all kinds of birds ywrought
Well tune their voice with warble small, as nature hath them taught.'
Thus prickèd me my lust the sluggish house to leave,
And for my health I thought it best such counsel to receive.
So on a morrow forth, unwist of any wight,
I went to prove how well it would my heavy burden light.
And when I felt the air so pleasant round about,
Lord, to myself how glad I was that I had gotten out!
There might I see how Ver had every blossom hent,
And eke the new betrothèd birds y-coupled how they went.
And in their songs methought they thankèd Nature much
That by her licence all that year to love, their hap was such,
Right as they could devise to choose them feres throughout:
With much rejoicing to their Lord, thus flew they all about.
Which when I gan revolve, and in my head conceive,
What pleasant life, what heaps of joy, these little birds receive,
And saw in what estate I, weary man, was brought
By want of that they had at will, and I reject at nought;
Lord, how I gan in wrath unwisely me demean!
I cursèd Love, and him defied: I thought to turn the stream.
But when I well beheld he had me under awe,
I askèd mercy for my fault that so transgrest his law.
'Thou blinded god,' quoth I, 'forgive me this offence:
Unwittingly I went about to malice thy pretence.'
Wherewith he gave a beck, and thus methought he swore:
'Thy sorrow ought suffice to purge thy fault, if it were more.'
The virtue of which sound mine heart did so revive
That I, methought, was made as whole as any man alive.
But here I may perceive mine error, all and some,
For that I thought that so it was, yet was it still undone;
And all that was no more but mine empressèd mind,
That fain would have some good relief of Cupid well assigned.
I turnèd home forthwith, and might perceive it well
That he aggrievèd was right sore with me for my rebell.
My harms have ever since increasèd more and more,
And I remain, without his help, undone for evermore.
A mirror let me be unto ye lovers all:
Strive not with Love, for if ye do, it will ye thus befall.

VI

LOVE that liveth and reigneth in my thought,
That built its seat within my captive breast,
Clad in the arms wherein with me he fought,
Oft in my face he doth his banner rest.
But she that taught me love, and suffer pain,
My doubtful hope and eke my hot desire
With shamefast cloak to shadow and refrain,
Her smiling grace converteth straight to ire.
And coward Love then to the heart apace
Taketh his flight, where he doth lurk and plain
His purpose lost, and dare not show his face.
For my lord's guilt thus faultless bide I pain.
Yet from my lord shall not my foot remove:
Sweet is his death that takes his end by love.

VII

IN Cyprus springs—whereas dame Venus dwelt—
A well so hot that whoso tastes the same,
Were he of stone, as thawèd ice should melt,
And kindled find his breast with secret flame;
Whose moist poison dissolvèd hath my hate.
This creeping fire my cold limbs so opprest,
That in the heart that harboured freedom late,
Endless despair long thraldom hath imprest.
One eke so cold in frozen snow is found
Whose chilling venom of repugnant kind
The fervent heat doth quench of Cupid's wound
And with the spot of change infects the mind,
Whereof my dear hath tasted, to my pain:
My service thus is grown into disdain.

VIII

FROM Tuscane came my lady's worthy race;
Fair Florence was sometime their ancient seat.
The western isle, whose pleasant shore doth face
Wild Camber's cliffs, did give her lively heat.
Fostered she was with milk of Irish breast:
Her sire an earl; her dame of prince's blood.
From tender years, in Britain she doth rest,
With a king's child, where she tastes ghostly food.
Hunsdon did first present her to mine eyen:
Bright is her hue, and Geraldine she hight;

Hampton me taught to wish her first for mine;
And Windsor, alas, doth chase me from her sight.
Beauty of kind her virtues from above,
Happy is he that may obtain her love.

IX

BRITTLE beauty, that Nature made so frail,
Whereof the gift is small, and short the season,
Flowering today, tomorrow apt to fail,
Tickle treasure, abhorred of reason,
Dangerous to deal with, vain, of none avail,
Costly in keeping, past not worth two peason,
Slipper in sliding as is an eel's tail,
Hard to obtain, once gotten not geason,
Jewel of jeopardy that peril doth assail,
False and untrue, enticèd oft to treason,
Enemy to youth: that most may I bewail.
Ah, bitter sweet, infecting as the poison!
Thou farest as fruit that with the frost is taken:
Today ready ripe, tomorrow all to shaken.

X

ALAS, so all things now do hold their peace:
Heaven and earth disturbèd in no thing:
The beasts, the air, the birds their song do cease;
The nightès car the stars about doth bring.
Calm is the sea, the waves work less and less:
So am not I, whom love, alas, doth wring,
Bringing before my face the great increase
Of my desires, whereat I weep and sing
In joy and woe, as in a doubtful ease.
For my sweet thoughts sometime do pleasure bring,
But, by and by, the cause of my disease
Gives me a pang that inwardly doth sting,
When that I think what grief it is again
To live and lack the thing should rid my pain.

XI

WHEN Windsor walls sustain'd my wearied arm,
My hand my chin, to ease my restless head,
The pleasant plot revested green with warm,
The blossom'd boughs with lusty Ver yspread,

The flower'd meads, the wedded birds so late,
Mine eyes discovered.   Then did to mind resort
The jolly woes, the hateless short debate,
The rakel life that 'longs to love's disport.
Wherewith, alas, the heavy charge of care
Heapt in my breast breaks forth, against my will,
In smoky sighs that overcast the air.
My vapour'd eyes such dreary tears distil,
The tender spring which quicken where they fall,
And I half-bent to throw me down withal.

XII

SET me whereas the sun doth parch the green,
Or where his beams may not dissolve the ice,
In temperate heat, where he is felt and seen;
With proud people, in presence sad and wise;
Set me in low, or yet in high degree;
In the long night, or in the shortest day;
In clear weather, or where clouds thickest be;
In lusty youth, or when my hairs be gray:
Set me in earth, in heaven, or yet in hell,
In hill, in dale, or in the foaming flood;
Thrall, or at large, alive whereso I dwell,
Sick, or in health, in ill fame or in good,
Yours will I be, and with this only thought
Comfort myself when that my hope is nought.

XIII

I NEVER saw you, madam, lay apart
Your cornet black, in cold nor yet in heat,
Sith first ye knew of my desire so great
Which other fancies chas'd clean from my heart.
Whiles to myself I did the thought reserve
That so unware did wound my woeful breast,
Pity I saw within your heart did rest:
But since ye knew I did you love and serve
Your golden treese was clad alway in black,
Your smiling looks were hid thus evermore,
All that withdrawn that I did crave so sore.
So doth this cornet govern me, alack,
In summer sun, in winter breath of frost,
Of your fair eyes whereby the light is lost.

XIV

THE golden gift that Nature did thee give,
To fasten friends and feed them at thy will
With form and favour, taught me to believe
How thou art made to show her greatest skill,
Whose hidden virtues are not so unknown
But lively dooms might gather at the first:
Where beauty so her perfect seed hath sown,
Of other graces follow needs there must.
Now certes, lady, since all this is true,
That from above thy gifts are thus elect,
Do not deface them then with fancies new,
Nor change of minds, let not the mind infect:
But mercy him thy friend that doth thee serve,
Who seeks alway thine honour to preserve.

XV

SO cruel prison how could betide, alas,
As proud Windsor, where I, in lust and joy,
With a king's son my childish years did pass,
In greater feast than Priam's sons of Troy.

Where each sweet place returns a taste full sour.
The large green courts, where we were wont to hove,
With eyes cast up unto the maiden's tower,
And easy sighs such as folk draw in love.

The stately seats, the ladies bright of hue,
The dances short, long tales of great delight,
With words and looks that tigers could but rue,
Where each of us did plead the other's right.

The palme-play, where, despoiled for the game,
With dazèd eyes oft we by gleams of love
Have miss'd the ball, and got sight of our dame,
To bait her eyes which kept the leads above.

The gravell'd ground, with sleeves tied on the helm.
On foaming horse, with swords and friendly hearts,
With chere as though one should another whelm,
Where we have fought and chasèd oft with darts.

With silver drops the mead yet spread for ruth,
In active games of nimbleness and strength,
Where we did strain (trailèd by swarms of youth)
Our tender limbs, that yet shot up in length.

The secret groves, which oft we made resound
Of pleasant plaint and of our ladies' praise,
Recording soft what grace each one had found,
What hope of speed, what dread of long delays.

The wild forest, the clothèd holt with green,
With reins availed and swift y-breathèd horse,
With cry of hounds and merry blasts between,
Where we did chase the fearful hart aforce.

The void walls eke, that harbour'd us each night:
Wherewith, alas, reviveth in my breast
The sweet accord, such sleeps as yet delight,
The pleasant dreams, the quiet bed of rest,

The secret thoughts imparted with such trust,
The wanton talk, the divers change of play;
The friendship sworn, each promise kept so just,
Wherewith we past the winter night away.

And with this thought the blood forsakes my face,
The tears berain my cheeks of deadly hue:
The which, as soon as sobbing sighs, alas,
Up-suppèd have, thus I my plaint renew:

'O place of bliss! renewer of my woes!
Give me accompt where is my noble fere
Whom in thy walls thou didst each night enclose,
To other lief, but unto me most dear.'

Echo, alas, that doth my sorrow rue,
Returns thereto a hollow sound of plaint.
Thus I, alone, where all my freedom grew,
In prison pine with bondage and restraint:

And with remembrance of the greater grief,
To banish the less, I find my chief relief.

XVI

WHEN raging love with extreme pain
Most cruelly distrains my heart,
When that my tears, as floods of rain,
Bear witness of my woeful smart,
When sighs have wasted so my breath
That I lie at the point of death:

I call to mind the navy great
That the Greeks brought to Troye town,
And how the boisterous winds did beat
Their ships, and rent their sails adown,
Till Agamemnon's daughter's blood
Appeased the gods that them withstood:

And how that in those ten years' war
Full many a bloody deed was done,
And many a lord that came full far
There caught his bane, alas, too soon,
And many a good knight overrun,
Before the Greeks had Helen won.

Then think I thus: 'Sith such repair,
So long time war of valiant men,
Was all to win a lady fair,
Shall I not learn to suffer then?
And to think my life well spent, to be
Serving a worthier wight than she?'

Therefore I never will repent,
But pains, contented, still endure;
For like as when, rough winter spent,
The pleasant spring straight draweth in ure;
So, after raging storms of care,
Joyful at length may be my fare.

XVII

[A LADY COMPLAINS OF HER LOVER'S ABSENCE]

O HAPPY dames, that may embrace
The fruit of your delight,
Help to bewail the woeful case
And eke the heavy plight
Of me, that wonted to rejoice
The fortunes of my pleasant choice.
Good ladies, help to fill my mourning voice.

In ship freight with rememberance
Of thoughts and pleasures past
He sails, that hath in governance
My life while it will last;
With scalding sighs, for lack of gale,
Furthering his hope, that is his sail,
Toward me, the sweet port of his avail.

Alas, how oft in dreams I see
Those eyes that were my food,
Which sometime so delighted me
That yet they do me good:
Wherewith I wake with his return
Whose absent flame did make me burn:
But when I find the lack, Lord how I mourn!

When other lovers, in arms across,
Rejoice their chief delight,
Drownèd in tears, to mourn my loss,
I stand the bitter night
In my window, where I may see
Before the winds how the clouds flee:
Lo, what a mariner love hath made of me!

And in green waves, when the salt flood
Doth rise by rage of wind,
A thousand fancies in that mood
Assail my restless mind.
Alas, now drencheth my sweet foe
That with the spoil of my heart did go,
And left me! But, alas, why did he so?

And when the seas wax calm again,
To chase fro me annoy,
My doubtful hope doth cause me plain:
So dread cuts off my joy.
Thus is my wealth mingled with woe,
And of each thought a doubt doth grow:
Now he comes! will he come? alas, no, no!

XVIII

IN winter's just return, when Boreas gan his reign,
And every tree unclothèd fast, as nature taught them plain,
In misty morning dark, as sheep are then in hold,
I hied me fast, it sat me on, my sheep for to unfold.

And as it is a thing that lovers have by fits,
Under a palm I heard one cry as he had lost his wits,
Whose voice did ring so shrill in uttering of his plaint,
That I amazèd was to hear how love could him attaint.
'Ah, wretched man,' quod he, 'come death and rid this woe;
A just reward, a happy end, if it may chance thee so.
Thy pleasures past have wrought thy woe without redress;
If thou hadst never felt no joy, thy smart had been the less.'
And reckless of his life, he gan both sigh and groan:
A rueful thing methought it was, to hear him make such moan.
'Thou cursed pen,' said he, 'woe worth the bird thee bare;
The man, the knife, and all that made thee, woe be to their share.
Woe worth the time and place where I so could indite,
And woe be it yet once again, the pen that so can write.
Unhappy hand, it had been happy time for me,
If, when to write thou learnèd first, unjointed hadst thou be.'
Thus cursèd he himself, and every other wight,
Save her alone whom love him bound to serve both day and night
Which when I heard, and saw, how he himself fordid,
Against the ground with bloody strokes himself e'en there to rid,
Had been my heart of flint, it must have melted tho;
For in my life I never saw a man so full of woe.
With tears for his redress I rashly to him ran
And in my arms I caught him fast, and thus I spake him than:
'What woful wight art thou, that in such heavy case
Torments thyself with such despite, here in this desert place?'
Wherewith as all aghast, fulfilled with ire and dread,
He cast on me a staring look, with colour pale and dead:
'Nay, what art thou,' quoth he, 'that in this heavy plight
Dost find me here, most woful wretch, that life hath in despite?'
'I am,' quoth I, 'but poor, and simple in degree;
A shepherd's charge I have in hand, unworthy though I be.'
With that he gave a sigh, as though the sky should fall,
And loud, alas, he shriekèd oft, and 'Shepherd' gan he call,
'Come, hie thee fast at once, and print it in thy heart,
So thou shalt know, and I shall tell thee, guiltless how I smart.'
His back against the tree, sore feebled all with faint,
With weary sprite he stretcht him up, and thus he told his plaint:
'Once in my heart,' quoth he, 'it chancèd me to love
Such one, in whom hath Nature wrought, her cunning for to prove.
And sure I cannot say, but many years were spent,
With such good will so recompensed, as both we were content.
Whereto then I me bound, and she likewise also,
The sun should run his course awry ere we this faith forgo.
Who joyèd then but I? who had this worldès bliss?
Who might compare a life to mine, that never thought on this?

But dwelling in this truth, amid my greatest joy,
Is me befall'n a greater loss than Priam had of Troy.
She is reversèd clean, and beareth me in hand,
That my deserts have given cause to break this faithful band,
And for my just excuse availeth no defence.
Now knowest thou all; I can no more.   But, Shepherd, hie thee hence
And give him leave to die that may no longer live:
Whose record, lo, I claim to have, my death I do forgive.
And eke, when I am gone, be bold to speak it plain,
Thou hast seen die the truest man that ever love did pain.'
Wherewith he turn'd him round, and gasping oft for breath,
Into his arms a tree he raught, and said, 'Welcome my death!
Welcome a thousandfold, now dearer unto me
Than should, without her love to live, an emperor to be.'
Thus in this woful state he yielded up the ghost,
And little knoweth his lady what a lover she hath lost:
Whose death when I beheld, no marvel was it, right
For pity though my heart did bleed, to see so piteous sight.
My blood from heat to cold oft changèd wonders sore;
A thousand troubles there I found I never knew before.
Tween dread and dolour so my sprites were brought in fear,
That long it was ere I could call to mind what I did there.
But as each thing hath end, so had these pains of mine:
The furies past, and I my wits restored by length of time.
Then as I could devise, to seek I thought it best
Where I might find some worthy place for such a corse to rest.
And in my mind it came, from thence not far away,
Where Cressid's love, king Priam's son, the worthy Troilus lay.
By him I made his tomb, in token he was true,
And as to him belongèd well, I cover'd it with blue.
Whose soul by angel's power departed not so soon,
But to the heavens, lo, it fled, for to receive his doom.

XIX

[THE LADY AGAIN COMPLAINS]

GOOD ladies, ye that have your pleasure in exile,
Step in your foot, come, take a place, and mourn with me awhile:
And such as by their lords do set but little price,
Let them sit still, it skills them not what chance come on the dice.
But ye whom love hath bound, by order of desire,
To love your lords whose good deserts none other would require,
Come ye yet once again, and set your foot by mine,
Whose woful plight and sorrows great no tongue may well define.

My love and lord, alas, in whom consists my wealth,
Hath fortune sent to pass the seas, in hazard of his health.
Whom I was wont t' embrace with well contented mind
Is now amid the foaming floods, at pleasure of the wind,
Where God him well preserve, and safely me him send,
Without which hope my life, alas, were shortly at an end,
Whose absence yet, although my hope doth tell me plain,
With short return he comes anon, yet ceaseth not my pain.
The fearful dreams I have, ofttimes they grieve me so
That when I wake I lie in doubt if they be true or no.
Sometime the roaring seas meseems do grow so high
That my sweet lord in danger great, alas, doth often lie.
Another time, the same doth tell me he is come,
And playing, where I shall him find, with his fair little son.
So forth I go apace to see that liefsome sight,
And with a kiss methinks I say, 'Now welcome home, my knight;
Welcome, my sweet, alas, the stay of my welfare;
Thy presence bringeth forth a truce betwixt me and my care.'
Then lively doth he look, and salueth me again,
And saith, 'My dear, how is it now that you have all this pain?'
Wherewith the heavy cares, that heapt are in my breast,
Break forth and me discharge clean of all my huge unrest.
But when I me awake, and find it but a dream,
The anguish of my former woe beginneth more extreme,
And me tormenteth so that unnethe may I find
Some hidden where to still the grief of my unquiet mind.
Thus, every way, you see with absence how I burn,
And for my wound no cure I find, but hope of good return,
Save when I feel by sour how sweet is felt the more:
It doth abate some of my pains that I abode before.
And then unto myself I say: 'When that we two shall meet,
But little time shall seem this pain, that joy shall be so sweet.'
Ye winds, I you conjure, in chiefest of your rage,
That ye my lord me safely send, my sorrows to assuage.
And that I may not long abide in this excess,
Do your good will to cure a wight that liveth in distress.

XX

GIVE place, ye lovers, here before
That spent your boasts and brags in vain;
My lady's beauty passeth more
The best of yours, I dare well sayen,
Than doth the sun the candle light,
Or brightest day the darkest night.

And thereto hath a troth as just
As had Penelope the fair;
For what she saith, ye may it trust,
As it by writing sealèd were:
And virtues hath she many moe
Than I with pen have skill to show.

I could rehearse, if that I would,
The whole effect of Nature's plaint
When she had lost the perfect mould,
The like to whom she could not paint:
With wringing hands how she did cry,
And what she said, I know it, I.

I know she swore with raging mind,
Her kingdom only set apart,
There was no loss by law of kind
That could have gone so near her heart.
And this was chiefly all her pain:
She could not make the like again.

Sith Nature thus gave her the praise
To be the chiefest work she wrought,
In faith, methink some better ways
On your behalf might well be sought
Than to compare, as ye have done,
To match the candle with the sun.

XXI

IF he that erst the form so lively drew
Of Venus' face, triumph'd in painter's art,
Thy father then what glory did ensue
By whose pencil a goddess made thou art!
Touchèd with flame that figure made some rue,
And with her love surprisèd many a heart.
There lackt yet that should cure their hot desire:
Thou canst inflame and quench the kindled fire.

XXII

ALTHOUGH I had a check,
To give the mate is hard,
For I have found a neck
To keep my men in guard.
And you that hardy are
To give so great assay
Unto a man of war,
To drive his men away.

I rede you take good heed
And mark this foolish verse,
For I will so provide
That I will have your ferse.
And when your ferse is had,
And all your war is done,
Then shall yourself be glad
To end that you begun.

For if by chance I win
Your person in the field,
Too late then come you in
Yourself to me to yield.
For I will use my power,
As captain full of might;
And such I will devour
As use to show me spite.

And for because you gave
Me check in such degree,
This vantage, lo, I have:
Now check, and guard to thee.
Defend it if thou may;
Stand stiff in thine estate;
For sure I will assay
If I can give thee mate.

XXIII

TOO dearly had I bought my green and youthful years,
If in mine age I could not find when craft for love appears.
And seldom though I come in court among the rest,
Yet can I judge in colours dim as deep as can the best.
Where grief torments the man that suff'reth secret smart,
To break it forth unto some friend it easeth well the heart.
So stands it now with me for my beloved friend.
This case is thine for whom I feel such torment of my mind,
And for thy sake I burn so in my secret breast
That till thou know my whole disease my heart can have no rest.
I see how thine abuse hath wrested so thy wits
That all it yields to thy desire, and follows thee by fits.
Where thou hast loved so long, with heart and all thy power,
I see thee fed with feignèd words, thy freedom to devour.
I know (though she say nay, and would it well withstand)
When in her grace thou held thee most, she bare thee but in hand.

I see her pleasant chere in chiefest of thy suit;
When thou art gone I see him come that gathers up the fruit.
And eke in thy respect I see the base degree
Of him to whom she gave the heart that promised was to thee.
I see (what would you more?) stood never man so sure
On woman's word, but wisdom would mistrust it to endure.

XXIV

O LOATHSOME place! where I
Have seen and heard my dear,
When in my heart her eye
Hath made her thought appear,
By glimsing with such grace
As fortune it ne would
That lasten any space
Between us longer should.

As fortune did advance
To further my desire,
Even so hath fortune's chance
Thrown all amidst the mire;
And that I have deserved
With true and faithful heart
Is to his hands reserved
That never felt the smart.

But happy is that man
That scapèd hath the grief
That love well teach him can,
By wanting his relief.
A scourge to quiet minds
It is, who taketh heed,
A common plage that binds;
A travail without meed.

This gift it hath also:
Whoso enjoys it most,
A thousand troubles grow,
To vex his wearied ghost.
And last it may not long;
The truest thing of all:
And sure the greatest wrong,
That is within this thrall.

But since that, desert place,
Canst give me no account
Of my desirèd grace,
That I to have was wont;
Farewell! thou hast me taught,
To think me not the first
That love hath set aloft,
And casten in the dust.

XXV

AS oft as I behold and see
The sovereign beauty that me bound,
The nigher my comfort is to me,
Alas, the fresher is my wound.

As flame doth quench by rage of fire,
And running streams consume by rain,
So doth the sight that I desire
Appease my grief and deadly pain.

Like as the fly that seeth the flame
And thinks to play her in the fire,
That found her woe, and sought her game
Where grief did grow by her desire,

When first I saw these crystal streams
Whose beauty made this mortal wound;
I little thought within their beams
So sweet a venom to have found:

Wherein is hid the cruel bit
Whose sharp repulse none can resist,
And eke the spur that strains each wit
To run the race against his list.

But wilful will did prick me forth;
Blind Cupid did me whip and guide;
Force made me take my grief in worth;
My fruitless hope my harm did hide.

As cruel waves full oft be found
Against the rocks to roar and cry,
So doth my heart full oft rebound
Against my breast full bitterly.

And as the spider draws her line,
With labour lost I frame my suit:
The fault is hers, the loss is mine,
Of ill-sown seed such is the fruit.

I fall and see mine own decay,
As he that bears flame in his breast
Forgets for pain to cast away
The thing that breedeth his unrest.

XXVI

THOUGH I regarded not
The promise made by me;
Or passèd not to spot
My faith and honesty,
Yet were my fancy strange,
And wilful will to wite,
If I sought now to change
A falcon for a kite.

All men might well dispraise
My wit and enterprise
If I esteemed a pese
Above a pearl in price,
Or judged the owl in sight
The sparhawk to excel,
Which flieth but in the night,
As all men know right well;

Or if I sought to sail
Into the brittle port
Where anchor hold doth fail
To such as do resort,
And leave the haven sure
Where blows no blustering wind,
Nor fickleness in ure,
So far forth as I find.

No, think me not so light,
Nor of so churlish kind,
Though it lay in my might
My bondage to unbind,
That I would leave the hind
To hunt the gander's foe.
No, no! I have no mind
To make exchanges so,

Nor yet to change at all;
For think, it may not be
That I should seek to fall
From my felicity,
Desirous for to win,
And loth for to forgo,
Or new change to begin.
How may all this be so?

The fire it cannot freeze,
For it is not his kind;
Nor true love cannot lese
The constance of the mind.
Yet as soon shall the fire
Want heat to blaze and burn;
As I, in such desire,
Have once a thought to turn.

XXVII

WRAPT in my careless cloak, as I walk to and fro,
I see how Love can show what force there reigneth in his bow:
And how he shooteth eke a hardy heart to wound;
And where he glanceth by again, that little hurt is found.
For seldom is it seen he woundeth hearts alike;
The one may rage, when t'other's love is often far to seek.
All this I see, with more, and wonder thinketh me
How he can strike the one so sore and leave the other free.
I see that wounded wight that suffereth all this wrong,
How he is fed with yeas and nays, and liveth all too long.
In silence though I keep such secrets to myself,
Yet do I see how she sometime doth yield a look by stealth,
As though it seem'd iwis, 'I will not lose thee so,'
When in her heart so sweet a thought did never truly grow.
Then say I thus: alas, that man is far from bliss
That doth receive for his relief none other gain but this.
And she that feeds him so, I feel and find it plain,
Is but to glory in her power that over such can reign.
Nor are such graces spent but when she thinks that he,
A wearied man, is fully bent such fancies to let flee.
Then, to retain him still, she wrasteth new her grace,
And smileth, lo, as though she would forthwith the man embrace.
But when the proof is made to try such looks withal,
He findeth then the place all void, and freighted full of gall.

Lord, what abuse is this! Who can such women praise
That for their glory do devise to use such crafty ways?
I, that among the rest do sit and mark the row,
Find that in her is greater craft than is in twenty mo.
Whose tender years, alas, with wiles so well are sped,
What will she do when hoary hairs are powdered in her head?

XXVIII

[A WOMAN'S ANSWER: AUTHORSHIP UNCERTAIN]

GIRT in my guiltless gown, as I sit here and sew,
I see that things are not indeed as to the outward show.
And who so list to look and note things somewhat near
Shall find, where plainness seems to haunt, nothing but craft appear.
For with indifferent eyes myself can well discern
How some to guide a ship in storms stick not to take the stern
Whose skill and courage tried in calm to steer a barge
They would soon show, you should soon see, it were too great a charge
And some I see again sit still and say but small
That can do ten times more than they that say they can do all.
Whose goodly gifts are such, the more they understand
The more they seek to learn and know, and take less charge in hand.
And, to declare more plain, the time flits not so fast
But I can bear right well in mind the song now sung and past,
The author whereof came, wrapt in a crafty cloak,
In will to force a flaming fire where he could raise no smoke.
If power and will had met, as it appeareth plain,
The truth nor right had ta'en no place, their virtues had been vain.
So that you may perceive, and I may safely see,
The innocent that guiltless is condemnèd should have be.
Much like untruth to this the story doth declare,
Where the elders laid to Susan's charge meet matter to compare.
They did her both accuse and eke condemn her too,
And yet no reason, right, nor truth, did lead them so to do.
And she thus judged to die, toward her death went forth
Fraughted with faith, a patient pace, taking her wrong in worth.
But He that doth defend all those that in Him trust
Did raise a child for her defence to shield her from the unjust.
And Daniel chosen was then of this wrong to weet
How, in what place, and eke with whom, she did this crime commit.
He caused the elders part the one from the other's sight,
And did examine one by one and charged them both say right.
Under a mulberry tree it was, first said the one,
The next named a pomegranate tree: whereby the truth was known.

Then Susan was discharged, and they condemned to die,
As right required and they deserved that framed so foul a lie.
And He that her preserved, and lett them of their lust,
Hath me defended hitherto, and will do still I trust.

XXIX

SINCE fortune's wrath envieth the wealth
Wherein I reignèd, by the sight
Of that that fed mine eyes by stealth
With sour, sweet, dread, and delight,
Let not my grief move you to moan,
For I will weep and wail alone.

Spite drave me into Boreas' reign,
Where hoary frosts the fruits do bite,
When hills were spread and every plain
With stormy winter's mantle white;
And yet, my dear, such was my heat,
When others froze, then did I sweat.

And now, though on the sun I drive,
Whose fervent flame all things decays;
His beams in brightness may not strive
With light of your sweet golden rays;
Nor from my breast this heat remove
The frozen thoughts graven by love.

Ne may the waves of the salt flood
Quench that your beauty set on fire,
For though mine eyes forbear the food
That did relieve the hot desire,
Such as I was, such will I be—
Your own.   What would ye more of me?

XXX

[OF A LADY THAT REFUSED TO DANCE WITH HIM]

EACH beast can choose his fere according to his mind,
And eke can show a friendly chere, like to their beastly kind.
A lion saw I late, as white as any snow,
Which seemèd well to lead the race, his port the same did show.
Upon the gentle beast to gaze it pleasèd me,
For still methought he seemèd well of noble blood to be.

And as he pranced before, still seeking for a make,
As who would say 'There is none here, I trow, will me forsake'
I might perceive a wolf as white as whalèsbone,
A fairer beast, a fresher hue, beheld I never none,
Save that her looks were fierce and froward eke her grace:
Toward the which this gentle beast gan him advance apace,
And with a beck full low he bowèd at her feet
In humble wise, as who would say 'I am too far unmeet'.
But such a scornful chere wherewith she him rewarded
Was never seen, I trow, the like, to such as well deservèd.
With that she start aside well near a foot or twain,
And unto him thus gan she say, with spite and great disdain:
'Lion,' she said, 'if thou hadst known my mind beforne,
Thou hadst not spent thy travail thus, nor all thy pain forlorne.
Do way! I let thee weet thou shalt not play with me:
Go range about, where thou mayst find some meeter fere for thee.'
Forthwith he beat his tail, his eyes began to flame;
I might perceive his noble heart much movèd by the same.
Yet saw I him refrain, and eke his wrath assuage,
And unto her thus gan he say, when he was past his rage:
'Cruel, you do me wrong to set me thus so light,
Without desert for my goodwill to show me such despite.
How can ye thus intreat a lion of the race,
That with his paws a crownèd king devourèd in the place,
Whose nature is to prey upon no simple food,
As long as he may suck the flesh, and drink of noble blood?
If you be fair and fresh, am I not of your hue?
And for my vaunt I dare well say my blood is not untrue.
For you yourself have heard, it is not long ago
Sith that, for love, one of the race did end his life in woe,
In tower both strong and high, for his assurèd truth,
Whereas in tears he spent his breath, alas, the more the ruth.
This gentle beast so died, whom nothing could remove,
But willingly to lose his life for loss of his true love.
Other there be whose lives, to linger still in pain,
Against their wills preservèd are that would have died right fain.
But now I do perceive that nought it moveth you,
My good intent, my gentle heart, nor yet my kind so true,
But that your will is such to lure me to the trade,
As other some full many years to trace by craft ye made.
And thus behold my kinds, how that we differ far:
I seek my foes, and you your friends do threaten still with war:
I fawn where I am fled, you slay that seeks to you;
I can devour no yielding prey, you kill where you subdue.
My kind is to desire the honour of the field,
And you, with blood to slake your thirst on such as to you yield.

Wherefore I would you wist, that for your coy looks
I am no man that will be trained nor tangled by such hooks.
And though some list to bow where blame full well they might,
And to such beastès currant fawn that should have travail bright,
I will observe the law that Nature gave to me,
To conquer such as will resist, and let the rest go free.
And as a falcon free, that soareth in the air,
Which never fed on hand or lure nor for no stale doth care,
While that I live and breathe, such shall my custom be,
In wildness of the woods to seek my prey where pleaseth me;
Where many one shall rue that never made offence:
Thus your refuse against my power shall boot them no defence.
And for revenge thereof I vow and swear thereto
A thousand spoils I shall commit I never thought to do.
And if to light on you my luck so good shall be,
I shall be glad to feed on that that would have fed on me.
And thus farewell, unkind, to whom I bent too low:
I would you wist the ship is safe that bare his sails so low.
Sith that a lion's heart is for a wolf no prey,
With bloody mouth go slake your thirst on simple sheep, I say,
With more despite and ire than I can now express,
Which to my pain, though I refrain, the cause you may well guess
As for because myself was author of this game,
It boots me not that for my wrath I should disturb the same.'

XXXI

IF care do cause men cry, why do not I complain?
If each man do bewail his woe, why show not I my pain?
Since that amongst them all I dare well say is none
So far from weal, so full of woe, or hath more cause to moan.
For all things having life sometime have quiet rest:
The bearing ass, the drawing ox, and every other beast,
The peasant and the post, that serve at all assays,
The ship-boy and the galley-slave, have time to take their ease:
Save I, alas, whom care of force doth so constrain
To wail the day and wake the night continually in pain,
From pensiveness to plaint, from plaint to bitter tears,
From tears to painful plaint again; and thus my life it wears.
No thing under the sun that I can hear or see
But moveth me for to bewail my cruel destiny.
For where men do rejoice, since that I cannot so,
I take no pleasure in that place, it doubleth but my woe.
And when I hear the sound of song or instrument,
Methinks each tune there doleful is and helps me to lament.

And if I see some have their most desirèd sight,
Alas, think I, each man hath weal save I, most woful wight!
Then, as the stricken deer withdraws himself alone,
So do I seek some secret place where I may make my moan.
There do my flowing eyes show forth my melting heart
So that the streams of those two wells right well declare my smart.
And in those cares so cold, I force myself a heat
(As sick men in their shaking fits procure themselves to sweat)
With thoughts that for the time do much appease my pain:
But yet they cause a farther fear, and breed my woe again.
Methinks within my thought I see right plain appear
My heart's delight, my sorrow's leech, mine earthly goddess here,
With every sundry grace that I have seen her have:
Thus I within my woful breast her picture paint and grave.
And in my thought I roll her beauties to and fro,
Her laughing chere, her lively look, my heart that piercèd so;
Her strangeness when I sued her servant for to be;
And what she said, and how she smiled, when that she pitied me.
Then comes a sudden fear, that riveth all my rest,
Lest absence cause forgetfulness to sink within her breast.
For when I think how far this earth doth us divide,
Alas, meseems love throws me down; I feel how that I slide.
But then I think again: 'Why should I thus mistrust
So sweet a wight, so sad and wise, that is so true and just?
For loth she was to love, and wavering is she not;
The farther off the more desired.'   Thus lovers tie their knot.
So in despair and hope plunged am I both up and down,
As is the ship with wind and wave when Neptune list to frown.
But as the watery showers delay the raging wind,
So doth good hope clean put away despair out of my mind
And bids me for to serve and suffer patiently,
For what wot I the after weal that fortune wills to me?
For those that care do know and tasted have of trouble,
When passèd is their woful pain each joy shall seem them double,
And bitter sends she now, to make me taste the better
The pleasant sweet when that it comes, to make it seem the sweeter.
And so determine I to serve until my death;
Yea, rather die a thousand times than once to false my faith.
And if my feeble corpse through weight of woful smart
Do fail or faint, my will it is that still she keep my heart.
And when this carcass here to earth shall be refared,
I do bequeath my wearied ghost to serve her afterward.

POEMS ON VARIOUS THEMES

The Happy Life

MARTIAL, the things that do attain
The happy life be these, I find:
The riches left, not got with pain;
The fruitful ground, the quiet mind:

The equal friend, no grudge nor strife;
No charge of rule nor governance;
Without disease, the healthful life;
The household of continuance:

The mean diet, no delicate fare;
True wisdom join'd with simpleness;
The night dischargèd of all care,
Where wine the wit may not oppress:

The faithful wife, without debate;
Such sleeps as may beguile the night:
Contented with thine own estate
Ne wish for death, ne fear his might.

The Golden Mean

OF thy life, Thomas, this compass well mark:
Not aye with full sails the high seas to beat;
Ne by coward dread, in shunning storms dark,
On shallow shores thy keel in peril freat.
Whoso gladly halseth the golden mean,
Void of dangers advisedly hath his home,
Not with loathsome muck as a den unclean,
Nor palace-like, whereat disdain may glome.
The lofty pine the great wind often rives;
With violenter sway fallen turrets steep;
Lightnings assault the high mountains and clives.
A heart well stay'd, in overthwartes deep,
Hopeth amends; in sweet, doth fear the sour.
God that sendeth, withdraweth winter sharp.
Now ill, not aye thus: once Phoebus to lower
With bow unbent shall cease, and frame to harp

His voice; in strait estate appear thou stout;
And so wisely, when lucky gale of wind
All thy puft sails shall fill, look well about;
Take in a reef: haste is waste, proof doth find.

In Praise of Wyatt's Psalms

THE great Macedon, that out of Persia chased
Darius, of whose huge power all Asia rang,
In the rich ark Dan Homer's rhymes he placed,
Who feignèd gests of heathen princes sang.
What holy grave, what worthy sepulture,
To Wyatt's Psalms should Christians then purchase?
Where he doth paint the lively faith and pure,
The steadfast hope, the sweet return to grace,
Of just David, by perfect penitence;
Where rulers may see, in a mirror clear,
The bitter fruit of false concupiscence:
How Jewry bought Uriah's death full dear.
In princes' hearts God's scourge yprinted deep
Mought them awake out of their sinful sleep.

The Death of Wyatt

DIVERS thy death do diversely bemoan.
Some, that in presence of thy livelihed
Lurked, whose breasts envy with hate had sown,
Yield Caesar's tears upon Pompeius' head.
Some, that watchèd with the murderer's knife,
With eager thirst to drink thy guiltless blood,
Whose practice brake by happy end of life,
Weep envious tears to hear thy fame so good.
But I that knew what harbour'd in that head,
What virtues rare were temper'd in that breast,
Honour the place that such a jewel bred,
And kiss the ground whereas thy corse doth rest,
With vapour'd eyes: from whence such streams availe
As Pyramus did on Thisbe's breast bewail.

Tribute to Wyatt

WYATT resteth here, that quick could never rest:
Whose heavenly gifts increasèd by disdain;
And virtue sank the deeper in his breast:
Such profit he by envy could obtain.

A head where wisdom mysteries did frame;
Whose hammers beat still in that lively brain
As on a stithe, where that some work of fame
Was daily wrought, to turn to Britain's gain.

A visage stern and mild, where both did grow,
Vice to contemn, in virtue to rejoice:
Amid great storms, whom grace assurèd so,
To live upright, and smile at fortune's choice.

A hand that taught what might be said in rhyme:
That reft Chaucer the glory of his wit.
A mark the which (unperfected, for time)
Some may approach but never none shall hit.

A tongue that served in foreign realms his king;
Whose courteous talk to virtue did inflame
Each noble heart; a worthy guide to bring
Our English youth by travail unto fame.

An eye whose judgment none affect could blind,
Friends to allure, and foes to reconcile;
Whose piercing look did represent a mind
With virtue fraught, reposèd, void of guile.

A heart where dread was never so imprest
To hide the thought that might the truth advance;
In neither fortune lost, nor yet represt,
To swell in wealth, or yield unto mischance.

A valiant corse where force and beauty met,
Happy, alas, too happy, but for foes,
Lived, and ran the race that nature set;
Of manhood's shape, where she the mould did lose.

But to the heavens that simple soul is fled,
Which left, with such as covet Christ to know,
Witness of faith that never shall be dead;
Sent for our health but not receivèd so.

Thus, for our guilt, this jewel have we lost;
The earth his bones, the heavens possess his ghost.

Another Tribute to Wyatt

IN the rude age, when knowledge was not rife,
If Jove in Crete and other were that taught
Arts to convert to profit of our life
Ween'd after death to have their temples sought:
If Virtue yet, no void unthankful time,
Failèd of some to blast her endless fame
(A goodly mean both to deter from crime
And to her steps our sequel to inflame):
In days of truth if Wyatt's friends then wail
(The only debt that dead of quick may claim)
That rare wit spent, employed to our avail,
Where Christ is taught, we led to Virtue's train.
His lively face their breasts how did it freat,
Whose cinders yet with envy they do eat.

Epitaph on Thomas Clere

NORFOLK sprung thee, Lambeth holds thee dead,
Clere, of the County of Cleremont, though hight.
Within the womb of Ormond's race thou bred,
And saw'st thy cousin crownèd in thy sight.
Shelton for love, Surrey for lord thou chase
(Ay me! whilst life did last that league was tender),
Tracing whose steps thou sawest Kelsal blaze,
Laundersey burnt, and batter'd Bullen render.
At Muttrel gates, hopeless of all recure,
Thine Earl, half dead, gave in thy hand his will;
Which cause did thee this pining death procure,
Ere summers four times seven thou couldst fulfil.
Ah, Clere, if love had booted, care or cost,
Heaven had not won, nor earth so timely lost.

Sardanapalus

THE Assyrian king—in peace, with foul desire
And filthy lusts that stained his regal heart—
In war, that should set princely hearts on fire,
Did yield vanquisht for want of martial art.
The dint of swords from kisses seemèd strange;
And harder than his lady's side, his targe:
From glutton feasts to soldier's fare, a change;
His helmet, far above a garland's charge.

Who scarce the name of manhood did retain,
Drenchèd in sloth and womanish delight.
Feeble of sprite, unpatient of pain,
When he had lost his honour and his right
(Proud, time of wealth: in storms, appall'd with dread)
Murder'd himself, to show some manful deed.

Youth and Age

LAID in my quiet bed, in study as I were,
I saw within my troubled head a heap of thoughts appear.
And every thought did show so lively in mine eyes,
That now I sigh'd, and then I smiled, as cause of thought did rise.
I saw the little boy in thought how oft that he
Did wish of God to scape the rod, a tall young man to be.
The young man, eke, that feels his bones with pains opprest,
How he would be a rich old man, to live and lie at rest.
The rich old man, that sees his end draw on so sore,
How he would be a boy again, to live so much the more.
Whereat full oft I smiled, to see how all these three,
From boy to man, from man to boy, would chop and change degree.
And, musing thus, I think the case is very strange
That man from wealth, to live in woe, doth ever seek to change.
Thus thoughtful as I lay, I saw my wither'd skin,
How it doth show my dinted jaws, the flesh was worn so thin.
And eke my toothless chaps, the gates of my right way,
That opes and shuts as I do speak, do thus unto me say:
'Thy white and hoarish hairs, the messengers of age,
That show, like lines of true belief, that this life doth assuage,
Bid thee lay hand, and feel them hanging on thy chin;
The which do write two ages past, the third now coming in.
Hang up therefore the bit of thy young wanton time:
And thou that therein beaten art, the happiest life define.'
Whereat I sigh'd, and said: 'Farewell, my wonted joy!
Truss up thy pack, and trudge from me to every little boy,
And tell them thus from me: their time most happy is,
If, to their time, they reason had to know the truth of this.'

Bonum est mihi quod humiliasti me

THE storms are past, the clouds are overblown,
And humble chere great rigour hath represt.
For the default is set a pain foreknown,
And patience graft in a determined breast.

And in the heart, where heaps of griefs were grown,
The sweet revenge hath planted mirth and rest.
No company so pleasant as mine own.

     *   *   *   *   *   *

Thraldom at large hath made this prison free.
Danger well past, remembered, works delight.
Of lingering doubts such hope is sprung, pardie!
That nought I find displeasant in my sight
But when my glass presenteth unto me
The cureless wound that bleedeth day and night.
To think, alas, such hap should granted be
Unto a wretch, that hath no heart to fight,
To spill that blood that hath so oft been shed
For Britain's sake, alas, and now is dead!

Lines to Ratclif

MY Ratclif, when thy reckless youth offends,
Receive thy scourge by others' chastisement;
For such calling, when it works none amends,
Then plagues are sent without advertisement.
Yet Solomon said, the wrongèd shall recure:
But Wyatt said true, the scar doth aye endure.

The Restless Heart

THE fancy, which that I have servèd long,
That hath alway been enemy to mine ease,
Seemèd of late to rue upon my wrong,
And bade me fly the cause of my miscase.
And I forthwith did press out of the throng,
That thought by flight my painful heart to please
Some other way, till I saw faith more strong.
And to myself I said, 'Alas, those days
In vain were spent, to run the race so long.'
And with that thought I met my guide, that plain
Out of the way wherein I wander'd wrong
Brought me amidst the hills in base Bullayne:
Where I am now, as restless to remain,
Against my will, full pleasèd with my pain.

A Satire on London

LONDON, hast thou accusèd me
Of breach of laws, the root of strife,
Within whose breast did boil to see,
So fervent hot, thy dissolute life
That even the hate of sins that grow
Within thy wicked walls so rife,
For to break forth did convert so
That terror could it not repress?
The which, by words, since preachers know
What hope is left for to redress,
By unknown means, it likèd me
My hidden burden to express.
Whereby it might appear to thee
That secret sin hath secret spite;
From justice' rod no fault is free,
But that all such as work unright
In most quiet, are next ill rest.
In secret silence of the night
This made me, with a reckless breast,
To wake thy sluggards with my bow:
A figure of the Lord's behest,
Whose scourge for sin the Scriptures show.
That as the fearful thunder clap
By sudden flame at hand we know,
Of pebble stones the soundless rap,
The dreadful plague might make thee see
Of God's wrath that doth thee enwrap.
That pride might know, from conscience free,
How lofty works may her defend;
And envy find, as he hath sought,
How other seek him to offend:
And wrath taste of each cruel thought,
The just shape higher in the end:
And idle sloth, that never wrought,
To heaven his spirit lift may begin:
And greedy lucre live in dread
To see what hate ill got goods win.
The lechers, ye that lusts do feed,
Perceive what secrecy is in sin:
And gluttons' hearts for sorrow bleed,
Awakèd, when their fault they find:
In loathsome vice each drunken wight,
To stir to God, this was my mind.
Thy windows had done me no spight;

But proud people that dread no fall,
Clothèd with falsehood and unright
Bred in the closures of thy wall.
But wrested to wrath in fervent zeal
Thou hast to strife my secret call.
Indurèd hearts no warning feel.
O shameless whore! is dread then gone?
Be such thy foes, as mean thy weal?
O member of false Babylon!
The shop of craft! the den of ire!
Thy dreadful doom draws fast upon.
Thy martyrs' blood, by sword and fire,
In heaven and earth for justice call.
The Lord shall hear their just desire!
The flame of wrath shall on thee fall!
With famine and pest lamentably
Stricken shall be thy lechers all.
Thy proud towers, and turrets high
Enemies to God, beat stone from stone:
Thine idols burnt that wrought iniquity:
When none thy ruin shall bemoan,
But render unto the righteous Lord,
That so high judgèd Babylon.
Immortal praise with one accord.

TRANSLATION

The Second Book of Virgil's Aeneid

THEY whisted all, with fixèd face attent,
When prince Aeneas from the royal seat
Thus gan to speak.   O Queen, it is thy will
I should renew a woe cannot be told,
How that the Greeks did spoil and overthrow
The Phrygian wealth and wailful realm of Troy,
Those ruthful things that I myself beheld,
And whereof no small part fell to my share:
Which to express, who could refrain from tears?
What Myrmidon? or yet what Dolopes?
What stern Ulysses' wagèd soldiar?
And lo, moist night now from the welkin falls,
And stars declining counsel us to rest,
But since so great is thy delight [1] to hear
Of our mishaps and Troyès last decay,
Though to record the same my mind abhors
And plaint eschews, yet thus will I begin.

The Greeks' chieftains, all irkèd with the war
Wherein they wasted had so many years
And oft repulst by fatal destiny,
By the divine science of Minerva
A huge horse made, high raisèd like a hill,
For their return a feignèd sacrifice:
The fame whereof so wandered it at point.
Of cloven fir compacted were his ribs:
In the dark bulk they closed bodies of men
Chosen by lot, and did enstuff by stealth
The hollow womb with armèd soldiars.

There stands in sight an isle, hight Tenedon,
Rich, and of fame, while Priam's kingdom stood;
Now but a bay, and road unsure for ship.
Hither them secretly the Greeks withdrew,
Shrouding themselves under the desert shore.
And, weening we they had been fled and gone
And with that wind had fet the land of Greece,
Troyè discharged her long continued dole.
The gates cast up, we issued out to play,

[1] See Notes.

The Greekish camp desirous to behold,
The places void, and the forsaken coasts.
Here Pyrrhus' band; there fierce Achilles pight;
Here rode their ships; there did their battles join.
Astonied, some the scatheful gift beheld,
Behight by vow unto the chaste Minerve,
All wondering at the hugeness of the horse.
   The first of all Timoetes gan advise
Within the walls to lead and draw the same,
And place it eke amid the palace court:
Whether of guile, or Troyès fate it would.
Capys, with some of judgment more discreet,
Will'd it to drown, or underset with flame
The suspect present of the Greeks' deceit,
Or bore and gauge the hollow caves uncouth:
So diverse ran the giddy people's mind.
   Lo, foremost of a rout that followed him,
Kindled Laocoon hasted from the tower,
Crying far off: 'O wretched citizens!
What so great kind of frenzy fretteth you?
Deem ye the Greeks our enemies to be gone?
Or any Greekish gifts can you suppose
Devoid of guile?   Is so Ulysses known?
Either the Greeks are in this timber hid,
Or this an engine is to annoy our walls,
To view our towers, and overwhelm our town.
Here lurks some craft.   Good Troyans, give no trust
Unto this horse, for whatsoever it be,
I dread the Greeks—yea, when they offer gifts!'
And with that word, with all his force a dart
He lancèd then into that crooked womb
Which trembling stuck, and shook within the side:
Wherewith the caves gan hollowly resound.
And, but for Fates, and for our blind forecast,
The Greeks' device and guile had he descried:
Troy yet had stood, and Priam's towers so high.
   Therewith behold, whereas the Phrygian herds
Brought to the king with clamour, all unknown
A young man, bound his hands behind his back,
Who willingly had yielden prisoner
To frame this guile and open Troyès gates
Unto the Greeks, with courage fully bent
And mind determèd either of the twain:
To work his feat, or willing yield to death.
Near him, to gaze, the Trojan youth gan flock,
And strave who most might at the captive scorn.

The Greeks' deceit behold, and by one proof
Imagine all the rest.
For in the press as he unarmèd stood,
With troubled chere, and Phrygian routs beset,
'Alas!' quod he, 'what earth now, or what seas
May me receive? caitiff, what rests me now?
For whom in Greece doth no abode remain.
The Trojans eke offended seek to wreak
Their heinous wrath, with shedding of my blood.'
With this regret our hearts from rancour moved.
The bruit appeased, we ask'd him of his birth,
What news he brought, what hope made him to yield.
   Then he, all dread removèd, thus began:
'O King, I shall, whatever me betide,
Say but the truth: ne first will me deny
A Grecian born; for though Fortune hath made
Sinon a wretch, she cannot make him false.
If ever came unto your ears the name,
Nobled by fame, of the sage Palamede,
Whom traitorously the Greeks condemn'd to die,
Guiltless, by wrongful doom, for that he did
Dissuade the wars: whose death they now lament:
Underneath him my father, bare of wealth,
Into his band young, and near of his blood,
In my prime years unto the war me sent.
While that by fate his state in stay did stand,
And when his realm did flourish by advice,
Of glory, then, we bare some fame and bruit.
But since his death by false Ulysses' sleight,
(I speak of things to all men well beknown)
A dreary life in doleful plaint I led,
Repining at my guiltless friend's mischance.
Ne could I, fool, refrain my tongue from threats,
That if my chance were ever to return
Victor to Arge, to follow my revenge.
With such sharp words procurèd I great hate.
Here sprang my harm.   Ulysses ever sith
With new found crimes began me to affray.
In common ears false rumours gan he sow:
Weapons of wreak his guilty mind gan seek.
Ne rested aye till he by Calchas mean——
But whereunto these thankless tales in vain
Do I rehearse, and linger forth the time,
In like estate if all the Greeks ye price?
It is enough ye here rid me at once.
Ulysses, Lord! how he would this rejoice!

Yea, and either Atride would buy it dear.'
This kindled us more eager to inquire,
And to demand the cause; without suspect
Of so great mischief thereby to ensue,
Or of Greeks' craft.   He then, with forgèd words
And quivering limbs, thus took his tale again.

'The Greeks ofttimes intended their return
From Troyè town, with long wars all ytired,
And to dislodge: which would God they had done!
But oft the winter storms of raging seas,
And oft the boisterous winds, did them to stay;
And, chiefly, when of clinchèd ribs of fir
This horse was made, the storms roar'd in the air.
Then we in doubt to Phoebus' temple sent
Euripilus, to weet the prophecy.
From whence he brought these woful news again.
"With blood, O Greeks! and slaughter of a maid,
Ye peased the winds, when first ye came to Troy.
With blood likewise ye must seek your return:
A Greekish soul must offer'd be therefore."

'But when this sound had pierced the people's ears,
With sudden fear astonied were their minds;
The chilling cold did overrun their bones,
To whom that fate was shaped, whom Phoebus would.
Ulysses then amid the press brings in
Calchas with noise, and will'd him to discuss
The god's intent.   Then some gan deem to me
The cruel wreak of him that framed the craft,
Foreseeing secretly what would ensue.
In silence then, yshrouding him from sight,
But days twice five he whisted, and refused
To death, by speech, to further any wight.
At last, as forced by false Ulysses' cry,
Of purpose he brake forth, assigning me
To the altar; whereto they granted all:
And that that erst each one dread to himself
Returnèd all unto my wretched death.
And now at hand drew near the woful day:
All things prepared wherewith to offer me:
Salt, corn, fillets my temples for to bind.
I scaped the death, I grant, and brake the bands,
And lurkèd in a marish all the night
Among the ooze, while they did set their sails;
If it so be that they indeed so did.
Now rests no hope my native land to see,
My children dear, nor long desirèd sire,

On whom, perchance, they shall wreak my escape:
Those harmless wights shall for my fault be slain.
  'Then, by the gods, to whom all truth is known,
By faith unfiled, if any anywhere
With mortal folk remains, I thee beseech,
O King, thereby rue on my travail great:
Pity a wretch that guiltless suffereth wrong.'
  Life to these tears, with pardon eke, we grant.
And Priam first himself commands to loose
His gyves, his bands, and friendly to him said:
'Whoso thou art, learn to forget the Greeks:
Henceforth be ours; and answer me with truth:
Whereto was wrought the mass of this huge horse?
Whose the devise? and whereto should it tend?
What holy vow? or engine for the wars?'
  Then he, instruct with wiles and Greekish craft,
His loosèd hands lift upward to the stars:
'Ye everlasting lamps! I testify,
Whose power divine may not be violate,
The altar and sword,' quoth he, 'that I have scaped,
Ye sacred bands I wore as yielden host;
Lawful be it for me to break mine oath
To Greeks; lawful to hate their nation;
Lawful be it to sparkle in the air
Their secrets all, whatso they keep in close:
For free am I from Greece and from their laws.
So be it, Troy, and saved by me from scathe,
Keep faith with me, and stand to thy behest;
If I speak truth, and opening things of weight,
For grant of life requite thee large amends.
The Greeks' whole hope of undertaken war
In Pallas' help consisted evermore.
But sith the time that wicked Diomed,
Ulysses eke, that forger of all guile,
Adventured from the holy sacred fane
For to bereave Dame Pallas' fatal form,
And slew the watches of the chiefest tower,
And then away the holy statue stole,
That were so bold with hands embrued in blood,
The virgin goddess' veils for to defile—
Sith then their hope gan fail, their hope to fall,
Their power appair, their goddess' grace withdraw;
Which with no doubtful signs she did declare.
Scarce was the statue to our tents ybrought
But she gan stare with sparkled eyes of flame;
Along her limbs the salt sweat trickled down:

Yea thrice herself—a hideous thing to tell—
In glances bright she glitter'd from the ground,
Holding in hand her targe and quivering spear.
Calchas by sea then bade us haste our flight,
Whose engines might not break the walls of Troy,
Unless at Greece they would renew their lots,
Restore the god that they by sea had brought
In warpèd keels.   To Arge sith they be come,
They pease their gods, and war afresh prepare,
And 'cross the seas unlookèd for eftsoons
They will return.   This order Calchas set.

'This figure made they for the aggrievèd god
In Pallas' stead, to cleanse their heinous fault.
Which mass he willèd to be rearèd high
Toward the skies, and ribbèd all with oak,
So that your gates ne wall might it receive;
Ne yet your people might defencèd be
By the good zeal of old devotion.
For if your hands did Pallas' gift defile,
To Priam's realm great mischief should befall:
Which fate the gods first on himself return.
But had your own hands brougnt it in your town,
Asia should pass, and carry offered war
In Greece, even to the walls of Pelops' town,
And we and ours that destiny endure.'

By suchlike wiles of Sinon, the forsworn,
His tale with us did purchase credit; some
Trapt by deceit, some forcèd by his tears,
Whom neither Diomed nor great Achille,
Nor ten years' war ne a thousand sail could daunt.

Us caitiffs then a far more dreadful chance
Befell, that troubled our unarmèd breasts.
Whiles Laocoon, that chosen was by lot
Neptunus' priest, did sacrifice a bull
Before the holy altar, suddenly
From Tenedon, behold in circles great
By the calm seas come fleeting adders twain,
Which plied towards the shore (I loathe to tell)
With rearèd breast lift up above the seas:
Whose bloody crests aloft the waves were seen.
The hinder part swam hidden in the flood;
Their grisly backs were linkèd manifold.
With sound of broken waves they gat the strand,
With glowing eyen, tainted with blood and fire;
Whose waltring tongues did lick their hissing mouths.
We fled away; our face the blood forsook;

But they with gait direct to Lacon ran.
And first of all each serpent doth enwrap
The bodies small of his two tender sons,
Whose wretched limbs they bit, and fed thereon.
Then raught they him, who had his weapon caught
To rescue them; twice winding him about,
With folded knots and circled tails, his waist:
Their scalèd backs did compass twice his neck,
With rearèd heads aloft and stretchèd throats.
He with his hands strave to unloose the knots
Whose sacred fillets all besprinkled were
With filth of gory blood and venom rank,
And to the stars such dreadful shouts he sent,
Like to the sound the roaring bull forth lows
Which from the altar wounded doth astart,
The swerving axe when he shakes from his neck.
The serpents twain, with hasted trail they glide
To Pallas' temple, and her towers of height:
Under the feet of the which goddess stern,
Hidden behind her target's boss they crept.
New gripes of dread then pierce our trembling breasts.
They said Lacon's deserts had dearly bought
His heinous deed that piercèd had with steel
The sacred bulk, and thrown the wicked lance.
The people cried with sundry greeing shouts
To bring the horse to Pallas' temple blive,
In hope thereby the goddess' wrath to appease.
We cleft the walls and closures of the town,
Whereto all help, and underset the feet
With sliding rolls, and bound his neck with ropes.
This fatal gin thus overclamb our walls,
Stuft with arm'd men, about the which there ran
Children and maids, that holy carols sang;
And well were they whose hands might touch the cords.
With threatening cheer thus slided through our town
The subtil tree, to Pallas' temple-ward.
O native land! Ilion! and of the gods
The mansion place! O warlike walls of Troy!
Four times it stopt in the entry of our gate;
Four times the harness clatter'd in the womb.
But we go on, unsound of memory,
And blinded eke by rage persever still:
This fatal monster in the fane we place.
   Cassandra then, inspired with Phoebus' sprite,
Her prophet's lips, yet never of us [be]leev'd,
Disclosèd eft, forespeaking things to come.

We wretches, lo, that last day of our life
With boughs of feast the town and temples deck.
　　With this the sky gan whirl about the sphere:
The cloudy night gan thicken from the sea,
With mantles spread that cloakèd earth and skies,
And eke the treason of the Greekish guile.
The watchmen lay disperst, to take their rest,
Whose wearied limbs sound sleep had then oppresst.
When well in order comes the Grecian fleet
From Tenedon, toward the coasts well known,
By friendly silence of the quiet moon.
When the king's ship put forth his mark of fire,
Sinon, preserved by froward destiny,
Let forth the Greeks enclosèd in the womb:
The closures eke of pine by stealth unpinn'd,
Whereby the Greeks restorèd were to air.
With joy down hasting from the hollow tree,
With cords let down did slide unto the ground
The great captains: Sthenel, and Thessander,
And fierce Ulysses, Athamas, and Thoas,
Machaon first, and then king Menelae,
Epeus eke that did the engine forge,
And straight invade the town yburied then
With wine and sleep. And first the watch is slain:
Then gates unfold to let their fellows in,
They join themselves with the conjurèd bands.
　　It was the time when, granted from the gods,
The first sleep creeps most sweet in weary folk.
Lo, in my dream before mine eyes, methought,
With rueful chere I saw where Hector stood,
(Out of whose eyes there gushèd streams of tears)
Drawn at a cart as he of late had been,
Distain'd with bloody dust, whose feet were bowln
With the strait cords wherewith they halèd him.
Ay me, what one! that Hector how unlike,
Which erst return'd clad with Achilles' spoils,
Or when he threw into the Greekish ships,
The Trojan flame, so was his beard defiled,
His crispèd locks all cluster'd with his blood,
With all such wounds, as many he received
About the walls of that his native town!
Whom frankly, thus, methought I spake unto,
With bitter tears and doleful deadly voice:
'O Troyan light! O only hope of thine!
What lets so long thee staid? or from what coasts,
Our most desirèd Hector, dost thou come?

Whom, after slaughter of thy many friends
And travail of the people and thy town,
All-wearied, lord, how gladly we behold!
What sorry chance hath stained thy lively face?
Or why see I these wounds, alas so wide?'
He answer'd nought, nor in my vain demands
Abode, but from the bottom of his breast
Sighing he said: 'Flee, flee, O goddess' son!
And save thee from the fury of this flame.
Our enemies now are masters of the walls,
And Troye town now falleth from the top.
Sufficeth that is done for Priam's reign.
If force might serve to succour Troyé town,
This right hand well mought have been her defence.
But Troyé now commendeth to thy charge
Her holy reliques, and her privy gods.
Them join to thee, as fellows of thy fate.
Large walls rear thou for them: for so thou shalt,
After time spent in the overwander'd flood.'
This said, he brought forth Vesta in his hands,
Her fillets eke, and everlasting flame.

In this mean while, with diverse plaint the town
Throughout was spread; and louder more and more
The din resound, with rattling of arms,
Although mine old father Anchises' house
Removèd stood, with shadow hid of trees,
I waked: therewith to the house-top I clamb,
And hearkening stood I: like as when the flame
Lights in the corn by drift of boisterous wind,
Or the swift stream that driveth from the hill
Roots up the fields and presseth the ripe corn
And plowèd ground, and overwhelms the grove,
The silly herdman all astonied stands,
From the high rock while he doth hear the sound.

Then the Greeks' faith, then their deceit appear'd.
Of Deiphobus the palace large and great
Fell to the ground, all overspread with flash.
His next neighbour Ucalegon afire:
The Sygean seas did glister all with flame.
Upsprang the cry of men, and trumpets' blast.
Then, as distraught, I did my armour on,
Ne could I tell yet whereto arms availed.
But with our feres to throng out from the press
Toward the tower, our hearts brent with desire.
Wrath prickt us forth, and unto us it seem'd
A seemly thing to die arm'd in the field.

Wherewith Panthus, scapte from the Greekish darts,
Otreus' son, Phoebus' priest, brought in hand
The sacred reliques and the vanquisht gods,
And in his hand his little nephew led;
And thus, as phrentic, to our gates he ran.
'Panthus,' quod I, 'in what estate stand we?
Or for refuge what fortress shall we take?'
Scarce spake I this, when wailing thus he said:
'The latter day and fate of Troy is come;
The which no plaint or prayer may avail.
Troyans we were, and Troyè was sometime,
And of great fame the Teucrian glory erst:
Fierce Jove to Greece hath now transposèd all.
The Greeks are lords over this firèd town.
Yonder huge horse that stands amid our walls
Sheds armèd men: and Sinon, victor now,
With scorn of us doth set all things on flame.
And, rushèd in at our unfolded gates,
Are thousands moe than ever came from Greece.
And some with weapons watch the narrow streets,
With bright swords drawn, to slaughter ready bent.
And scarce the watches of the gate began
Them to defend, and with blind fight resist.'
    Through Panthus' words, and lightning of the gods,
Amid the flame and arms ran I in press,
As fury guided me, and whereas I had heard
The cry greatest that made the air resound.
Into our band then fell old Iphytus,
And Rhipeus, that met us by moonlight;
Dymas and Hypanis joining to our side,
With young Chorebus, Mygdonius' son;
Which in those days at Troyè did arrive
(Burning with rage of dame Casandra's love)
In Priam's aid and rescue of his town.
Unhappy he! that would no credit give
Unto his spouse's words of prophecy.
    Whom when I saw, assembled in such wise,
So desperately the battle to desire,
Then furthermore thus said I unto them:
'O ye young men, of courage stout in vain,
For nought ye strive to save the burning town.
What cruel fortune hath betid, ye see:
The gods out of the temples all are fled,
Through whose might long this empire was maintain'd:
Their altars eke are left both waste and void.
But if your will be bent with me to prove

That uttermost that now may us befall,
Then let us die, and run amid our foes:
To vanquisht folk, despair is only hope.'
  With this the young men's courage did increase,
And through the dark, like to the ravening wolves
Whom raging fury of their empty maws
Drives from their den, leaving with hungry throats
Their whelps behind, among our foes we ran,
Upon their swords, unto apparent death;
Holding alway the chief street of the town,
Cover'd with the close shadows of the night.
  Who can express the slaughter of that night,
Or tell the number of the corpses slain,
Or can in tears bewail them worthily?
The ancient famous city falleth down
That many years did hold such seignory.
With senseless bodies every street is spread,
Each palace, and sacred porch of the gods.
Nor yet alone the Troyan blood was shed.
Manhood ofttimes into the vanquisht breast
Returns, whereby some victors Greeks are slain.
Cruel complaints and terror everywhere,
And plenty of grisly pictures of death.
  And, first with us Androgeus there met,
Fellowèd with a swarming rout of Greeks,
Deeming us, unware, of that fellowship,
With friendly words whom thus he call'd unto:
'Haste ye, my friends! what sloth hath tarried you?
Your feres now sack and spoil the burning Troy:
From the tall ships were ye but newly come?'
  When he had said, and heard no answer made
To him again, whereto he might give trust,
Finding himself chancèd amid his foes,
Mazed he withdrew his foot back with his word.
Like him that wandering in the bushes thick
Treads on the adder with his reckless foot,
Rearèd for wrath, swelling her speckled neck,
Dismay'd, gives back all suddenly for fear:
Androgeus so, fear'd of that sight, stept back,
And we gan rush amid the thickest rout;
When, here and there we did them overthrow,
Stricken with dread, unskilful of the place.
Our first labour thus luckèd well with us.
  Chorebus then, encouraged by this chance,
Rejoicing said: 'Hold forth the way of health,
My feres, that hap and manhood hath us taught.

Change we our shields; the Greeks' arms do we on.
Craft or manhood with foes what recks it which:
The slain to us their armour they shall yield.'
And with that word Androgeus' crested helm
And the rich arms of his shield did he on;
A Greekish sword he girded by his side.
Like gladly Dimas and Rhipeus did:
The whole youth gan them clad in the new spoils.
Mingled with Greeks, for no good luck to us,
We went, and gave many onsets that night,
And many a Greek we sent to Pluto's court.
Other there fled and hasted to their ships,
And to their coasts of safeguard ran again.
And some there were for shameful cowardry,
Clamb up again unto the hugy horse,
And did them hide in his well knowen womb.

Ay me! bootless it is for any wight
To hope on aught against will of the gods.
Lo, where Cassandra, Priam's daughter dear,
From Pallas' church was drawn with sparkled tress,
Lifting in vain her flaming eyen to heaven!
Her eyen, for fast her tender wrists were bound.
Which sight Chorebus raging could not bear,
Reckless of death, but thrust amid the throng;
And after we through thickest of the swords.

Here were we first ybatter'd with the darts
Of our own feres, from the high temples' top;
Whereby of us great slaughter did ensue,
Mistaken by our Greekish arms and crests.
Then flockt the Greeks movèd with wrath and ire
Of the virgin from them so rescuèd:
The fell Ajax, and either Atrides,
And the great band clepèd the Dolopes.
As wrestling winds out of dispersèd whirl
Befight themselves, the west with southern blast,
And gladsome east proud of Aurora's horse;
The woods do whiz and foamy Nereus
Raging in fury with three-forked mace
From bottom's depth doth welter up the seas:
So came the Greeks.   And such, as by deceit
We sparkled erst in shadow of the night,
And drave about our town, appearèd first:
Our feignèd shields and weapons then they found,
And, by sound, our discording voice they knew.
We went to wreck with number overlaid.
And by the hand of Peneleus first

Chorebus fell before the altar dead
Of armèd Pallas; and Rhipeus eke,
The justest man among the Troians all,
And he that best observèd equity.
But otherwise it pleasèd now the gods.
There Hypanis, and Dymas, both were slain,
Through piercèd with the weapons of their feres.
Nor thee, Panthus, when thou wast overthrown,
Pity, nor zeal of good devotion,
Nor habit yet of Phoebus hid from scathe.
   Ye Troyan ashes, and last flames of mine,
I call in witness, that at your last fall
I fled no stroke of any Greekish sword,
And if the fates would I had fallen in fight,
That with my hand I did deserve it well.
   With this from thence I was recoilèd back
With Iphytus and Pelias alone:
Iphytus weak, and feeble all for age,
Pelias lamèd by Ulysses' hand.
To Priam's palace cry did call us then.
Here was the fight right hideous to behold,
As though there had no battle been but there,
Or slaughter made elsewhere throughout the town.
A fight of rage and fury there we saw.
The Greeks toward the palace rushèd fast,
And, cover'd with engines, the gates beset,
And rearèd up ladders against the walls;
Under the windows scaling by their steps,
Fencèd with shields in their left hands, whereon
They did receive the darts, while their right hands
Gripèd for hold the embattle of the wall.
The Troyans on the other part rend down
The turrets high and eke the palace roof;
With such weapons they shope them to defend,
Seeing all lost, now at the point of death.
The gilt spars and the beams then threw they down,
Of old fathers the proud and royal works.
And with drawn swords some did beset the gates,
Which they did watch, and keep in routs full thick.
Our sprites restored to rescue the king's house,
To help them, and to give the vanquisht strength.
   A postern with a blind wicket there was,
A common trade to pass through Priam's house,
On the back side whereof waste houses stood:
Which way eftsithes, while that our kingdom dured,
The infortunate Andromache alone

Resorted to the parents of her make,
With young Astyanax, his grandsire to see.
Here passèd I up to the highest tower,
From whence the wretched Troyans did throw down
Darts, spent in waste.   Unto a turret then
We stept, the which stood in a place aloft,
The top whereof did reach well near the stars,
Where we were wont all Troyé to behold,
The Greekish navy, and their tents also.
With instruments of iron gan we, pick,
To seek where we might find the joining shrunk
From that high seat; which we razed, and threw down:
Which falling, gave forthwith a rushing sound,
And large in breadth on Greekish routs it light.
But soon another sort stept in their stead;
No stone unthrown, nor yet no dart uncast.

   Before the gate stood Pyrrhus in the porch
Rejoicing in his darts, with glittering arms.
Like to the adder with venomous herbès fed,
Whom cold winter all bolne hid under ground,
And shining bright, when she her slough had slung,
Her slipper back doth roll, with forkèd tongue
And raisèd breast lift up against the sun.
With that together came great Periphas;
Automedon eke, that guided had some time
Achilles' horse, now Pyrrhus' armour bare;
And eke with him the warlike Scyrian youth
Assail'd the house, and threw flame to the top.
And he an axe before the foremost raught,
Wherewith he gan the strong gates hew and break;
From whence he beat the staples out of brass,
He brake the bars, and through the timber pierced
So large a hole whereby they might discern
The house, the court, the secret chambers eke
Of Priamus and ancient kings of Troy,
And armèd foes in the entry of the gate.

   But the palace within confounded was
With wailing, and with rueful shrieks and cries;
The hollow halls did howl of women's plaint;
The clamour strake up to the golden stars.
Fray'd mothers, wandering through the wide house,
Embracing pillars, did them hold and kiss.
Pyrrhus assaileth with his father's might,
Whom the closures ne keepers might hold out.
With often pushèd ram the gate did shake;
The posts beat down, removèd from their hooks;

By force they made the way, and the entry brake.
And now the Greeks let in, the foremost slew:
And the large palace with soldiers gan to fill.
Not so fiercely doth overflow the fields
The foaming flood, that breaks out of his banks,
Whose rage of waters bears away what heaps
Stand in his way, the cotes, and eke the herds,
As in the entry of slaughter furious
I saw Pyrrhus, and either Atrides.

There Hecuba I saw, with a hundred moe
Of her sons' wives, and Priam at the altar,
Sprinkling with blood his flame of sacrifice.
Fifty bedchambers of his children's wives,
With loss of so great hope of his offspring,
The pillars eke, proudly beset with gold
And with the spoils of other nations,
Fell to the ground: and whatso that with flame
Untouchèd was, the Greeks did all possess.

Percase you would ask what was Priam's fate?
When of his taken town he saw the chance,
And the gates of his palace beaten down,
His foes amid his secret chambers eke,
The old man in vain did on his shoulders then,
Trembling for age, his cuirass long disused:
His bootless sword he girded him about,
And ran amid his foes ready to die.

Amid the court, under the heaven, all bare,
A great altar there stood, by which there grew
An old laurel tree, bowing thereunto,
Which with his shadow did embrace the gods.
Here Hecuba, with her young daughters all
About the altar swarmèd were in vain
(Like doves that flock together in the storm),
The statues of the gods embracing fast.
But when she saw Priam had taken there
His armour, like as though he had been young:
'What furious thought, my wretched spouse,' quod she,
'Did move thee now such weapons for to wield?
Why hastest thou?   This time doth not require
Such succour, ne yet such defenders now:
No, though Hector my son were here again.
Come hither; this altar shall save us all,
Or we shall die together.'   Thus she said.
Wherewith she drew him back to her, and set
The aged man down in the holy seat.

But lo, Polites, one of Priam's sons,

Escapèd from the slaughter of Pyrrhus,
Comes fleeing through the weapons of his foes,
Searching, all wounded, the long galleries
And the void courts; whom Pyrrhus all in rage
Followed fast to reach a mortal wound;
And now in hand, well near strikes with his spear.
Who fleeing forth till he came now in sight
Of his parents, before their face fell down
Yielding the ghost, with flowing streams of blood.
Priamus then, although he were half dead,
Might not keep in his wrath, nor yet his words;
But crieth out: 'For this thy wicked work,
And boldness eke such thing to enterprise,
If in the heavens any justice be,
That of such things takes any care or keep,
According thanks the gods may yield to thee;
And send thee eke thy just deservèd hire,
That made me see the slaughter of my child,
And with his blood defile the father's face.
But he, by whom thou feign'st thyself begot,
Achilles, was to Priam not so stern.
For lo, he tendering my most humble suit
The right and faith, my Hector's bloodless corpse
Render'd, for to be laid in sepulture,
And sent me to my kingdom home again.'
    Thus said the aged man, and therewithal
Forceless he cast his weak unwieldy dart.
Which, repulst from the brass where it gave dint,
Without sound hung vainly in the shieldès boss.
Quod Pyrrhus: 'Then thou shalt this thing report:
On message to Pelide my father go:
Show unto him my cruel deeds, and how
Neoptolem is swervèd out of kind.
Now shalt thou die,' quod he.   And with that word
At the altar him trembling gan he draw
Wallowing through the bloodshed of his son:
And his left hand all claspèd in his hair,
With his right arm drew forth his shining sword,
Which in his side he thrust up to the hilt.
Of Priamus this was the fatal fine,
The woeful end that was allotted him,
When he had seen his palace all on flame,
With ruin of his Troyan turrets eke.
That royal prince of Asia, which of late
Reigned over so many peoples and realms,
Like a great stock now lieth on the shore;

His head and shoulders parted been in twain,
A body now without renown and fame.
 Then first in me enter'd the grisly fear:
Dismay'd I was. Wherewith came to my mind
The image eke of my dear father, when
I thus beheld the king of equal age
Yield up the sprite with wounds so cruelly.
Then thought I of Creusa left alone,
And of my house in danger of the spoil,
And the estate of young Iulus eke.
I lookèd back to seek what number then
I might discern about me of my feres:
But wearied they had left me all alone.
Some to the ground were lopen from above,
Some in the flame their irkèd bodies cast.
 There was no moe but I left of them all,
When that I saw in Vesta's temple sit
Dame Helen, lurking in a secret place;
Such light the flame did give as I went by
While here and there I cast mine eyen about:
For she in dread lest that the Troians should
Revenge on her the ruin of their walls,
And of the Greeks the cruel wreaks also,
The fury eke of her forsaken make,
The common bane of Troy, and eke of Greece,
Hateful she sat beside the altars hid.
Then boiled my breast with flame, and burning wrath,
To revenge my town, unto such ruin brought;
With worthy pains on her to work my will.
Thought I: 'Shall she pass to the land of Sparte
All safe, and see Mycene her native land,
And like a queen return with victory
Home to her spouse, her parents, and children,
Followed with a train of Troyan maids,
And servèd with a band of Phrygian slaves;
And Priam eke with iron murder'd thus,
And Troyè town consumèd all with flame,
Whose shore hath been so oft forbathed in blood?
No! no! for though on women the revenge
Unseemly is (such conquest hath no fame),
To give an end unto such mischief yet
My just revenge shall merit worthy praise;
And quiet eke my mind, for to be wroke
On her which was the causer of this flame,
And satisfy the cinder of my feres.'
 With furious mind while I did argue thus,

My blessed mother then appear'd to me,
Whom erst so bright mine eyes had never seen,
And with pure light she glistred in the night,
Disclosing her in form a goddess like,
As she doth seem to such as dwell in heaven.
My right hand then she took, and held it fast,
And with her rosy lips thus did she say:
'Son! what fury hath thus provokèd thee
To such untamèd wrath? what ragest thou?
Or where is now become the care of us?
Wilt thou not first go see where thou hast left
Anchises, thy father fordone with age?
Doth Creusa live, and Ascanius thy son?
Whom now the Greekish bands have round beset,
And were they not defencèd by my cure,
Flame had them raught and enemies' sword ere this.
Not Helen's beauty hateful unto thee,
Nor blamèd Paris yet, but the gods' wrath
Reft you this wealth, and overthrew your town.
Behold! and I shall now the cloud remove
Which overcast thy mortal sight doth dim,
Whose moisture doth obscure all things about:
And fear not thou to do thy mother's will,
Nor her advice refuse thou to perform.
Here, where thou seest the turrets overthrown,
Stone beat from stone, smoke rising mixt with dust,
Neptunus there shakes with his mace the walls
And eke the loose foundations of the same,
And overwhelms the whole town from his seat:
And cruel Juno with the foremost here
Doth keep the gate that Scea clepèd is,
Near woode for wrath, whereas she stands, and calls
In harness bright the Greeks out of their ships:
And in the turrets high behold where stands
Bright shining Pallas, all in warlike weed,
And with her shield, where Gorgon's head appears:
And Jupiter, my father, distributes
Availing strength and courage to the Greeks:
Yet evermore, against the Troyan power
He doth provoke the rest of all the gods.
Flee then, my son, and give this travail end;
Ne shall I thee forsake, in safeguard till
I have thee brought unto thy father's gate.'
This did she say: and therewith gan she hide
Herself in shadow of the close night.
      Then dreadful figures gan appear to me

And great gods eke aggrievèd with our town.
I saw Troyè fall down in burning gledes,
Neptunus' town clean razèd from the soil.
Like as the elm forgrown in mountains high,
Round hewen with axe, that husbandmen
With thick assaults strive to tear up, doth threat;
And hackt beneath trembling doth bend his top,
Till yold with strokes, giving the latter crack,
Rent from the height, with ruin it doth fall.
  With this I went, and guided by a god
I passèd through my foes, and eke the flame:
Their weapons and the fire eke gave me place.
And when that I was come before the gates
And ancient building of my father's house,
My father, whom I hopèd to convey
To the next hills, and did him thereto 'treat,
Refusèd either to prolong his life,
Or bide exile after the fall of Troy.
'All ye,' quod he, 'in whom young blood is fresh,
Whose strength remains entire and in full power,
Take ye your flight.
For if the gods my life would have prorogued,
They had reserv'd for me this wonning-place.
It was enough, alas, and eke too much,
To see the town of Troy thus razèd once;
To have lived after the city taken.
When ye have said, this corpse laid out forsake;
My hand shall seek my death, and pity shall
Mine enemies move, or else hope of my spoil.
As for my grave, I weigh the loss but light:
For I my years, disdainful to the gods,
Have linger'd forth, unable to all needs,
Since that the sire of gods and king of men
Strake me with thunder and with levening blast.'
Such things he gan rehearse, thus firmly bent:
But we besprent with tears, my tender son,
And eke my sweet Creusa, with the rest
Of the household, my father gan beseech
Not so with him to perish all at once,
Nor so to yield unto the cruel fate:
Which he refus'd, and stack to his intent.
  Driven I was to harness then again,
Miserably my death for to desire.
For what advice, or other hope was left?
'Father, thought'st thou that I may once remove,'
Quod I, 'a foot, and leave thee here behind?

May such a wrong pass from a father's mouth?
If gods' will be, that nothing here be saved
Of this great town, and thy mind bent to join
Both thee and thine to ruin of this town,
The way is plain this death for to attain.
Pyrrhus shall come, besprent with Priam's blood,
That gored the son before the father's face
And slew the father at the altar eke.
O sacred mother! was it then for this
That you me led through flame and weapons sharp,
That I might in my secret chamber see
Mine enemies; and Ascanius my son,
My father, with Creusa my sweet wife,
Murder'd, alas, the one in the other's blood?
Why, servants, then, bring me my arms again.
The latter day us vanquishèd doth call.
Render me now to the Greeks' sight again,
And let me see the fight begun of new:
We shall not all unwroken die this day.'
    About me then I girt my sword again,
And eke my shield on my left shoulder cast,
And bent me so to rush out of the house.
Lo! in my gate my spouse, clasping my feet,
Forgainst his father young Iulus set.
'If thou wilt go,' quod she, 'and spill thyself,
Take us with thee in all that may betide.
But as expert if thou in arms have set
Yet any hope, then first this house defend,
Whereas thy son, and eke thy father dear,
And I, sometime thine own dear wife, are left.'
Her shrill loud voice with plaint thus filled the house,
When that a sudden monstrous marvel fell:
For in their sight, and woful parents' arms,
Behold a light out of the button sprang
That in tip of Iulus' cap did stand;
With gentle touch whose harmless flame did shine
Upon his hair, about his temples spread.
And we afraid, trembling for dreadful fear,
Bet out the fire from his blazing tress,
And with water gan quench the sacred flame.
    Anchises glad his eyen lift to the stars;
With hands his voice to heaven thus he bent.
'If by prayer, almighty Jupiter,
Inclinèd thou mayst be, behold us then
Of ruth at least, if we so much deserve.
Grant eke thine aid, Father! confirm this thing.'

Scarce had the old man said, when that the heavens
With sudden noise thunder'd on the left hand:
Out of the sky, by the dark night there fell
A blazing star, dragging a brand of flame,
Which, with much light gliding on the house top,
In the forest of Ida hid her beams;
The which full bright kindling a furrow, shone,
By a long tract appointing us the way:
And round about of brimstone rose a fume.
  My father, vanquisht then, beheld the skies,
Spake to the gods, and the holy star adored:
'Now, now,' quod he, 'no longer I abide:
Follow I shall where ye me guide at hand.
O native gods, your family defend!
Preserve your line! This warning comes of you,
And Troyë stands in your protection now.
Now give I place, and whereso that thou go,
Refuse I not, my son, to be thy fere.'
  This did he say; and by that time more clear
The cracking flame was heard throughout the walls.
And more and more the burning heat drew near.
'Why then, have done, my father dear,' quod I,
'Bestride my neck forthwith, and sit thereon,
And I shall with my shoulders thee sustain,
Ne shall this labour do me any dere.
What so betide, come peril, come welfare,
Like to us both and common there shall be.
Young Iulus shall bear me company,
And my wife shall follow far off my steps.
Now ye, my servants, mark well what I say:
Without the town ye shall find, on a hill,
An old temple there stands, whereas some time
Worship was done to Ceres the goddess;
Beside which grows an aged cypress tree,
Preservèd long by our forefathers' zeal:
Behind which place let us together meet.
And thou, Father, receive into thy hands
The reliques all, and the gods of the land:
The which it were not lawful I should touch,
That come but late from slaughter and bloodshed,
Till I be washèd in the running flood.'
  When I had said these words, my shoulders broad
And laied neck with garments gan I spread,
And thereon cast a yellow lion's skin;
And thereupon my burden I receive.
Young Iulus, claspèd in my right hand,

Followeth me fast with unegal pace;
And at my back my wife.   Thus did we pass
By places shadowèd most with the night.
And me, whom late the dart which enemies threw,
Nor press of Argive routs could make amazed,
Each whispering wind hath power now to fray,
And every sound to move my doubtful mind:
So much I dread my burden, and my fere.

And now we gan draw near unto the gate,
Right well escapte the danger, as methought,
When that at hand a sound of feet we heard.
My father then, gazing throughout the dark,
Crièd on me, 'Flee, son!   They are at hand.'
With that bright shields and shene armours I saw.
But then, I know not what unfriendly god
My troubled wit from me bereft for fear:
For while I ran by the most secret streets,
Eschewing still the common haunted track,
From me caitiff, alas! bereavèd was
Creusa then, my spouse, I wot not how,
Whether by fate, or missing of the way,
Or that she was by weariness retain'd,
But never sith these eyes might her behold;
Nor did I yet perceive that she was lost,
Ne never backward turnèd I my mind,
Till we came to the hill, whereas there stood
The old temple dedicate to Ceres.

And when that we were there assembled all,
She was only away, deceiving us
Her spouse, her son, and all her company.
What god or man did I not then accuse,
Near woode for ire, or what more cruel chance
Did hap to me, in all Troy's overthrow?
Ascanius to my feres I then betook,
With Anchises, and eke the Troyan gods.
And left them hid within a valley deep.
And to the town I gan me hie again,
Clad in bright arms, and bent for to renew
Aventures past, to search throughout the town,
And yield my head to perils once again.

And first the walls and dark entry I sought
Of the same gate whereat I issued out;
Holding backward the steps where we had come
In the dark night, looking all round about:
In every place the ugsome sights I saw;
The silence self of night aghast my sprite.

From hence again I pass'd unto our house,
If she by chance had been returnèd home.
The Greeks were there, and had it all beset:
The wasting fire, blown up by drift of wind,
Above the roof in blazing flame sprang up,
The sound whereof with fury pierced the skies.
To Priam's palace and the castle then
I made; and there at Juno's sanctuair,
In the void porches, Phenix, Ulysses eke,
Stern guardians stood, watching of the spoil.
The riches here were set, reft from the brent
Temples of Troy: the tables of the gods,
The vessels eke that were of massy gold,
And vestures spoil'd, were gather'd all in heap.
The children orderly, and mothers pale for fright,
Long rangèd on a row stood round about.
    So bold was I to show my voice that night
With clepes and cries to fill the streets throughout,
With Creuse' name in sorrow, with vain tears;
And oftensithes the same for to repeat.
The town restless with fury as I sought,
The unlucky figure of Creusa's ghost,
Of stature more than wont, stood fore mine eyen.
Abashèd then I woxe: therewith my hair
Gan start right up: my voice stack in my throat,
When with such words she gan my heart remove:
'What helps to yield unto such furious rage,
Sweet spouse?' quod she.   'Without will of the gods
This chancèd not: ne lawful was for thee
To lead away Creusa hence with thee:
The King of the high heaven suffereth it not.
A long exile thou art assign'd to bear,
Long to furrow large space of stormy seas:
So shalt thou reach at last Hesperian land,
Where Lydian Tiber with his gentle stream
Mildly doth flow along the fruitful fields.
There mirthful wealth, there kingdom is for thee;
There a king's child prepar'd to be thy make.
For thy beloved Creusa stint thy tears:
For now shall I not see the proud abodes
Of Myrmidons, nor yet of Dolopes:
Ne I, a Troyan lady and the wife
Unto the son of Venus the goddess,
Shall go a slave to serve the Greekish dames.
Me here the god's great mother holds——
And now farewell: and keep in father's breast

The tender love of thy young son and mine.'
  This having said, she left me all in tears
And minding much to speak; but she was gone,
And subtly fled into the weightless air.
Thrice raught I with mine arms to accoll her neck:
Thrice did my hands vain hold the image escape,
Like nimble winds, and like the flying dream.
So, night spent out, return I to my feres;
And there wondering I find together swarm'd
A number of mates, mothers, and men,
A rout exiled, a wretched multitude,
From each-where flock together, prest to pass
With heart and goods to whatsoever land
By sliding seas me listed them to lead.
And now rose Lucifer above the ridge
Of lusty Ide, and brought the dawning light.
The Greeks held the entries of the gates beset:
Of help there was no hope.   Then gave I place,
Took up my sire, and hasted to the hill.

SIR PHILIP SIDNEY

1554–86

SIDNEY, born two years later than Ralegh, precedes him in this volume by virtue of his much earlier death: Ralegh survived him by twenty-two years. His poetical work consists of the hundred and eight sonnets and eleven songs of *Astrophel and Stella*, metrical versions of the Psalms (of which the extent of his authorship is uncertain), the songs and sonnets and pastorals that occur at intervals throughout the prose romance *Arcadia* in its various versions, and two or three fugitive pieces. Sidney's poetry at its best is beyond praise, but he wrote copiously and unequally, as greater poets have done; and not the most avid reader will quarrel with the exclusion, from this edition, of the *Psalms* and of all but three or four of the experiments in classical metres ordained by Gabriel Harvey. Here will be found all the sonnets and all but two of the songs of *Astrophel and Stella*, and a generous selection from the Arcadian and other pieces. Except in the matter of spelling and punctuation our text is based mainly on Grosart, who in 1877 first brought the scattered poems together. But Feuillerat's monumental edition (1912–26) of Sidney's Works has also been consulted, and now and again a variant reading rejected by Grosart has been preferred.

ASTROPHEL AND STELLA

I

LOVING in truth, and fain in verse my love to show,
That She, dear She, might take some pleasure of my pain,
Pleasure might cause her read, reading might make her know,
Knowledge might pity win, and pity grace obtain,
I sought fit words to paint the blackest face of woe;
Studying inventions fine, her wits to entertain,
Oft turning others' leaves, to see if thence would flow
Some fresh and fruitful showers upon my sun-burn'd brain.
But words came halting out, wanting Invention's stay;
Invention, Nature's child, fled stepdame Study's blows;
And others' feet still seem'd but strangers in my way.
Thus, great with child to speak, and helpless in my throes,
Biting my truand pen, beating myself for spite,
'Fool,' said my Muse to me, 'look in thy heart and write.'

II

NOT at the first sight, nor with a dribb'd shot,
Love gave the wound which while I breathe will bleed;
But known worth did in tract of time proceed
Till by degrees it had full conquest got.
I saw and liked; I liked but lovèd not;
I loved, but did not straight what Love decreed:
At length to Love's decrees I, forc'd, agreed,
Yet with repining at so partial lot.
Now, even that footstep of lost liberty
Is gone, and now, like slave-borne Muscovite,
I call it praise to suffer tyranny;
And now employ the remnant of my wit
To make myself believe that all is well,
While with a feeling skill I paint my hell.

III

LET dainty wits cry on the Sisters nine,
That bravely maskt, their fancies may be told;
Or Pindar's apes flaunt they in phrases fine,
Enamelling with pied flowers their thoughts of gold;

Or else let them in statelier glory shine,
Ennobling new-found tropes with problems old,
Or with strange similes enrich each line,
Of herbs or beasts which Ind or Afric hold.
For me, in sooth, no Muse but one I know,
Phrases and problems from my reach do grow,
And strange things cost too dear for my poor sprites.
How then? even thus—in Stella's face I read
What Love and Beauty be, then all my deed
But ccpying is, what in her Nature writes.

IV

VIRTUE, alas, now let me take some rest:
Thou set'st a bate between my will and wit.
In vain Love have my simple soul opprest,
Leave what thou lik'st not, deal not thou with it.
Thy sceptre use in some old Cato's breast,
Churches or schools are for thy seat more fit:
I do confess—pardon a fault confest—
My mouth too tender is for thy hard bit.
But if that needs thou wilt usurping be
The little reason that is left in me,
And still th' effect of thy persuasions prove,
I swear my heart such one shall show to thee,
That shrines in flesh so true a deity,
That, Virtue, thou thyself shalt be in love.

V

IT is most true that eyes are form'd to serve
The inward light, and that the heavenly part
Ought to be King, from whose rules who do swerve,
Rebels to nature, strive for their own smart.
It is most true, what we call Cupid's dart
An image is, which for ourselves we carve,
And, fools, adore in temple of our heart,
Till that good god make church and churchmen starve.
True, that true beauty virtue is indeed,
Whereof this beauty can be but a shade,
Which elements with mortal mixture breed.
True that on earth we are but pilgrims made,
And should in soul up to our country move:
True, and yet true that I must Stella love.

VI

SOME lovers speak, when they their Muses entertain,
Of hopes begot by fear, of wot not what desires,
Of force of heavenly beams infusing hellish pain,
Of living deaths, dear wounds, fair storms, and freezing fires:
Some one his song in Jove and Jove's strange tales attires,
Bord'red with bulls and swans, powdred with golden rain:
Another, humbler wit, to shepherd's pipe retires,
Yet hiding royal blood full oft in rural vein.
To some a sweetest plaint a sweetest style affords:
While tears pour out his ink, and sighs breathe out his words,
His paper pale despair, and pain his pen doth move.
I can speak what I feel, and feel as much as they,
But think that all the map of my state I display
When trembling voice brings forth that I do Stella love.

VII

WHEN Nature made her chief work, Stella's eyes,
In colour black why wrapt she beams so bright?
Would she in beamy black, like painter wise,
Frame daintiest lustre mixt of shades and light?
Or did she else that sober hue devise,
In object best to knit and strength our sight;
Lest if no veil these brave gleams did disguise
They sunlike should more dazzle than delight?
Or would she her miraculous power show,
That, whereas black seems Beauty's contrary,
She even in black doth make all beauties flow?
Both so and thus: she, minding Love should be
Placed ever there, gave him this mourning weed
To honour all their deaths who for her bleed.

VIII

LOVE, born in Greece, of late fled from his native place,
Forced, by a tedious proof, that Turkish hardned heart
Is not fit mark to pierce with his fine-pointed dart,
And pleas'd with our soft peace stay'd here his flying race:
But, finding these north climes too coldly him embrace,
Not used to frozen clips, he strave to find some part
Where with most ease and warmth he might employ his art.
At length he perch'd himself in Stella's joyful face,

Whose fair skin, beamy eyes, like morning sun on snow,
Deceiv'd the quaking boy, who thought from so pure light
Effects of lively heat must needs in nature grow:
But she, most fair, most cold, made him thence take his flight
To my close heart, where, while some firebrands he did lay,
He burnt unwares his wings, and cannot fly away.

IX

QUEEN Virtue's Court, which some call Stella's face,
Prepar'd by Nature's choicest furniture,
Hath his front built of alabaster pure;
Gold is the covering of that stately place.
The door by which sometimes comes forth her grace
Red porphir is, which lock of pearl makes sure,
Whose porches rich—which name of cheeks endure—
Marble, mixt red and white, do interlace.
The windows now, through which this heavenly guest
Looks over the world and can find nothing such
Which dare claim from those lights the name of best,
Of touch they are, that without touch do touch,
Which Cupid's self, from Beauty's mine did draw:
Of touch they are, and poor I am their straw.

X

REASON, in faith thou art well serv'd that still
Wouldst brabbling be with Sense and Love in me.
I rather wisht thee climb the Muses' hill,
Or reach the fruit of Nature's choicest tree,
Or seek heaven's course or heaven's inside to see:
Why shouldst thou toil our thorny soil to till?
Leave Sense, and those which Sense's objects be:
Deal thou with powers of thoughts, leave Love to Will.
But thou wouldst needs fight both with Love and Sense,
With sword of wit giving wounds of dispraise,
Till downright blows did foil thy cunning fence;
For, soon as they strake thee with Stella's rays,
Reason, thou kneeld'st, and offered'st straight to prove,
By reason good, good reason her to love.

XI

IN truth, O Love, with what a boyish kind
Thou dost proceed in thy most serious ways,
That when the heaven to thee his best displays,
Yet of that best thou leav'st the best behind!
For, like a child that some fair book doth find

With gilded leaves or colour'd vellum plays,
Or at the most on some fine picture stays
But never heeds the fruit of writer's mind,
So when thou saw'st, in Nature's cabinet,
Stella, thou straight lookt'st babies in her eyes:
In her cheeks' pit thou didst thy pitfold set,
And in her breast bo-peep or crouching lies,
Playing and shining in each outward part;
But, fool, seekst not to get into her heart.

XII

CUPID, because thou shin'st in Stella's eyes,
That from her looks thy day-nets none scapes free,
That those lips swell'd so full of thee they be,
That her sweet breath makes oft thy flames to rise,
That in her breast thy pap well sug'red lies,
That her grace gracious makes thy wrongs, that she,
What words soe'er she speak, persuades for thee,
That her clear voice lifts thy fame to the skies—
Thou countest Stella thine: like those whose powers
Having got up a breach by fighting well,
Cry 'Victory, this fair day all is ours!'
O no! Her heart is such a citadel,
So fortified with wit, stor'd with disdain,
That to win it is all the skill and pain.

XIII

PHOEBUS was judge between Jove, Mars, and Love,
Of those three gods, whose arms the fairest were.
Jove's golden shield did eagle sables bear,
Whose talons held young Ganymede above:
But in vert field Mars bare a golden spear
Which through a bleeding heart his point did shove.
Each had his crest; Mars carried Venus' glove;
Jove on his helmet the thunderbolt did rear.
Cupid then smiles, for on his crest there lies
Stella's fair hair; her face he makes his shield,
Where roses gules are borne in silver field.
Phoebus drew wide the curtains of the skies
To blaze these last, and sware devoutly then
The first, thus matcht, were scantly gentlemen.

XIV

ALAS, have I not pain enough, my friend,
Upon whose breast a fiercer grip doth tire
Than did on him who first stale down the fire,
While Love on me doth all his quiver spend?
But with your rhubarb words ye must contend
To grieve me worse, in saying that Desire
Doth plunge my well-form'd soul even in the mire
Of sinful thoughts, which do in ruin end.
If that be sin which doth the manners frame,
Well stay'd with truth in word and faith of deed,
Ready of wit, and fearing nought but shame;
If that be sin which in fixt hearts doth breed
A loathing of all loose unchastity—
Then love is sin, and let me sinful be.

XV

YOU that do search for every purling spring
Which from the ribs of old Parnassus flows,
And every flower, not sweet perhaps, which grows
Near thereabouts, into your poesy wring;
Ye that do dictionary's method bring
Into your rimes, running in rattling rows;
You that poor Petrarch's long-deceasèd woes
With new-born sighs and denizen'd wit do sing;
You take wrong ways; those far-fet helps be such
As do bewray a want of inward touch,
And sure, at length, stol'n goods do come to light.
But if, both for your love and skill, your name
You seek to nurse at fullest breasts of Fame,
Stella behold, and then begin to indite.

XVI

IN nature apt to like, when I did see
Beauties which were of many carats fine,
My boiling sprites did thither then incline,
And, Love, I thought that I was full of thee.
But finding not those restless flames in me
Which others said did make their souls to pine,
I thought those babes of some pin's hurt did whine,
By my soul judging what Love's pain might be.
But while I thus with this young lion play'd,

Mine eyes—shall I say curst or blest?—beheld
Stella: now she is nam'd, need more be said?
In her sight I a lesson new have spell'd.
I now have learn'd love right, and learn'd even so
As they that being poison'd poison know.

XVII

HIS mother dear, Cupid offended late,
Because that Mars, grown slacker in her love,
With pricking shot he did not throughly move·
To keep the place of their first loving state.
The boy refused for fear of Mars's hate,
Who threatned stripes if he his wrath did prove;
But she, in chafe, him from her lap did shove,
Brake bowe, brake shafts, while Cupid weeping sate:
Till that his grandam Nature, pitying it,
Of Stella's brows made him two better bows,
And in her eyes of arrows infinit.
O how for joy he leaps! O how he crows!
And straight therewith, like wags new got to play,
Falls to shrewd turns! And I was in his way.

XVIII

WITH what sharp checks I in myself am shent
When into Reason's audit I do go,
And by just counts myself a bankrout know
Of all those goods which heaven to me hath lent;
Unable quite to pay even Nature's rent,
Which unto it by birthright I do owe;
And, which is worse, no good excuse can show,
But that my wealth I have most idly spent!
My youth doth waste, my knowledge brings forth toys,
My wit doth strive those passions to defend
Which, for reward, spoil it with vain annoys.
I see my course to lose myself doth bend;
I see—and yet no greater sorrow take
Than that I lose no more for Stella's sake.

XIX

ON Cupid's bow how are my heart-strings bent,
That see my wrack and yet embrace the same!
When most I glory, then I feel most shame;
I willing run, yet while I run repent;

My best wits still their own disgrace invent,
My very ink turns straight to Stella's name,
And yet my words, as them my pen doth frame,
Avise themselves that they are vainly spent.
For though she pass all things, yet what is all
That unto me, who fare like him that both
Looks to the skies and in a ditch doth fall?
O let me prop my mind, yet in his growth,
And not in nature for best fruits unfit.
'Scholar', saith Love, 'bend hitherward your wit.'

XX

FLY, fly, my friends! I have my death's wound—fly!
See there that boy, that murthring boy I say,
Who like a thief hid in dark bush doth lie,
Till bloody bullet get him wrongful prey.
So tyrant he no fitter place could spy,
Nor so fair level in so secret stay,
As that sweet black which veils the heavenly eye:
There with his shot himself he close doth lay.
Poor passenger, pass now thereby I did,
And stay'd, pleas'd with the prospect of the place,
While that black hue from me the bad guest hid.
But straight I saw motions of lightning grace,
And then described the glistrings of his dart:
But ere I could fly thence, it pierc'd my heart.

XXI

YOUR words (my friend), right healthful caustiks, blame
My young mind marred, whom Love doth windlass so,
That mine own writings, like bad servants, show
My wits quick in vain thoughts, in virtue lame;
That Plato I read for nought but if he tame
Such coltish years; that to my birth I owe
Nobler desires, lest else that friendly foe,
Great expectation, wear a train of shame:
For since mad March great promise made of me,
If now the May of my years much decline,
What can be hoped my harvest-time will be?
Sure, you say well, 'Your wisdom's golden mine
Dig deep with Learning's spade.' Now tell me this—
Hath this world aught so fair as Stella is?

XXII

IN highest way of heaven the sun did ride,
Progressing then from fair Twins' golden place,
Having no mask of clouds before his face,
But streaming forth of heat in his chief pride;
When some fair ladies, by hard promise tied,
On horseback met him in his furious race;
Yet each prepar'd with fans' well-shading grace
From that foe's wounds their tender skins to hide.
Stella alone with face unarmèd marcht,
Either to do like him which open shone,
Or careless of the wealth, because her own.
Yet were the hid and meaner beauties parcht:
Her dainties bare went free.   The cause was this—
The sun, that others burn'd, did her but kiss.

XXIII

THE curious wits, seeing dull pensiveness
Bewray itself in my long-settled eyes
Whence those same fumes of melancholy rise,
With idle pains and missing aim do guess.
Some, that know how my spring I did address,
Deem that my Muse some fruit of knowledge plies;
Others, because the prince my service tries,
Think that I think State errors to redress.
But harder judges judge ambition's rage—
Scourge of itself, still climbing slippery place—
Holds my young brain captiv'd in golden cage.
O fools, or over-wise!   Alas, the race
Of all my thoughts hath neither stop nor start
But only Stella's eyes and Stella's heart.

XXIV

RICH fools there be whose base and filthy heart
Lies hatching still the goods wherein they flow,
And damning their own selves to Tantal's smart,
Wealth breeding want—more rich, more wretched grow.
Yet to those fools Heaven doth such wit impart
As what their hands do hold, their heads do know,
And knowing love, and loving lay apart
As sacred things, far from all danger's show.
But that rich fool who by blind Fortune's lot

The richest gem of love and life enjoys,
And can with foul abuse such beauties blot,
Let him, depriv'd of sweet but unfelt joys,
Exiled for aye from those high treasures which
He knows not, grow in only folly rich!

XXV

THE wisest scholar of the wight most wise
By Phoebus' doom, with sug'red sentence says
That virtue, if it once met with our eyes,
Strange flames of love it in our souls would raise.
But—for that man with pain this truth descries
Whiles he each thing in Sense's balance weighs,
And so nor will nor can behold those skies
Which inward sun to heroic mind displays—
Virtue of late, with virtuous care to stir
Love of herself, took Stella's shape that she
To mortal eyes might sweetly shine in her.
It is most true; for since I her did see,
Virtue's great beauty in that face I prove,
And find the effect: for I do burn in love.

XXVI

THOUGH dusty wits dare scorn Astrology,
And fools can think those lamps of purest light—
Whose numbers, ways, greatness, eternity,
Promising wonders, wonder do invite—
To have for no cause birthright in the sky
But for to spangle the black weed of Night,
Or for some brawl which in that chamber high
They should still dance to please a gazer's sight:
For me, I do Nature unidle know,
And know great causes great effects procure;
And know those bodies high reign on the low.
And if these rules did fail, proof makes me sure
Who oft foresee my after-following race,
By only those two stars in Stella's face.

XXVII

BECAUSE I oft in dark abstracted guise
Seem most alone in greatest company,
With dearth of words, or answers quite awry,
To them that would make speech of speech arise;

They deem, and of their doom the rumour flies,
That poison foul of bubbling pride doth lie
So in my swelling breast that only I
Fawn on myself, and others do despise.
Yet pride I think doth not my soul possess
(Which looks too oft in his unflattering glass):
But one worse fault, ambition, I confess,
That makes me oft my best friends overpass,
Unseen, unheard, while thought to highest place
Bends all his powers, even unto Stella's grace.

XXVIII

YOU that with Allegory's curious frame
Of others' children changelings use to make,
With me those pains, for God's sake, do not take:
I list not dig so deep for brazen fame.
When I say Stella I do mean the same
Princess of beauty for whose only sake
The reins of Love I love, though never slake,[1]
And joy therein, though nations count it shame.
I beg no subject to use eloquence,
Nor in hid ways to guide philosophy:
Look at my hands for no such quintessence,
But know that I in pure simplicity
Breathe out the flames which burn within my heart,
Love only reading unto me this art.

XXIX

LIKE some weak lords, neighbour'd by mighty kings,
To keep themselves and their chief cities free
Do easily yield that all their coasts may be
Ready to store their camps of needful things,
So Stella's heart, finding what power Love brings
To keep itself in life and liberty,
Doth willing grant that in the frontiers he
Use all to help his other conquerings.
And thus her heart escapes, but thus her eyes
Serve him with shot, her lips his heralds are,
Her breasts his tents, legs his triumphal car,
Her flesh his food, her skin his armour brave.
And I, but for because my prospect lies
Upon that coast, am given up for slave.

[1] slack

XXX

WHETHER the Turkish new moon minded be
To fill her horns this year on Christian coast:
How Poles' right king means without leave of host
To warm with ill-made fire cold Muscovy:
If French can yet three parts in one agree:
What now the Dutch in their full diets boast:
How Holland hearts, now so good towns be lost,
Trust in the shade of pleasant Orange-tree:
How Ulster likes of that same golden bit
Wherewith my father once made it half tame:
If in the Scotch Court be no weltring yet:
These questions busy wits to me do frame.
I, cumbred with good manners, answer do,
But know not how.   For still I think of you.

XXXI

WITH how sad steps, O Moon, thou climbst the skies!
How silently, and with how wan a face!
What, may it be that even in heavenly place
That busy archer his sharp arrows tries?
Sure, if that long-with-love-acquainted eyes
Can judge of love, thou feel'st a lover's case:
I read it in thy looks: thy languisht grace,
To me that feel the like, thy state descries.
Then even of fellowship, O Moon, tell me,
Is constant love deem'd there but want of wit?
Are beauties there as proud as here they be?
Do they above love to be lov'd, and yet
Those lovers scorn whom that love doth possess?
Do they call virtue there ungratefulness?

XXXII

MORPHEUS, the lively son of deadly Sleep,
Witness of life to them that living die,
A prophet oft and oft an history,
A poet eke, as humours fly or creep;
Since thou in me so sure a power dost keep,
That never I with closed-up sense do lie
But by thy work my Stella I descry,
Teaching blind eyes both how to smile and weep;
Vouchsafe, of all acquaintance, this to tell,
Whence hast thou ivory, rubies, pearl, and gold,

To show her skin, lips, teeth, and head so well?
'Fool!' answers he, 'no Inds such treasures hold;
But from thy heart, while my sire charmeth thee,
Sweet Stella's image I do steal to me.'

XXXIII

I MIGHT—unhappy word!—O me, I might,
And then would not, or could not, see my bliss,
Till now wrapt in a most infernal night,
I find how heavenly day, wretch! I did miss.
Heart, rent thyself, thou dost thyself but right:
No lovely Paris made thy Helen his,
No force, no fraud robb'd thee of thy delight,
Nor Fortune of thy fortune author is,
But to myself myself did give the blow,
While too much wit, forsooth, so troubled me
That I respects for both our sakes must show,
And yet could not by rising morn foresee
How fair a day was near.   O punisht eyes,
That I had been more foolish, or more wise!

XXXIV

COME, let me write. And to what end?   To ease
A burthened heart.   How can words ease, which are
The glasses of thy daily-vexing care?
Oft cruel fights well pictured-forth do please.
Art not asham'd to publish thy disease?
Nay, that may breed my fame, it is so rare.
But will not wise men think thy words fond ware?
Then be they close, and so none shall displease.
What idler thing than speak and not be heard?
What harder thing than smart and not to speak?
Peace, foolish wit! with wit my wit is marr'd.
Thus write I, while I doubt to write, and wreak
My harms in ink's poor loss.   Perhaps some find
Stella's great powers that so confuse my mind.

XXXV

WHAT may words say, or what may words not say,
Where Truth itself must speak like Flattery?
Within what bounds can one his liking stay,
Where Nature doth with infinite agree?

What Nestor's counsel can my flames allay,
Since Reason's self doth blow the coal in me?
And, ah, what hope that Hope should once see day,
Where Cupid is sworn page to Chastity?
Honour is honour'd that thou dost possess
Him as thy slave, and now long-needy Fame
Doth even grow rich, meaning my Stella's name.
Wit learns in thee perfection to express:
Not thou by praise, but praise in thee is rais'd.
It is a praise to praise, when thou art prais'd.

XXXVI

STELLA, whence doth these new assaults arise,
A conquer'd yielding ransackt heart to win,
Whereto long since, through my long-battered eyes,
Whole armies of thy beauties enterèd in?
And there, long since, Love thy lieutenant lies;
My forces razed, thy banners rais'd within:
Of conquest do not these effects suffice,
But wilt new war upon thine own begin?
With so sweet voice, and by sweet Nature so
In sweetest strength, so sweetly skill'd withal
In all sweet stratagems sweet Art can show,
That not my soul, which at thy foot did fall
Long since, forc'd by thy beams, but stone nor tree,
By Sense's privilege, can scape from thee!

XXXVII

MY mouth doth water, and my breast doth swell,
My tongue doth itch, my thoughts in labour be.
Listen then, lordings, with good ear to me,
For of my life I must a riddle tell.
Toward Aurora's Court a nymph doth dwell,
Rich in all beauties which man's eye can see;
Beauties so far from reach of words that we
Abase her praise saying she doth excel;
Rich in the treasure of deserv'd renown,
Rich in the riches of a royal heart,
Rich in those gifts which give th' eternal crown;
Who, though most rich in these and every part
Which make the patents of true worldly bliss,
Hath no misfortune but that Rich she is.

XXXVIII

THIS night, while sleep begins with heavy wings
To hatch mine eyes, and that unbitted thought
Doth fall to stray, and my chief powers are brought
To leave the scepter of all subject things,
The first that straight my fancy's error brings
Unto my mind is Stella's image, wrought
By Love's own self, but with so curious draught
That she, methinks, not only shines but sings.
I start, look, heark: but what in closed-up sense
Was held, in open'd sense it flies away,
Leaving me nought but wailing eloquence.
I, seeing better sights in sight's decay,
Call'd it anew, and wooèd Sleep again:
But him, her host, that unkind guest had slain.

XXXIX

COME, Sleep, O Sleep, the certain knot of peace,
The baiting-place of wit, the balm of woe,
The poor man's wealth, the prisoner's release,
The indifferent judge between the high and low!
With shield of proof shield me from out the prease
Of those fierce darts Despair at me doth throw.
O make in me those civil wars to cease:
I will good tribute pay, if thou do so.
Take thou of me smooth pillows, sweetest bed,
A chamber deaf of noise and blind of light,
A rosy garland and a weary head:
And if these things, as being thine in right,
Move not thy heavy grace, thou shalt in me,
Livelier than elsewhere, Stella's image see.

XL

AS good to write, as for to lie and groan.
O Stella dear, how much thy power hath wrought,
That hast my mind—now of the basest—brought
My still-kept course, while others sleep, to moan!
Alas, if from the height of Virtue's throne
Thou canst vouchsafe the influence of a thought
Upon a wretch that long thy grace hath sought,
Weigh then how I by thee am overthrown,
And then think thus—although thy beauty be
Made manifest by such a victory,

Yet noble conquerors do wrecks avoid.
Since then thou hast so far subduèd me
That in my heart I offer still to thee,
O do not let thy temple be destroy'd!

XLI

HAVING this day my horse, my hand, my lance
Guided so well that I obtain'd the prize,
Both by the judgment of the English eyes
And of some sent from that sweet enemy France;
Horsemen my skill in horsemanship advance,
Townfolks my strength; a daintier judge applies
His praise to sleight which from good use doth rise;
Some lucky wits impute it but to chance;
Others, because of both sides I do take
My blood from them who did excel in this,
Think Nature me a man-at-arms did make.
How far they shot awry!   The true cause is,
Stella lookt on, and from her heavenly face
Sent forth the beams which made so fair my race.

XLII

O EYES which do the spheres of beauty move,
Whose beams be joys, whose joys all virtues be,
Who, while they make Love conquer, conquer Love;
The schools where Venus hath learn'd chastity:
O eyes, where humble looks most glorious prove,
Only-lov'd tyrants, just in cruelty,
Do not, O do not, from poor me remove:
Keep still my zenith, ever shine on me.
For though I never see them but straightways
My life forgets to nourish languisht sprites,
Yet still on me, O eyes, dart down your rays!
And if from majesty of sacred lights
Oppressing mortal sense my death proceed,
Wracks triumphs be which Love high-set doth breed.

XLIII

FAIR eyes, sweet lips, dear heart, that foolish
Could hope, by Cupid's help, on you to prey,
Since to himself he doth your gifts apply,
As his main force, choice sport and easeful stay!
For when he will see who dare him gainsay,

Then with those eyes he looks: lo, by and by
Each soul doth at Love's feet his weapons lay,
Glad if for her he give them leave to die.
When he will play, then in her lips he is,
Where, blushing red that Love's self them doth love,
With either lip he doth the other kiss;
But when he will, for quiet's sake, remove
From all the world, her heart is then his room,
Where well he knows no man to him can come.

LXIV

MY words I know do well set forth my mind;
My mind bemoans his sense of inward smart;
Such smart may pity claim of any heart;
Her heart, sweet heart, is of no tiger's kind:
And yet she hears and yet no pity I find,
But more I cry, less grace she doth impart.
Alas, what cause is there so overthwart
That nobleness itself makes thus unkind?
I much do guess, yet find no truth save this,
That when the breath of my complaints doth touch
Those dainty doors unto the Court of Bliss,
The heavenly nature of that place is such
That, once come there, the sobs of mine annoys
Are metamorphos'd straight to tunes of joys.

XLV

STELLA oft sees the very face of woe
Painted in my beclouded stormy face,
But cannot skill to pity my disgrace,
Not though thereof the cause herself she know:
Yet, hearing late a fable which did show
Of lovers never known a grievous case,
Pity thereof gat in her breast such place
That, from that sea deriv'd, tears' spring did flow.
Alas, if Fancy, drawn by imag'd things
Though false, yet with free scope, more grace doth breed
Than servants' wrack, where new doubts honour brings!
Then think, my dear, that you in me do read
Of lovers' ruin some thrice-sad tragedy.
I am not I: pity the tale of me.

XLVI

I CURST thee oft, I pity now thy case,
Blind-hitting Boy, since she that thee and me
Rules with a beck so tyranniseth thee
That thou must want or food or dwelling-place,
For she protests to banish thee her face.
Her face! O Love, a rogue thou then shouldst be
If Love learn not alone to love and see
Without desire to feed of further grace.
Alas, poor wag, that now a scholar art
To such a schoolmistress, whose lessons new
Thou needs must miss, and so thou needs must smart.
Yet, dear, let me his pardon get of you,
That he so long may sport him with desire,
Till without fuel you can make hot fire.

XLVII

WHAT, have I thus betray'd my liberty?
Can those black beams such burning marks engrave
In my free side, or am I born a slave,
Whose neck becomes such yoke of tyranny?
Or want I sense to feel my misery,
Or sprite, disdain of such disdain to have,
Who for long faith, tho' daily help I crave,
May get no alms but scorn of beggary?
Virtue, awake! Beauty but beauty is.
I may, I must, I can, I will, I do
Leave following that which it is gain to miss.
Let her go! Soft, but here she comes! Go to,
Unkind, I love you not! O me, that eye
Doth make my heart to give my tongue the lie!

XLVIII

SOUL'S joy, bend not those morning stars from me
Where Virtue is made strong by Beauty's might:
Where Love is chasteness Pain doth learn delight,
And Humbleness grows one with Majesty.
Whatever may ensue, O let me be
Co-partner of the riches of that sight.
Let not mine eyes be hell-driv'n from that light:
O look, O shine, O let me die, and see.
For though I oft myself of them bemoan
That through my heart their beamy darts be gone

Whose cureless wounds even now most freshly bleed,
Yet since my death-wound is already got,
Dear killer, spare not thy sweet-cruel shot:
A kind of grace it is to slay with speed.

XLIX

I ON my horse, and Love on me, doth try
Our horsemanships, while by strange work I prove
A horseman to my horse, a horse to Love,
And now man's wrongs in me, poor beast, descry.
The reins wherewith my rider doth me tie
Are humbled thoughts, which bit of reverence move,
Curb'd-in with fear, but with gilt boss above
Of hope, which makes it seem fair to the eye.
The wand is will; thou, Fancy, saddle art,
Girt fast by Memory; and while I spur
My horse, he spurs with sharp desire my heart.
He sits me fast, however I do stir,
And now hath made me to his hand so right
That in the manage myself take delight.

L

STELLA, the fullness of my thoughts of thee
Cannot be stay'd within my panting breast
But they do swell and struggle forth of me
Till that in words thy figure be exprest:
And yet, as soon as they so formèd be,
According to my lord Love's own behest,
With sad eyes I their weak proportions see
To portrait that which in this world is best.
So that I cannot choose but write my mind,
And cannot choose but put out what I write,
While these poor babes their death in birth do find.
And now my pen these lines had dashèd quite
But that they stopt his fury from the same,
Because their forefront bare sweet Stella's name.

LI

PARDON mine ears, both I and they do pray,
So may your tongue still flauntingly proceed
To them that do such entertainment need,
So may you still have somewhat new to say.

On silly me do not the burthen lay
Of all the grave conceits your brain doth breed,
But find some Hercules to bear, insteed
Of Atlas tired, your wisdom's heavenly sway.
For me, while you discourse of courtly tides,
Of cunningest fishers in most troubled streams,
Of straying ways, when valiant Error guides,
Meanewhile my heart confers with Stella's beams,
And is e'en woe that so sweet comedy
By such unsuited speech should hind'red be.

LII

A STRIFE is grown between Virtue and Love,
While each pretends that Stella must be his:
Her eyes, her lips, her all, saith Love, do this,
Since they do wear his badge, most firmly prove.
But Virtue thus that title doth disprove,
That Stella—O dear name!—that Stella is
That virtuous soul, sure heir of heavenly bliss,
Not this fair outside which our heart doth move.
And therefore, though her beauty and her grace
Be Love's indeed, in Stella's self he may
By no pretence claim any manner place.
Well, Love, since this demur our suit doth stay,
Let Virtue have that Stella's self; yet thus,
That Virtue but that body grant to us.

LIII

IN martial sports I had my cunning tried,
And yet to break more staves did me address,
While, with the people's shouts, I must confess,
Youth, luck, and praise even fill'd my veins with pride;
When Cupid, having me his slave descried
In Mars's livery prancing in the press,
'What now, Sir Fool!' said he (I would no less)
'Look here, I say!' I look'd, and Stella spied,
Who, hard by, made a window send forth light.
My heart then quak'd, then dazzled were mine eyes,
One hand forgat to rule, th' other to fight,
Nor trumpet's sound I heard, nor friendly cries:
My foe came on, and beat the air for me,
Till that her blush taught me my shame to see.

LIV

BECAUSE I breathe not love to every one,
Nor do not use set colours for to wear,
Nor nourish special locks of vowèd hair,
Nor give each speech a full point of a groan,
The courtly nymphs, acquainted with the moan
Of them which in their lips Love's standard bear,
'What, he!' say they of me, 'now I dare swear
He cannot love!   No, no, let him alone.'
And think so still, so Stella know my mind;
Profess indeed I do not Cupid's art;
But you, fair maids, at length this true shall find,
That his right badge is but worn in the heart.
Dumb swans, not chattering pies, do lovers prove:
They love indeed who quake to say they love.

LV

MUSES, I oft invoked your holy aid,
With choicest flowers my speech to engarland so,
That it, despised, in true but naked show
Might win some grace in your sweet grace array'd:
And oft whole troops of saddest words I stay'd,
Striving abroad a-foraging to go,
Until by your inspiring I might know
How their black banner might be best display'd.
But now I mean no more your help to try,
Nor other sugaring of my speech to prove,
But on her name incessantly to cry:
For let me but name her whom I do love,
So sweet sounds straight mine ear and heart do hit
That I well find no eloquence like it.

LVI

FIE, school of Patience, fie!   Your lesson is
Far, far too long to learn it without book:
What, a whole week without one piece of look,
And think I should not your large precepts miss!
When I might read those letters fair of bliss
Which in her face teach virtue, I could brook
Somewhat thy leaden counsels, which I took
As of a friend that meant not much amiss.
But now that I, alas, do want her sight,

What, dost thou think that I can ever take
In thy cold stuff a phlegmatic delight?
No, Patience; if thou wilt my good, then make
Her come and hear with patience my desire,
And then with patience bid me bear my fire.

LVII

WOE having made, with many fights, his own
Each sense of mine, each gift, each power of mind;
Grown now his slaves, he forced them out to find
The thoroughest words fit for Woe's self to groan,
Hoping that when they might find Stella alone,
Before she could prepare to be unkind,
Her soul, arm'd but with such a dainty rind,
Should soon be pierc'd with sharpness of the moan.
She heard my plaints, and did not only hear,
But them, so sweet is she, most sweetly sing,
With that fair breast making Woe's darkness clear.
A pretty case! I hopèd her to bring
To feel my grief, and she, with face and voice,
So sweets my pains that my pains me rejoice.

LVIII

DOUBT there hath been, when with his golden chain
The orator so far men's hearts doth bind
That no pace else their guidèd steps can find
But as he them more short or slack doth rein,
Whether with words this sovranty he gain,
Cloth'd with fine tropes, with strongest reasons lin'd,
Or else pronouncing grace, wherewith his mind
Prints his own lively form in rudest brain.
Now judge by this: in piercing phrases late
The anatomy of all my woes I wrate;
Stella's sweet breath the same to me did read.
O voice! O face! Maugre my speech's might,
Which wooèd woe, most ravishing delight
Even those sad words even in sad me did breed.

LIX

DEAR, why make you more of a dog than me?
If he do love, I burn, I burn in love;
If he wait well, I never thence would move;
If he be fair, yet but a dog can be.

Little he is, so little worth is he;
He barks, my songs thine own voice oft doth prove;
Bidd'n, perhaps he fetchèd thee a glove,
But I, unbid, fetch even my soul to thee.
Yet, while I languish, him that bosom clips,
That lap doth lap, nay lets, in spite of spite,
This sour-breath'd mate taste of those sugared lips.
Alas, if you grant only such delight
To witless things, then Love, I hope—since wit
Becomes a clog—will soon ease me of it.

LX

WHEN my good angel guides me to the place
Where all my good I do in Stella see,
That heaven of joys throws only down on me
Thundering disdains and lightnings of disgrace;
But when the ruggedst step of Fortune's race
Makes me fall from her sight, then sweetly she,
With words wherein the Muses' treasures be,
Shows love and pity to my absent case.
Now I, wit-beaten long by hardest fate,
So dull am that I cannot look into
The ground of this fierce love and lovely hate.
Then, some good body, tell me how I do,
Whose presence absence, absence presence is:
Blest in my curse, and cursèd in my bliss.

LXI

OFT with true sighs, oft with uncallèd tears,
Now with slow words, now with dumb eloquence,
I Stella's eyes assay'd, invade her ears;
But this, at last, is her sweet-breath'd defence:
That who indeed in-felt affection bears
So captives to his saint both soul and sense
That, wholly hers, all selfness he forbears,
Then his desires he learns, his life's course thence.
Now, since her chaste mind hates this love in me,
With chastened mind I straight must show that she
Shall quickly me from what she hates remove.
O Doctor Cupid, thou for me reply;
Driven else to grant, by angel's sophistry,
That I love not without I leave to love,

LXII

LATE tired with woe, even ready for to pine
With rage I love, I call'd my Love unkind;
She in whose eyes love, though unfelt, doth shine
Sweet said that I true love in her should find.
I joy'd; but straight thus waterèd was my wine:
That love she did, but loved a love not blind,
Which would not let me whom she loved decline
From nobler course fit for my birth and mind,
And therefore, by her love's authority,
Will'd me these tempests of vain love to fly,
And anchor fast myself on Virtue's shore.
Alas, if this the only metal be
Of love new-coin'd to help my beggary,
Dear, love me not, that you may love me more.

LXIII

O GRAMMAR-RULES, O now your virtues show,
So children still read you with awful eyes,
As my young dove may in your precepts wise
Her grant to me by her own virtue know.
For late, with heart most high, with eyes most low,
I craved the thing which ever she denies:
She, lightning love, displaying Venus' skies,
Lest once should not be heard, twice said, 'No, no!'
Sing then, my Muse, now Io Paean sing;
Heavens envy not at my high triumphing,
But grammar's force with sweet success confirm:
For grammar says—O this, dear Stella, say!—
For grammar says—to grammar who says nay?—
That in one speech two negatives affirm.

LXIV

NO more, my dear, no more these counsels try;
O give my passions leave to run their race;
Let Fortune lay on me her worst disgrace;
Let folk o'ercharged with brain against me cry;
Let clouds bedim my face, break in mine eye;
Let me no steps but of lost labour trace;
Let all the earth with scorn recount my case—
But do not will me from my love to fly.
I do not envy Aristotle's wit,

Nor do aspire to Cæsar's bleeding fame,
Nor aught do care though some above me sit,
Nor hope nor wish another course to frame,
But that which once may win thy cruel heart:
Thou art my wit and thou my virtue art.

LXV

LOVE, by sure proof I may call thee unkind
That giv'st no better ear to my just cries,
Thou whom to me such my good turns should bind
As I may well recount but none can prize:
For when, nak'd Boy, thou couldst no harbour find
In this old world grown now so too too wise,
I lodg'd thee in my heart, and being blind
By nature born, I gave to thee mine eyes.
Mine eyes! my light, my heart, my life, alas!
If so great services may scornèd be,
Yet let this thought thy tigerish courage pass,
That I perhaps am somewhat kin to thee,
Since in thine arms, if learn'd fame truth hath spread,
Thou bear'st the arrow, I the arrow-head.

LXVI

AND do I see some cause a hope to feed,
Or doth the tedious burden of long woe
In weaken'd minds quick apprehending breed
Of every image which may comfort show?
I cannot brag of word, much less of deed;
Fortune wheels still with me in one sort slow;
My wealth no more, and no whit less my need;
Desire still on stilts of Fear doth go.
And yet amid all fears a hope there is,
Stol'n to my heart since last fair night, nay day,
Stella's eyes sent to me the beams of bliss,
Looking on me while I lookt other way:
But when mine eyes back to their heaven did move,
They fled with blush which guilty seem'd of love.

LXVII

HOPE, art thou true, or dost thou flatter me?
Doth Stella now begin with piteous eye
The ruins of her conquest to espy?
Will she take time before all wrackèd be?

Her eyes-speech is translated thus by thee,
But failst thou not in phrase so heavenly high?
Look on again, the fair text better pry:
What blushing notes dost thou in margin see?
With sighs stol'n out, or kill'd before full-born?
Hast thou found such and such-like arguments,
Or art thou else to comfort me forsworn?
Well, howso thou interpret the contents,
I am resolv'd thy error to maintain,
Rather than by more truth to get more pain.

LXVIII

STELLA, the only planet of my light,
Light of my life, and life of my desire,
Chief good whereto my hope doth only aspire,
World of my wealth, and heaven of my delight,
Why dost thou spend the treasures of thy sprite
With voice more fit to wed Amphion's lyre,
Seeking to quench in me the noble fire
Fed by thy worth, and kindled by thy sight?
And all in vain: for while thy breath most sweet
With choicest words, thy words with reasons rare,
Thy reasons firmly set on Virtue's feet,
Labours to kill in me this killing care,
O think I then, what paradise of joy
It is, so fair a virtue to enjoy!

LXIX

O JOY too high for my low style to show!
O bliss fit for a nobler state than me!
Envy, put out thine eyes, lest thou do see
What oceans of delight in me do flow!
My friend, that oft saw through all masks my woe,
Come, come, and let me pour myself on thee.
Gone is the Winter of my misery:
My Spring appears: O see what here doth grow!
For Stella hath, with words where faith doth shine,
Of her high heart given me the monarchy.
I, I, oh I, may say that she is mine,
And though she give but thus conditionly
This realm of bliss, while virtuous course I take,
No kings be crown'd but they some covenants make.

LXX

MY Muse may well grudge at my heavenly joy,
If still I force her in sad rimes to creep:
She oft hath drunk my tears, now hopes to enjoy
Nectar of mirth, since I Jove's cup do keep.
Sonnets be not bound prentice to annoy;
Trebles sing high, so well as basses deep;
Grief but Love's winter-livery is; the boy
Hath cheeks to smile, so well as eyes to weep.
Come then, my Muse, show thou height of delight
In well-rais'd notes; my pen, the best it may,
Shall paint out joy, though but in black and white.
Cease, eager Muse.   Peace, pen, for my sake stay.
I give you here my hand for truth of this—
Wise silence is best music unto bliss.

LXXI

WHO will in fairest book of Nature know
How virtue may best lodg'd in beauty be,
Let him but learn of Love to read in thee,
Stella, those fair lines which true goodness show.
There shall he find all vice's overthrow,
Not by rude force, but sweetest sovranty
Of reason, from whose light those night-birds fly,
That inward sun in thine eyes shineth so.
And, not content to be Perfection's heir
Thyself, dost strive all minds that way to move
Who mark in thee what is in thee most fair.
So while thy beauty draws the heart to love,
As fast thy virtue bends that love to good.
But ah, Desire still cries: 'Give me some food!'

LXXII

DESIRE, though thou my old companion art,
And oft so clingst to my pure love that I
One from the other scarcely can descry,
While each doth blow the fire of my heart,
Now from thy fellowship I needs must part:
Venus is taught with Dian's wings to fly.
I must no more in thy sweet passions lie:
Virtue's gold now must head my Cupid's dart.
Service and honour, wonder with delight,

Fear to offend, will worthy to appear,
Care shining in mine eyes, faith in my sprite,
These things are left me by my only Dear.
But thou, Desire, because thou wouldst have all,
Now banisht art—but yet, alas, how shall?

LXXIII

LOVE still a boy and oft a wanton is,
School'd only by his mother's tender eye:
What wonder then if he his lesson miss,
When for so soft a rod dear play he try?
And yet my Star, because a sugared kiss
In sport I suckt while she asleep did lie,
Doth lower, nay chide, nay threat for only this.
Sweet, it was saucy Love, not humble I.
But no 'scuse serves.   She makes her wrath appear
In Beauty's throne.   See now, who dares come near
Those scarlet judges threatening bloody pain?
O heavenly fool, thy most kiss-worthy face
Anger invests with such a lovely grace
That Anger's self I needs must kiss again.

LXXIV

I NEVER drank of Aganippe well,
Nor ever did in shade of Tempe sit,
And Muses scorn with vulgar brains to dwell;
Poor layman I, for sacred rites unfit.
Some do I hear of poets' fury tell,
But, God wot, wot not what they mean by it;
And this I swear by blackest brook of hell,
I am no pick-purse of another's wit.
How falls it then, that with so smooth an ease
My thoughts I speak, and what I speak doth flow
In verse, and that my verse best wits doth please?
Guess we the cause?   What, is it this?   Fie, no.
Or so?   Much less.   How then?   Sure thus it is:
My lips are sweet, inspired with Stella's kiss.

LXXV

OF all the kings that ever here did reign,
Edward, named fourth, as first in praise I name:
Not for his fair outside nor well-lined brain,
Although less gifts imp feathers oft on fame:

Nor that he could, young-wise, wise-valiant, frame
His sire's revenge join'd with a kingdom's gain,
And gain'd by Mars could yet mad Mars so tame
That balance weigh'd what sword did late obtain:
Nor that he made the fleur-de-luce so 'fraid
　—Though strongly hedg'd—of bloody lions' paws,
That witty Lewis to him a tribute paid:
Nor this, nor that, nor any such small cause,
But only for this worthy knight durst prove
To lose his crown rather than fail his love.

LXXVI

SHE comes, and straight therewith her shining twins do move
Their rays to me, who in their tedious absence lay
Benighted in cold woe; but now appears my day,
The only light of joy, the only warmth of love.
She comes with light and warmth which, like Aurora, prove
Of gentle force, so that mine eyes dare gladly play
With such a rosy morn whose beams, most freshly gay,
Scorch not, but only do dark chilling sprites remove.
But, lo, while I do speak, it groweth noon with me,
Her flamy-glistring lights increase with time and place,
My heart cries, oh it burns, mine eyes now dazzled be;
No wind, no shade can cool: what help then in my case?
But with short breath, long looks, staid feet, and aching head,
Pray that my sun go down with meeker beams to bed.

LXXVII

THOSE looks, whose beams be joy, whose motion is delight,
That face whose lecture shows what perfect beauty is,
That presence which doth give dark hearts a living light,
That grace which Venus weeps that she herself doth miss,
That hand which without touch holds more then Atlas might,
Those lips which make death's pay a mean price for a kiss,
That skin whose past-praise hue scorns this poor term of white,
Those words which do sublime the quintessence of bliss,
That voice which makes the soul plant himself in the ears,
That conversation sweet where such high comforts be
As, conster'd in true speech, the name of heaven it bears:
Makes me in my best thoughts and quietest judgments see
That in no more but these I might be fully blest.
Yet, ah, my maiden Muse doth blush to tell the best.

LXXVIII

O HOW the pleasant airs of true love be
Infected by those vapours which arise
From out that noisome gulf which gaping lies
Between the jaws of hellish Jealousy!
A monster, others' harm, self-misery,
Beauty's plague, Virtue's scourge, succour of lies,
Who his own joy to his own hurt applies,
And only cherish doth with injury;
Who since he hath by Nature's special grace
So piercing paws as spoil when they embrace,
So nimble feet as stir still, though on thorns,
So many eyes aye seeking their own woe,
So ample ears as never good news know:
Is it not evil that such a devil wants horns?

LXXIX

SWEET kiss, thy sweets I fain would sweetly indite
Which even of sweetness sweetest sweetener art,
Pleasingst consort, where each sense holds a part,
Which, coupling doves, guides Venus' chariot right;
Best charge and bravest retrait in Cupid's fight,
A double key which opens to the heart,
Most rich when most his riches it impart;
Nest of young joys, schoolmaster of delight,
Teaching the means at once to take and give;
The friendly fray, where blows both wound and heal,
The pretty death, while each in other live.
Poor hope's first wealth, hostage of promist weal,
Breakfast of love.   But lo, lo, where she is,
Cease we to praise: now pray we for a kiss.

LXXX

SWEET-SWELLING lip, well mayst thou swell in pride,
Since best wits think it wit thee to admire;
Nature's praise, Virtue's stall; Cupid's cold fire,
Whence words, not words but heavenly graces slide;
The new Parnassus, where the Muses bide;
Sweetener of music, Wisdom's beautifier,
Breather of life, and fastner of desire,
Where Beauty's blush in Honour's grain is dyed.
Thus much my heart compell'd my mouth to say;
But now, spite of my heart, my mouth will stay,

Loathing all lies, doubting this flattery is:
And no spur can his resty race renew
Without, how far this praise is short of you,
Sweet lip, you teach my tongue with one sweet kiss.

LXXXI

O KISS, which dost those ruddy gems impart,
Or gems or fruits of new-found Paradise,
Breathing all bliss and sweetning to the heart,
Teaching dumb lips a nobler exercise;
O kiss which souls, even souls, together ties
By links of love and only Nature's art,
How fain would I paint thee to all men's eyes,
Or of thy gifts at least shade out some part!
But she forbids: with blushing words she says
She builds her fame on higher-seated praise.
But my heart burns: I cannot silent be.
Then, since, dear life, you fain would have me peace,
And I, mad with delight, want wit to cease,
Stop you my mouth with still, still kissing me.

LXXXII

NYMPH of the garden where all beauties be,
Beauties which do in excellency pass
His who till death lookt in a watery glass,
Or hers whom nakd the Troian boy did see;
Sweet garden-nymph, which keeps the cherry-tree
Whose fruit doth far the Hesperian taste surpass,
Most sweet-fair, most fair-sweet, do not, alas,
From coming near those cherries banish me.
For though, full of desire, empty of wit,
Admitted late by your best-gracèd grace,
I caught at one of them, and hungry bit,
Pardon that fault; once more grant me the place;
And I do swear, even by the same delight,
I will but kiss, I never more will bite.

LXXXIII

[*To a Sparrow*]

GOOD brother Philip, I have borne you long.
I was content you should in favour creep,
While craftily you seem'd your cut to keep,
As though that fair soft hand did you great wrong:

I bare, with envy, yet I bare your song,
When in her neck you did love-ditties peep;
Nay—more fool I—oft suffer'd you to sleep
In lilies' nest where Love's self lies along.
What, doth high place ambitious thoughts augment?
Is sauciness reward of courtesy?
Cannot such grace your silly self content
But you must needs with those lips billing be,
And through those lips drink nectar from that tongue?
Leave that, Sir Phip, lest off your neck be wrung!

LXXXIV

HIGHWAY, since you my chief Parnassus be,
And that my Muse, to some ears not unsweet,
Tempers her words to trampling horses' feet
More oft than to a chamber-melody,
Now, blessed you, bear onward blessed me
To her where I my heart, safe-left, shall meet:
My Muse and I must you of duty greet
With thanks and wishes, wishing thankfully.
Be you still careful kept by public heed,
By no encroachment wrong'd, nor time forgot,
Nor blamed for blood, nor shamed for sinful deed,
And, that you know I envy you no lot
Of highest wish, I wish you so much bliss,
Hundreds of years you Stella's feet may kiss!

LXXXV

I SEE the house.   My heart thyself contain!
Beware full sails drown not thy tottering barge,
Lest joy, by nature apt sprites to enlarge,
Thee to thy wrack beyond thy limits strain;
Nor do like lords whose weak confusèd brain,
Not 'pointing to fit folks each undercharge,
While every office themselves will discharge,
With doing all leave nothing done but pain.
But give apt servants their due place: let eyes
See beauty's total sum summ'd in her face,
Let ears hear speech which wit to wonder ties,
Let breath suck up those sweets, let arms embrace
The globe of weal, lips Love's indentures make:
Thou but of all the kingly tribute take.

LXXXVI

ALAS, whence came this change of looks?   If I
Have chang'd desert let mine own conscience be
A still-felt plague to self-condemning me,
Let woe gripe on my heart, shame load mine eye:
But if all faith like spotless ermine lie
Safe in my soul, which only doth to thee
As his sole object of felicity
With wings of love in air of wonder fly,
O ease your hand, treat not so hard your slave:
In justice pains come not till faults do call.
Or if I needs, sweet judge, must torments have,
Use something else to chasten me withal
Than those blest eyes where all my hopes do dwell:
No doom should make man's heaven become his hell.

LXXXVII

WHEN I was forced from Stella ever dear—
Stella, food of my thoughts, heart of my heart—
Stella whose eyes make all my tempests clear—
By Stella's laws of duty to depart,
Alas, I found that she with me did smart:
I saw that tears did in her eyes appear,
I saw that sighs her sweetest lips did part,
And her sad words my sadded sense did hear.
For me, I wept to see pearls scatterèd so,
I sigh'd her sighs and wailèd for her woe,
Yet swam in joy, such love in her was seen.
Thus, while the effect most bitter was to me,
And nothing than the cause more sweet could be,
I had been vext, if vext I had not been.

LXXXVIII

OUT, traitor Absence, darest thou counsel me
From my dear captainess to run away
Because in brave array here marcheth she
That to win me oft shows a present pay?
Is faith so weak?   Or is such force in thee?
When sun is hid, can stars such beams display?
Cannot heaven's food, once felt, keep stomachs free
From base desire on earthly cates to prey?
Tush, Absence!   While thy mists eclipse that light,
My orphan sense flies to the inward sight,

Where memory sets forth the beams of love,
That, where before heart loved and eyes did see,
In heart both sight and love now coupled be:
United powers make each the stronger prove.

LXXXIX

NOW that of absence the most irksome night
With darkest shade doth overcome my day,
Since Stella's eyes, wont to give me my day,
Leaving my hemisphere leave me in night,
Each day seems long and longs for long-stay'd night:
The night, as tedious, woos the approach of day;
Tired with the dusty toils of busy day,
Languisht with horrors of the silent night;
Suffering the evils both of day and night,
While no night is more dark than is my day,
Nor no day hath less quiet than my night:
With such bad-mixture of my night and day,
That living thus in blackest winter night,
I feel the flames of hottest summer day.

XC

STELLA, think not that I by verse seek fame
Who seek, who hope, who love, who live but thee;
Thine eyes my pride, thy lips mine history:
If thou praise not, all other praise is shame.
Nor so ambitious am I as to frame
A nest for my young praise in laurel tree:
In truth I swear, I wish not there should be
Graved in my epitaph a poet's name.
Ne, if I would, could I just title make,
That any laud thereof to me should grow,
Without my plumes from others' wings I take:
For nothing from my wit or will doth flow,
Since all my words thy beauty doth indite,
And Love doth hold my hand and makes me write.

XCI

STELLA, while now by Honour's cruel might
I am from you, light of my life, misled,
And whiles—fair you, my sun, thus overspread
With Absence' veil—I live in Sorrow's night,

If this dark place yet show like candle-light
Some beauty's piece, as amber-colour'd head,
Milk hands, rose cheeks, or lips more sweet, more red;
Or seeing jets black but in blackness bright;
They please, I do confess they please mine eyes.
But why? Because of you they models be,
Models such be wood-globes of glist'ring skies.
Dear, therefore be not jealous over me,
If you hear that they seem my heart to move:
Not them, O no, but you in them I love.

XCII

BE your words made, good Sir, of Indian ware,
That you allow me them by so small rate?
Or do you curted Spartans imitate?
Or do you mean my tender ears to spare,
That to my questions you so total are?
When I demand of Phoenix-Stella's state,
You say, forsooth, you left her well of late.
O God, think you that satisfies my care?
I would know whether she did sit or walk;
How cloth'd; how waited on; sigh'd she, or smiled;
Whereof, with whom, how often did she talk;
With what pastimes Time's journey she beguiled;
If her lips deign'd to sweeten my poor name.
Say all, and, all well said, still say the same.

XCIII

O FATE, O fault, O curse, child of my bliss!
What sobs can give words grace my grief to show?
What ink is black enough to paint my woe?
Through me—wretch me—even Stella vexèd is.
Yet, Truth—if caitiff's breath may call thee—this
Witness with me, that my foul stumbling so
From carelessness did in no manner grow,
But wit confused with too much care did miss.
And do I, then, myself this vain 'scuse give?
I have—live I, and know this—harmèd thee;
Tho' worlds 'quite me, shall I myself forgive?
Only with pains my pains thus easèd be,
That all thy hurts in my heart's wrack I read:
I cry thy sighs, my dear, thy tears I bleed.

XCIV

GRIEF, find the words, for thou hast made my brain
So dark with misty vapours which arise
From out thy heavy mould that inbent eyes
Can scarce discern the shape of mine own pain.
Do thou then—for thou canst—do thou complain
For my poor soul, which now that sickness tries
Which even to sense sense of itself denies,
Though harbingers of death lodge there his train.
Of if thy love of plaint yet mine forbears,
As of a caitiff worthy so to die,
Yet wail thyself, and wail with causeful tears,
That though in wretchedness thy life doth lie,
Yet growest more wretched than thy nature bears
By being placed in such a wretch as I.

XCV

YET sighs, dear sighs, indeed true friends you are,
That do not leave your left friend at the worst,
But as you with my breast I oft have nurst,
So, grateful now, you wait upon my care.
Faint coward Joy no longer tarry dare,
Seeing Hope yield when this woe strake him first;
Delight exclaims he is for my fault curst,
Though oft himself my mate in arms he sware;
Nay, Sorrow comes with such main rage, that he
Kills his own children, tears, finding that they
By Love were made apt to consort with me.
Only, true sighs, you do not go away.
Thank may you have for such a thankful part,
Thank-worthiest yet when you shall break my heart.

XCVI

THOUGHT, with good cause thou likest so well the night,
Since kind or chance gives both one livery:
Both sadly black, both blackly darknèd be,
Night barr'd from sun, thou from thy own sunlight.
Silence in both displays his sullen might,
Slow heaviness in both holds one degree,
That full of doubts, thou of perplexity,
Thy tears express Night's native moisture right.
In both amazeful solitariness:
In night, of spirits the ghastly powers do stir,

In thee, or spirits or spirited ghastliness.
But, but, alas, Night's side the odds hath fur,
For that, at length, yet doth invite some rest:
Thou, though still tired, yet still dost it detest.

XCVII

DIAN, that fain would cheer her friend the Night,
Shows her oft, at the full, her fairest face,
Bringing with her those starry nymphs, whose chace
From heavenly standing hits each mortal wight.
But ah, poor Night, in love with Phoebus' light,
And endlessly despairing of his grace,
Herself, to show no other joy hath place,
Silent and sad in mourning weeds doth dight.
Even so, alas, a lady, Dian's peer,
With choice delights and rarest company
Would fain drive clouds from out my heavy cheer;
But, woe is me, though Joy herself were she,
She could not show my blind brain ways of joy,
While I despair my sun's sight to enjoy.

XCVIII

AH, bed! the field where Joy's peace some do see,
The field where all my thoughts to war be train'd,
How is thy grace by my strange fortune strain'd!
How thy lee-shores by my sighs stormèd be!
With sweet soft shades thou oft invitest me
To steal some rest; but, wretch, I am constrain'd—
Spurr'd with Love's spur, though gall'd, and shortly rein'd
With Care's hard hand—to turn and toss in thee,
While the black horrors of the silent night
Paint Woe's black face so lively to my sight
That tedious leisure marks each wrinkled line.
But when Aurora leads out Phoebus' dance
Mine eyes then only wink: for spite, perchance,
That worms should have their sun, and I want mine.

XCIX

WHEN far-spent Night persuades each mortal eye,
To whom nor Art nor Nature granteth light,
To lay his then mark-wanting shafts of sight,
Clos'd with their quivers, in Sleep's armoury,

With windows ope then most my mind doth lie
Viewing the shape of darkness, and delight
Takes in that sad hue which with the inward night
Of his mazed powers keeps perfect harmony.
But when birds charm and that sweet air which is
Morn's messenger with rose-enamell'd skies
Calls each wight to salute the flower of bliss,
In tomb of lids then buried are mine eyes,
Forced by their lord, who is asham'd to find
Such light in sense with such a darkened mind.

C

O TEARS! no tears, but rain from Beauty's skies,
Making those lilies and those roses grow
Which, aye most fair, now more than most fair show,
While graceful Pity Beauty beautifies.
O honied sighs! which from that breast do rise,
Whose pants do make unspilling cream to flow,
Wing'd with whose breath so pleasing zephyrs blow
As might refresh the hell where my soul fries.
O plaints! conserv'd in such a sugared phrase
That Eloquence itself envies your praise,
While sobb'd-out words a perfect music give.
Such tears, sighs, plaints, no sorrow is, but joy.
Or, if such heavenly signs must prove annoy,
All mirth farewell, let me in sorrow live.

CI

STELLA is sick, and in that sick-bed lies
Sweetness which breathes and pants as oft as she:
And Grace, sick too, such fine conclusion tries
That Sickness brags itself best graced to be.
Beauty is sick, but sick in so fair guise
That in that paleness Beauty's white we see,
And Joy, which is inseparate from those eyes,
Stella, now learns, strange case, to weep in me.
Love moans thy pain, and like a faithful page,
As thy looks stir, runs up and down to make
All folks prest at thy will thy pain to swage.
Nature with care sweats for her darling's sake,
Knowing worlds pass ere she enough can find
Of such heaven-stuff to clothe so heavenly a mind.

CII

WHERE be those roses gone which sweetened so our eyes?
Where those red cheeks which oft with fair increase did frame
The height of honour in the kindly badge of shame?
Who hath the crimson weeds stol'n from my morning skies?
How doth the colour vade of those vermilion dyes,
Which Nature' self did make and self-ingrain'd the same?
I would know by what right this paleness overcame
That hue whose force my heart still unto thraldom ties?
Galen's adoptive sons, who by a beaten way
Their judgments hackney on, the fault of sickness lay;
But feeling proof makes me say they mistake it fur:
It is but love which makes this paper perfect white,
To write therein more fresh the story of delight,
Whiles Beauty's reddest ink Venus for him doth stir.

CIII

O HAPPY Thames that didst my Stella bear,
I saw thee with full many a smiling line
Upon thy cheerful face Joy's livery wear,
While those fair planets on thy streams did shine.
The boat for joy could not to dance forbear,
While wanton winds, with beauties so divine
Ravisht, stay'd not till in her golden hair
They did themselves, O sweetest prison, twine.
And fain those Aeol's youth there would their stay
Have made, but forced by Nature still to fly,
First did with puffing kiss those locks display:
She, so dishevell'd, blusht: from window I
With sight thereof cried out: 'O fair disgrace,
Let Honour's self to thee grant highest place.'

CIV

ENVIOUS wits, what hath been mine offence
That with such poisonous care my looks you mark,
That to each word, nay sigh of mine, you hark,
As grudging me my sorrow's eloquence?
Ah, is it not enough that I am thence,
Thence, so far thence, that scantly any spark
Of comfort dare come to this dungeon dark,
Where Rigour's exile locks up all my sense?
But if I by a happy window pass,

If I but stars upon mine armour bear,
Sick, thirsty, glad (though but of empty glass),
Your moral notes straight my hid meaning tear
From out my ribs, and puffing proves that I
Do Stella love: fools, who doth it deny?

CV

UNHAPPY sight, and hath she vanisht by
So near, in so good time, so free a place?
Dead glass, dost thou thy object so embrace
As what my heart still sees thou canst not spy?
I swear, by her I love and lack, that I
Was not in fault who bent thy dazzling race
Only unto the heaven of Stella's face,
Counting but dust what in the way did lie.
But cease, mine eyes, your tears do witness well
That you, guiltless thereof, your nectar miss'd:
Curst be the page from whom the bad torch fell:
Curst be the night which did your strife resist:
Curst be the coachman that did drive so fast,
With no less curse than absence makes me taste.

CVI

O ABSENT presence! Stella is not here.
False-flattering hope, that with so fair a face
Bare me in hand, that in this orphan place
Stella, I say my Stella, should appear:
What sayst thou now? where is that dainty cheer
Thou told'st mine eyes should help their famisht case?
But thou art gone, now that self-felt disgrace
Doth make me most to wish thy comfort near.
But here I do store of fair ladies meet
Who may with charm of conversation sweet
Make in my heavy mould new thoughts to grow.
Sure they prevail as much with me as he
That bad his friend, but then new-maim'd, to be
Merry with him, and so forget his woe.

CVII

STELLA, since thou so right a princess art
Of all the powers which life bestows on me,
That ere by them aught undertaken be
They first resort unto that sovereign part,

Sweet, for a while give respite to my heart,
Which pants as though it still should leap to thee,
And on my thoughts give thy lieutenancy
To this great cause, which needs both use and art.
And as a queen, who from her presence sends
Whom she employs, dismiss from thee my wit,
Till it have wrought what thy own will attends:
On servants' shame oft master's blame doth sit.
O, let not fools in me thy works reprove,
And scorning say, 'See what it is to love!'

CVIII

WHEN Sorrow, using mine own fire's might,
Melts down his lead into my boiling breast,
Through that dark furnace to my heart opprest
There shines a joy from thee my only light:
But soon as thought of thee breeds my delight,
And my young soul flutters to thee his nest,
Most rude Despair, my daily unbidden guest,
Clips straight my wings, straight wraps me in his night,
And makes me then bow down my head and say:
'Ah, what doth Phoebus' gold that wretch avail
Whom iron doors do keep from use of day?'
So strangely, alas, thy works in me prevail,
That in my woes for thee thou art my joy,
And in my joys for thee my only annoy.

Doubt you to whom?

DOUBT you to whom my Muse these notes intendeth
Which now my breast, o'ercharged, to music lendeth?
    To you, to you, all song of praise is due:
Only in you my song begins and endeth.

Who hath the eyes which marry state with pleasure?
Who keeps the key of Nature's chiefest treasure?
    To you, to you, all song of praise is due:
Only for you the heaven forgat all measure.

Who hath the lips where wit in fairness reigneth?
Who womankind at once both decks and staineth?
    To you, to you, all song of praise is due:
Only by you Cupid his crown maintaineth.

Who hath the feet whose step all sweetness planteth?
Who else for whom Fame worthy trumpets wanteth?
   To you, to you, all song of praise is due:
Only to you her sceptre Venus granteth.

Who hath the breast whose milk doth patience nourish?
Whose grace is such that when it chides doth cherish?
   To you, to you, all song of praise is due:
Only through you the tree of life doth flourish.

Who hath the hand which without stroke subdueth?
Who long-dead beauty with increase reneweth?
   To you, to you, all song of praise is due:
Only at you all envy hopeless rueth.

Who hath the hair which loosest, fastest, tieth?
Who makes a man live then glad, when he dieth?
   To you, to you, all song of praise is due:
Only of you the flatterer never lieth.

Who hath the voice which soul from senses sunders?
Whose force but yours the bolts of beauty thunders?
   To you, to you, all song of praise is due:
Only with you not miracles are wonders.

Doubt you to whom my Muse these notes intendeth
Which now my breast o'ercharged to music lendeth?
   To you, to you, all song of praise is due:
Only in you my song begins and endeth.

Stella sleeping

   HAVE I caught my heavenly jewel
   Teaching Sleep most fair to be?
   Now will I teach her that she,
   When she wakes, is too too cruel.

   Since sweet Sleep her eyes hath charmèd,
   The two only darts of Love,
   Now will I with that Boy prove
   Some play while he is disarmèd.

   Her tongue, waking, still refuseth,
   Giving frankly niggard no:
   Now will I attempt to know
   What no her tongue, sleeping, useth.

See the hand that, waking, guardeth,
Sleeping, grants a free resort.
Now will I invade the fort—
Cowards Love with loss rewardeth.

But, O fool, think of the danger
Of her just and high disdain!
Now will I, alas, refrain.
Love fears nothing else but anger.

Yet those lips, so sweetly swelling,
Do invite a stealing kiss.
Now will I but venture this.
Who will read must first learn spelling.

Oh, sweet kiss! but ah, she's waking!
Lowring beauty chastens me.
Now will I for fear hence flee:
Fool, more fool, for no more taking!

If Orpheus' voice

IF Orpheus' voice had force to breathe such music's love
Through pores of senseless trees as it could make them move,
If stones good measure danced the Theban walls to build
To cadence of the tunes which Amphion's lyre did yield,
More cause a like effect at leastwise bringeth:
O stones, O trees, learn hearing—Stella singeth.

If love might sweeten so a boy of shepherd brood
To make a lizard dull to taste love's dainty food,
If eagle fierce could so in Grecian maid delight,
As her eyes were his light, her death his endless night—
Earth gave that love, heaven I trow love refineth—
O birds, O beasts, look, love—lo, Stella shineth.

The birds, beasts, stones, and trees feel this, and feeling love;
And if the trees nor stones stir not the same to prove,
Nor beasts nor birds do come unto this blessèd gaze,
Know that small love is quick, and great love doth amaze.
They are amazed, but you, with reason armèd,
O eyes, O ears of men, how are you charmèd!

Only Joy, now here you are

ONLY Joy, now here you are,
Fit to hear and ease my care.
Let my whispering voice obtain
Sweet reward for sharpest pain:
Take me to thee, and thee to me.
 '*No, no, no, no, my dear, let be.*'

Night hath closed all in her cloak,
Twinkling stars love-thoughts provoke,
Danger hence good care doth keep,
Jealousy himself doth sleep;
Take me to thee, and thee to me.
 '*No, no, no, no, my dear, let be.*'

Better place no wit can find,
Cupid's knot to loose or bind;
These sweet flowers, our fine bed too,
Us in their best language woo:
Take me to thee, and thee to me.
 '*No, no, no, no, my dear, let be.*'

This small light the moon bestows
Serves thy beams but to disclose,
So to raise my hap more high,
Fear not else, none can us spy:
Take me to thee, and thee to me.
 '*No, no, no, no, my dear, let be.*'

That you heard was but a mouse,
Dumb sleep holdeth all the house:
Yet asleep, methinks, they say
'Young fools, take time while you may.'
Take me to thee, and thee to me.
 '*No, no, no, no, my dear, let be.*'

Niggard Time threats, if we miss
This large offer of our bliss,
Long stay ere he grant the same:
Sweet, then, while each thing doth frame,
Take me to thee, and thee to me.
 '*No, no, no, no, my dear, let be.*'

Your fair mother is a-bed,
Candles out and curtains spread;
She thinks you do letters write;
Write, but let me first indite.
Take me to thee, and thee to me.
   '*No, no, no, no, my dear, let be.*'

Sweet, alas, why strive you thus?
Concord better fitteth us.
Leave to Mars the force of hands:
Your power in your beauty stands.
Take thee to me, and me to thee.
   '*No, no, no, no, my dear, let be.*'

Woe to me, and do you swear
Me to hate but [1] I forbear?
Cursèd be my destines all
That brought me so high to fall.
Soon with my death I will please thee.
   '*No, no, no, no, my dear, let be.*'

O you that hear this voice

O YOU that hear this voice,
O you that see this face,
Say whether [2] of the choice
Deserves the former place:
Fear not to judge this bate,
For it is void of hate.

This side doth Beauty take,
For that doth Music speak,
Fit orators to make
The strongest judgments weak:
The bar to plead their right
Is only true delight.

Thus doth the voice and face,
These gentle lawyers, wage,
Like loving brothers' case,
For father's heritage;
That each, while each contends,
Itself to other lends.

   [1] *unless*   [2] *which*

For Beauty beautifies
With heavenly hue and grace
The heavenly harmonies,
And in this faultless face
The perfect beauties be
A perfect harmony.

Music more lusty swells
In speeches nobly placed,
Beauty as far excels
In action aptly graced.
A friend each party draws
To countenance his cause.

Love more affected seems
To Beauty's lovely light,
And Wonder more esteems
Of Music's wondrous might:
But both to both so bent,
As both in both are spent.

Music doth witness call
The ear his truth to try,
Beauty brings to the hall
The judgment of the eye:
Both in their objects such
As no exceptions touch.

The common sense which might
Be arbiter of this,
To be forsooth upright,
To both sides partial is:
He lays on this chief praise,
Chief praise on that he lays.

Then Reason, princess high,
Whose throne is in the mind,
Which Music can in sky
And hidden beauties find—
Say, whether thou wilt crown
With limitless renown?

In a grove most rich of shade

IN a grove most rich of shade,
Where birds wanton music made,
May, then young, his pied weeds showing,
New-perfumed with flowers fresh growing,

Astrophel with Stella sweet
Did for mutual comfort meet,
Both within themselves oppressèd,
But each in the other blessèd.

Him great harms had taught much care;
Her fair neck a foul yoke bare:
But her sight his cares did banish;
In his sight her yoke did vanish.

Wept they had, alas the while!
But now tears themselves did smile,
While their eyes, by love directed;
Interchangeably reflected.

Sigh they did, but now betwixt
Sighs of woe were glad sighs mixt,
With arms crossed yet testifying
Restless rest and living dying.

Their ears hungry of each word
Which the dear tongue would afford,
But their tongues restrain'd from walking
Till their hearts had ended talking.

But, when their tongues could not speak,
Love itself did silence break;
Love did set his lips asunder,
Thus to speak in love and wonder:

'Stella, sovereign of my joy,
Fair triumpher of annoy,
Stella, star of heavenly fire,
Stella, lodestar of desire,

'Stella, in whose shining eyes
Are the lights of Cupid's skies,
Whose beams, where they once are darted,
Love therewith is straight imparted,

'Stella whose voice, when it speaks,
Senses all asunder break,
Stella whose voice, when it singeth,
Angels to acquaintance bringeth,

'Stella, in whose body is
Writ each character of bliss,
Whose face all, all beauty passeth,
Save thy mind, which yet surpasseth:

'Grant, O grant—but speech, alas,
Fails me, fearing on to pass!—
Grant, O me! what am I saying?
But no fault there is in praying.

'Grant, O dear, on knees I pray,'
(Knees on ground he then did stay)
'That, not I, but, since I love you,
Time and place for me may move you.

'Never season was more fit,
Never room more apt for it;
Smiling air allows my reason;
These birds sing, "Now use the season."

'This small wind, which so sweet is,
See how it the leaves doth kiss;
Each tree in his best attiring
Sense of love to love inspiring.

'Love makes earth the water drink,
Love to earth makes water sink;
And, if dumb things be so witty,
Shall a heavenly grace want pity?'

There his hands, in their speech, fain
Would have made tongue's language plain;
But her hands, his hands repelling,
Gave repulse all grace excelling.

Then she spake; her speech was such,
As not ears but heart did touch:
While suchwise she love denièd,
As yet love she signifièd.

'Astrophel,' said she, 'my love,
Cease in these effects to prove;
Now be still, yet still believe me,
Thy grief more than death would grieve me.

'If that any thought in me
Can taste comfort but of thee,
Let me, fed with hellish anguish,
Joyless, hopeless, endless languish.

'If those eyes you praisèd be
Half so dear as you to me,
Let me home return, stark blinded
Of those eyes, and blinder minded.

'If to secret of my heart
I do any wish impart
Where thou art not foremost placèd,
Be both wish and I defacèd.

'If more may be said, I say
All my bliss in thee I lay;
If thou love, my love, content thee,
For all love, all faith, is meant thee.

'Trust me, while I thee deny,
In myself the smart I try.
Tyrant honour doth thus use thee:
Stella's self might not refuse thee.

'Therefore, dear, this no more move,
Lest, though I leave not thy love,
Which too deep in me is framèd,
I should blush when thou art namèd.'

Therewithal away she went,
Leaving him to passion, rent
With what she had done and spoken,
That therewith my song is broken.

Go, my flock

GO, my flock, go get you hence.
Seek a better place of feeding,
Where you may have some defence
Fro the storms in my breast breeding,
And showers from mine eyes proceeding.

Leave a wretch in whom all woe
Can abide to keep no measure;
Merry flock, such one forgo,
Unto whom mirth is displeasure,
Only rich in mischief's treasure.

Yet, alas, before you go,
Hear your woeful master's story,
Which to stones I else would show:
Sorrow only then hath glory
When 'tis excellently sorry.

Stella, fiercest shepherdess,
Fiercest but yet fairest ever,
Stella whom, O heavens, still bless,
Though against me she persever,
Though I bliss inherit never,

Stella hath refusèd me:
Stella who more love hath provèd
In this caitiff heart to be
Than can in good ewes be movèd
Toward lambkins best belovèd.

Stella hath refusèd me,
Astrophel, that so well servèd
In this pleasant spring (Muse) see,
While in pride flowers be preservèd,
Himself only winter-starvèd.

Why, alas, doth she then swear
That she loveth me so dearly,
Seeing me so long to bear
Coals of love that burn so clearly,
And yet leave me helpless merely?

Is that love? forsooth I trow,
If I saw my good dog grievèd,
And a help for him did know,
My love should not be believèd
But he were by me relievèd.

No, she hates me (wellaway!)
Feigning love somewhat to please me,
For she knows if she display
All her hate death soon would seize me
And of hideous torments ease me.

Then adieu, dear flock, adieu!
But, alas, if in your straying
Heavenly Stella meet with you,
Tell her, in your piteous blaying,
Her poor slave's unjust decaying.

O dear life, when shall it be?

O DEAR life, when shall it be
That mine eyes thine eyes shall see,
And in them thy mind discover
Whether absence have had force
Thy remembrance to divorce
From the image of thy lover?

Or if I myself find not
After parting aught forgot,
Nor debarr'd from beauty's treasure,
Let not tongue aspire to tell
In what high joys I shall dwell:
Only thought aims at the pleasure.

Thought, therefore, will I send thee
To take up the place for me:
Long I will not after tarry.
There, unseen, thou mayst be bold
Those fair wonders to behold
Which in them my hopes do carry

Thought, see thou no place forbear;
Enter bravely everywhere;
Seize on all to her belonging.
But if thou wouldst guarded be,
Fearing her beams, take with thee
Strength of liking, rage of longing.

Think of that most grateful time
When my leaping heart will climb
In thy lips to have his biding,
There those roses for to kiss
Which do breathe a sugared bliss,
Opening rubies, pearls dividing.

Think of my most princely power
When I blessèd shall devour
With my greedy licorous senses
Beauty, music, sweetness, love,
While she doth against me prove
Her strong darts but weak defences.

Think, think of those dallyings
When with dovelike murmurings,
With glad moaning, passèd anguish,
We change eyes, and heart for heart
Each to other do depart,
Joying till joy makes us languish.

O my thought, my thoughts surcease!
Thy delights my woes increase:
My life melts with too much thinking.
Think no more, but die in me,
Till thou shalt revivèd be
At her lips, my nectar drinking.

Lovers' Dialogue

'WHO is it that this dark night
Underneath my window plaineth?'
It is one who from thy sight
Being, ah, exiled, disdaineth
Every other vulgar light.

'Why, alas, and are you he?
Be not yet those fancies changèd?'
Dear, when you find change in me,
Though from me you be estrangèd,
Let my change to ruin be.

'Well, in absence this will die;
Leave to see and leave to wonder.'
Absence sure will help, if I
Can learn how myself to sunder
From what in my heart doth lie.

'But time will these thoughts remove,
Time doth work what no man knoweth.'
Time doth as the subject prove;
With time still the affection groweth
In the faithful turtle dove.

'What if we new beauties see,
Will not they stir new affection?'
I will think they pictures be,
Image-like of saints' perfection,
Poorly counterfeiting thee.

'But your reason's purest light
Bids you leave such minds to nourish.'
Dear, do reason no such spite;
Never doth thy beauty flourish
More than in my reason's sight.

'But the wrongs love bears will make
Love at length leave undertaking.'
No, the more fools it do shake,
In a ground of so firm making
Deeper still they drive the stake.

'Peace, I think that some give ear;
Come no more lest I get anger.'
Bliss, I will my bliss forbear,
Fearing, sweet, you to endanger;
But my soul shall harbour there.

'Well, begone, begone I say,
Lest that Argus' eyes perceive you.'
O unjust is Fortune's sway,
Which can make me thus to leave you,
And from louts to run away.

POEMS FROM ARCADIA

Sapphics

IF mine eyes can speak to do hearty errand,
Or mine eyes' language she do hap to judge of,
So that eyes' message be of her receivèd,
　　　　Hope, we do live yet.

But if eye fail then, when I most do need them,
Or if eyes' language be not unto her known,
So that eyes' message do return rejected,
　　　　Hope, we do both die.

Yet, dying and dead, do we sing her honour;
So become our tombs monuments of her praise;
So becomes our loss the triumph of her gain;
　　　　Hers be the glory.

If the spheres senseless do yet hold a music
If the swan's sweet voice be not heard but at death,
If the mute timber when it hath the life lost
　　　　Yieldeth a lute's tune,

Are then human minds privileg'd so meanly
As that hateful Death can abridge them of power
With the vow of truth to record to all worlds
　　　　That we be her spoils?

Thus, not ending, ends the due praise of her praise;
Fleshly veil consumes, but a soul hath his life
Which is held in love: love it is that hath join'd
　　　　Life to this our soul.

But if eyes can speak to do hearty errand,
Or mine eyes' language she do hap to judge of,
So that eyes' message be of her receivèd,
　　　　Hope, we do live yet.

A Shepherd's Tale

A SHEPHERD'S tale no height of style desires,
To raise in words what in effect is low:
A plaining song plain-singing voice requires,
For warbling notes from inward cheering flow.
I then, whose burd'ned breast but thus aspires
Of shepherds two the seely care to show,
Need not the stately Muses' help invoke
For creeping rimes, which often sighings choke.

But you, O you, that think not tears too dear
To spend for harms, although they touch you not,
And deign to deem your neighbours' mischief near,
Although they be of meaner parents got,
You I invite with easy ears to hear
The poor-clad truth of Love's wrong-ord'red lot.
Who may be glad, be glad you be not such;
Who share in woe, weigh others have as much.

There was (O seldom-blessèd word of was!)
A pair of friends, or rather one call'd two,
Train'd in the life which no short-bitten grass
In shine or storm must set the clouted shoe:
He that the other in some years did pass,
And in those gifts that years distribute do,
Was Klaius call'd (ah, Klaius, woful wight!);
The later born—yet too soon—Strephon hight.

Epeirus high was honest Klaius' nest,
To Strephon Aeole's land first breathing lent,
But East and West were join'd by friendship's hest.
As Strephon's ear and heart to Klaius bent,
So Klaius' soul did in his Strephon rest:
Still both their flocks flocking together went,
As if they would of owners' humour be;
As eke their pipes did well as friends agree.

Klaius, for skill of herbs and shepherd's art,
Among the wisest was accounted wise;
Yet not so wise as of unstainèd heart.
Strephon was young, yet markt with humble eyes
How elder rul'd their flocks and cur'd their smart,
So that the grave did not his words despise.
Both free of mind, both did clear-dealing love,
And both had skill in verse their voice to move.

Their cheerful minds, till pois'ned was their cheer,
The honest sports of earthy lodging prove;
Now for a clod-like hare in form they peer,
Now bolt and cudgel squirrel's leap do move.
Now the ambitious lark with mirror clear
They catch, while he, fool, to himself makes love:
And now at keels they try a harmless chance,
And now their cur they teach to fetch and dance.

When merry May first early calls the morn,
With merry maids a-Maying they do go;
Then do they pull from sharp and niggard thorn
The plenteous sweets (can sweets so sharply grow?);
Then some green gowns are by the lasses worn
In chastest plays, till home they walk a-row,
While dance about the May-pole is begun,
When, if need were, they could at quintain run.

While thus they ran a low but levell'd race,
While thus they lived (this was indeed a life)
With Nature pleas'd, content with present case,
Free of proud fears, brave begg'ry, smiling strife
Of climb-fall Court, the envy-hatching place;
While those restless desires, in great men rife,
To visit of folks so low did much disdain,
This while, though poor, they in themselves did reign.

One day (O day, that shined to make them dark!)
While they did ward sunbeams with shady bay,
And Klaius, taking for his youngling cark,
Lest greedy eyes to them might challenge lay,
Busy with ochre did their shoulders mark
(His mark a pillar was, devoid of stay,
As bragging that free of all passions' moan,
Well might he others' bear, but lean to none),

Strephon with leavy twigs of laurel-tree
A garland made on temples for to wear,
For he then chosen was the dignity
Of village-lord that Whitsuntide to bear,
And full, poor fool, of boyish bravery,
With triumphs' shows would show he nought did fear.
But fore-accounting oft makes builders miss:
They found, they felt, they had no lease of bliss.

For ere that either had his purpose done,
Behold (beholding well it doth deserve),
They saw a maid who thitherward did run
To catch a sparrow which from her did swerve,
As she a black-silk cap on him begun
To set, for foil of his milk-white to serve.
She chirping ran; he peeping flew away;
Till hard by them both he and she did stay.

Well for to see, they kept themselves unseen,
And saw this fairest maid of fairer mind,
By fortune mean, in Nature born a queen,
How well apaid she was her bird to find;
How tenderly her tender hands between
In ivory cage she did the micher bind;
How rosy moistened lips about his beak
Moving, she seem'd at once to kiss and speak.

Chastened but thus, and thus his lesson taught,
The happy wretch she put into her breast,
Which to their eyes the bowls of Venus brought,
For they seem'd made even of sky metal best,
And that the bias of her blood was wrought:
Betwixt them two the peeper took his nest,
Where snugging well he well appear'd content,
So to have done amiss, so to be shent.

This done, but done with captive-killing grace,
Each motion seeming shot from Beauty's bow,
With length laid down she deckt the lonely place.
Proud grew the grass that under her did grow:
The trees spread out their arms to shade her face.
But she, on elbow lean'd, with sighs did show
No grass, no trees, nor yet her sparrow, might
To long-perplexèd mind breed long delight.

She troubled was (alas that it mought be!)
With tedious brawlings of her parents dear,
Who would have her in will and word agree
To wed Antaxius, their neighbour near.
A herdman rich of much account was he,
In whom no ill did reign, nor good appear.
In sum, such one she liked not his desire,
Fain would be free, but dreadeth parents' ire.

Kindly, sweet soul, she did unkindness take
That baggèd baggage of a miser's mud
Should price of her, as in a market, make:
But gold can gild a rotten piece of wood.
To yield, she found her noble heart did ache:
To strive, she fear'd how it with virtue stood.
Thus doubting, clouds o'er-casting heavenly brain,
At length in rows of kiss-cheek tears they rain.

Cupid, the wag, that lately conquer'd had
Wise counsellors, stout captains, puissant kings,
And tied them fast to lead his triumph bad,
Glutted with them now plays with meanest things.
So oft in feasts with costly changes clad
To crammèd maws a sprat new stomach brings:
So lords, with sport of stag and heron full,
Sometimes, we see, small birds from nests do pull.

So now for prey these shepherds two he took,
Whose metal stiff he knew he could not bend
With hearsay pictures, or a window-look,
With one good dance, or letter finely penn'd
(That were in Court a well-proportion'd hook,
Where piercing wits do quickly apprehend):
Their senses rude plain objects only move,
And so must see great cause before they love.

Therefore Love arm'd in her now takes the field,
Making her beams his bravery and might;
Her hands which pierced the soul's seven-double shield
Were now his darts, leaving his wonted fight;
Brave crest to him her scorn-gold hair did yield;
His complete harness was her purest white;
But, fearing lest all white might seem too good,
In cheeks and lips the tyrant threatens blood.

Besides this force, within her eyes he kept
A fire, to burn the prisoners he gains,
Whose boiling heat increasèd as she wept:
For even in forge cold water fire maintains.
Thus proud and fierce unto the hearts he stept
Of them, poor souls, and cutting Reason's reins,
Made them his own before they had it wist.
But if they had, could sheephooks this resist?

Klaius straight felt and groanèd at the blow,
And call'd, now wounded, purpose to his aid:
Strephon, fond boy, delighted did not know
That it was Love that shined in shining maid,
But, licorous, poison'd, fain to her would go,
If him new-learnèd manners had not stay'd.
For then Urania homeward did arise,
Leaving in pain their well-fed hungry eyes.

She went, they stay'd, or, rightly for to say,
She stay'd in them, they went in thought with her.
Klaius indeed would fain have pull'd away
This mote from out his eye, this inward bur,
And now, proud rebel, 'gan for to gainsay
The lesson which but late he learn'd too fur;
Meaning with absence to refresh the thought
To which her presence such a fever brought.

Strephon did leap with joy and jollity,
Thinking it just more therein to delight
Than in good dog, fair field, or shading tree.
So have I seen trim books in velvet dight
With golden leaves and painted babery,
Of seely boys please unacquainted sight.
But when the rod began to play his part,
Fain would, but could not, fly from golden smart.

He quickly learn'd Urania was her name,
And straight for failing, graved it in his heart:
He knew her haunt, and haunted in the same,
And taught his sheep her sheep in food to thwart,
Which soon as it did bateful question frame,
He might on knees confess his faulty part,
And yield himself unto her punishment,
While nought but game the self-hurt wanton meant.

Nay even unto her home he oft would go,
Where bold and hurtless many play he tries,
Her parents liking well it should be so,
For simple goodness shinèd in his eyes.
There did he make her laugh in spite of woe,
So as good thoughts of him in all arise,
While into none doubt of his love did sink,
For not himself to be in love did think.

But glad Desire, his late-embosom'd guest,
Yet but a babe, with milk of sight he nurst:
Desire, the more he sucks, more sought the breast,
Like dropsy-folk still drink to be athirst.
Till one fair even, an hour ere sun did rest,
Who then in lion's cave did enter first,
By neighbours pray'd she went abroad thereby,
At barly-brake her sweet swift foot to try.

Never the Earth on his round shoulders bare
A maid train'd up from high or low degree
That in her doings better could compare
Mirth with respect, few words with courtesy,
A careless comeliness with comely care,
Self-guard with mildness, sport with majesty:
Which made her yield to deck this shepherd's band,
And still, believe me, Strephon was at hand.

Afield they go, where many lookers be,
And thou seek-sorrow Klaius them among:
Indeed thou saidst it was thy friend to see,
Strephon, whose absence seem'd unto thee long;
While most with her he less did keep with thee.
No, no, it was in spite of wisdom's song
Which absence wish'd: Love play'd a victor's part:
The heaven-love lodestone drew thy iron heart.

Then couples three be straight allotted there;
They of both ends, the middle two do fly;
The two that in mid place, Hell, callèd were
Must strive with waiting foot and watching eye
To catch of them, and them to Hell to bear,
That they, as well as they, Hell may supply:
Like some which seek to salve their blotted name
With others' blot, till all do taste of shame.

There may you see, soon as the middle two
Do couplèd towards either couple make,
They false and fearful do their hands undo,
Brother his brother, friend doth friend forsake,
Heeding himself, cares not how fellow do,
But of a stranger mutual help doth take,
As perjured cowards in adversity
With sight of fear from friends to fremd do fly.

These sports shepherds devised such faults to show.
Geron, though old yet gamesome, kept one end
With Cosma, for whose love Pas past in woe.
Fair Nous with Pas the lot to Hell did send,
Pas thought it Hell, while he was Cosma fro.
At other end Uran did Strephon lend
Her happy-making hand, of whom one look
From Nous and Cosma all their beauty took.

The play began: Pas durst not Cosma chase,
But did intend next bout with her to meet;
So he with Nous to Geron turn'd their race,
With whom to join, fast ran Urania sweet,
But light-legg'd Pas had got the middle space.
Geron strave hard, but agèd were his feet,
And therefore finding force now faint to be,
He thought grey hairs afforded subtilty,

And so when Pas' hand reachèd him to take,
The fox on knees and elbows tumbled down;
Pas could not stay, but over him did rake,
And crown'd the earth with his first-touching crown:
His heels grown proud did seem at heaven to shake,
But Nous, that slipt from Pas, did catch the clown.
So laughing all, yet Pas to ease some-dell,
Geron with Uran were condemn'd to Hell.

Cosma this while to Strephon safely came,
And all to second barly-brake are bent:
The two in Hell did toward Cosma frame,
Who should to Pas, but they would her prevent.
Pas, mad with fall, and madder with the shame,
Most mad with beams which he thought Cosma sent,
With such mad haste he did to Cosma go
That to her breast he gave a noisome blow.

She, quick and proud, and who did Pas despise,
Up with her fist and took him on the face:
'Another time,' quoth she, 'become more wise.'
Thus Pas did kiss her hand with little grace
And, each way luckless yet in humble guise,
Did hold her fast for fear of more disgrace,
While Strephon might with pretty Nous have met,
But all this while another course he fet;

For as Urania after Cosma ran,
He, ravishèd with sight how gracefully
She moved her limbs and drew the agèd man,
Left Nous, to coast the lovèd beauty nigh.
Nous cried and chafed, but he no other can,
Till Uran, seeing Pas to Cosma fly,
And Strephon single, turnèd after him.
Strephon, so chased, did seem in milk to swim.

He ran, but ran with eye o'er shoulder cast,
More marking her than how himself did go:
Like Numid lions by the hunters chased,
Though they do fly, yet backwardly do glow
With proud aspèct, disdaining greater haste:
What rage in them, that love in him, did show.
But God gives them instinct the man to shun,
And he, by law of barley-break, must run.

But as his heat with running did augment,
Much more his sight increast his hot desire.
So is in her the best of Nature spent,
The air her sweet race moved doth blow the fire:
Her feet be pursevants from Cupid sent,
With those fine steps all loves and joys conspire.
The hidden beauties seem'd in wait to lie,
To drown proud hearts that would not willing die.

Thus fast he fled from her he follow'd sore,
Still shunning Nous to lengthen pleasing race,
Till that he spied old Geron could no more;
Then did he slack his love-instructed pace,
So that Uran, whose arm old Geron bore,
Laid hold on him with most lay-holding grace.
So caught, him seem'd he caught of joys the bell,
And thought it heaven so to be drawn to Hell.

To Hell he goes, and Nous with him must dwell:
Nous sware it was not right, for his default
Who would be caught, that she should go to Hell:
But so she must.   And now the third assault
Of barley-break among the six befell.
Pas Cosma matcht, yet angry with his fault;
The other end Geron with Uran guard.
I think you think Strephon bent thitherward.

Nous counsell'd Strephon Geron to pursue,
For he was old and easy would be caught:
But he drew her as love his fancy drew,
And so to take the gem Urania sought.
While Geron old came safe to Cosma true,
Though him to meet at all she stirrèd nought.
For Pas, whether it were for fear or love,
Moved not himself, nor suffered her to move.

So they three did together idly stay,
While dear Uran, whose course was Pas to meet,
(He staying thus) was fain abroad to stray
With larger round, to shun the following feet.
Strephon, whose eyes on her back-parts did play,
With love drawn on, so fast with pace unmeet
Drew dainty Nous, that she not able so
To run, brake from his hands, and let him go.

He single thus hop'd soon with her to be
Who, nothing earthly, but of fire and air,
Though with soft legs, did run as fast as he.
He thrice reacht, thrice deceiv'd, when her to bear
He hopes, with dainty turns she doth him flee.
So on the downs we see, near Wilton fair,
A hastened hare from greedy greyhound go,
And past all hope his chaps to frustrate so.

But this strange race more strange conceits did yield.
Who victor seem'd was to his ruin brought:
Who seem'd o'erthrown was mistress of the field.
She fled, and took: he followed, and was caught.
So have I heard, to pierce pursuing shield
By parents train'd the Tartars wild are taught,
With shafts shot out from their back-turnèd bow.
But, ah, her darts did far more deeply go.

As Venus' bird, the white, swift, lovely dove,
(O happy dove that art compar'd to her!)
Doth on her wings her utmost swiftness prove,
Finding the gripe of falcon fierce not fur;
So did Uran the narre, the swifter move
(Yet beauty still as fast as she did stir),
Till with long race dear she was breathless brought,
And then the phoenix fearèd to be caught.

Among the rest that there did take delight
To see the sports of double-shining day,
And did the tribute of their wondring sight
To Nature's heir, the fair Urania, pay,
I told you Klaius was the hapless wight
Who earnest found what they accounted play.
He did not there do homage of his eyes,
But on his eyes his heart did sacrifice.

With gazing looks, short sighs, unsettled feet,
He stood, but turn'd, as girasol, to sun;
His fancies still did her in half-way meet,
His soul did fly as she was seen to run.
In sum, proud Boreas never rulèd fleet
(Who Neptune's web on Danger's distaff spun)
With greater power, than she did make them wend
Each way as she, that age's praise, did bend.

Till spying well she wellnigh weary was,
And surely taught by his love-open eye
(His eye, that even did mark her trodden grass)
That she would fain the catch of Strephon fly,
Giving his reason passport for to pass
Whither it would, so it would let him die,
He that before shunn'd her (to shun such harms),
Now runs and takes her in his clipping arms.

For with pretence from Strephon her to guard,
He met her full, but full of warefulness,
With inbow'd bosom well for her prepar'd,
When Strephon, cursing his own backwardness,
Came to her back and so with double ward
Imprison'd her, who both them did possess
As heart-bound slaves: and happy then embrace
Virtue's proof, Fortune's victor, Beauty's place.

Her race did not her beauty's beams augment,
For they were ever in the best degree,
But yet a setting-forth it some way lent,
As rubies' lustre when they rubbèd be.
The dainty dew on face and body went,
As on sweet flowers when morning's drops we see;
Her breath, then short, seem'd loth from home to pass;
Which more it moved, the more it sweeter was.

Happy, O happy, if they so might bide,
To see her eyes, with how true humbleness
They lookèd down to triumph over pride;
With how sweet sauce she blamed their sauciness,
To feel the panting heart, which through her side
Did beat their hands, which durst so near to press,
To see, to feel, to hear, to taste, to know
More than, besides her, all the earth could show.

But never did Medea's golden weed
On Creon's child his poison sooner throw
Than those delights through all their sinews breed
A creeping, serpent-like, of mortal woe:
Till she brake from their arms—although indeed
Going from them, from them she could not go—
And farewelling the flock, did homeward wend:
And so that even the barley-break did end.

It ended, but the other woe began
Began at least to be conceiv'd as woe.
For then wise Klaius found no absence can
Help him, who can no more her sight forgo.
He found man's virtue is but part of man,
And part must follow where whole man doth go.
He found that Reason's self now reasons found
To fasten knots which Fancy first had bound.

So doth he yield; so takes he on his yoke,
Not knowing who did draw with him therein.
Strephon, poor youth, because he saw no smoke,
Did not conceive what fire he had within;
But after this to greater rage it broke,
Till of his life it did full conquest win.
First killing mirth, then banishing all rest,
Filling his eyes with tears, with sighs his breast.

Then sports grew pains, all talking tedious;
On thoughts he feeds, his looks their figure change,
The day seems long, but night is odious;
No sleeps but dreams, no dreams but visions strange:
Till, finding still his evil increasing thus,
One day he with his flock abroad did range,
And, coming where he hoped to be alone,
Thus on a hillock set he made his moan:

'Alas, what weights are these that load my heart!
I am as dull as winter-starvèd sheep,
Tired as a jade in over-loaden cart;
Yet thoughts do fly, though I can scarcely creep.
All visions seem; at every bush I start;
Drowsy am I, and yet can rarely sleep.
Sure I bewitchèd am—it is even that!
Late near a cross I met an ugly cat!—

'For, but by charms, how fall these things on me,
That from those eyes, where heavenly apples bene,—
Those eyes (which nothing like themselves can see)
Of fair Urania, fairer than a green
Proudly bedeckt in April's livery,
A shot unheard gave me a wound unseen?
He was invisible that hurt me so,
And none invisible but spirits can go.

'When I see her, my sinews shake for fear,
And yet, dear soul, I know she hurteth none;
Amid my flock with woe my voice I tear,
And, but bewitch'd, who to his flock would moan?
Her cherry lips, milk hands, and golden hair
I still do see, though I be still alone:
Now make me think that there is not a fiend
Who, hid in angel's shape, my life would end.

'The sports wherein I wonted to do well,
Come she and sweet the air with open breast,
Then so I fail when most I would excel,
That at me, so amaz'd, my fellows jest.
Sometimes to her news of myself to tell
I go about, but then is all my best
Wry words and stammering, or else doltish dumb:
Say then, can this but of enchantment come?

'Nay, each thing is bewitcht to know my case:
The nightingales for woe their songs refrain;
In river, as I look'd my pining face,
As pin'd a face as mine I saw again;
The courteous mountains, griev'd at my disgrace,
Their snowy hair tear off in melting pain;
And now the dropping trees do weep for me,
And now fair evenings blush my shame to see.

'But you, my pipe, whilom my chief delight,
Till strange delight delight to nothing ware;
And you, my flock, care of my careful sight
While I was I, and so had cause to care;
And thou, my dog, whose truth and valiant might
Made wolves (not inward wolves) my ewes to spare—
Go you not from your maister in his woe:
Let it suffice that he himself forgo.

'For though like wax this magic makes me waste,
Or like a lamb whose dam away is fet,
Stol'n from her young by thieves' unchoosing haste,
He treble baas for help but none can get,
Though thus and worse, though now I am at last,
Of all the games that here ere now I met,
Do you remember still you once were mine,
Till mine eyes had their curse from blessèd eyne.

'Be you with me while I unheard do cry,
While I do score my losses on the wind,
While I in heart my will write ere I die,
In which by will my will and wits I bind
Still to be hers, about her aye to fly,
As this same sprite about my fancies blind
Doth daily haunt; but so that mine become
As much more loving as less cumbersome.

'Alas, a cloud hath overcast mine eyes,
And yet I see her shine amid the cloud.
Alas, of ghosts I hear the ghastly cries,
Yet there, meseems, I hear her singing loud:
This song she sings in most commanding wise:
"Come, shepherd's boy, let now thy heart be bow'd,
To make itself to my least look a slave:
Leave sleep, leave all, I will no piecing have."

'I will, I will, alas, alas, I will!
Wilt thou have more? more have, if more I be?
Away ragg'd rams, care I what murrain kill!
Out, shrieking pipe, made of some witchèd tree!
Go, bawling cur, thy hungry maw go fill
On yon foul flock, belonging not to me!'
With that his dog he henced, his flock he curst,
With that (yet kissèd first) his pipe he burst.

This said, this done, he rose, even tired with rest,
With heart as carefull as with careless grace,
With shrinking legs but with a swelling breast,
With eyes which threatened they would drown his face,
Fearing the worst, not knowing what were best,
And giving to his sight a wandering race,
He saw behind a bush where Klaius sate,
His well-known friend, but yet his unknown mate.

Klaius the wretch, who lately yielden was
To bear the bonds which time nor wit could break,
(With blushing soul at sight of judgment's glass,
While guilty thoughts accused his reason weak),
This morn alone to lonely walk did pass,
Within himself of her dear self to speak;
Till Strephon's plaining voice him nearer drew,
Where by his words his self-like case he knew.

For hearing him so oft with words of woe
Urania name, whose force he knew so well,
He quickly knew what witchcraft gave the blow,
Which made his Strephon think himself in hell:
Which when he did in perfect image show
To his own wit, thought upon thought did swell,
Breeding huge storms within his inward part,
Which thus breath'd out with earthquake of his heart.

In vain, mine eyes

IN vain, mine eyes, you labour to amend
With flowing tears your fault of hasty sight,
Since to my heart her shape you so did send
That her I see, though you did lose your light.
In vain, my heart, now you with sight are burn'd,
With sighs you seek to cool your hot desire,
Since sighs (into mine inward furnace turn'd)
For bellows serve to kindle more the fire.
Reason, in vain, now you have lost my heart,
My head you seek, as to your strongest fort,
Since there mine eyes have play'd so false a part,
That to your strength your foes have sure resort.
Then since in vain I find were all my strife,
To this strange death I vainly yield my life.

Old Age

LET not old age disgrace my high desire,
O heavenly soul, in human shape contain'd:
Old wood inflamed doth yield the bravest fire,
When younger doth in smoke his virtue spend.
Ne let white hairs, which on my face do grow,
Seem to your eyes of a disgraceful hue,
Since whiteness doth present the sweetest show,
Which makes all eyes do homage unto you.
Old age is wise and full of constant truth;
Old age well stay'd from ranging humour lives;
Old age hath known what ever was in youth;
Old age o'ercome, the greater honour gives:
And to old age since you yourself aspire,
Let not old age disgrace my high desire.

Since so mine eyes

SINCE so mine eyes are subject to your sight
That in your sight they fixèd have my brain,
Since so my heart is fillèd with that light
That only light doth all my life maintain,
Since in sweet you all goods so richly reign
That where you are no wishèd good can want,
Since so your living image lives in me
That in myself yourself true love doth plant:
How can you him unworthy then decree,
In whose chief part your worths implanted be?

My sheep are thoughts

MY sheep are thoughts, which I both guide and serve;
Their pasture is fair hills of fruitless love.
On barren sweets they feed, and feeding sterve.
I wail their lot but will not other prove;
My sheephook is wanhope, which all upholds;
My weeds desire, cut out in endless folds;
What wool my sheep shall bear, whiles thus they live,
In you it is, you must the judgment give.

What tongue can her perfections tell?

WHAT tongue can her perfections tell
In whose each part all pens may dwell?
Her hair fine threads of finest gold,
In curlèd knots man's thought to hold,
But that her forehead says 'In me
A whiter beauty you may see.'
Whiter indeed, more white than snow
Which on cold Winter's face doth grow:
That doth present those even brows
Whose equal line their angles bows;
Like to the Moon, when, after change,
Her hornèd head abroad doth range,
And arches be two heavenly lids,
Whose wink each bold attempt forbids.
For the black stars those spheres contain,
The matchless pair even praise doth stain;
No lamp whose light by Art is got,
No sun which shines and seeth not,
Can liken them, without all peer
Save one as much as other clear;
Which only thus unhappy be
Because themselves they cannot see.
Her cheeks with kindly claret spread,
Aurora-like new out of bed;
Or like the fresh queen-apple's side,
Blushing at sight of Phoebus' pride.
Her nose, her chin, pure ivory wears,
No purer then the pretty ears,
So that therein appears some blood,
Like wine and milk that mingled stood;
In whose incirclets if ye gaze
Your eyes may tread a lover's maze,
But with such turns the voice to stray,
No talk untaught can find the way.
The tip no jewel needs to wear,
The tip is jewel of the ear.
But who those ruddy lips can miss,
Which, blessèd, still themselves do kiss?
Rubies, cherries, and roses new,
In worth, in taste, in perfect hue,
Which never part but that they show
Of precious pearl the double row;

The second sweetly-fencèd ward,
Her heavenly-dewèd tongue to guard,
Whence never word in vain did flow.
Fair under these doth stately grow
The handle of this precious work,
The neck, in which strange graces lurk.
Such be I think the sumptuous towers
Which skill doth make in princes' bowers.
So good assay invites the eye
A little downward to espy
The lively clusters of her breasts,
Of Venus' babe the wanton nests:
Like pommels round of marble clear,
Where azured veins well-mixt appear,
With dearest tops of porphyry.
Betwixt these two a way doth lie,
A way more worthy Beauty's fame
Than that which bears the milky name:
This leads into the joyous field
Which only still doth lilies yield;
But lilies such whose native smell
The Indian odours doth excel:
Waist it is call'd, for it doth waste
Men's lives until it be embraced.
There may one see, and yet not see,
Her ribs in white all armèd be;
More white than Neptune's foamy face
When struggling rocks he would embrace.
In those delights the wandering thought
Might of each side astray be brought,
But that her navel doth unite
In curious circle busy sight:
A dainty seal of virgin-wax,
Where nothing but impression lacks.
Her belly then glad sight doth fill,
Justly entitled Cupid's hill,
A hill most fit for such a master,
A spotless mine of alablaster:
Like alablaster fair and sleek,
But soft and supple satin-like.
In that sweet seat the boy doth sport;
Loath I must leave his chief resort,
For such a use the world hath gotten,
The best things still must be forgotten.
Yet never shall my song omit
Her thighs, for Ovid's song more fit,

Which flankèd with two sugared flanks,
Lift up her stately-swelling banks,
That Albion clives [1] in whiteness pass,
With haunches smooth as looking-glass.
But, bow all knees!   Now of her knees
My tongue doth tell what fancy sees,
The knots of joy, the gems of love,
Whose motion makes all graces move,
Whose bought incaved doth yield such sight
Like cunning painter shadowing white.
The gartering-place, with child-like sign,
Shows easy print in metal fine;
But then again the flesh doth rise
In her brave calves, like crystal skies,
Whose Atlas is a smallest small,
More white than whitest bone of all.
Thereout steals out that round clean foot,
This noble cedar's precious root,
In show and scent pale violets;
Whose step on earth all beauty sets.
But back unto her back, my Muse!—
Where Leda's swan his feathers mews,
Along whose ridge such bones are met,
Like comfits round in marchpane set.
Her shoulders be like two white doves,
Perching within square royal rooves,
Which leaded are with silver skin,
Passing the hate-sport ermelin.
And thence those arms derivèd are:
The phoenix' wings are not so rare
For faultless length and stainless hue.
Ah, woe is me, my woes renew,
Now course doth lead me to her hand,
Of my first love the fatal band,
Where whiteness doth for ever sit:
Nature herself enamell'd it.
For there with strange compact doth lie
Warm snow, moist pearl, soft ivory;
There fall those sapphire-colour'd brooks,
Which conduit-like with curious crooks
Sweet islands make in that sweet land.
As for the fingers of the hand,
The bloody shafts of Cupid's war,
With amethysts they headed are.

[1] *cliffs*

Thus hath each part his beauty's part.
But how the Graces do impart
To all her limbs a special grace,
Becoming every time and place,
Which doth even beauty beautify,
And most bewitch the wretched eye:
How all this is but a fair inn
Of fairer guests which dwell therein,
Of whose high praise and praiseful bliss
Goodness the pen, heaven paper is,
The ink immortal fame doth lend—I
As I began so must I end:
No tongue can her perfections tell,
In whose each part all tongues may dwell.

Cupid

POOR painters oft with silly poets join
To fill the world with strange but vain conceits:
One brings the stuff, the other stamps the coin,
Which breeds naught else but glosses of deceits.
Thus painters Cupid paint; thus poets do
A naked god, blind, young, with arrows two.

Is he a god, that ever flies the light?
Or naked he, diguis'd in all untruth?
If he be blind, how hitteth he so right?
How is he young, that tamed old Phoebus' youth?
But arrows two, and tipt with gold or lead?
Some, hurt, accuse a third with horny head.

No, nothing so: an old, false knave he is,
By Argus got on Io, then a cow,
What time for her Juno her Jove did miss,
And charge of her to Argus did allow.
Mercury kill'd his false sire for this act;
His dam, a beast, was pardon'd beastly fact.

With father's death and mother's guilty shame,
With Jove's disdain at such a rival's seed,
The wretch, compell'd, a runagate became,
And learn'd what ill a miser-state [1] doth breed.
To lie, to steal, to pry, and to accuse,
Naught in himself, each other to abuse.

[1] miserable state

Yet bears he still his parents' stately gifts,
A hornèd head, cloven feet, and thousand eyes
Some gazing still, some winking wily shifts,
With long large ears where never rumour dies.
His hornèd head doth seem the heaven to spite,
His cloven foot doth never tread aright.

Thus, half a man, with men he daily haunts,
Cloth'd in the shape which soonest may deceive:
Thus, half a beast, each beastly vice he plants
In those weak hearts that his advice receive.
He prowls each place, still in new colours deckt
Sucking one's ill, another to infect.

To narrow breasts he comes all wrapt in gain;
To swelling hearts he shines in Honour's fire:
To open eyes all beauties he doth rain,
Creeping to each with flattering of desire.
But, for that love is worst which rules the eyes,
Thereon his name, there his chief triumph lies.

Millions of years this old drivel Cupid lives,
While still more wretch, more wicked he doth prove;
Till now at length that Jove him office gives,
At Juno's suit who much did Argus love,
In this our world a hangman for to be
Of all those fools that will have all they see.

Complaint of Love

LOVED I am, and yet complain of Love,
As, loving not, accus'd in love I die.
When pity most I crave I cruel prove;
Still seeking love, love found, as much I fly.
Burnt in myself I muse at others' fire,
What I call wrong I do the same and more;
Barr'd of my will, I have beyond desire;
I wail for want and yet am choked with store.
This is thy work, thou god for ever blind,
Though thousands old, a Boy entitled still:
Thus children do the silly birds they find
With stroking hurt and too much cramming kill.
Yet thus much love, O Love, I crave of thee:
Let me be loved, or else not lovèd be.

Love and Jealousy

WITH two strange fires of equal heat possest,
The one of Love, the other of Jealousy,
Both still do work, in neither I find rest,
For both, alas, their strengths together tie:
The one aloft doth hold, the other high.
Love wakes the jealous eye lest thence it moves;
The jealous eye, the more it looks it loves.

These fires increase, in these I daily burn;
They feed on me and with my wings do fly;
My lovely joys to doleful ashes turn,
Their flames mount up, my powers prostrate lie;
They live in force, I quite consumèd die.
One wonder yet far passeth my conceit,—
The fuel small, how be the fires so great?

Echo

FAIR rocks, goodly rivers, sweet woods, when shall I see peace? *Peace.*
Peace! what bars me my tongue? who is it that comes me so nigh? *I.*
Oh, I do know what guest I have met, it is Echo. *'Tis Echo.*
Well met, Echo, approach; then tell me thy will too. *I will too.*
Echo, what do I get yielding my sprite to my grieves? *Grieves.*
What medicine may I find for a grief that draws me to death? *Death.*
O poisonous medicine! what worse to me can be than it? *It.*
In what state was I then, when I took this deadly disease? *Ease.*
And what manner a mind which had to that humour a vein? *Vain.*
Hath not reason enough vehemence the desire to reprove? *Prove.*
Oft prove I: but what salve, when reason seeks to be gone? *One.*
Oh, what is it? what is it that may be a salve to my love? *Love.*
What do lovers seek for, long seeking for to enjoy? *Joy.*
What be the joys which for to enjoy they went to the pains? *Pains.*
Then to an earnest love what doth best victory lend? *End.*
End! but I can never end, Love will not give me leave? *Leave.*
How be the minds dispos'd that cannot taste thy physick? *Sick.*
Yet say again thy advice for the evils that I told thee? *I told thee.*
Doth the infected wretch of his harm the extremity know? *No.*
But if he know not his harms, what guides hath he whilst he be blind?
    Blind.
What blind guides can he have that leans to a fancy? *A fancy.*
Can fancies want eyes, or he fall that steppeth aloft? *Oft.*
What causes first made these torments on me to light? *Light.*
Can then a cause be so light that forceth a man to go die? *Ay.*
Yet tell what light thing I had in me to draw me to die? *Eye.*

Eyesight made me to yield; but what first pierced to my eyes?　*Eye.*
Eyes hurters, eyes hurt; but what from them to me falls?　*Falls.*
But when I first did fall, what brought most fall to my heart?　*Art.*
Art! what can be that art that thou dost mean by thy speech?　*Spee*
What be the fruits of speaking art? what grows by the words?　*Wor*
O, much more than words: those words served more me to ble*
　Less.
Oh, when shall I be known where most to be known I do long?　*Lo*
Long be thy woes for such news; but how recks she my thought
　Oughts.
Then, then, what do I gain, since unto her will I do wind?　*Wind.*
Wind, tempests, and storms, yet in end what gives she desire?　*Ir*
Silly reward! yet among women hath she of virtue the most.　*Mos*
What great name may I give to so heav'nly a woman?　*A wo-man.*
Woe but seems to me joy, that agrees to my thought so.　*I thought*
Think so, for of my desirèd bliss it is only the course.　*Curse.*
Curs'd be thyself for cursing that which leads me to joys.　*Toys.*
What be the sweet creatures where lowly demands be not heard?　*Ha*
What makes them be unkind? speak, for thou hast narrowly prie*
　Pride.
Whence can pride come there, since springs of beauty be thenc*
　Thence.
Horrible is this blasphemy unto the most holy.　*O lie.*
Thou liest, false Echo! their minds as virtue be just.　*Just.*
Mock'st thou those diamonds which only be matcht by the god*
　Odds.
Odds! what an odds is there! since them to the heavens I prefer.　*E*
Tell yet again me the names of these fair form'd to do evils?　*Dev*
Devils! if in hell such devils do abide, to the hell I do go.　*Go.*

Love and Reason

REASON, tell me thy mind, if here be reason
In this strange violence to make resistance,
Where sweet graces erect the stately banner
Of Virtue's regiment, shining in harness
Of Fortune's diadems, by Beauty mustrèd:
Say, then, Reason, I say, what is thy counsel?

Her loose hairs be the shot, the breasts the pikes be,
Scouts each motion is, the hands be horsemen,
Her lips are the riches the wars to maintain,
Where well-couchèd abides a coffer of pearl,
Her legs carriage is of all the sweet camp:
Say, then, Reason, I say, what is thy counsel?

Her cannons be her eyes, mine eyes the walls be,
Which at first volley gave too open entry;
Nor rampire did abide, my brain was up blown,
Undermined with a speech, the piercer of thoughts;
Thus weakened by myself, no help remaineth:
Say, then, Reason, I say, what is thy counsel?

And now fame, the herald of her true honour,
Doth proclaim with a sound made all by men's mouths,
That Nature, sovereign of earthly dwellers,
Commands all creatures to yield obeisance
Under this, this her own, her only dearling:
Say, then, Reason, I say, what is thy counsel?

Reason sighs, but in end he thus doth answer:
Nought can reason avail in heavenly matters.
Thus, Nature's diamond, receive thy conquest;
Thus, pure pearl, I do yield my senses and soul;
Thus, sweet pain, I do yield whate'er I yield.
Reason, look to thyself! I serve a goddess.

Solitariness

O SWEET woods, the delight of solitariness
O how much I do like your solitariness!
Where man's mind hath a freed consideration
Of goodness to receive lovely direction;
Where senses do behold the order of heavenly host,
And wise thoughts do behold what the Creator is.
Contemplation here holdeth his only seat,
Bounded with no limits, borne with a wing of hope,
Climbs even unto the stars; Nature is under it.
Nought disturbs thy quiet, all to thy service yields;
Each sight draws on a thought (thought, mother of science);
Sweet birds kindly do grant harmony unto thee;
Fair trees' shade is enough fortification,
Nor danger to thyself if be not in thyself.

O sweet woods, the delight of solitariness!
O how much I do like your solitariness!
Here nor treason is hid, veilèd in innocence,
Nor envy's snaky eye finds any harbour here,
Nor flatterers' venomous insinuations,
Nor cunning humorists' puddled opinions,

Nor courteous ruin of proffered usury,
Nor time prattled away, cradle of ignorance,
Nor causeless duty, nor cumber of arrogance,
Nor trifling title of vanity dazzleth us,
Nor golden manacles stand for a paradise.
Here wrong's name is unheard, slander a monster is.
Keep thy sprite from abuse, here no abuse doth haunt:
What man grafts in a tree dissimulation?

O sweet woods, the delight of solitariness!
O how well I do like your solitariness!
Yet dear soil, if a soul closed in a mansion
As sweet as violets, fair as a lily is,
Straight as a cedar, a voice stains the canary bird's,
Whose shade safety doth hold, danger avoideth her:
Such wisdom that in her lives speculation:
Such goodness that in her simplicity triumphs;
Where envy's snaky eye winketh or else dieth,
Slander wants a pretext, flattery gone beyond:
Oh, if such a one have bent to a lonely life
Her steps, glad we receive, glad we receive her eyes,
And think not she doth hurt our solitariness,
For such company decks such solitariness.

The Wronged Lover

THE Fire to see my wrongs for anger burneth,
The Air in rain for my affliction weepeth,
The Sea to ebb for grief his flowing turneth,
The Earth with pity dull his centre keepeth;
    Fame is with wonder blazed,
    Time runs away for sorrow,
    Place standeth still amazed
To see my night of evils, which hath no morrow:
    Alas, a lonely she no pity taketh
To know my miseries, but, chaste and cruel,
    My fall her glory maketh;
Yet still her eyes give to my flames their fuel.

Fire, burn me quite, till sense of burning leave me;
Air, let me draw thy breath no more in anguish;
Sea, drown'd in thee, of tedious life bereave me;
Earth, take this earth wherein my spirits languish;

Fame, say I was not born;
Time, haste my dying hour;
Place, see my grave uptorn:
Fire, air, sea, earth, fame, time, place, show your power.
Alas, from all their helps I am exilèd,
For hers am I, and Death fears her displeasure:
Fie, Death, thou art beguilèd!
Though I be hers, she makes of me no treasure.

A sweeter saint I serve

PHOEBUS, farewell! A sweeter saint I serve.
The high conceits thy heavenly wisdoms breed
My thoughts forget, my thoughts which never swerve
From her in whom is sown their freedom's seed,
And in whose eyes my daily doom I read.

Phoebus, farewell! A sweeter saint I serve.
Thou art far off, thy kingdom is above:
She heaven on earth with beauties doth preserve.
Thy beams I like, but her clear rays I love:
Thy force I fear, her force I still do prove.
Phoebus, yield up thy title in my mind;
She doth possess, thy image is defaced;
But if thy rage some brave revenge will find
On her who hath in me thy temple raste,
Employ thy might that she my fires may taste:
And, how much more her worth surmounteth thee,
Make her as much more base by loving me.

Arcadian Duologue

[SHE SINGS]

MY true love hath my heart and I have his,
By just exchange one for the other given:
I hold his dear, and mine he cannot miss,
There never was a better bargain driven.
His heart in me keeps me and him in one;
My heart in him his thoughts and senses guides:
He loves my heart, for once it was his own;
I cherish his because in me it bides.

His heart his wound receivèd from my sight;
My heart was wounded with his wounded heart;
For as from me on him his hurt did light,
So still methought in me his hurt did smart.
Both, equal hurt, in this change sought our bliss,
My true love hath my heart and I have his.

[HE ANSWERS]

O words which fall like summer dew on me,
O breath more sweet than is the growing bean,
O tongue in which all honey'd liquors be,
O voice that doth the thrush in shrillness stain:
Do you say still, this is her promise due,
That she is mine as I to her am true.

Gay hair, more gay than straw when harvest lies,
Lips red and plump as cherry's ruddy side,
Eyes fair and great like fair great ox's eyes,
O breast in which two white sheep swell in pride:
Join you with me, to seal this promise due,
That she be mine as I to her am true.

But thou white skin, as white as cruds well prest,
As smooth as sleekstone like it smooths each part,
And thou dear flesh, as soft as wool new drest,
And yet as hard as brawn made hard by art:
First four but say, next four their saying seal,
But you must pay the gage of promist weal.

Another Version[1]

MY true love hath my heart and I have his,
By just exchange one for another given:
I hold his dear, and mine he cannot miss,
There never was a better bargain driven.
My true love hath my heart and I have his.

His heart in me keeps him and me in one,
My heart in him his thoughts and senses guides.
He loves my heart, for once it was his own:
I cherish his, because in me it bides.
My true love hath my heart and I have his.

[1] See Notes

Graven Thoughts

DO not disdain, O straight up-raisèd pine,
That wounding thee my thoughts in thee I grave,
Since that my thoughts, as straight as straightness thine,
No smaller wound—alas, far deeper—have,
Deeper engraved, which salve nor time can save,
Given to my heart by my sore-wounded eyne.
Thus cruel to myself, how canst thou crave
My inward hurt should spare thy outward rine?
Yet still, fair tree, lift up thy stately line,
Live long, and long witness my chosen smart
Which barr'd desires (barr'd by myself) impart,
And in this growing bark grow verses mine.
My heart my word, my word hath given my heart.
The giver given from gift shall never part.

Sleep

LOCK up, fair lids, the treasure of my heart,
Preserve those beams, this age's only light;
To her sweet sense, sweet Sleep, some ease impart,
Her sense, too weak to bear her spirit's might.
And while, O Sleep, thou closest up her sight
(Her sight where Love did forge his fairest dart),
O harbour all her parts in easeful plight;
Let no strange dream make her fair body start.
But yet, O Dream, if thou wilt not depart
In this rare subject from thy common right,
But wilt thyself in such a seat delight,
Then take my shape and play a lover's part:
Kiss her from me and say unto her sprite
Till her eyes shine I live in darkest night.

Madrigal

WHY dost thou haste away,
O Titan fair, the giver of the day?
        Is it to carry news
To western wights what stars in east appear?
        Or dost thou think that here
Is left a sun whose beams thy place may use?
        Yet stay, and well peruse

What be her gifts that make her equal thee;
    Bend all thy light to see
In earthly clothes enclosed a heavenly spark.
Thy running course cannot such beauties mark;
    No, no, thy motions be
Hastened from us with bar of shadow dark,
Because that thou, the author of our sight,
Disdain'st we see thee stain'd with other's light.

When two suns do appear

WHEN two suns do appear,
Some say it doth betoken wonders near,
    As prince's loss or change.
Two gleaming suns of splendour like I see,
    And seeing feel in me
Of prince's heart quite lost the ruin strange.
    But now each where doth range
With ugly cloak the dark envious Night,
    Who, full of guilty spite,
Such living beams should her black seat assail,
Too weak for them our weaker sight doth vail.
    No, says fair Moon, my light
Shall bar that wrong, and though it not prevail
Like to my brother's rays, yet those I send
Hurt not the face which nothing can amend.

Contentment

GET hence, foul Grief, the canker of the mind;
Farewell, Complaint, the miser's only pleasure;
Away, vain Cares, by which few men do find
    Their sought-for treasure.

Ye helpless sighs, blow out your breath to nought;
Tears, drown yourselves, for woe your cause is wasted;
Thought, think to end—too long the fruit of thought
    My mind hath tasted.

But thou, sure Hope, tickle my leaping heart,
Comfort, step thou in place of wonted sadness;
Fore-felt Desire, begin to savour part
    Of coming gladness.

Let voice of sighs into clear music run;
Eyes, let your tears with gazing now be mended;
Instead of thought true pleasure be begun,
        And never ended.

Epithalamium

LET mother Earth now deck herself in flowers,
To see her offspring seek a good increase,
Where justest love doth vanquish Cupid's powers,
And war of thoughts is swallow'd up in peace,
        Which never may decrease,
        But, like the turtles fair,
Live one in two, a well-united pair,
        Which that no chance may stain,
O Hymen, long their coupled joys maintain!

O heaven, awake, show forth thy stately face;
Let not these slumbering clouds thy beauties hide,
But with thy cheerful presence help to grace
The honest Bridegroom and the bashful Bride;
        Whose loves may ever bide,
        Like to the elm and vine,
With mutual embracements them to twine:
        In which delightful pain,
O Hymen, long their coupled joys maintain!

Ye Muses all, which chaste affects allow,
And have to Thyrsis showed your secret skill,
To this chaste love your sacred favours bow,
And so to him and her your gifts distil,
        That they all vice may kill,
        And, like to lilies pure,
May please all eyes, and spotless may endure,
        Where that all bliss may reign:
O Hymen, long their coupled joys maintain!

Ye Nymphs which in the waters empire have,
Since Thyrsis' music oft doth yield you praise,
Grant to the thing which we for Thyrsis crave;
Let one time—but long first—close up their days,
        One grave their bodies seize;
        And like two rivers sweet,
When they though divers do together meet,
        One stream both streams contain:
O Hymen, long their coupled joys maintain!

Pan, father Pan, the god of silly sheep,
Whose care is cause that they in number grow,
Have much more care of them that them do keep—
Since from these good the others' good doth flow—
　　　And make their issue show
　　　In number like the herd
Of younglings which thyself with love hast rear'd,
　　　Or like the drops of rain.
O Hymen, long their coupled joys maintain!

Virtue, if not a god, yet God's chief part,
Be thou the knot of this their open vow,
That still he be her head, she be his heart,
He lean to her, she unto him do bow,
　　　Each other still allow:
　　　Like oak and mistletoe,
Her strength from him, his praise from her do grow:
　　　In which most lovely train,
O Hymen, long their coupled joys maintain!

But thou, foul Cupid, sire to lawless lust,
Be thou far hence with thy empoison'd dart,
Which, though of glittering gold, shall here take rust
Where simple love, which chasteness doth impart,
　　　Avoids thy hurtful art,
　　　Not needing charming skill
Such minds with sweet affections for to fill:
　　　Which being pure and plain,
O Hymen, long their coupled joys maintain!

All churlish words, shrewd answers, crabbèd looks,
All privateness, self-seeking, inward spite,
All waywardness which nothing kindly brooks,
All strife for toys and claiming master's right,
　　　Be hence aye put to flight!
　　　All stirring husband's hate
Gainst neighbours good, for womanish debate,
　　　Be fled, as things most vain!
O Hymen, long their coupled joys maintain!

All peacock pride, and fruits of peacock's pride,
Longing to be with loss of substance gay;
With recklessness what may the house betide,
So that you may on higher slippers stay,

For ever hence away:
　　Yet let not sluttery,
The sink of filth, be counted huswifery,
　　But keeping whole your mean,
O Hymen, long their coupled joys maintain!

But above all, away vile jealousy,
The evil of evils, just cause to be unjust;
How can he love suspecting treachery?
How can she love where love cannot win trust?
　　Go, snake, hide thee in dust,
　　Ne dare once show thy face
Where open hearts do hold so constant place
　　That they thy sting restrain:
O Hymen, long their coupled joys maintain

The earth is deckt with flowers, the heavens display'd.
Muses grant gifts, nymphs long and joinèd life,
Pan store of babes, virtue their thoughts well staid;
Cupid's lust gone, and gone is bitter strife.
　　Happy man, happy wife!
　　No pride shall them oppress,
Nor yet shall yield to loathsome sluttishness,
　　And jealousie is slain;
For Hymen will their coupled joys maintain.

A Tale for Husbands

A NEIGHBOUR mine not long ago there was
(But nameless he, for blameless he shall be),
That married had a trick and bonny lass
As in a summer-day a man might see;
But he himself a foul unhandsome groom,
And far unfit to hold so good a room.

Now, whether moved with self-unworthiness,
Or with her beauty fit to make a prey,
Fell jealousy did so his brain oppress
That if he absent were but half a day
He guess'd the worst (you wot what is the worst),
And in himself new doubting causes nurst.

While thus he fear'd the silly innocent,
Who yet was good because she knew none ill,
Unto his house a jolly shepherd went,
To whom our prince did bear a great good will,
Because in wrestling and in pastoral
He far did pass the rest of shepherds all.

And therefore he a courtier was benamed,
And as a courtier was with cheer received;
For they have tongues to make a poor man blamed,
If he to them his duty misconceived:
And for this courtier should well like his table,
The good man bade his wife be serviceable.

And so she was, and all with good intent;
But few days past, while she good manner used,
But that her husband thought her service bent
To such an end as he might be abused:
Yet, like a coward, fearing stranger's pride,
He made the simple wench his wrath abide.

With chumpish looks, hard words, and secret nips,
Grumbling at her when she his kindness sought,
Asking her how she tasted courtier's lips,
He forced her think that which she never thought.
In fine, he made her guess there was some sweet
In that which he so fear'd that she should meet.

When once this entered was in woman's heart,
And that it had inflam'd a new desire,
There rested then to play a woman's part,
Fuel to seek, and not to quench the fire:
But for his jealous eye she well did find,
She studied cunning how the same to blind.

And thus she did: one day to him she came,
And, though against his will, on him she lean'd,
And out gan cry: 'Ah, well-away for shame,
If you help not, our wedlock will be stain'd!'
The goodman, starting, askt what her did move.
She sigh'd and said: The bad guest sought her love.

He, little looking that she should complain
Of that whereto he fear'd she was inclined,
Bussing her oft, and in his heart full fain,
He did demand what remedy to find;
How they might get that guest from them to wend,
And yet the prince, that loved him, not offend.

'Husband,' quoth she, 'go to him by and by,
And tell him you do find I do him love;
And therefore pray him that of courtesy
He will absent himself, lest he should move
A young girl's heart to that were shame for both:
Whereto, you know, his honest heart were loth.

'Thus shall you show that him you do not doubt,
And as for me, sweet husband, I must bear.'
Glad was the man when he had heard her out,
And did the same, although with mickle fear.
For fear he did, lest he the young man might
In choler put, with whom he would not fight.

The courtly shepherd, much aghast at this,
Not seeing erst such token in the wife,
Though full of scorn would not his duty miss,
Knowing that ill becomes a household strife,
Did go his way, but sojourn'd near thereby,
That yet the ground hereof he might espy.

The wife thus having settled husband's brain—
Who would have sworn his spouse Diana was—
Watchèd when she a further point might gain,
Which little time did fitly bring to pass:
For to the Court her man was call'd by name,
Whither he needs must go for fear of blame.

Three days before that he must sure depart
She written had, but in a hand disguised,
A letter such, which might from either part,
Seem to proceed, so well it was devised.
She seal'd it first, then she the sealing brake.
And to her jealous husband did it take.

With weeping eyes (her eyes she taught to weep)
She told him that the Courtier had it sent:
'Alas,' quoth she.   Thus women's shame doth creep!
The goodman read on both sides the content.
It title had: *Unto my only Love.*
Subscription was: *Yours most, if you will prove.*

The pistle' self such kind of words it had:
'My sweetest joy, the comfort of my sprite,
So may thy flocks' increase thy dear heart glad;
So may each thing even as thou wishest light,
As thou wilt deign to read, and gently rede
This mourning ink in which my heart doth bleed.

'Long have I loved (alas thou worthy art);
Long have I loved (alas love craveth love);
Long have I loved thyself, alas my heart
Doth break, now tongue unto thy name doth move:
And think not that thy answer answer is,
But that it is my doom of bale or bliss.

'The jealous wretch must now to Court be gone:
Ne can he fail, for Prince hath for him sent.
Now is the time we may be here alone,
And give a long desire a sweet content.
Thus shall you both reward a lover true,
And eke revenge his wrong-suspecting you.'

And this was all, and this the husband read
With chafe enough, till she him pacified,
Desiring that no grief in him be bred,
Now that he had her words so truely tried,
But that he would to him the letter show,
That with his fault he might her goodness know.

That straight was done with many a boisterous threat,
That to the King he would his sin declare:
But now the Courtier 'gan to smell the feat,
And with some words which showèd little care,
He stay'd until the goodman was departed,
Then gave he him the blow which never smarted.

Thus may you see the jealous wretch was made
The pandar of the thing he most did fear.
Take heed, therefore, how you ensue that trade,
Lest the same marks of jealousy you bear:
For sure no jealousy can that prevent
Whereto two parties once be full content.

Advice to the Same

WHO doth desire that chaste his wife should be,
First be he true, for truth doth truth deserve:
Then such be he as she his worth may see,
And one man still credit with her preserve.
Not toying kind nor causelessly unkind,
Not stirring thoughts nor yet denying right,
Not spying faults nor in plain errors blind,
Never hard hand nor ever reins too light.

As far from want, as far from vain expense
(The one doth force, the latter doth entice),
Allow good company, but keep from thence
All filthy mouths that glory in their vice.
This done, thou hast no more, but leave the rest
To virtue, fortune, time, and woman's breast.

A Country Song

THE lad Philisides
Lay by a river side,
In flowery field a gladder eye to please:
His pipe was at his foot,
His lambs were him beside,
A widow turtle near on barèd root
Sat wailing without boot.
Each thing both sweet and sad
Did draw his boiling brain
To think and think with pain
Of Mira's beams, eclipst by absence bad.
And thus, with eyes made dim
With tears, he said, or sorrow said for him:
'O earth, once answer give,
So may thy stately grace
By north or south still rich adornèd live;
So Mira long may be
On thy then blessed face,
Whose foot doth set a heaven on cursèd thee;
I ask, now answer me,
If the author of thy bliss,
Phoebus, that shepherd high,
Do turn from thee his eye,
Doth not thyself, when he long absent is,
Like rogue, all ragged go,
And pine away with daily wasting woe?
Tell me, you wanton brook;
So may your sliding race
Shun loathèd-loving banks with cunning crook;
So in you ever new
Mira may look her face,
And make you fair with shadow of her hue;
So when to pay your due
To mother sea you come,

She chide you not for stay,
Not beat you for your play;
Tell me, if your diverted springs become
Absented quite from you,
Are you not dried? Can you yourselves renew?
Tell me, you flowers fair,
Cowslip and columbine,
So may your make this wholesome springtime air
With you embracèd lie,
And lately thence untwine,
But with dew drops engender children high;
So may you never die,
But, pull'd by Mira's hand,
Dress bosom hers, or head,
Or scatter on her bed;
Tell me, if husband Springtime leave your land
When he from you is sent,
Wither not you, languisht with discontent?
Tell me, my silly pipe;
So may thee still betide
A cleanly cloth thy moistness for to wipe;
So may the cherries red
Of Mira's lips divide
Their sugared selves to kiss thy happy head;
So may her ears be led—
Her ears where music lives—
To hear and not despise
Thy lyribliring cries;
Tell if that breath, which thee thy sounding gives,
Be absent far from thee,
Absent alone canst thou, then, piping be?
Tell me, my lamb of gold;
So mayst thou long abide
The day well fed, the night in faithful fold;
So grow thy wool of note
In time, that, richly dyed,
It may be part of Mira's petticoat;
Tell me, if wolves the throat
Have caught of thy dear dam,
Or she from thee be stay'd,
Or thou from her be stray'd,
Canst thou, poor lamb, become another's lamb,
Or rather, till thou die,
Still for thy dam with baa-waymenting cry?
Tell me, O turtle true;
So may no fortune breed

To make thee nor thy better-lovèd rue;
        So may thy blessings swarm,
        That Mira may thee feed
With hand and mouth, with lap and breast keep warm;
        Tell me if greedy arm
        Do fondly take away,
        With traitor lime, the one,
        The other left alone,
Tell me, poor wretch, parted from wretched prey,
        Disdain not you the green,
Wailing till death shun you not to be seen?
Earth, brook, flowers, pipe, lamb, dove
        Say all, and I with them,
Absence is death, or worse, to them that love.
        So I, unlucky lad,
        Whom hills from her do hem,
What fits me now but tears and sighings sad!
        O Fortune, too too bad!
        I rather would my sheep
        Th'adst killèd with a stroke,
        Burnt cabin, lost my cloak,
Than want one hour those eyes which my joys keep.
        O, what doth wailing win?
Speech without end were better not begin.
        My song, climb thou the wind
Which Holland sweet now gently sendeth in,
That on his wings the level thou mayst find
        To hit, but kissing hit
        Her ears the weights of wit.
If thou know not for whom thy master dies,
        These marks shall make thee wise:
She is the herdress fair that shines in dark,
And gives her kids no food but willow's bark.
        This said, at length he ended
        His oft sigh-broken ditty,
Then raise, but raise on legs with faintness bended,
        With skin in sorrow dyed,
        With face the plot of pity,
With thoughts, which thoughts, their own tormentors, tried.
        He rose, and straight espied
        His ram, who to recover
        The ewe another loved,
        With him proud battle proved.
He envied such a death in sight of lover,
        And always westward eyeing,
More envied Phoebus for his western flying.

Shepherd Song

AS I my little flock on Ister bank
(A little flock, but well my pipe they couth)
Did piping lead, the sun already sank
Beyond our world, and ere I got my booth,
Each thing with mantle black the night doth scoth,
Saving the glow-worm, which would courteous be
Of that small light oft watching shepherds see.

The welkin had full niggardly enclosed
In coffer of dim clouds his silver groats,
Iclepèd stars; each thing to rest disposed;
The caves were full, the mountains void of goats;
The bird's eye closed, closèd their chirping notes:
As for the nightingale, wood-music's king,
It August was, he deign'd not then to sing.

Amid my sheep, though I saw naught to fear,
Yet (for I nothing saw) I fearèd sore;
Then found I which thing is a charge to bear:
As for my sheep I dradded mickle more
Than ever for myself since I was bore.
I sat me down, for see to go ne could,
And sang unto my sheep lest stray they should.

The song I sang old Lanquet had me taught:
Lanquet, the shepherd best swift Ister knew,
For clerkly rede, and hating what is naught,
For faithful heart, clean hands, and mouth as true.
With his sweet skill my skill-less youth he drew
To have a feeling taste of Him that sits
Beyond the heaven, far more beyond our wits.

He said, the music best thilk powers pleas'd
Was jump concord between our wit and will,
Where highest notes to godliness are rais'd,
And lowest sink not down to jot of ill;
With old true tales he wont mine ears to fill,
How shepherds did of yore, how now they thrive,
Spoiling their flock, erewhile twixt them they strive.

He likèd me, but pitied lustful youth;
His good strong staff my slippery years upbore;
He still hop'd well because I lovèd truth;
Till, forced to part, with heart and eyes even sore
To worthy Coridon he gave me o'er.
But thus in oak's true shade recounted he
Which now in night's deep shade sheep heard of me.

Such manner time there was (what time I n'ot)
When all this earth, this dam or mould of ours,
Was only wonned with such as beasts begot.
Unknown as then were they that builded towers.
The cattle wild or tame, in Nature's bowers
Might freely roam, or rest, as seemèd them;
Man was not made their dwellings in to hem.

The beasts had sure some beastly policy—
For nothing can endure where order n'is—
For once the lion by the lamb did lie,
The fearful hind the leopard did kiss,
Hurtless was tiger's paw and serpent's hiss:
This think I well, the beasts with courage clad,
Like senators a harmless empire had:

At which whether the others did repine
(For envy harboureth most in feeblest hearts),
Or that they all to changing did incline
(As even in beasts their dams love changing parts),
The multitude to Jove a suit imparts,
With neighing, blaying, braying, and barking,
Roaring and howling for to have a king.

A king, in language theirs, they said they would,
For then their language was a perfect speech;
The birds likewise with chirps and pewing could,
Cackling and chattering, that of Jove beseech.
Only the owl still warn'd them not to seech
So hastily that which they would repent:
But saw they would, and he to deserts went.

Jove wisely said (for wisdom wisely says),
O beasts, take heed what you of me desire:
Rulers will think all things made them to please,
And soon forget the swink due to their hire;
But, since you will, part of my heavenly fire
I will you lend; the rest yourselves must give,
That it both seen and felt may with you live.

Full glad they were, and took the naked sprite,
Which straight the earth yclothèd in his clay;
The lion heart, the ounce gave active might,
The horse good shape, the sparrow lust to play,
Nightingale voice, enticing songs to say;
Elephant gave a perfect memory,
And parrot ready tongue, that to apply.

The fox gave craft, the dog gave flattery,
Ass patience, the mole a working thought,
Eagle high look, wolf secret cruelty,
Monkey sweet breath, the cow her fair eyes brought,
The ermine whitest skin, spotted with naught;
The sheep mild-seeming face, climbing the bear,
The stag did give the harm-eschewing fear.

The hare her sleights, the cat his melancholy,
Ant industry, and cony skill to build;
Cranes order, storks to be appearing holy;
Chameleon ease to change, duck ease to yield;
Crocodile, tears which might be falsely spill'd;
Ape great thing gave, though he did mowing stand,
The instrument of instruments, the hand.

Each other beast likewise his present brings,
And (but they drad their Prince they aught should want)
They all consented were to give him wings;
And aye more awe towards him for to plant,
To their own work this privilege they grant,
That from thenceforth to all eternity
No beast should freely speak, but only he.

Thus Man was made, thus Man their lord became:
Who at the first, wanting or hiding pride,
He did to beasts best use his cunning frame,
With water drink, herbs meat, and naked hide,
And fellow-like, let his dominion slide,
Not in his sayings saying *I*, but *we*,
As if he meant his lordship common be.

But when his seat so rooted he had found
That they now skill'd not how from him to wend,
Then gan in guiltless earth full many a wound,
Iron to seek, which gainst itself should bend,
To tear the bowels that good corn should send:
But yet the common dam none did bemoan,
Because, though hurt, they never heard her groan.

Then gan he factions in the beasts to breed;
Where helping weaker sort, the nobler beasts,
As tigers, leopards, bears, and lion's seed,
Disdain'd with this, in deserts sought their rests,
Where famine ravine taught their hungry chests.
Thus craftily he forced them to do ill,
Which being done, he afterwards would kill.

For murther done—which never erst was seen—
By those great beasts, as for the weakers' good,
He chose themselves his guarders for to been
Gainst those of might, of whom in fear they stood,
As horse and dog, not great, but gentle blood:
Blithe were the common cattle of the field,
The when they saw their foen of greatness kill'd.

But they or spent, or made of slender might,
Then, quickly did the meaner cattle find
The great beams gone, the house on shoulders light.
For by and by the horse fair bits did bind;
The dog was in a collar taught his kind;
As for the gentle birds, like case may rue,
When falcon they and goshawk saw in mew.

Worst fell to smallest birds and meanest herd,
Whom now his own, full like his own he used.
Yet first but wool or feathers off he tear'd:
And when they were well used to be abused,
For hungry teeth their flesh with teeth he bruised.
At length for glutton taste he did them kill:
At last for sport their silly lives did spill.

But yet, O man, rage not beyond thy need;
Deem it no glory to swell in tyranny.
Thou art of blood: joy not to see things bleed.
Thou fearest death: think they are loth to die.
A plaint of guiltless hurt doth pierce the sky:
And you, poor beasts, in patience bide your hell,
Or know your strengths, and then you shall do well.

Thus did I sing and pipe, eight sullen hours,
To sheep whom love not knowledge made to bear
Now fancy's fits, now fortune's baleful flowers.
But then I homewards call'd my lambkins dear:
For to my dimmèd eyes began to appear
The night grown old, her black head waxen gray,
Sure shepherd's sign that morn should soon fetch day.

Geron and Histor

GERON

IN faith, good Histor, long is your delay
From holy marriage, sweet and surest mean,
Our foolish lust in honest rules to stay.
I pray thee do to Lalus' sample lean:
Thou seest how frisk and jolly now he is,
That last day seem'd he could not chew a bean.
Believe me, man, there is no greater bliss
Than is the quiet joy of living wife,
Which whoso wants, half of himself doth miss.
Friend without change, play-fellow without strife,
Food without fullness, counsel without pride,
Is this sweet doubling of our single life.

HISTOR

No doubt, to whom so good chance did betide,
As for to find a pasture strew'd with gold,
He were a fool if there he did not bide:
Who would not have a phoenix if he could?
The humming wasp, if it had not a sting,
Before all flies the wasp accept I would.
But this bad world few golden fields doth bring—
Phoenix but one, of crows we millions have;
The wasp seems gay, but is a cumbrous thing.
If many Kalaes our Arcadia gave,
Lalus' example I would soon ensue,
And think I did myself from a sorrow save.
But of such wives we find a slender crew,
Shrewdness so stirs, pride so puffs up the heart;
They seldom ponder what to them is due:
With meagre looks, as if they still did smart,
Puling or whimpering, or else scolding flat,
Make home more pain than following of the cart.
Either dull silence, or eternal chat,
Still contrary to what her husband says;
If he do praise the dog, she likes the cat.
Austere she is when he would honest plays,
And gamesome then when he thinks on his sheep;
She bids him go, and yet from journey stays:
She war doth ever with his kinsfolk keep,

And makes them fremd who friends by nature are,
Envying shallow toys with malice deep.
And if, forsooth, there come some new-found ware,
The little coin his sweating brows have got
Must go for that, if for her lours he care;
Or else—'Nay, faith, mine is the lucklest lot
That ever fell to honest woman yet!
No wife but I hath such a man, God wot!'
Such is their speech who be of sober wit;
But who do let their tongues show well their rage,
Lord, what by-words they speak, what spite they spit!
The house is made a very loathsome cage,
Wherein the bird doth never sing, but cry
With such a will as nothing can assuage.
Dearly the servants do their wages buy,
Reviled for each small fault, sometimes for none:
They better live that in a jail do lie.
Let other, fouler spots away be blown,
For I seek not their shame; but still methinks
A better life it is to lie alone.

GERON

Who for each fickle fear from virtue shrinks
Shall in this life embrace no worthy thing;
No mortal man the cup of surety drinks;
The heavens do not good haps in handfuls bring.
But let us pick our good from out much bad,
That still our little world may know his king.
But certainly so long we may be glad
While that we do what Nature doth require,
And for the event we never ought be sad.
Man oft is plagu'd with air, is burnt with fire,
In water drown'd, in earth his burial is;
And shall we not, therefore, their use desire?
Nature above all things requireth this,
That we our kind do labour to maintain,
Which drawn-out line doth hold all human bliss.
The father justly may of thee complain
If thou do not repay his deeds for thee
In granting unto him a grandsire's gain.
Thy commonwealth may rightly grievèd be
Which must by this immortal be preserved,
If thus thou murther thy posterity.
His very being he hath not deserved

Who for a self-conceit will that forbear
Whereby that being aye must be conserved.
And God forbid women such cattle were
As you paint them; but well in you I find
No man doth speak aright who speaks in fear:
Who only sees the ill is worse than blind.
These fifty winters married have I been,
And yet find no such fault in womankind.
I have a wife worthy to be a queen,
So well she can command and yet obey,
In ruling of a house so well she's seen:
And yet, in all this time betwixt us tway
We bear our double yoke with such consent
That never pass'd foul word, I dare well say.
But these are your love-toys which still are spent
In lawless games and love not as you should,
But with much study learn late to repent.
How well last day before our Prince you could
Blind Cupid's works with wonder testify,
Yet now the root of him abase you would!
Go to, go to, and Cupid now apply
To that where thou thy Cupid mayst avow,
And thou shalt find in women virtues lie:
Sweet supple minds which soon to wisdom bow
Where they by wisdom's rule directed are,
And are not forced fond thraldom to allow.
As we to get are framed, so they to spare;
We made for pain, our pains they made to cherish;
We care abroad, and they of home have care.
O Histor, seek within thyself to flourish;
Thy house by thee must live, or else be gone,
And then who shall the name of Histor nourish?
Riches of children pass a prince's throne,
Which touch the father's heart with secret joy,
When without shame he saith: 'These be mine own.'
Marry, therefore; for marriage will destroy
Those passions which to youthful head do climb—
Mothers and nurses of all vain annoy.

HISTOR

Perchance I will, but now methinks it time
To go unto the bride, and use this day
To speak with her while freely speak we may.

Night

O NIGHT, the ease of care, the pledge of pleasure,
Desire's best mean, harvest of hearts affected,
The seat of peace, the throne which is erected
Of human life to be the quiet measure;
Be victor still of Phoebus' golden treasure,
Who hath our sight with too much sight infected;
Whose light is cause we have our lives neglected,
Turning all Nature's course to self-displeasure.
These stately stars in their now shining faces,
With sinless Sleep, and Silence, Wisdom's mother,
Witness his wrong which by thy help is eased:
Thou art, therefore, of these our desart places
The sure refuge; by thee and by no other
My soul is blest, sense joy'd, and fortune raised.

Why fear to die?

SINCE Nature's works be good, and death doth serve
As Nature's work, why should we fear to die?
Since fear is vain but when it may preserve,
Why should we fear that which we cannot fly?
Fear is more pain than is the pain it fears,
Disarming human minds of native might;
While each conceit an ougly figure bears,
Which were not evil, well view'd in reason's light
Our only eyes, which dimm'd with passions be,
And scarce discern the dawn of coming day,
Let them be clear'd, and now begin to see
Our life is but a step in dusty way:
Then let us hold the bliss of peaceful mind,
Since this we feel, great loss we cannot find.

OTHER SONGS AND SONNETS

A Farewell

OFT have I mused, but now at length I find,
Why those that die, men say they do depart.
Depart!—a word so gentle, to my mind,
Weakly did seem to paint Death's ougly dart.
But now the stars, with their strange course, do bind
Me one to leave, with whom I leave my heart:
I hear a cry of spirits faint and blind,
That, parting thus, my chiefest part I part.
Part of my life, the loathèd part to me,
Lives to impart my weary clay some breath:
But that good part, wherein all comforts be,
Now dead, doth show departure is a death—
Yea, worse than death: death parts both woe and joy:
From joy I part, still living in annoy.

Absence

FINDING those beams (which I must ever love)
To mar my mind, and with my hurt to please,
I deem'd it best some absence, for to prove
If farther place might further me to ease.
My eyes, thence drawn where livèd all their light,
Blinded forthwith in dark despair did lie,
Like to the mole, with want of guiding sight,
Deep plung'd in earth, deprivèd of the sky.
In absence blind, and wearied with that woe,
To greater woes, by presence, I return:
Even as the fly which to the flame doth go,
Pleas'd with the light that his small corse doth burn.
Fair choice I have, either to live or die:
A blinded mole, or else a burnèd fly.

The Nightingale

THE nightingale, as soon as April bringeth
Unto her rested sense a perfect waking,
While late bare earth, proud of new clothing, springeth,
Sings out her woes, a thorn her song-book making;

And, mournfully bewailing,
Her throat in tunes expresseth
What grief her breast oppresseth
For Tereus' force on her chaste will prevailing.
O Philomela fair, O take some gladness,
That here is juster cause of plaintful sadness:
Thine earth now springs, mine fadeth;
Thy thorn without, my thorn my heart invadeth.

Alas, she hath no other cause of anguish
But Tereus' love, on her by strong hand wroken,
Wherein she suffering, all her spirits languish,
Full womanlike complains her will was broken.
But I, who, daily craving,
Cannot have to content me,
Have more cause to lament me,
Since wanting is more woe than too much having.
O Philomela fair, O take some gladness,
That here is juster cause of plaintful sadness:
Thine earth now springs, mine fadeth;
Thy thorn without, my thorn my heart invadeth.

Ring out your bells

RING out your bells, let mourning shows be spread;
For Love is dead.
All Love is dead, infected
With plague of deep disdain:
Worth, as nought worth, rejected,
And Faith fair scorn doth gain.
From so ungrateful fancy,
From such a female franzy,
From them that use men thus,
Good Lord, deliver us!

Weep, neighbours, weep! do you not hear it said
That Love is dead?
His death-bed, peacock's folly;
His winding-sheet is shame;
His will, false-seeming holy;
His sole executor, blame.
From so ungrateful fancy,
From such a female franzy,
From them that use men thus,
Good Lord, deliver us!

Let dirge be sung and trentals rightly read,
    For Love is dead.
    Sir Wrong his tomb ordaineth
    My mistress' marble heart,
    Which epitaph containeth:
    'Her eyes were once his dart.'
    From so ungrateful fancy.
    From such a female franzy,
    From them that use men thus,
    Good Lord, deliver us !

Alas, I lie ! rage hath this error bred.
    Love is not dead.
    Love is not dead, but sleepeth
    In her unmatchèd mind,
    Where she his counsel keepeth
    Till due desert she find.
    Therefore from so vile fancy,
    To call such wit a franzy,
    Who Love can temper thus,
    Good Lord, deliver us !

Song

O FAIR ! O sweet ! when I do look on thee,
In whom all joys so well agree,
Heart and soul do sing in me.
This you hear is not my tongue,
Which once said what I conceivèd,
For it was of use bereavèd,
With a cruel answer stung.
No, though tongue to roof be cleavèd,
Fearing lest he chastised be,
Heart and soul do sing in me.

O fair ! O sweet ! when I do look on thee,
In whom all joys so well agree,
Heart and soul do sing in me.
Just accord all music makes:
In thee just accord excelleth.
Where each part in such peace dwelleth,
One of other, beauty takes.
Since, then, truth to all minds telleth
That in thee lives harmony,
Heart and soul do sing in me.

O fair! O sweet! when I do look on thee,
In whom all joys so well agree,
Heart and soul do sing in me.
They that heaven have known do say
That whoso that grace obtaineth
To see what fair sight there reigneth
Forcèd are to sing alway:
So, then, since that heaven remaineth
In thy face I plainly see,
Heart and soul do sing in me.

O fair! O sweet! when I do look on thee,
In whom all joys so well agree,
Heart and soul do sing in me.
Sweet, think not I am at ease,
For because my chief part singeth:
This song from death's sorrow springeth,
As to swan in last disease.
For no dumbness nor death bringeth
Stay to true love's melody:
Heart and soul do sing in me.

Like as the Dove

LIKE as the Dove, which seelèd up doth fly,
Is neither freed nor yet to service bound,
But hopes to gain some help by mounting high,
Till want of force do force her fall to ground,
Right so my mind, caught by his guiding eye,
And thence cast off, where his sweet hurt he found,
Hath neither leave to live nor doom to die,
Nor held in evil, nor suffered to be sound;
But with his wings of fancies up he goes,
To high conceits whose fruits are oft but small,
Till wounded, blind, and wearied, spirit lose
Both force to fly and knowledge where to fall.
O happy Dove, if she no bondage tried:
More happy I, might I in bondage bide!

Song

WHO hath his fancy pleasèd
With fruits of happy sight,
Let here his eyes be raisèd
On Nature's sweetest light:
A light which doth dissever
And yet unite the eyes,
A light which, dying never,
Is cause the looker dies.

She never dies, but lasteth
In life of lover's heart:
He ever dies that wasteth
In love his chiefest part.
Thus is her life still guarded
In never-dying faith:
Thus in his death rewarded,
Since she lives in his death.

Look, then, and die: the pleasure
Doth answer well the pain.
Small loss of mortal treasure,
Who may immortal gain.
Immortal be her graces,
Immortal is her mind:
They, fit for heavenly places,
This, heaven in it doth bind.

But eyes these beauties see not,
Nor sense that grace descries:
Yet eyes deprivèd be not
From sight of her fair eyes,
Which, as of inward glory
They are the outward seal,
So may they live still sorry,
Which die not in that weal.

But who hath fancies pleasèd
With fruits of happy sight,
Let here his eyes be raisèd
On Nature's sweetest light.

Song

NO, no, no, no, I cannot hate my foe,
    Although with cruel fire
    First thrown on my desire
She sacks my rendered sprite:
For so fair a flame embraces
    All the places
Where that heat of all heats springeth,
    That it bringeth
To my dying heart some pleasure,
    Since his treasure
Burneth bright in fairest light.
    No, no, no, no.

No, no, no, no, I cannot hate my foe,
    Although with cruel fire
    First thrown on my desire
She sacks my rendered sprite:
Since our lives be not immortal,
    But to mortal
Fetters tied, to wait the hour
    Of death's power,
They have no cause to be sorry,
    Who with glory
End the way, where all men stay.
    No, no, no, no.

No, no, no, no, I cannot hate my foe,
    Although with cruel fire
    First thrown on my desire
She sacks my rendered sprite:
No man doubts, whom beauty killeth
    Fair death feeleth,
And in whom fair death proceedeth
    Glory breedeth:
So that I, in her beams dying,
    Glory trying,
Though in pain cannot complain.
    No, no, no, no.

Desire

THOU blind man's mark, thou fool's self-chosen snare,
Fond fancy's scum, and dregs of scattered thought;
Band of all evils, cradle of causeless care;
Thou web of will, whose end is never wrought:
Desire! Desire! I have too dearly bought,
With price of mangled mind, thy worthless ware;
Too long, too long, asleep thou hast me brought,
Who shouldst my mind to higher things prepare.
But yet in vain thou hast my ruin sought,
In vain thou mad'st me to vain things aspire,
In vain thou kindlest all thy smoky fire,
For Virtue hath this better lesson taught:
Within myself to seek my only hire,
Desiring nought but how to kill Desire.

Splendidis longum valedico nugis [1]

LEAVE me, O love which reachest but to dust,
And thou, my mind, aspire to higher things.
Grow rich in that which never taketh rust:
Whatever fades but fading pleasure brings.
Draw in thy beams, and humble all thy might
To that sweet yoke where lasting freedoms be;
Which breaks the clouds and opens forth the light
That doth both shine and give us sight to see.
O take fast hold; let that light be thy guide
In this small course which birth draws out to death,
And think how evil becometh him to slide
Who seeketh heaven and comes of heavenly breath.
Then farewell, world! thy uttermost I see:
Eternal Love, maintain thy life in me.

[1] See Notes

SIR WALTER RALEGH

1552–1618

THE poems of Ralegh were 'first collected and authenticated' by Archdeacon Hannah, in 1845, and by the same editor reprinted with additional pieces (including the then newly discovered MS of the fragment *Cynthia*) in 1870. Earlier collections, uncritical and haphazard, contained much that we now know to be by other hands. Ralegh's apparent indifference to the fate of his poems, coupled with the textual liberties habitually taken by Elizabethan anthologists (in whose volumes most of them first saw the light), has left us with insoluble problems of text and authorship. It is broadly true to say that each poem has as many versions as sources; and therefore, except in rare instances where one source has clear priority over others, a present-day editor is free—or rather, is forced—to take his choice among variant readings. This Everyman text, while based broadly on Hannah, is the result of such choice. All the poems have been re-punctuated. Readers who want a catalogue of the numerous variant readings, or who care to examine the pros and cons of this ascription or that, are referred to Agnes M. C. Latham's *Poems of Sir Walter Ralegh* (Constable, 1929). The present volume contains all finished (and some unfinished) poems known to have been written by Ralegh, and, with one exception, the best of those others that are plausibly but less confidently attributed to him. The exception is the famous ballad: *As ye came from the holy land*. It is one of the most beautiful of all English poems; but in some form or another it certainly existed before Ralegh arrived on the scene; Ralegh's connexion with it is largely a matter of conjecture; and it is too well known to need reprinting here for its own sake.

In Commendation of George Gascoigne's Steel Glass (1576)

SWEET were the sauce would please each kind of taste;
The life likewise were pure that never swerved:
For spiteful tongues in canker'd stomachs placed
Deem worst of things which best (percase) deserved.
But what for that? This medicine may suffice
To scorn the rest, and seek to please the wise.

Though sundry minds in sundry sort do deem,
Yet worthiest wights yield praise for every pain;
But envious brains do nought, or light, esteem
Such stately steps as they cannot attain:
For whoso reaps renown above the rest,
With heaps of hate shall surely be opprest.

Wherefore, to write my censure of this book,
This Glass of Steel unpartially doth show
Abuses all to such as in it look,
From prince to poor, from high estate to low.
As for the verse, who list like trade to try,
I fear me much, shall hardly reach so high.

The Excuse

CALLING to mind, my *eyes* went long about
To cause my heart for to forsake my breast,
All in a rage I sought to pull them out,
As who had been such traitors to my rest:
What could they say to win again my grace?—
Forsooth, that they had seen my mistress' face.

Another time, my *heart* I called to mind,
Thinking that he this woe on me had wrought.
Because he had his fort to Love resign'd,
When of such wars my fancy never thought:
What could he say when I would him have slain?—
That he was hers, and had forgone my chain.

At last, when I perceived both eyes and heart
Excuse themselves, as guiltless of my ill,
I found *myself* the cause of all my smart,
And told myself that I myself would kill:
Yet when I saw myself to you was true,
I loved myself, because myself loved you.

Epitaph on Sir Philip Sidney

TO praise thy life or wail thy worthy death,
And want thy wit—thy wit high, pure, divine—
Is far beyond the power of mortal line,
Nor any one hath worth that draweth breath;

Yet rich in zeal (though poor in learning's lore),
And friendly care obscured in secret breast,
And love that envy in thy life supprest—
Thy dear life done—and death hath doubled more.

And I, that in thy time and living state
Did only praise thy virtues in my thought,
As one that seeld the rising sun hath sought,
With words and tears now wail thy timeless fate.

Drawn was thy race aright from princely line;
Nor less than such, by gifts that nature gave—
The common mother that all creatures have—
Doth virtue show, and princely lineage shine.

A king gave thee thy name; a kingly mind,
That God thee gave, who found it now too dear
For this base world, and hath resumed it near,
To sit in skies, and sort with powers divine.

Kent thy birth-days, and Oxford held thy youth;
The heavens made haste, and stay'd nor years nor time;
The fruits of age grew ripe in thy first prime;
Thy will, thy words; thy words the seals of truth.

Great gifts and wisdom rare employ'd thee thence,
To treat from kings with those more great than kings;
Such hope men had to lay the highest things
On thy wise youth, to be transported hence.

Whence to sharp wars sweet honour did thee call,
Thy country's love, religion, and thy friends;
Of worthy men the marks, the lives, and ends,
And her defence for whom we labour all.

There didst thou vanquish shame and tedious age,
Grief, sorrow, sickness, and base fortune's might;
Thy rising day saw never woeful night,
But pass'd with praise from off this worldly stage.

Back to the camp by thee that day was brought,
First thine own death; and after, thy long fame;
Tears to the soldiers; the proud Castilian's shame;
Virtue exprest, and honour truly taught.

What hath he lost that such great grace hath won?
Young years for endless years, and hope ensure
Of fortune's gifts for wealth that still shall dure:
O happy race, with so great praises run!

England doth hold thy limbs, that bred the same;
Flanders thy valour, where it last was tried;
The camp thy sorrow, where thy body died;
Thy friends thy want; the world thy virtue's fame;

Nations thy wit; our minds lay up thy love;
Letters thy learning; thy loss years long to come;
In worthy hearts sorrow hath made thy tomb;
Thy soul and spright enrich the heavens above.

Thy liberal heart embalm'd in grateful tears,
Young sighs, sweet sighs, sage sighs, bewail thy fall;
Envy her sting, and spite hath left her gall;
Malice herself a mourning garment wears.

That day their Hannibal died, our Scipio fell:
Scipio, Cicero, and Petrarch of our time,
Whose virtues, wounded by my worthless rhyme,
Let angels speak, and heaven thy praises tell.

Of Spenser's Faery Queen

METHOUGHT I saw the grave where Laura lay,
Within that temple where the vestal flame
Was wont to burn: and, passing by that way,
To see that buried dust of living fame,
Whose tomb fair Love and fairer Virtue kept,
All suddenly I saw the Fairy Queen,
At whose approach the soul of Petrarch wept;
And from thenceforth those graces were not seen,
For they this Queen attended; in whose stead
Oblivion laid him down on Laura's hearse.
Hereat the hardest stones were seen to bleed,
And groans of buried ghosts the heavens did pierce:
Where Homer's spright did tremble all for grief,
And curst the access of that celestial thief.

Another of the Same

THE praise of meaner wits this work like profit brings,
As doth the cuckoo's song delight when Philumena sings.
If thou hast formèd right true Virtue's face herein,
Virtue herself can best discern to whom they written bin.
If thou hast beauty praised, let her sole looks divine
Judge if aught therein be amiss, and mend it by her eyne.
If Chastity want aught, or Temperance her due,
Behold her princely mind aright, and write thy Queen anew.
Meanwhile she shall perceive how far her virtues soar
Above the reach of all that live, or such as wrote of yore:
And thereby will excuse and favour thy good will,
Whose virtue cannot be express'd but by an angel's quill.
Of me no lines are loved nor letters are of price,
Of all which speak our English tongue, but those of thy device.

The Nymphs Reply to the Passionate Shepherd

I. The Shepherd's Plea

[BY CHRISTOPHER MARLOWE]

COME live with me, and be my love,
And we will all the pleasures prove
That hills and valleys, dales and fields,
Woods, or steepy mountain yields.

And we will sit upon the rocks,
And see the shepherds feed their flocks
By shallow rivers, to whose falls
Melodious birds sing madrigals.

And I will make thee beds of roses,
And a thousand fragrant posies;
A cap of flowers, and a kirtle
Embroider'd all with leaves of myrtle;

A gown made of the finest wool
Which from our pretty lambs we pull;
Fair-linèd slippers for the cold,
With buckles of the purest gold;

A belt of straw and ivy-buds,
With coral clasps and amber-studs:
And if these pleasures may thee move,
Come live with me, and be my love.

The shepherd-swains shall dance and sing
For thy delight each May-morning;
If these delights thy mind may move,
Then live with me, and be my love.

II. The Nymph's Reply

[BY SIR WALTER RALEGH]

IF all the world and love were young,
And truth in every shepherd's tongue,
These pretty pleasures might me move
To live with thee and be thy love.

But Time drives flocks from field to fold,
When rivers rage and rocks grow cold;
And Philomel becometh dumb;
The rest complains of cares to come.

The flowers do fade, and wanton fields
To wayward Winter reckoning yields:
A honey tongue, a heart of gall,
Is fancy's spring, but sorrow's fall.

Thy gowns, thy shoes, thy beds of roses,
Thy cap, thy kirtle, and thy posies,
Soon break, soon wither, soon forgotten
In folly ripe, in reason rotten.

Thy belt of straw and ivy buds,
Thy coral clasps and amber studs—
All those in me no means can move
To come to thee and be thy love.

But could youth last, and love still breed;
Had joys no date, nor age no need;
Then those delights my mind might move
To live with thee and be thy love.

Like Hermit Poor

LIKE to a hermit poor, in place obscure
I mean to spend my days of endless doubt,
To wail such woes as time cannot recure,
Where none but Love shall ever find me out.

My food shall be of care and sorrow made;
My drink nought else but tears fall'n from mine eyes;
And for my light, in such obscurèd shade,
The flames shall serve which from my heart arise.

A gown of grief my body shall attire,
And broken hope shall be my strength and stay;
And late repentance, linkt with long desire,
Shall be the couch whereon my limbs I 'll lay.

And at my gate Despair shall linger still,
To let in Death when Love and Fortune will.

Farewell to the Court

LIKE truthless dreams, are so my joys expired,
And past return are all my dandled days,
My love misled, and fancy quite retired:
Of all which past, the sorrow only stays.

My lost delights, now clean from sight of land,
Have left me all alone in unknown ways,
My mind to woe, my life in Fortune's hand:
Of all which past, the sorrow only stays.

As in a country strange without companion,
I only wail the wrong of death's delays,
Whose sweet spring spent, whose summer well nigh done;
Of all which past, the sorrow only stays:

Whom care forewarns, ere age and winter cold,
To haste me hence to find my fortune's fold.

The Advice

MANY desire, but few or none deserve,
To win the fort of thy most constant will:
Therefore take heed, let fancy never swerve
But unto him that will defend thee still.
For this be sure, the fort of fame once won,
Farewell the rest, thy happy days are done!

Many desire, but few or none deserve,
To pluck the flowers, and let the leaves to fall:
Therefore take heed, let fancy never swerve
But unto him that will take leaves and all.
For this be sure, the flower once pluckt away,
Farewell the rest, thy happy days decay!

Many desire, but few or none deserve,
To cut the corn, not subject to the sickle:
Therefore take heed, let fancy never swerve.
But constant stand, for mowers' minds are fickle.
For this be sure, the crop being once obtain'd,
Farewell the rest, the soil will be disdain'd.

False Love

FAREWELL, false Love, the oracle of lies!
A mortal foe and enemy to rest,
An envious boy, from whom all cares arise,
A bastard vile, a beast with rage possest,
A way of error, a temple full of treason,
In all effects contrary unto reason:

A poison'd serpent covered all with flowers,
Mother of sighs and murtherer of repose,
A sea of sorrows from whence are drawn such showers
As moisture lend to every grief that grows,
A school of guile, a net of deep deceit,
A gilded hook that holds a poison'd bait:

A fortress foil'd which reason did defend,
A siren song, a fever of the mind,
A maze wherein affection finds no end,
A ranging cloud that runs before the wind,
A substance like the shadow of the sun,
A goal of grief for which the wisest run:

A quenchless fire, a nurse of trembling fear,
A path that leads to peril and mishap,
A true retreat of sorrow and despair,
An idle boy that sleeps in pleasure's lap,
A deep mistrust of that which certain seems,
A hope of that which reason doubtful deems:

Sith, then, thy trains my younger years betray'd
And for my faith ingratitude I find,
And sith repentance hath my wrongs bewray'd
Whose course was ever contrary to kind,
False love, Desire, and Beauty frail, adieu!
Dead is the root whence all these fancies grew.

The Wood, the Weed, the Wag

THREE things there be that prosper all apace
And flourish, while they grow asunder far;
But on a day, they meet all in a place,
And when they meet they one another mar.

And they be these: the Wood, the Weed, the Wag.
The Wood is that that makes the gallows tree;
The Weed is that that strings the hangman's bag;
The Wag, my pretty knave, betokens thee.

Now mark, dear boy—while these assemble not,
Green springs the tree, hemp grows, the wag is wild;
But when they meet, it makes the timber rot,
It frets the halter, and it chokes the child.

Then bless thee, and beware, and let us pray
We part not with thee at this meeting-day.

A Prognostication upon Cards and Dice

BEFORE the sixth day of the next new year,
Strange wonders in this kingdom shall appear.
Four kings shall be assembled in this isle,
Where they shall keep great tumult for awhile.
Many men then shall have an end of crosses,
And many likewise shall sustain great losses.
Many that now full joyful are and glad
Shall at that time be sorrowful and sad.
Full many a Christian's heart shall quake for fear,
The dreadful sound of trump when he shall hear.
Dead bones shall then be tumbled up and down
In every city and in every town.
By day or night this tumult shall not cease,
Until an herald shall proclaim a peace:
An herald strange, the like was never born,
Whose very beard is flesh and mouth is horn.

Epitaph on the Earl of Leicester

HERE lies the noble Warrior that never blunted sword;
Here lies the noble Courtier that never kept his word;
Here lies his Excellency that govern'd all the state;
Here lies the Lord of Leicester that all the world did hate.

A Poem put into my Lady Laiton's Pocket

LADY, farewell, whom I in silence serve!
Would God thou knewest the depth of my desire:
Then mought I wish, though nought I can deserve,
Some drops of grace to slake my scalding fire.
But sith to live alone I have decreed,
I'll spare to speak, that I may spare to speed.

On the Snuff of a Candle

COWARDS fear to die: but Courage stout,
Rather than live in snuff, will be put out.

To His Mistress

OUR passions are most like to floods and streams:
The shallow murmur, but the deep are dumb.
So, when affections yield discourse, it seems
The bottom is but shallow whence they come.
They that are rich in words must needs discover
That they are poor in that which makes a lover.

Wrong not, dear empress of my heart,
The merit of true passion,
With thinking that he feels no smart
That sues for no compassion;
Since, if my plaints serve not to prove
The conquest of your beauty,
It comes not from defect of love,
But from excess of duty.

For, knowing that I sue to serve
A saint of such perfection,
As all desire, but none deserve,
A place in her affection,
I rather choose to want relief
Then venture the revealing;
Where glory recommends the grief,
Despair distrusts the healing.

Thus those desires that aim too high
For any mortal lover,
When reason cannot make them die,
Discretion will them cover.
Yet, when discretion doth bereave
The plaints that they should utter,
Then your discretion may perceive
That silence is a suitor.

Silence in love bewrays more woe
Than words, though ne'er so witty:
A beggar that is dumb, you know,
Deserveth double pity.
Then misconceive not, dearest heart,
My true though secret passion:
He smarteth most that hides his smart
And sues for no compassion.

Love and Time

NATURE, that washt her hands in milk
And had forgot to dry them,
Instead of earth took snow and silk
At Love's request, to try them
If she a mistress could compose
To please Love's fancy out of those.

Her eyes he would should be of light,
A violet breath, and lips of jelly,
Her hair not black nor over-bright,
And of the softest down her belly:
As for her inside, he 'ld have it
Only of wantonness and wit.

At Love's entreaty, such a one
Nature made, but with her beauty
She hath framed a heart of stone,
So as Love, by ill destiny,
Must die for her whom Nature gave him,
Because her darling would not save him.

But Time, which Nature doth despise,
And rudely gives her love the lie,
Makes Hope a fool and Sorrow wise,
His hands doth neither wash nor dry,
But, being made of steel and rust,
Turns snow and silk and milk to dust.

The light, the belly, lips and breath,
He dims, discolours, and destroys,
With those he feeds (but fills not) Death
Which sometimes were the food of Joys:
Yea, Time doth dull each lively wit,
And dries all wantonness with it.

O cruel Time, which takes in trust
Our youth, our joys, and all we have,
And pays us but with age and dust;
Who in the dark and silent grave,
When we have wandered all our ways,
Shuts up the story of our days.

Conceit begotten by the Eyes

CONCEIT begotten by the eyes
Is quickly born and quickly dies;
For while it seeks our hearts to have,
Meanwhile, there reason makes his grave;
For many things the eyes approve,
Which yet the heart doth seldom love.

For as the seeds in springtime sown
Die in the ground ere they be grown,
Such is conceit, whose rooting fails,
As child that in the cradle quails,
Or else within the mother's womb
Hath his beginning and his tomb.

Affection follows Fortune's wheels,
And soon is shaken from her heels;
For, following beauty or estate,
Her liking still is turn'd to hate;
For all affections have their change,
And fancy only loves to range.

Desire himself runs out of breath,
And, getting, doth but gain his death:
Desire nor reason hath nor rest,
And, blind, doth seldom choose the best:
Desire attain'd is not desire,
But as the cinders of the fire.

As ships in ports desired are drown'd,
As fruit, once ripe, then falls to ground,
As flies that seek for flames are brought
To cinders by the flames they sought:
So fond desire when it attains,
The life expires, the woe remains.

And yet some poets fain would prove
Affection to be perfect love;
And that desire is of that kind,
No less a passion of the mind;
As if wild beasts and men did seek
To like, to love, to choose alike.

The Lie

GO, Soul, the body's guest,
Upon a thankless arrant:
Fear not to touch the best;
The truth shall be thy watrant:
Go, since I needs must die,
And give the world the lie.

Say to the court, it glows
And shines like rotten wood;
Say to the church, it shows
What 's good, and doth no good:
If church and court reply,
Then give them both the lie.

Tell potentates, they live
Acting by others' action;
Not loved unless they give,
Not strong but by a faction:
If potentates reply,
Give potentates the lie.

Tell men of high condition,
That manage the estate,
Their purpose is ambition,
Their practice only hate:
And if they once reply,
Then give them all the lie.

Tell them that brave it most,
They beg for more by spending,
Who, in their greatest cost,
Seek nothing but commending:
And if they make reply,
Then give them all the lie.

Tell zeal it wants devotion;
Tell love it is but lust:
Tell time it is but motion;
Tell flesh it is but dust:
And wish them not reply,
For thou must give the lie.

Tell age it daily wasteth;
Tell honour how it alters;
Tell beauty how she blasteth;
Tell favour how it falters:
And as they shall reply,
Give every one the lie.

Tell wit how much it wrangles
In tickle points of niceness;
Tell wisdom she entangles
Herself in over-wiseness:
And when they do reply,
Straight give them both the lie.

Tell physic of her boldness;
Tell skill it is pretension;
Tell charity of coldness;
Tell law it is contention:
And as they do reply,
So give them still the lie.

Tell fortune of her blindness;
Tell nature of decay;
Tell friendship of unkindness;
Tell justice of delay:
And if they will reply,
Then give them all the lie.

Tell arts they have no soundness,
But vary by esteeming;
Tell schools they want profoundness,
And stand too much on seeming:
If arts and schools reply,
Give arts and schools the lie.

Tell faith it 's fled the city;
Tell how the country erreth;
Tell manhood shakes off pity
And virtue least preferreth:
And if they do reply,
Spare not to give the lie.

So when thou hast, as I
Commanded thee, done blabbing
—Although to give the lie
Deserves no less than stabbing—
Stab at thee he that will,
No stab the soul can kill.

The Pilgrimage

GIVE me my scallop-shell of quiet,
My staff of faith to walk upon,
My scrip of joy, immortal diet,
My bottle of salvation,
My gown of glory, hope's true gage;
And thus I 'll take my pilgrimage.

Blood must be my body's balmer;
No other balm will there be given;
Whilst my soul, like a white palmer,
Travels to the land of heaven;
Over the silver mountains,
Where spring the nectar fountains:
      There will I kiss
      The bowl of bliss;
And drink mine everlasting fill
On every milken hill.
My soul will be a-dry before;
But, after, it will thirst no more.

Then by that happy blissful day,
More peaceful pilgrims I shall see,
That have cast off their rags of clay,
And walk apparelled fresh like me.
      I 'll take them first
      To quench their thirst
And taste of nectar suckets,
      At those clear wells
      Where sweetness dwells,
Drawn up by saints in crystal buckets.

And when our bottles and all we
Are filled with immortality,
Then the blessed paths we 'll travel,
Strowed with rubies thick as gravel;
Ceilings of diamonds, sapphire floors,
High walls of coral and pearly bowers.
From thence to heaven's bribeless hall,
Where no corrupted voices brawl;
No conscience molten into gold,
No forged accuser bought or sold,
No cause deferred, no vain-spent journey,
For there Christ is the King's Attorney,
Who pleads for all without degrees,
And He hath angels, but no fees.
And when the grand twelve-million jury
Of our sins, with direful fury,
Against our souls black verdicts give,
Christ pleads His death, and then we live.

Be Thou my speaker, taintless pleader,
Unblotted lawyer, true proceeder!
Thou givest salvation even for alms;
Not with a bribèd lawyer's palms.

And this is mine eternal plea
To Him that made heaven, earth, and sea,
That, since my flesh must die so soon,
And want a head to dine next noon,
Just at the stroke, when my veins start and spread,
Set on my soul an everlasting head!
Then am I ready, like a palmer fit,
To tread those blest paths which before I writ.

What is our life?

WHAT is our life?　A play of passion.
And what our mirth but music of division?
Our mother's wombs the tiring-houses be
Where we are drest for this short comedy.
Heaven the judicious sharp spectator is
Who sits and marks what here we do amiss.
The graves that hide us from the searching sun
Are like drawn curtains when the play is done.
Thus playing post we to our latest rest,
And then we die, in earnest, not in jest.

To the Translator of Lucan's Pharsalia (1614)

HAD Lucan hid the truth to please the time,
He had been too unworthy of thy pen,
Who never sought nor ever cared to climb
By flattery, or seeking worthless men.
For this thou hast been bruis'd; but yet those scars
Do beautify no less than those wounds do
Receiv'd in just and in religious wars;
Though thou hast bled by both, and bear'st them too.
Change not!　To change thy fortune 'tis too late:
Who with a manly faith resolves to die
May promise to himself a lasting state,
Though not so great, yet free from infamy.
Such was thy Lucan, whom so to translate,
Nature thy muse like Lucan's did create.

Sweet Unsure

SWEET were the joys that both might like and last;
Strange were the state exempt from all distress;
Happy the life that no mishap should taste;
Blessed the chance might never change success.
Were such a life to lead or state to prove,
Who would not wish that such a life were love?

But O the soury sauce of sweet unsure,
When pleasures flit, and fly with waste of wind;
The trustless trains that hoping hearts allure,
When sweet delights do but allure the mind;
When care consumes and wastes the wretched wight,
While fancy feeds and draws of her delight.

What life were love, if love were free from pain?
But O that pain with pleasure matcht should meet!
Why did the course of nature so ordain
That sugared sour must sauce the bitter sweet?
Which sour from sweet might any means remove,
What hap, what heaven, what life, were like to love?

The Shepherd's Praise of Diana

PRAISED be Diana's fair and harmless light;
Praised be the dews wherewith she moists the ground;
Praised be her beams, the glory of the night;
Praised be her power, by which all powers abound.

Praised be her nymphs, with whom she decks the woods;
Praised be her knights, in whom true honour lives;
Praised be that force, by which she moves the floods;
Let that Diana shine which all these gives.

In heaven queen she is among the spheres;
She mistress-like makes all things to be pure;
Eternity in her oft change she bears;
She beauty is; by her the fair endure.

Time wears her not; she doth his chariot guide;
Mortality below her orb is placed;
By her the virtues of the stars down slide;
In her is virtue's perfect image cast.

A knowledge pure it is her worth to know:
With Circes let them dwell that think not so.

If Cynthia be a Queen

IF Cynthia be a Queen, a princess, and supreme,
Keep these among the rest, or say it was a dream;
For those that like, expound, and those that loathe, express
Meanings according as their minds are movèd more or less.
For writing what thou art, or showing what thou were,
Adds to the one disdain, to the other but despair.
Thy mind of neither needs, in both seeing it exceeds.

My Body in the Walls captived

MY body in the walls captivèd
Feels not the wounds of spiteful envy;
But my thrall'd mind, of liberty deprivèd,
Fast fetter'd in her ancient memory.
Doth nought behold but sorrow's dying face;
Such prison erst was so delightful
As it desired no other dwelling place,
But time's effects and destinies despiteful
Have changèd both my keeper and my fare.
Love's fire and beauty's light I then had store;
But now, close kept, as captives wonted are,
That food, that heat, that light, I find no more.

Despair bolts up my doors, and I alone
Speak to dead walls: but those hear not my moan.

THE OCEAN'S LOVE TO CYNTHIA

SUFFICETH it to you, my joys interred,
In simple words that I my woes complain,
You that then died when first my fancy erred,
Joys under dust.that never live again?

If to the living were my muse addressed
Or did my mind her own spirit still inhold,
Were not my living passion so repressed
As to the dead the dead did these unfold,

Some sweeter words, some more becoming verse
Should witness my mishap in higher kind;
But my love's wounds, my fancy in the hearse,
The idea but resting of a wasted mind,

The blossoms fallen, the sap gone from the tree,
The broken monuments of my great desires—
From these so lost what may the affections be?
What heat in cinders of extinguisht fires?

Lost in the mud of those high-flowing streams
Which through more fairer fields their courses bend,
Slain with self-thoughts, amazed in fearful dreams,
Woes without date, discomforts without end:

From fruitful trees I gather withered leaves
And glean the broken ears with miser's hands:
Who sometime did enjoy the weighty sheaves
I seek fair flowers amid the brinish sand.

All in the shade, even in the fair sun days,
Under those healthless trees I sit alone,
Where joyful birds sing neither lovely lays,
Nor Philomel recounts her direful moan.

No feeding flocks, no shepherd's company
That might renew my dolorous conceit,
While happy then, while love and fantasy
Confined my thoughts on that fair flock to wait;

No pleasing streams fast to the ocean wending,
The messengers sometimes of my great woe,
But all on earth, as from the cold storms bending,
Shrink from my thoughts in high heavens and below.

O hopeful love my object and invention!
O true desire the spur of my conceit!
O worthiest spirit, my mind's impulsion!
O eyes transpersant, my affection's bait!

O princely form, my fancy's adamant!
Divine conceit, my painès acceptance!
O all in one, O heaven on earth transparent!
The seat of joys and lovès abundance!

Out of that mass of miracles, my muse
Gathered those flowers, to her pure senses pleasing;
Out of her eyes, the store of joys, did choose
Equal delights, my sorrow's counterpeising.

Her regal looks my vigorous sighs suppressed;
Small drops of joys sweeten'd great worlds of woes;
One gladsome day a thousand cares redressed;
Whom love defends, what fortune overthrows?

When she did well, what did there else amiss?
When she did ill, what empires could have pleased?
No other power effecting woe or bliss,
She gave, she took, she wounded, she appeased.

The honour of her love love still devising,
Wounding my mind with contrary conceit,
Transferr'd itself sometime to her aspiring,
Sometime the trumpet of her thought's retreat.

To seek new worlds for gold, for praise, for glory,
To try desire, to try love sever'd far,
When I was gone, she sent her memory,
More strong than were ten thousand ships of war,

To call me back, to leave great honour's thought,
To leave my friends, my fortune, my attempt,
To leave the purpose I so long had sought,
And hold both cares and comforts in contempt.

Such heat in ice, such fire in frost remained,
Such trust in doubt, such comfort in despair,
Which, like the gentle lamb, though lately weaned,
Plays with the dug, though finds no comfort there.

But as a body violently slain
Retaineth warmth although the sprite be gone,
And by a power in nature moves again
Till it be laid below the fatal stone;

Or as the earth, even in cold winter days,
Left for a time by her life-giving sun,
Doth by the power remaining of his rays
Produce some green, though not as it hath done;

Or as a wheel, forced by the falling stream,
Although the course be turn'd some other way,
Doth for a time go round upon the beam,
Till, wanting strength to move, it stands at stay:

So my forsaken heart, my withered mind,
Widow of all the joys it once possest,
My hopes clean out of sight with forcèd wind,
To kingdoms strange, to lands far-off addrest,

Alone, forsaken, friendless, on the shore
With many wounds, with death's cold pangs embraced,
Writes in the dust, as one that could no more,
Whom love, and time, and fortune, had defaced;

Of things so great, so long, so manifold,
With means so weak, the soul even then depicting
The weal, the woe, the passages of old,
And worlds of thoughts describ'd by one last sighing.

As if, when after Phoebus is descended,
And leaves a light much like the past day's dawning,
And, every toil and labour wholly ended,
Each living creature draweth to his resting,

We should begin by such a parting light
To write the story of all ages past,
And end the same before the approaching night.

Such is again the labour of my mind,
Whose shroud, by sorrow woven now to end,
Hath seen that ever shining sun declin'd,
So many years that so could not descend,

But that the eyes of my mind held her beams
In every part transferr'd by love's swift thought;
Far off or near, in waking or in dreams,
Imagination strong their lustre brought.

Such force her angelic appearance had
To master distance, time, or cruelty;
Such art to grieve, and after to make glad;
Such fear in love, such love in majesty.

My weary limbs her memory embalmed;
My darkest ways her eyes make clear as day.
What storms so great but Cynthia's beams appeased?
What rage so fierce, that love could not allay?

Twelve years entire I wasted in this war;
Twelve years of my most happy younger days;
But I in them, and they, now wasted are:
'Of all which past, the sorrow only stays'—

So wrote I once, and my mishap foretold,
My mind still feeling sorrowful success,
Even as before a storm the marble cold
Doth by moist tears tempestuous times express.

So felt my heavy mind my harms at hand,
Which my vain thought in vain sought to recure:
At middle day my sun seemed under land,
When any little cloud did it obscure.

And as the icicles in a winter's day
Whenas the sun shines with unwonted warm

*   *   *   *   *

So did my joys melt into secret tears;
So did my heart dissolve in wasting drops:
And as the season of the year outwears,
And heaps of snow from off the mountain tops

With sudden streams the valleys overflow,
So did the time draw on my more despair:
Then floods of sorrow and whole seas of woe
The banks of all my hope did overbear

And drown'd my mind in depths of misery:
Sometime I died; sometime I was distract,
My soul the stage of fancy's tragedy;
Then furious màdness, where true reason lackt,

Wrote what it would, and scourged mine own conceit.
Oh, heavy heart! who can thee witness bear?
What tongue, what pen, could thy tormenting treat,
But thine own mourning thoughts which present were?

What stranger mind believe the meanest part?
What altered sense conceive the weakest woe,
That tare, that rent, that piercèd thy sad heart?

And as a man distract, with triple might
Bound in strong chains doth strive and rage in vain,
Till tired and breathless he is forced to rest,
Finds by contention but increase of pain,
And fiery heat inflam'd in swollen breast:

So did my mind in change of passion
From woe to wrath, from wrath return to woe,
Struggling in vain from love's subjection;

Therefore, all lifeless and all helpless bound,
My fainting spirits sunk, and heart appaled,
My joys and hopes lay bleeding on the ground,
That not long since the highest heaven scaled.

I hated life and cursèd destiny;
The thoughts of passèd times, like flames of hell,
Kindled afresh within my memory
The many dear achievements that befell

In those prime years and infancy of love,
Which to describe were but to die in writing;
Ah, those I sought, but vainly, to remove,
And vainly shall, by which I perish living.

And though strong reason hold before mine eyes
The images and forms of worlds past,
Teaching the cause why all those flames that rise
From forms external can no longer last

Than that those seeming beauties hold in prime
Love's ground, his essence, and his empery,
All slaves to age, and vassals unto time,
Of which repentance writes the tragedy:

But this my heart's desire could not conceive,
Whose love outflew the fastest flying time,
A beauty that can easily deceive
The arrest of years, and creeping age outclimb.

A spring of beauties which time ripeth not—
Time that but works on frail mortality;
A sweetness which woe's wrongs outwipeth not
Whom love hath chose for his divinity;

A vestal fire that burns but never wasteth,
That loseth nought by giving light to all,
That endless shines each where, and endless lasteth,
Blossoms of pride that can nor fade nor fall;

These were those marvellous perfections,
The parents of my sorrow and my envy,
Most deathful and most violent infections;
These be the tyrants that in fetters tie

Their wounded vassals, yet nor kill nor cure,
But glory in their lasting misery—
That, as her beauties would, our woes should dure—
These be the effects of powerful empery.

Yet have these wounders want, which want compassion;
Yet hath her mind some marks of human race;
Yet will she be a woman for a fashion,
So doth she please her virtues to deface.

And like as that immortal power doth seat
An element of waters, to allay
The fiery sunbeams that on earth do beat,
And temper by cold night the heat of day,

So hath perfection, which begat her mind,
Added thereto a change of fantasy,
And left her the affections of her kind,
Yet free from every evil but cruelty.

But leave her praise; speak thou of naught but woe;
Write on the tale that sorrow bids thee tell;
Strive to forget, and care no more to know
Thy cares are known, by knowing those too well.

Describe her now as she appears to thee;
Not as she did appear in days fordone:
In love, those things that were no more may be
For fancy seldom ends where it begun.

And as a stream, by strong hand bounded in
From nature's course where it did sometime run,
By some small rent or loose part doth begin
To find escape, till it a way hath won,

Doth then all unawares in sunder tear
The forcèd bounds, and, raging, run at large
In the ancient channels as they wonted were:
Such is of women's love the careful charge

Held and maintain'd with multitude of woes;
Of long erections such the sudden fall:
One hour diverts, one instant overthrows,
For which our lives, for which our fortune's thrall

So many years those joys have dearly bought;
Of which when our fond hopes do most assure,
All is dissolv'd; our labours come to nought
Nor any mark thereof there doth endure:

No more than when small drops of rain do fall
Upon the parchèd ground by heat updried;
No cooling moisture is perceiv'd at all,
Nor any show or sign of wet doth bide.

But as the fields, clothèd with leaves and flowers,
The banks of roses smelling precious sweet,
Have but their beauty's date and timely hours,
And then, defaced by winter's cold and sleet,

*   *   *   *   *

So far as neither fruit nor form of flower
Stays for a witness what such branches bare,
But as time gave, time did again devour,
And change our rising joy to falling care:

So of affection which our youth presented,
When she that from the sun reaves power and light
Did but decline her beams as discontented,
Converting sweetest days to saddest night,

All droops, all dies, all trodden under dust,
The person, place, and passages forgotten;
The hardest steel eaten with softest rust,
The firm and solid tree both rent and rotten.

Those thoughts, so full of pleasure and content,
That in our absence were affection's food,
Are razèd out and from the fancy rent;
In highest grace and heart's dear care that stood,

Are cast for prey to hatred and to scorn,
Our dearest treasures and our heart's true joys;
The tokens hung on breast and kindly worn
Are now elsewhere disposed or held for toys.

And those which then our jealousy removed,
And others for our sakes then valu'd dear,
The one forgot, the rest are dear beloved,
When all of ours doth strange or vild appear.

Those streams seem standing puddles, which before
We saw our beauties in, so were they clear;
Belphoebe's course is now observ'd no more;

That fair resemblance weareth out of date;
Our ocean seas are but tempestuous waves,
And all things base, that blessèd were of late . . .

And as a field wherein the stubble stands
Of harvest past the ploughman's eye offends,
He tills again, or tears them up with hands,
And throws to fire as foil'd and fruitless ends

And takes delight another seed to sow:
So doth the mind root up all wonted thought
And scorns the care of our remaining woes;
The sorrows which themselves for us have wrought

Are burnt to cinders by new kindled fires;
The ashes are disperst into the air;
The sighs, the groans of all our past desires
Are clean outworn, as things that never were.

With youth is dead the hope of love's return,
Who looks not back to hear our after-cries:
Where he is not, he laughs at those that mourn;
Whence he is gone, he scorns the mind that dies.

When he is absent, he believes no words;
When reason speaks, he careless stops his ears;
Whom he hath left, he never grace affords,
But bathes his wings in our lamenting tears.

Unlasting passion, soon outworn conceit
Whereon I built and on so dureless trust!
My mind had wounds, I dare not say deceit,
Where I resolv'd her promise was not just.

Sorrow was my revenge and woe my hate;
I powerless was to alter my desire;
My love is not of time or bound to date;
My heart's internal heat and living fire

Would not, or could, be quencht with sudden showers;
My bound respect was not confin'd to days;
My vowèd faith not set to ended hours;
I love the bearing and not bearing sprays

Which now to others do their sweetness send;
The incarnate, snow-driven white, and purest azure,
Who from high heaven doth on their fields descend,
Filling their barns with grain, and towers with treasure.

Erring or never erring, such is love
As, while it lasteth, scorns the account of those
Seeking but self-contentment to improve,
And hides, if any be, his inward woes,

And will not know, while he knows his own passion,
The often and unjust perseverance
In deeds of love and state, and every action
From that first day and year of their joy's entrance.

But I, unblessèd and ill-born creature,
That did embrace the dust her body bearing,
That loved her, both by fancy and by nature,
That drew, even with the milk in my first sucking,

Affection from the parent's breast that bare me,
Have found her as a stranger so severe,
Improving my mishap in each degree;
But love was gone: so would I my life were!

A queen she was to me—no more Belphoebe;
A lion then—no more a milk-white dove;
A prisoner in her breast I could not be:
She did untie the gentle chains of love.

    *   *   *   *   *

Love was no more the love of hiding . . .

All trespass and mischance for her own glory:
It had been such; it was still for the elect;
But I must be the example in love's story;
This was of all forepast the sad effect.

But thou, my weary soul and heavy thought,
Made by her love a burthen to my being,
Dost know my error never was forethought,
Or ever could proceed from sense of loving.

Of other cause if then it had proceeding,
I leave the excuse, sith judgment hath been given;
The limbs divided, sundered, and a-bleeding,
Cannot complain the sentence was uneven.

This did that nature's wonder, virtue's choice,
The only paragon of time's begetting,
Divine in words, angelical in voice,
That spring of joys, that flower of love's own setting.

The idea remaining of those golden ages,
That beauty, braving heavens and earth embalming,
Which after worthless worlds but play on stages,
Such didst thou her long since describe, yet sighing

That thy unable spirit could not find aught,
In heaven's beauties or in earth's delight,
For likeness fit to satisfy thy thought:
But what hath it avail'd thee so to write?

She cares not for thy praise, who knows not theirs;
It 's now an idle labour, and a tale
Told out of time, that dulls the hearer's ears;
A merchandise whereof there is no sale.

Leave them, or lay them up with thy despairs!
She hath resolv'd, and judg'd thee long ago.
Thy lines are now a murmuring to her ears,
Like to a falling stream which passing slow
Is wont to nourish sleep and quietness;

So shall thy painful labours be perused,
And draw on rest, which sometime had regard;
But those her cares thy errors have excused.
Thy days fordone have had their day's reward;

So her hard heart, so her estrangèd mind,
In which above the heavens I once reposed;
So to thy error have her ears inclin'd,

And have forgotten all thy past deserving,
Holding in mind but only thine offence;
And only now affecteth thy depraving,
And thinks all vain that pleadeth thy defence.

Yet greater fancy beauty never bred;
A more desire the heart-blood never nourisht;
Her sweetness an affection never fed,
Which more in any age hath ever flourisht.

The mind and virtue never have begotten
A firmer love, since love on earth had power;
A love obscured, but cannot be forgotten;
Too great and strong for Time's jaws to devour;

Containing such a faith as ages wound not,
Care, wakeful ever of her good estate,
Fear, dreading loss, which sighs and joys not,
A memory of the joys her grace begat;

A lasting gratefulness for those comforts past,
Of which the cordial sweetness cannot die:
These thoughts, knit up by faith, shall ever last;
These time assays, but never can untie,

Whose life once livèd in her pearl-like breast,
Whose joys were drawn but from her happiness,
Whose heart's high pleasure, and whose mind's true rest
Proceeded from her fortune's blessedness;

Who was intentive, wakeful, and dismay'd
In fears, in dreams, in feverous jealousy,
Who long in silence servèd and obey'd
With secret heart and hidden loyalty

Which never change to sad adversity,
Which never age, or nature's overthrow,
Which never sickness or deformity,
Which never wasting care or wearing woe
(If subject unto these she could have been),

Which never words or wits malicious,
Which never honour's bait, or world's fame,
Achievèd by attempts adventurous,
Or aught beneath the sun or heaven's frame

Can so dissolve, dissever, or destroy
The essential love of no frail parts compounded,
Though of the same now buried be the joy,
The hope, the comfort, and the sweetness ended,

But that the thoughts and memories of these
Work a relapse of passion, and remain
Of my sad heart the sorrow-sucking bees;
The wrongs receiv'd, the scorns persuade in vain.

And though these medicines work desire to end,
And are in others the true cure of liking,
The salves that heal love's wounds, and do amend
Consuming woe, and slake our hearty sighing,

They work not so in thy mind's long decease;
External fancy time alone recureth:
All whose effects do wear away with ease
Love of delight, while such delight endureth;
Stays by the pleasure, but no longer stays . . .

But in my mind so is her love enclosèd,
And is thereof not only the best part,
But into it the essence is disposèd:
Oh love! (the more my woe) to it thou art

Even as the moisture in each plant that grows;
Even as the sun unto the frozen ground;
Even as the sweetness to the incarnate rose;
Even as the centre in each perfect round:

As water to the fish, to men as air,
As heat to fire, as light unto the sun;
O love, it is but vain to say thou were!
Ages and times cannot thy power outrun.

Thou art the soul of that unhappy mind
Which, being by nature made an idle thought,
Began even then to take immortal kind,
When first her virtues in thy spirits wrought.

From thee therefore that mover cannot move,
Because it is become thy cause of being;
Whatever error may obscure that love,
Whatever frail effect in mortal living,

Whatever passion from distemper'd heart,
What absence, time, or injuries effect,
What faithless friends or deep dissembled art
Present to feed her most unkind suspect.

Yet as the air in deep caves underground
Is strongly drawn when violent heat hath rent
Great clefts therein, till moisture do abound,
And then the same, imprison'd and up-pent,

Breaks out in earthquakes tearing all asunder,
So, in the centre of my cloven heart—
My heart, to whom her beauties were such wonder—
Lies the sharp poison'd head of that love's dart

Which, till all break and all dissolve to dust,
Thence drawn it cannot be, or therein known:
There, mixt with my heart-blood, the fretting rust
The better part hath eaten and outgrown.

But what of those or these? or what of aught
Of that which was, or that which is, to treat?
What I possess is but the same I sought:
My love was false, my labours were deceit.

Nor less than such they are esteem'd to be;
A fraud bought at the price of many woes;
A guile, whereof the profits unto me—
Could it be thought premeditate for those?

Witness those withered leaves left on the tree,
The sorrow-worren face, the pensive mind;
The external shows what may the internal be:
Cold care hath bitten both the root and rind.

But stay, my thoughts, make end: give fortune way:
Harsh is the voice of woe and sorrow's sound:
Complaints cure not, and tears do but allay
Griefs for a time, which after more abound.

To seek for moisture in the Arabian sand
Is but a loss of labour and of rest:
The links which time did break of hearty bands

Words cannot knit, or wailings make anew.
Seek not the sun in clouds when it is set. . . .
On highest mountains, where those cedars grew,
Against whose banks the troubled ocean

And were the marks to find thy hopèd port.
Into a soil far off themselves remove.
On Sestus' shore, Leander's late resort,
Hero hath left no lamp to guide her love.

Thou lookest for light in vain, and storms arise;
She sleeps thy death, that erst thy danger sithèd;
Strive then no more; bow down thy weary eyes—
Eyes which to all these woes thy heart have guided.

She is gone, she is lost, she is found, she is ever fair:
Sorrow draws weakly where love draws not too:
Woe's cries sound nothing, but only in love's ear.
Do then by dying what life cannot do.

Unfold thy flocks and leave them to the fields,
To feed on hills, or dales, where likes them best,
Of what the summer or the springtime yields;
For love, and time, hath given thee leave to rest.

Thy heart which was their fold, now in decay,
By often storms and winter's many blasts
All torn and rent, becomes misfortune's prey;
False hope, my shepherd's staff, now age hath brast.

My pipe, which love's own hand gave my desire
To sing her praises and my woe upon,
Despair hath often threatened to the fire,
As vain to keep now all the rest are gone.

Thus home I draw, as death's long night draws on;
Yet every foot, old thoughts turn back mine eyes:
Constraint me guides, as old age draws a stone
Against the hill, which over-weighty lies

For feeble arms or wasted strength to move;
My steps are backward, gazing on my loss;
My mind's affection and my soul's sole love,
Not mixt with fancy's chaff or fortune's dross,

To God I leave it, who first gave it me,
And I her gave, and she return'd again,
As it was hers; so let His mercies be
Of my last comforts the essential mean,

But be it so or not, the effects are past;
Her love hath end; my woe must ever last.

A Poem entreating of Sorrow

[Unfinished]

MY days' delights, my springtime joys fordone,
Which in the dawn and rising sun of youth
Had their creation, and were first begun,

Do in the evening and the winter sad
Present my mind, which takes my time's accompt,
The grief remaining of the joy it had.

My times that then ran o'er themselves in these,
And now run out in others' happiness,
Bring unto those new joys and new-born days.

So could she not if she were not the sun,
Which sees the birth and burial of all else,
And holds that power with which she first begun,

Leaving each withered body to be torn
By fortune, and by times tempestuous,
Which, by her virtue, once fair fruit have born;

Knowing she can renew, and can create
Green from the ground, and flowers even out of stone,
By virtue lasting over time and date,

Leaving us only woe, which, like the moss,
Having compassion of unburied bones,
Cleaves to mischance and unrepairèd loss.

For tender stalks—

[*MS ends here*]

His Petition to Queen Anne of Denmark (*1618*)

O HAD truth power, the guiltless could not fall,
Malice win glory, or revenge triumph;
But truth alone cannot encounter all.

Mercy is fled to God, which mercy made;
Compassion dead, faith turn'd to policy,
Friends know not those who sit in sorrow's shade.

For what we sometime were, we are no more:
Fortune hath changed our shape, and destiny
Defaced the very form we had before.

All love, and all desert of former times,
Malice hath covered from my sovereign's eyes,
And largely laid abroad supposèd crimes.

But kings call not to mind what vassals were,
But know them now, as envy hath described them:
So can I look on no side from despair.

Cold walls, to you I speak, but you are senseless:
Celestial Powers, you hear but have determined,
And shall determine, to the greatest happiness.

Then unto whom shall I unfold my wrong,
Cast down my tears, or hold up folded hands?
To her to whom remorse doth most belong;

To her who is the first and may alone
Be justly call'd the Empress of the Bretanes.
Who should have mercy if a Queen have none?

Save those that would have died for your defence!
Save him whose thoughts no treason ever tainted!
For lo, destruction is no recompense.

If I have sold my duty, sold my faith
To strangers, which was only due to one,
Nothing I should esteem so dear as death:

But if both God and Time shall make you know
That I your humblest vassal am opprest,
Then cast your eyes on undeservèd woe

That I and mine may never mourn the miss
Of her we had, but praise our living Queen,
Who brings us equal, if not greater, bliss.

Even such is Time

EVEN such is Time, that takes in trust
Our youth, our joys, our all we have,
And pays us but with earth and dust;
Who, in the dark and silent grave,
When we have wandered all our ways,
Shuts up the story of our days.
But from this earth, this grave, this dust,
My God shall raise me up, I trust.

Lines from Catullus

THE sun may set and rise;
But we, contrariwise,
Sleep after our short light
One everlasting night.

SIR JOHN DAVIES

1569–1626

SIR JOHN DAVIES'S reputation as a poet rests on *Orchestra* and *Nosce Teipsum*; and though the latter poem, admirable in its way as it is, could with some benefit to the reader's patience have been represented by selected passages, both are given here (*Nosce Teipsum* for the first time since 1876) in full. For the rest we content ourselves (and, it is hoped, the reader) with a selection: four (out of ten) *Sonnets to Philomel*, the ingenuous sententious *Contention betwixt a Wife, a Widow, and a Maid*, and a few of the few pieces first brought to light by Grosart. Except in spelling and punctuation our text mainly follows Grosart. Re-punctuation, here as throughout this volume, has been necessary because, especially where sixteenth-century syntax is in question, both clarity and fluency are as much impeded by the laborious and too weighty grammar-book punctuation current in the nineteenth century as by the erratic practice of the Elizabethans themselves. The poet's spelling of *reall* is retained, to remind the reader that it carries two syllables.

Dedications

[of ORCHESTRA]

I

TO HIS VERY FRIEND, MASTER RICHARD MARTIN

TO whom shall I this dancing poem send,
This sudden, rash, half-capriole of my wit?
To you, first mover and sole cause of it,
Mine-own-selve's better half, my dearest friend.
Oh would you yet my Muse some honey lend
From your mellifluous tongue, whereon doth sit
Suada in majesty, that I may fit
These harsh beginnings with a sweeter end!
You know the modest sun full fifteen times
Blushing did rise and blushing did descend
While I in making of these ill-made rimes
My golden hours unthriftily did spend:
Yet, if in friendship you these numbers praise,
I will mispend another fifteen days.

II

TO THE PRINCE

SIR, whatsoever you are pleas'd to do
It is your special praise that you are bent
And sadly set your princely mind thereto:
Which makes you in each thing so excellent.
Hence is it that you came so soon to be
A man-at-arms in every point aright;
The fairest flower of noble chivalry,
And of Saint George his band, the bravest knight.
And hence it is, that all your youthful train
In activeness and grace you do excel;
When you do courtly dancings entertain
Then Dancing's praise may be presented well
To you, whose action adds more praise thereto
Than all the Muses with their pens can do.

ORCHESTRA

or, a Poem on Dancing

WHERE lives the man that never yet did hear
Of chaste Penelope, Ulysses' queen?
Who kept her faith unspotted twenty year,
Till he return'd, that far away had been,
And many men and many towns had seen;
Ten year at siege of Troy he lingering lay,
And ten year in the midland sea did stray.

Homer, to whom the Muses did carouse
A great deep cup with heavenly nectar fill'd:
The greatest deepest cup in Jove's great house
(For Jove himself had so expressly will'd)
He drank off all, ne let one drop be spill'd;
Since when his brain, that had before been dry,
Became the wellspring of all poetry.

Homer doth tell in his abundant verse
The long laborious travels of the man,
And of his lady too he doth rehearse
How she illudes with all the art she can
The ungrateful love which other lords began;
For of her lord false fame long since had sworn
That Neptune's monsters had his carcass torn.

All this he tells, but one thing he forgot,
One thing most worthy his eternal song;
But he was old and blind and saw it not,
Or else he thought he should Ulysses wrong
To mingle it his tragic acts among;
Yet was there not, in all the world of things,
A sweeter burden for his Muse's wings.

The courtly love Antinous did make—
Antinous, that fresh and jolly knight
Which of the gallants that did undertake
To win the widow had most wealth and might,
Wit to persuade, and beauty to delight—
The courtly love he made unto the queen
Homer forgot, as if it had not been.

Sing then, Terpischore, my light Muse, sing
His gentle art and cunning courtesy!
You, lady, can remember everything,
For you are daughter of Queen Memory;
But sing a plain and easy melody,
For the soft mean that warbleth but the ground
To my rude ear doth yield the sweetest sound.

Only one night's discourse I can report:
When the great torchbearer of heaven was gone
Down in a mask unto the Ocean's court
To revel it with Tethys, all alone
Antinous, disguisèd and unknown,
Like to the spring in gaudy ornament,
Unto the castle of the princess went.

The sovereign castle of the rocky isle,
Wherein Penelope the princess lay,
Shone with a thousand lamps which did exile
The shadows dark and turn'd the night to day.
Not Jove's blue tent, what time the sunny ray
Behind the bulwark of the earth retires,
Is seen to sparkle with more twinkling fires.

That night the queen came forth from far within,
And in the presence of her court was seen;
For the sweet singer Phemius did begin
To praise the worthies that at Troy had been;
Somewhat of her Ulysses she did ween
In his grave hymn the heavenly man would sing,
Or of his wars, or of his wandering.

Pallas that hour with her sweet breath divine
Inspired immortal beauty in her eyes,
That with celestial glory she did shine
Brighter than Venus when she doth arise
Out of the waters to adorn the skies.
The wooers, all amazèd, do admire
And check their own presumptuous desire.

Only Antinous, when at first he view'd
Her star-bright eyes that with new honour shined,
Was not dismay'd, but therewithal renew'd
The noblesse and the splendour of his mind;
And as he did fit circumstances find,
Unto the throne he boldly 'gan advance,
And with fair manners woo'd the queen to dance:

'Goddess of women, sith your heavenliness
Hath now vouchsafed itself to represent
To our dim eyes, which though they see the less,
Yet are they blest in their astonishment,
Imitate heaven, whose beauties excellent
Are in continual motion day and night,
And move thereby more wonder and delight.

'Let me the mover be, to turn about
Those glorious ornaments that youth and love
Have fixèd in you, every part throughout;
Which if you will in timely measure move,
Not all those precious gems in heaven above
Shall yield a sight more pleasing to behold,
With all their turns and tracings manifold.'

With this the modest princess blusht and smiled,
Like to a clear and rosy eventide,
And softly did return this answer mild:
'Fair sir! you needs must fairly be denied,
Where your demand cannot be satisfied.
My feet, which only nature taught to go,
Did never yet the art of footing know.

'But why persuade you me to this new rage?
For all disorder and misrule is new,
For such misgovernment in former age
Our old divine forefathers never knew;
Who if they lived, and did the follies view
Which their fond nephews make their chief affairs,
Would hate themselves that had begot such heirs.'

'Sole heir of virtue and of beauty both!
Whence cometh it', Antinous replies,
'That your imperious virtue is so loth
To grant your beauty her chief exercise?
Or from what spring doth your opinion rise
That dancing is a frenzy and a rage,
First known and used in this new-fangled age?

'Dancing, bright lady, then began to be
When the first seeds whereof the world did spring,
The fire air earth and water, did agree
By Love's persuasion, nature's mighty king,
To leave their first discorded combating
And in a dance such measure to observe
As all the world their motion should preserve.

'Since when they still are carried in a round,
And changing come one in another's place;
Yet do they neither mingle nor confound,
But every one doth keep the bounded space
Wherein the dance doth bid it turn or trace.
This wondrous miracle did Love devise,
For dancing is love's proper exercise.

'Like this he framed the gods' eternal bower,
And of a shapeless and confusèd mass,
By his through-piercing and digesting power,
The turning vault of heaven formèd was,
Whose starry wheels he hath so made to pass,
As that their movings do a music frame,
And they themselves still dance unto the same.

'Or if this all, which round about we see,
As idle Morpheus some sick brains hath taught,
Of individed motes compacted be,
How was this goodly architecture wrought?
Or by what means were they together brought?
They err that say they did concur by chance;
Love made them meet in a well-ordered dance!

'As when Amphion with his charming lyre
Begot so sweet a siren of the air
That with her rhetoric made the stones conspire
The ruins of a city to repair,
A work of wit and reason's wise affair,
So Love's smooth tongue the motes such measure taught
That they joined hands, and so the world was wrought.

'How justly then is dancing termèd new
Which with the world in point of time began?
Yea, Time itself, whose birth Jove never knew,
And which is far more ancient than the sun,
Had not one moment of his age outrun
When out leaped Dancing from the heap of things
And lightly rode upon his nimble wings.

'Reason hath both their pictures in her treasure,
Where Time the measure of all moving is
And Dancing is a moving all in measure.
Now if you do resemble that to this,
And think both one, I think you think amiss;
But if you judge them twins, together got,
And Time first born, your judgment erreth not.

'Thus doth it equal age with Age enjoy
And yet in lusty youth forever flowers;
Like Love his sire, whom painters make a boy,
Yet is he eldest of the heavenly powers;
Or like his brother Time whose wingèd hours,
Going and coming, will not let him die
But still preserve him in his infancy.'

This said, the queen with her sweet lips divine
Gently began to move the subtle air,
Which gladly yielding did itself incline
To take a shape between those rubies fair,
And, being formèd, softly did repair
With twenty doublings in the empty way
Unto Antinous' ears, and thus did say:

'What eye doth see the heaven but doth admire
When it the movings of the heavens doth see?
Myself, if I to heaven may once aspire,
If that be dancing, will a dancer be;
But as for this, your frantic jollity,
How it began or whence you did it learn
I never could with reason's eye discern.'

Antinous answered: 'Jewel of the earth,
Worthy you are that heavenly dance to lead,
But, for you think our Dancing base of birth
And newly born but of a brain-sick head,
I will forthwith his antique gentry read,
And, for I love him, will his herald be,
And blaze his arms, and draw his pedigree.

'When Love had shaped this world, this great fair wight
That all wights else in this wide womb contains,
And had instructed it to dance aright
A thousand measures with a thousand strains
Which it should practise with delightful pains
Until that fatal instant should revolve
When all to nothing should again resolve,

'The comely order and proportion fair
On every side did please his wandering eye,
Till glancing through the thin transparent air
A rude disordered rout he did espy
Of men and women that most spitefully
Did one another throng and crowd so sore,
That his kind eye in pity wept therefore.

'And swifter than the lightning down he came,
Another shapeless chaos to digest:
He will begin another world to frame,
For Love, till all be well, will never rest.
Then with such words as cannot be exprest
He cuts the troops, that all asunder fling,
And ere they wist he casts them in a ring.

'Then did he rarefy the element,
And in the centre of the ring appear;
The beams that from his forehead spreading went
Begot a horror and religious fear
In all the souls that round about him were,
Which in their ears attentiveness procures,
While he with suchlike sounds their minds allures:

'"How doth Confusion's mother, headlong Chance,
Put Reason's noble squadron to the rout?
Or how should you that have the governance
Of Nature's children, heaven and earth throughout,
Prescribe them rules, and live yourselves without?
Why should your fellowship a trouble be,
Since man's chief pleasure is society?

'"If sense hath not yet taught you, learn of me
A comely moderation and discreet,
That your assemblies may well ordered be;
When my uniting power shall make you meet,
With heavenly tunes it shall be tempered sweet
And be the model of the world's great frame,
And you, earth's children, Dancing shall it name.

'"Behold the world, now it is whirlèd round!
And for it is so whirl'd, is namèd so;
In whose large volume many rules are found
Of this new art, which it doth fairly show.
For your quick eyes, in wandering to and fro
From east to west, on no one thing can glance
But, if you mark it well, it seems to dance.

'"First you see fixt in this huge mirror blue
Of trembling lights a number numberless;
Fixt they are named, but with a name untrue,
For they all move and in a dance express
The great long year that doth contain no less
Than threescore hundreds of those years in all
Which the sun makes with his course natural.

‘"What if to you these sparks disordered seem,
As if by chance they had been scattered there?
The gods a solemn measure do it deem
And see a just proportion everywhere,
And know the points whence first their movings were,
To which first points when all return again,
The axletree of heaven shall break in twain.

‘"Under that spangled sky five wandering flames,
Besides the king of day and queen of night,
Are wheel'd around, all in their sundry frames,
And all in sundry measures do delight;
Yet altogether keep no measure right;
For by itself each doth itself advance,
And by itself each doth a galliard dance.

‘"Venus, the mother of that bastard Love
Which doth usurp the world's great marshal's name,
Just with the sun her dainty feet doth move,
And unto him doth all her gestures frame;
Now after, now afore, the flattering dame
With divers cunning passages doth err,
Still him respecting [1] that respects not her.

‘"For that brave sun, the father of the day,
Doth love this earth, the mother of the night,
And like a reveller in rich array
Doth dance his galliard in his leman's sight,
Both back and forth and sideways passing light.
His gallant grace doth so the gods amaze
That all stand still and at his beauty gaze.

‘"But see the earth when she approacheth near,
How she for joy doth spring and sweetly smile;
But see again her sad and heavy cheer
When changing places he retires awhile.
But those black clouds he shortly will exile,
And make them all before his presence fly
As mists consumed before his cheerful eye.

‘"Who doth not see the measure of the moon?
Which thirteen times she danceth every year,
And ends her pavan thirteen times as soon
As doth her brother, of whose golden hair
She borroweth part and proudly doth it wear.
Then doth she coyly turn her face aside,
That half her cheek is scarce sometimes descried.

[1] See Notes

'"Next her, the pure, subtle, and cleansing fire
Is swiftly carried in a circle even,
Though Vulcan be pronounced by many a liar
The only halting god that dwells in heaven;
But that foul name may be more fitly given
To your false fire, that far from heaven is fall,
And doth consume, waste, spoil, disorder all.

'"And now behold your tender nurse, the air,
And common neighbour that aye runs around;
How many pictures and impressions fair
Within her empty regions are there found
Which to your senses dancing do propound?
For what are breath, speech, echoes, music, winds,
But dancings of the air, in sundry kinds?

'"For when you breathe the air in order moves
Now in, now out, in time and measure true,
And when you speak, so well she dancing loves
That doubling oft and oft redoubling new
With thousand forms she doth herself endue;
For all the words that from your lips repair
Are nought but tricks and turnings of the air.

'"Hence is her prattling daughter, Echo, born,
That dances to all voices she can hear.
There is no sound so harsh that she doth scorn,
Nor any time wherein she will forbear
The airy pavement with her feet to wear;
And yet her hearing sense is nothing quick,
For after time she endeth every trick.

'"And thou, sweet music, dancing's only life,
The ear's sole happiness, the air's best speech,
Lodestone of fellowship, charming rod of strife,
The soft mind's paradise, the sick mind's leech,
With thine own tongue thou trees and stones canst teach,
That when the air doth dance her finest measure
Then art thou born, the gods' and men's sweet pleasure.

'"Lastly, where keep the winds their revelry,
Their violent turnings and wild whirling hays,
But in the air's tralucent gallery
Where she herself is turn'd a hundred ways
While with those maskers wantonly she plays?
Yet in this misrule they such rule embrace
As two at once encumber not the place.

'"If then fire, air, wandering and fixèd lights,
In every province of th' imperial sky,
Yield perfect forms of dancing to your sights,
In vain I teach the ear that which the eye
With certain view already doth descry;
But for your eyes perceive not all they see,
In this I will your senses' master be.

'"For lo, the sea that fleets about the land
And like a girdle clips her solid waist
Music and measure both doth understand,
For his great crystal eye is always cast
Up to the moon and on her fixèd fast,
And as she danceth in her pallid sphere,
So danceth he about the centre here.

'"Sometimes his proud green waves in order set,
One after other, flow unto the shore;
Which when they have with many kisses wet
They ebb away in order, as before;
And to make known his courtly love the more
He oft doth lay aside his three-fork'd mace
And with his arms the timorous earth embrace.

'"Only the earth doth stand forever still:
Her rocks remove not, nor her mountains meet,
Although some wits enrich'd with learning's skill
Say heaven stands firm and that the earth doth fleet
And swiftly turneth underneath their feet;
Yet, though the earth is ever steadfast seen,
On her broad breast hath dancing ever been.

'"For those blue veins that through her body spread,
Those sapphire streams which from great hills do spring,
The earth's great dugs, for every wight is fed
With sweet fresh moisture from them issuing,
Observe a dance in their wild wandering;
And still their dance begets a murmur sweet,
And still the murmur with the dance doth meet.

'"Of all their ways, I love Meander's path,
Which, to the tunes of dying swans, doth dance
Such winding sleights.   Such turns and tricks he hath,
Such creeks, such wrenches, and such dalliance,
That, whether it be hap or heedless chance,
In his indented course and wriggling play
He seems to dance a perfect cunning hay.

'"But wherefore do these streams forever run?
To keep themselves forever sweet and clear.
For, let their everlasting course be done,
They straight corrupt and foul with mud appear.
O ye sweet nymphs, that beauty's loss do fear,
Contemn the drugs that physic doth devise
And learn of Love this dainty exercise.

'"See how those flowers, that have sweet beauty too,
The only jewels that the earth doth wear
When the young sun in bravery her doth woo,
As oft as they the whistling wind do hear
Do wave their tender bodies here and there;
And though their dance no perfect measure is,
Yet oftentimes their music makes them kiss.

'"What makes the vine about the elm to dance
With turnings, windings, and embracements round?
What makes the lodestone to the north advance
His subtle point, as if from thence he found
His chief attractive virtue to redound?
Kind nature first doth cause all things to love;
Love makes them dance, and in just order move.

'"Hark how the birds do sing, and mark then how,
Jump with the modulation of their lays,
They lightly leap and skip from bough to bough;
Yet do the cranes deserve a greater praise,
Which keep such measure in their airy ways
As when they all in order rankèd are
They make a perfect form triangular.

'"In the chief angle flies the watchful guide,
And all the followers their heads do lay
On their foregoers' backs, on either side;
But, for the captain hath no rest to stay
His head, forwearied with the windy way,
He back retires, and then the next behind
As his lieutenant leads them through the wind.

'"But why relate I every singular,
Since all the world's great fortunes and affairs
Forward and backward rapt and whirlèd are,
According to the music of the spheres;
And Chance herself her nimble feet upbears
On a round slippery wheel, that rolleth aye,
And turns all states with her impetuous sway?

'"Learn then to dance, you that are princes born,
And lawful lords of earthly creatures all;
Imitate them, and thereof take no scorn,
For this new art to them is natural.
And imitate the stars celestial;
For when pale Death your vital twist shall sever,
Your better parts must dance with them forever."

'*Thus Love persuades*, and all the crown [1] of men
That stands around doth make a murmuring,
As when the wind, loos'd from his hollow den,
Among the trees a gentle bass doth sing,
Or as a brook through pebbles wandering.
But in their looks they uttered this plain speech:
That they would learn to dance if Love would teach.

'Then first of all he doth demonstrate plain
The motions seven that are in nature found:
Upward and downward, forth and back again,
To this side and to that, and turning round:
Whereof a thousand brawls [2] he doth compound,
Which he doth teach unto the multitude,
And ever with a turn they must conclude.

'As when a nymph arising from the land
Leadeth a dance with her long watery train,
Down to the sea she wries to every hand,
And every way doth cross the fertile plain,
But when at last she falls into the main,
Then all her traverses concluded are
And with the sea her course is circular.

'Thus when at first Love had them marshallèd,
As erst he did the shapeless mass of things,
He taught them rounds and winding hays to tread,
And about trees to cast themselves in rings;
As the two Bears, whom the First Mover flings
With a short turn about heaven's axletree,
In a round dance for ever wheeling be.

'But after these, as man more civil grew,
He did more grave and solemn measures frame
With such fair order and proportion true
And correspondence every way the same
That no fault-finding eye did ever blame,
For every eye was movèd at the sight
With sober wondering and with sweet delight.

                    [1] See Notes   [2] *dances*

'Not those young students of the heavenly book,
Atlas the great, Prometheus the wise,
Which on the stars did all their lifetime look,
Could ever find such measures in the skies,
So full of change and rare varieties;
Yet all the feet whereon these measures go
Are only spondees, solemn, grave, and slow.

'But for more divers and more pleasing show,
A swift and wandering dance he did invent,
With passages uncertain, to and fro,
Yet with a certain answer and consent
To the quick music of the instrument.
Five was the number of the music's feet,
Which still the dance did with five paces meet.

'A gallant dance! that lively doth bewray
A spirit and a virtue masculine;
Impatient that her house on earth should stay,
Since she herself is fiery and divine.
Oft doth she make her body upward flyne
With lofty turns and caprioles in the air,
Which with the lusty tunes accordeth fair.

'What shall I name those current traverses,
That on a triple dactyl foot do run,
Close by the ground, with sliding passages?
Wherein that dancer greatest praise hath won,
Which with best order can all orders shun;
For everywhere he wantonly must range,
And turn, and wind, with unexpected change.

'Yet is there one, the most delightful kind,
A lofty jumping, or a leaping round,
When arm in arm two dancers are entwined,
And whirl themselves with strict embracements bound,
And still their feet an anapest do sound;
An anapest is all their music's song
Whose first two feet are short and third is long;

'As the victorious twins of Leda and Jove,
That taught the Spartans dancing on the sands
Of swift Eurotas, dance in heaven above,
Knit and united with eternal bands;
Among the stars their double image stands,
Where both are carried with an equal pace,
Together jumping in their turning race.

'This is the net wherein the sun's bright eye
Venus and Mars entangled did behold;
For in this dance their arms they so imply
As each doth seem the other to enfold.
What if lewd wits another tale have told,
Of jealous Vulcan, and of iron chains?
Yet this true sense that forgèd lie contains.

'These various forms of dancing Love did frame,
And besides these a hundred million mo,
And as he did invent he taught the same
With goodly gesture and with comely show,
Now keeping state, now humbly honouring low.
And ever for the persons and the place
He taught most fit and best according grace.

'For Love within his fertile working brain
Did then conceive those gracious virgins three
Whose civil moderation did maintain
All decent order and conveniency
And fair respect and seemly modesty;
And then he thought it fit they should be born,
That their sweet presence dancing might adorn.

'Hence is it that these Graces painted are
With hand in hand, dancing an endless round,
And with regarding eyes, that still beware
That there be no disgrace amongst them found;
With equal foot they beat the flowery ground,
Laughing or singing, as their passions will;
Yet nothing that they do becomes them ill.

'Thus Love taught men, and men thus learn'd of Love
Sweet music's sound with feet to counterfeit;
Which was long time before high-thundering Jove
Was lifted up to heaven's imperial seat;
For though by birth he were the prince of Crete,
Nor Crete nor heaven should that young prince have seen
If dancers with their timbrels had not been.

'Since when all ceremonious mysteries,
All sacred orgies and religious rites,
All pomps and triumphs and solemnities,
All funerals, nuptials, and like public sights,
All parliaments of peace. and warlike fights,
All learnèd arts, and every great affair,
A lively shape of dancing seems to bear.

'For what did he, who with his ten-tongued lute
Gave beasts and blocks an understanding ear,
Or rather into bestial minds and brutes
Shed and infused the beams of reason clear?
Doubtless for men that rude and savage were
A civil form of dancing he devised,
Wherewith unto their gods they sacrificed.

'So did Musaeus, so Amphion did,
And Linus with his sweet enchanting song,
And he whose hand the earth of monsters rid
And had men's ears fast chainèd to his tongue,
And Theseus too, his wood-born slaves among,
Used dancing as the finest policy
To plant religion and society.

'And therefore, now, the Thracian Orpheus' lyre
And Hercules himself are stellified,
And in high heaven, amidst the starry choir,
Dancing their parts, continually do slide;
So, on the zodiac, Ganymede doth ride,
And so is Hebe with the Muses nine,
For pleasing Jove with dancing, made divine.

'Wherefore was Proteus said himself to change
Into a stream, a lion, and a tree,
And many other forms fantastic strange,
As in his fickle thought he wish'd to be,
But that he danced with such facility
As like a lion he could pace with pride,
Ply like a plant, and like a river slide?

'And how was Caeneus made at first a man,
And then a woman, then a man again,
But in a dance? which when he first began,
He the man's part in measure did sustain,
But when he changed into a second strain
He danced the woman's part another space,
And then returned unto his former place.

'Hence sprang the fable of Tiresias
That he the pleasure of both sexes tried,
For in a dance he man and woman was,
By often change of place, from side to side;
But, for the woman easily did slide
And smoothly swim with cunning hidden art,
He took more pleasure in a woman's part.

'So to a fish Venus herself did change,
And swimming through the soft and yielding wave,
With gentle motions did so smoothly range
As none might see where she the water drave;
But this plain truth that falsèd fable gave,
That she did dance with sliding easiness,
Pliant and quick in wandering passages.

'And merry Bacchus practised dancing too,
And to the Lydian numbers rounds did make;
The like he did in the eastern India do,
And taught them all, when Phoebus did awake,
And when at night he did his coach forsake,
To honour heaven and heaven's great rolling eye
With turning dances and with melody.

'Thus they who first did found a commonweal,
And they who first religion did ordain,
By dancing first the people's hearts did steal;
Of whom we now a thousand tales do feign.
Yet do we now their perfect rules retain,
And use them still in such devices new
As in the world, long since their withering, grew.

'For after towns and kingdoms founded were,
Between great states arose well-ordered war,
Wherein most perfect measure doth appear;
Whether their well-set ranks respected are
In quadrant forms or semicircular,
Or else the march, when all the troops advance
And to the drum in gallant order dance.

'And after wars, when white-wing'd victory
Is with a glorious triumph beautified,
And every one doth *Io*, *Io!* cry,
While all in gold the conqueror doth ride,
The solemn pomp that fills the city wide
Observes such rank and measure everywhere
As if they all together dancing were.

'The like just order mourners do observe,
But with unlike affection and attire,
When some great man that nobly did deserve,
And whom his friends impatiently desire,
Is brought with honour to his latest fire.
The dead corpse too in that sad dance is moved,
As if both dead and living dancing loved.

'A diverse cause, but like solemnity,
Unto the temple leads the bashful bride,
Which blusheth like the Indian ivory
Which is with dip of Tyrian purple dyed;
A golden troop doth pass on every side
Of flourishing young men and virgins gay,
Which keep fair measure all the flowery way.

'And not alone the general multitude,
But those choice Nestors, which in council grave
Of cities and of kingdoms do conclude,
Most comely order in their sessions have;
Wherefore the wise Thessalians ever gave
The name of leader of their country's dance
To him that had their country's governance.

'And those great masters of the liberal arts
In all their several schools do dancing teach;
For humble grammar first doth set the parts
Of congruent and well-according speech,
Which rhetoric, whose state the clouds doth reach,
And heavenly poetry do forward lead,
And divers measures diversely do tread.

'For Rhetoric, clothing speech in rich array,
In looser numbers teacheth her to range
With twenty tropes, and turnings every way,
And various figures, and licentious change;
But poetry, with rule and order strange,
So curiously doth move each single pace,
As all is marred if she one foot misplace.

'These arts of speech the guides and marshals are,
But logic leadeth reason in a dance,
Reason, the cynosure and bright lodestar
In this world's sea, to avoid the rocks of chance;
For with close following and continuance
One reason doth another so ensue
As, in conclusion, still the dance is true.

'So music to her own sweet tunes doth trip,
With tricks of 3, 5, 8, 15, and more;
So doth the art of numbering seem to skip
From even to odd, in her proportioned score;
So do those skills, whose quick eyes do explore
The just dimension both of earth and heaven,
In all their rules observe a measure even.

'Lo! this is Dancing's true nobility,
Dancing, the child of Music and of Love;
Dancing itself, both love and harmony,
Where all agree and all in order move;
Dancing, the art that all arts do approve;
The fair character of the world's consent,
The heaven's true figure, and the earth's ornament.'

The queen, whose dainty ears had borne too long
The tedious praise of that she did despise,
Adding once more the music of the tongue
To the sweet speech of her alluring eyes,
Began to answer in such winning wise
As that forthwith Antinous' tongue was tied,
His eyes fast fixed, his ears were open wide.

'Forsooth,' quoth she, 'great glory you have won
To your trim minion, Dancing, all this while,
By blazing him Love's first begotten son,
Of every ill the hateful father vile,
That doth the world with sorceries beguile,
Cunningly mad, religiously profane,
Wit's monster, reason's canker, sense's bane.

'Love taught the mother that unkind desire
To wash her hands in her own infant's blood;
Love taught the daughter to betray her sire
Into most base unworthy servitude;
Love taught the brother to prepare such food
To feast his brothers that the all-seeing sun,
Wrapp'd in a cloud, the wicked sight did shun.

'And even this self-same Love hath dancing taught,
An art that showeth th' idea of his mind
With vainness, frenzy, and misorder fraught;
Sometimes with blood and cruelties unkind,
For in a dance Tereus' mad wife did find
Fit time and place, by murdering her son,
To avenge the wrong his traitorous sire had done.

'What mean the mermaids when they dance and sing
But certain death unto the mariner?
What tidings do the dancing dolphins bring
But that some dangerous storm approacheth near?
Then sith both Love and Dancing liveries bear
Of such ill hap, unhappy may they prove
That, sitting free, will either dance or love!'

Yet once again Antinous did reply:
'Great Queen! condemn not Love the innocent,
For this mischievous Lust, which traitorously
Usurps his name and steals his ornament;
For that true Love which dancing did invent
Is he that tuned the world's whole harmony
And linkt all men in sweet society.

'He first extracted from th' earth-mingled mind
That heavenly fire or quintessence divine
Which doth such sympathy in beauty find
As is between the elm and fruitful vine,
And so to beauty ever doth incline;
Life's life it is, and cordial to the heart,
And of our better part the better part.

'This is true Love, by that true Cupid got,
Which danceth galliards in your amorous eyes,
But to your frozen heart approacheth not;
Only your heart he dares not enterprise,
And yet through every other part he flies,
And everywhere he nimbly danceth now,
Though in yourself yourself perceive not how.

'For your sweet beauty daintily transfused
With due proportion throughout every part,
What is it but a dance where Love hath used
His finer cunning and more curious art?
Where all the elements themselves impart,
And turn, and wind, and mingle with such measure,
That the eye that sees it surfeits with the pleasure.

'Love in the twinkling of your eyelids danceth,
Love danceth in your pulses and your veins,
Love, when you sew, your needle's point advanceth,
And makes it dance a thousand curious strains
Of winding rounds, whereof the form remains,
To show that your fair hands can dance the hay,
Which your fine feet would learn as well as they.

'And when your ivory fingers touch the strings
Of any silver-sounding instrument,
Love makes them dance to those sweet murmurings
With busy skill and cunning excellent.
Oh that your feet those tunes would represent
With artificial motions to and fro,
That Love this art in every part might show!

'Yet your fair soul, which came from heaven above
To rule this house (another heaven below),
With divers powers in harmony doth move;
And all the virtues that from her do flow
In a round measure hand in hand do go;
Could I now see, as I conceive, this dance,
Wonder and love would cast me in a trance.

'The richest jewel in all the heavenly treasure
That ever yet unto the earth was shown
Is perfect concord, the only perfect pleasure
That wretched earth-born men have ever known;
For many hearts it doth compound in one,
That whatso one doth will, or speak, or do,
With one consent they all agree thereto.

'Concord's true picture shineth in this art,
Where divers men and women rankèd be,
And every one doth dance a several part,
Yet all as one in measure do agree,
Observing perfect uniformity:
All turn together, all together trace,
And all together honour and embrace.

'If they whom sacred Love hath linkt in one
Do as they dance, in all their course of life,
Never shall burning grief nor bitter moan
Nor factious difference nor unkind strife
Arise between the husband and the wife,
For whether forth, or back, or round he go,
As doth the man so must the woman do.

'What if by often interchange of place
Sometime the woman gets the upper hand?
That is but done for more delightful grace,
For on that part she doth not ever stand;
But as the measure's law doth her command
She wheels about, and ere the dance doth end
Into her former place she doth transcend.

'But not alone this correspondence meet
And uniform consent doth dancing praise,
For comeliness, the child of order sweet,
Enamels it with her eye-pleasing rays:
Fair comeliness ten hundred thousand ways
Through dancing sheds itself and makes it shine
With glorious beauty and with grace divine.

'For comeliness is a disposing fair
Of things and actions in fit time and place,
Which doth in dancing show itself most clear
When troops confused, which here and there do trace
Without distinguishment or bounded space,
By dancing rule into such ranks are brought,
As glads the eye and ravisheth the thought.

'Then why should reason judge that reasonless
Which is wit's offspring and the work of art,
Image of concord and of comeliness?
Who sees a clock moving in every part,
A sailing pinnace, or a wheeling cart,
But thinks that reason, ere it came to pass,
The first impulsive cause and mover was?

'Who sees an army all in rank advance
But deems a wise commander is in place
Which leadeth on that brave victorious dance?
Much more in dancing's art, in dancing's grace,
Blindness itself may reason's footsteps trace;
For of love's maze it is the curious plot,
And of man's fellowship the true-love knot.

'But if these eyes of yours, lodestars of love,
Showing the world's great dance to your mind's eye,
Cannot with all their demonstrations move
Kind apprehension in your fantasy
Of dancing's virtue and nobility,
How can my barbarous tongue win you thereto,
Which heaven and earth's fair speech could never do?

'O Love, my king, if all my wit and power
Have done you all the service that they can,
Oh be you present in this present hour
And help your servant and your true liegeman
End that persuasion which I erst began.
For who in praise of dancing can persuade
With such sweet force as Love, which dancing made?'

Love heard his prayer, and swifter than the wind,
Like to a page in habit, face, and speech,
He came, and stood Antinous behind,
And many secrets of his thoughts did teach.
At last a crystal mirror he did reach
Unto his hands, that he with one rash view
All forms therein by Love's revealing knew.

And, humbly honouring, gave it to the queen
With this fair speech: 'See, fairest queen,' quoth he,
'The fairest sight that ever shall be seen,
And the only wonder of posterity,
The richest work in nature's treasury;
Which she disdains to show on this world's stage,
And thinks it far too good for our rude age.

'But in another world divided far,
In the great fortunate triangled isle
Thrice twelve degrees remov'd from the north star,
She will this glorious workmanship compile,
Which she hath been conceiving all this while
Since the world's birth, and will bring forth at last
When six and twenty hundred years are past.'

Penelope the queen, when she had view'd
The strange eye-dazzling admirable sight,
Fain would have praised the state and pulchritude;
But she was stroken dumb with wonder quite.
Yet her sweet mind retain'd her thinking might;
Her ravisht mind in heavenly thoughts did dwell;
But what she thought no mortal tongue can tell.

You, lady Muse, whom Jove the counsellor
Begot of Memory, Wisdom's treasuress,
To your divining tongue is given a power
Of uttering secrets, large and limitless:
You can Penelope's strange thoughts express,
Which she conceiv'd and then would fain have told
When she the wondrous crystal did behold.

Her wingèd thoughts bore up her mind so high
As that she ween'd she saw the glorious throne
Where the bright moon doth sit in majesty.
A thousand sparkling stars about her shone,
But she herself did sparkle more alone
Than all those thousand beauties would have done
If they had been confounded all in one.

And yet she thought those stars moved in such mea
To do their sovereign honour and delight
As sooth'd her mind with sweet enchanting pleasure
Although the various change amazed her sight
And her weak judgment did entangle quite;
Beside, their moving made them shine more clear,
As diamonds moved more sparkling do appear.

This was the picture of her wondrous thought.
But who can wonder that her thought was so,
Sith Vulcan, king of fire, that mirror wrought
Which things to come, present, and past doth know,
And there did represent in lively show
Our glorious English court's divine image,
As it should be in this our golden age?

*

[Away, Terpsichore, light Muse, away!
And come, Urania, prophetess divine!
Come, Muse of heaven, my burning thirst allay:
Even now for want of sacred drink I tine.
In heavenly moisture dip this pen of mine
And let my mouth with nectar overflow,
For I must more than mortal glory show.

Oh that I had Homer's abundant vein,
I would hereof another *Ilias* make!
Or else the man of Mantua's charmèd brain,
In whose large throat great Jove the thunder spake.
Oh that I could old Geoffrey's muse awake,
Or borrow Colin's fair heroic style,
Or smooth my rhymes with Delia's servant's file!

Oh could I, sweet companion, sing like you,
Which of a shadow, under a shadow sing!
Or like fair Saluè's sad lover true,
Or like the bay, the marigold's darling,
Whose sudden verse Love covers with his wing.
Oh that your brains were mingled all with mine,
T' enlarge my wit for this great work divine!

Yet Astrophel might one for all suffice,
Whose supple Muse chameleon-like doth change
Into all forms of excellent device:
So might the swallow, whose swift muse doth range
Through rare Ideas and inventions strange,
And ever doth enjoy her joyful spring,
And sweeter than the nightingale doth sing.

Oh that I might that singing swallow hear
To whom I owe my service and my love!
His sugared tunes would so enchant mine ear,

And in my mind such sacred fury move
As I should knock at heaven's great gate above
With my proud rhymes, while of this heavenly state
I do aspire the shadow to relate.]

*

Here are wanting some stanzas describing Queen Elizabeth.
Then follow these:

Her brighter dazzling beams of majesty
Were laid aside, for she vouchsafed awhile
With gracious cheerful and familiar eye
Upon the rebels of her court to smile;
For so Time's journeys she doth oft beguile,
Like sight no mortal eye might elsewhere see,
So full of state, art, and variety.

For of her barons brave and ladies fair,
Who had they been elsewhere most fair had been,
Many an incomparable lovely pair
With hand in hand were interlinkèd seen,
Making fair honour to their sovereign Queen:
Forward they paced and did their pace apply
To a most sweet and solemn melody.

So subtile and curious was the measure,
With such unlookt-for change in every strain,
As that Penelope, rapt with sweet pleasure,
Ween'd she beheld the true proportion plain
Of her own web, weaved and unweaved again:
But that her art was somewhat less, she thought,
And on a mere ignoble subject wrought.

For here, like to the silkworm's industry,
Beauty itself out of itself did weave
So rare a work and of such subtilty
As did all eyes entangle and deceive
And in all minds a strange impression leaves
In this sweet labyrinth did Cupid stray,
And never had the power to pass away.

As, when the Indians, neighbours of the morning,
In honour of the cheerful rising sun
With pearl and painted plumes themselves adorning
A solemn stately measure have begun,
The god, well-pleas'd with that fair honour done,
Sheds forth his beams, and doth their faces kiss
With that immortal glorious face of his,

So ——

Two Poems of Dedication

[of NOSCE TEIPSUM]

I

To my most gracious dread sovereign

TO that clear majesty which in the north
Doth like another Sun in glory rise,
Which standeth fixt yet spreads her heavenly worth,
Lodestone to hearts and lodestar to all eyes:

Like heaven in all, like the earth in this alone,
That though great states by her support do stand,
Yet she herself supported is of none
But by the finger of the Almighty's hand:

To the divinest and the richest mind,
Both by art's purchase and by nature's dower,
That ever was from heaven to earth confined,
To show the utmost of a creature's power:

To that great Spirit which doth great kingdoms move,
The sacred spring whence right and honour streams,
Distilling virtue, shedding peace and love
In every place, as Cynthia sheds her beams:

I offer up some sparkles of that fire
Whereby we reason, live, and move, and be;
These sparks by nature evermore aspire,
Which makes them to so high an highness flee.

Fair Soul, since to the fairest body knit,
You give such lively life, such quickening power,
Such sweet celestial influences to it
As keeps it still in youth's immortal flower:

(As where the sun is present all the year,
And never doth retire his golden ray,
Needs must the Spring be everlasting there
And every season like the month of May.)

Oh many, many years may your remain,
A happy angel to this happy land;
Long, long may you on earth our empress reign,
Ere you in heaven a glorious angel stand.

Stay long (sweet spirit) ere thou to heaven depart,
Which mak'st each place a heaven wherein thou art.

Her Majesty s least and unworthiest subject

JOHN DAVIES.

II

[Inscribed in a manuscript gift-copy:] *To the right noble, valorous, and learned Prince Henry, Earle of Northumberland*

THE strongest and the noblest argument,
To prove the soul immortal, rests in this:
That in no mortal thing it finds content,
But seeks an object that eternal is.

If any soul hath this immortal sign
(As every soul doth show it, more or less),
It is your spirit, heroic and divine,
Which this true note most lively doth express;

For being a prince, and having princely blood,
The noblest of all Europe in your veins,
Having youth, wealth, pleasure, and every good,
Which all the world doth seek with endless pains,

Yet can you never fix your thoughts on these,
These cannot with your heavenly mind agree,
These momentary objects cannot please
Your wingèd spirit, which more aloft doth flee.

It only longs to learn and know the truth,
The truth of everything, which never dies;
The nectar which preserves the soul in youth,
The manna which doth minds immortalize.

These noble studies more ennoble you,
And bring more honour to your race and name,
Than Hotspur's fire, which did the Scots subdue,
Than Brabant's scion, or great Charles his name.

Then to what spirit shall I these notes commend
But unto that which doth them best express?
Who will to them more kind protection lend
Than He which did protect me in distress?

NOSCE TEIPSUM

OF HUMAN KNOWELDGE

WHY did my parents send me to the schools,
That I with knowledge might enrich my mind,
Since the desire to know first made men fools,
And did corrupt the root of all mankind?

For when God's hand had written in the hearts
Of the first Parents all the rules of good,
So that their skill infused did pass all arts
That ever were, before or since the Flood,

And when their reason's eye was sharp and clear,
And (as an eagle can behold the sun)
Could have approacht the Eternal Light as near
As the intellectual angels could have done:

Even then to them the Spirit of Lies suggests
That they were blind because they saw not ill,
And breathes into their incorrupted breasts
A curious wish, which did corrupt their will.

For that same ill they straight desired to know:
Which ill, being nought but a defect of good,
In all God's works the Devil could not show
While Man their lord in his perfection stood.

So that themselves were first to do the ill,
Ere they thereof the knowledge could attain,
Like him that knew not poison's power to kill,
Until (by tasting it) himself was slain.

Even so by tasting of that fruit forbid,
Where they sought knowledge they did error find:
Ill they desir'd to know, and ill they did,
And to give Passion eyes made Reason blind.

For then their minds did first in Passion see
Those wretched shapes of Misery and Woe,
Of Nakedness, of Shame, of Poverty,
Which then their own experience made them know.

But then grew Reason dark, that she no more,
Could the fair forms of Good and Truth discern:
Bats they became that eagles were before,
And this they got by their desire to learn.

But we their wretched offspring, what do we?
Do not we still taste of the fruit forbid
Whiles with fond fruitless curiosity,
In books profane we seek for knowledge hid?

What is this knowledge but the sky-stoln fire
For which the thief still chain'd in ice doth sit,
And which the poor rude Satyr did admire,
And needs would kiss but burnt his lips with it?

What is it but the cloud of empty rain
Which when Jove's guest embraced, he monsters got?
Or the false pails which, oft being fill'd with pain,
Receiv'd the water but retain'd it not?

Shortly, what is it but the fiery coach
Which the youth sought, and sought his death withal?
Or the boy's wings which, when he did approach
The sun's hot beams, did melt and let him fall?

And yet alas, when all our lamps are burn'd,
Our bodies wasted and our spirits spent,
When we have all the learnèd volumes turn'd
Which yield men's wits both help and ornament,

What can we know? or what can we discern?
When Error chokes the windows of the mind,
The divers forms of things how can we learn
That have been ever from our birthday blind?

When Reason's lamp, which like the sun in sky
Throughout Man's little world her beams did spread,
Is now become a sparkle, which doth lie
Under the ashes, half extinct and dead,

How can we hope that through the eye and ear
This dying sparkle in this cloudy place
Can re-collect these beams of knowledge clear
Which were infused in the first minds by grace?

So might the heir, whose father hath in play
Wasted a thousand pound of ancient rent,
By painful earning of a groat a day
Hope to restore the patrimony spent.

The wits that dived most deep and soar'd most high,
Seeking Man's powers, have found his weakness such:
'Skill comes so slow, and life so fast doth fly,
We learn so little and forget so much.'

For this the wisest of all mortal men
Said he knew nought but that he nought did know:
And the great mocking-master mockt not then,
When he said truth was buried deep below.

For how may we to others' things attain
When none of us his own soul understands?
For which the Devil mocks our curious brain
When 'Know thyself' his oracle commands.

For why should we the busy Soul believe
When boldly she concludes of that and this,
When of herself she can no judgment give,
Nor how, nor whence, nor where, nor what she is?

All things without, which round about we see,
We seek to know and how therewith to do;
But that whereby we reason, live, and be,
Within ourselves, we strangers are thereto.

We seek to know the moving of each sphere,
And the strange cause of the ebbs and floods of Nile;
But of that clock within our breasts we bear,
The subtle motions we forget the while.

We that acquaint ourselves with every Zone
And pass both Tropics and behold the Poles,
When we come home are to ourselves unknown,
And unacquainted still with our own Souls.

We study Speech, but others we persuade;
We leech-craft learn, but others cure with it;
We interpret laws, which other men have made,
But read not those which in our hearts are writ.

Is it because the mind is like the eye,
Through which it gathers knowledge by degrees,
Whose rays reflect not, but spread outwardly,
Not seeing itself when other things it sees?

No, doubtless; for the mind can backward cast
Upon herself her understanding light;
But she is so corrupt, and so defaced,
As her own image doth herself affright.

As in the fable of the Lady fair
Which for her lust was turn'd into a cow,
When thirsty to a stream she did repair
And saw herself transform'd (she wist not how),

At first she startles, then she stands amazed,
At last with terror she from thence doth fly;
And loathes the watery glass wherein she gazed,
And shuns it still though she for thirst do die:

Even so Man's Soul which did God's image bear,
And was at first fair, good, and spotless pure,
Since with her sins her beauties blotted were,
Doth of all sights her own sight least endure:

For even at first reflection she espies
Such strange chimeras and such monsters there;
Such toys, such antics, and such vanities,
As she retires, and shrinks for shame and fear.

And as the man loves least at home to be
That hath a sluttish house haunted with sprites,
So she, impatient her own faults to see,
Turns from herself and in strange things delights.

For this few know themselves: for merchants broke
View their estate with discontent and pain;
And seas are troubled when they do revoke
Their flowing waves into themselves again.

And while the face of outward things we find
Pleasing and fair, agreeable and sweet,
These things transport and carry out the mind,
That with herself her self can never meet.

Yet if Affliction once her wars begin,
And threat the feebler Sense with sword and fire,
The Mind contracts herself and shrinketh in,
And to herself she gladly doth retire—

As spiders, toucht, seek their webs' inmost part;
As bees in storms unto their hives return;
As blood, in danger, gathers to the heart;
As men seek towns when foes the country burn.

If aught can teach us aught, Affliction's looks,
Making us look into ourselves so near,
Teach us to know ourselves beyond all books,
Or all the learnèd Schools that ever were.

This mistress lately pluckt me by the ear,
And many a golden lesson hath me taught;
Hath made my Senses quick, and Reason clear,
Reform'd my Will and rectified my Thought.

So do the winds and thunders cleanse the air;
So working lees settle and purge the wine;
So lopt and prunèd trees do flourish fair;
So doth the fire the drossy gold refine.

Neither Minerva nor the learnèd Muse,
Nor rules of Art nor precepts of the wise,
Could in my brain those beams of skill infuse
As but the glance of this Dame's angry eyes.

So within lists my ranging mind hath brought
That now beyond myself I list not go:
Myself am centre of my circling thought,
Only myself I study, learn, and know.

I know my body's of so frail a kind
As force without, fevers within, can kill;
I know the heavenly nature of my mind,
But 'tis corrupted both in wit and will.

I know my Soul hath power to know all things,
Yet is she blind and ignorant in all;
I know I am one of Nature's little kings,
Yet to the least and vilest things am thrall.

I know my life's a pain and but a span,
I know my Sense is mockt with every thing:
And, to conclude; I know myself a MAN,
Which is a proud, and yet a wretched thing.

OF THE SOUL OF MAN AND THE IMMORTALITY THEREOF

THE lights of heaven, which are the World's fair eyes,
Look down into the World, the World to see;
And as they turn, or wander in the skies,
Survey all things that on this centre be.

And yet the lights which in my tower do shine,
Mine eyes which view all objects, nigh and far,
Look not into this little world of mine,
Nor see my face wherein they fixèd are.

Since Nature fails us in no needful thing,
Why want I means my inward self to see?
Which sight the knowledge of myself might bring
Which to true wisdom is the first degree.

That Power which gave me eyes the World to view,
To see myself infused an inward light
Whereby my Soul, as by a mirror true,
Of her own form may take a perfect sight,

But as the sharpest eye discerneth nought,
Except the sunbeams in the air do shine,
So the best Soul with her reflecting thought
Sees not herself without some light divine.

O Light which mak'st the light, which makes the day!
Which setst the eye without, and mind within!
'Lighten my spirit with one clear heavenly ray,
Which now to view itself doth first begin.

For her true form how can my spark discern
Which, dim by nature, Art did never clear,
When the great wits, of whom all skill we learn,
Are ignorant both what she is, and where?

One thinks the Soul is air, another fire,
Another blood, diffused about the heart;
Another saith, the elements conspire,
And to her essence each doth give a part.

Musicians think our Souls are harmonies,
Physicians hold that they complexions be;
Epicures make them swarms of atomies
Which do by chance into our bodies flee.

Some think one general Soul fills every brain,
As the bright sun sheds light in every star;
And others think the name of Soul is vain,
And that we only well-mixt bodies are.

In judgment of her substance thus they vary,
And thus they vary in judgment of her seat;
For some her chair up to the brain do carry,
Some thrust it down into the stomach's heat.

Some place it in the root of life, the heart;
Some in the liver, fountain of the veins;
Some say, she is all in all, and all in part;
Some say, she is not contain'd but all contains.

Thus these great clerks their little wisdom show,
While with their doctrines they at hazard play,
Tossing their light opinions to and fro,
To mock the lewd, as learn'd in this as they.

For no crazed brain could ever yet propound,
Touching the Soul, so vain and fond a thought,
But some among these masters have been found
Which in their Schools the selfsame thing have taught

God only wise, to punish pride of wit,
Among men's wits hath this confusion wrought,
As the proud tower whose points the clouds did hit
By tongues' confusion was to ruin brought.

But Thou which didst Man's soul of nothing make,
And when to nothing it was fallen agen,
'To make it new, the form of man didst take,
And, God with God, becam'st a Man with men.'

Thou that hast fashioned twice this Soul of ours,
So that she is by double title Thine,
Thou only knowest her nature and her powers,
Her subtle form Thou only canst define.

To judge herself she must herself transcend,
As greater circles comprehend the less;
But she wants power her ówn pówers to extend,
As fettered men cannot their strength express.

But Thou bright Morning Star, Thou rising Sun,
Which in these later times hast brought to light
Those mysteries that since the world begun
Lay hid in darkness and eternal night:

Thou like the sun dost with indifferent ray
Into the palace and the cottage shine,
And show'st the soul both to the clerk and lay,
By the clear lamp of Thy Oracle divine.

This Lamp through all the regions of my brain,
Where my soul sits, doth spread such beams of grace
As now, methinks, I do distinguish plain
Each subtle line of her immortal face.

What the Soul is

THE Soul a substance and a spirit is,
Which God Himself doth in the body make,
Which makes the Man: for every man from this
The nature of a Man and name doth take.

And though this spirit be to the body knit,
As an apt mean her powers to exercise,
Which are life, motion, sense, and will, and wit;
Yet she survives, although the body dies.

That the Soul is a thing subsisting by itself without the Body

SHE is a substance, and a reall thing,
Which hath itself an actual working might
Which neither from the Senses' power doth spring,
Nor from the body's humours, tempered right.

She is a vine, which doth no propping need
To make her spread herself or spring upright;
She is a star, whose beams do not proceed
From any sun, but from a native light.

For when she sorts things present with things past,
And thereby things to come doth oft foresee;
When she doth doubt at first, and choose at last,
These acts her own, without her body, be.

When of the dew, which the eye and ear do take
From flowers abroad and bring into the brain,
She doth within both wax and honey make:
This work is hers, this is her proper pain.

When she from sundry acts one skill doth draw,
Gathering from divers fights one art of war,
From many cases like, one rule of Law:
These *her* collections, not the Senses', are.

When in the effects she doth the causes know,
And seeing the stream, thinks where the spring doth rise,
And seeing the branch, conceives the root below,
These things she views without the body's eyes.

When she, without a Pegasus, doth fly
Swifter then lightning's fire from East to West,
About the Centre and above the sky,
She travels then, although the body rest.

When all her works she formeth first within,
Proportions them, and sees their perfect end
Ere she in act does any part begin,
What instruments doth then the body lend?

When without hands she thus doth castles build,
Sees without eyes, and without feet doth run;
When she digests the world, yet is not fill'd:
By her own power these miracles are done.

When she defines, argues, divides, compounds,
Considers virtue, vice, and general things,
And marrying divers principles and grounds,
Out of their match a true conclusion brings,

These actions in her closet all alone,
Retired within herself, she doth fulfill:
Use of her body's organs she hath none
When she doth use the powers of Wit and Will.

Yet in the body's prison so she lies ·
As through the body's windows she must look,
Her divers powers of sense to exercise
By gathering notes out of the World's great book.

Nor can herself discourse or judge of aught
But what the Sense collects and home doth bring;
And yet the power of her discoursing thought,
From these collections, is a diverse thing.

For though our eyes can nought but colours see,
Yet colours give them not their power of sight,
So, though these fruits of Sense her objects be,
Yet she discerns them by her proper light.

The workman on his stuff his skill doth show,
And yet the stuff gives not the man his skill;
Kings their affairs do by their servants know,
But order them by their own royal will.

So, though this cunning mistress and this queen
Doth as her instrument the Senses use,
To know all things that are felt, heard, or seen,
Yet she herself doth only judge and choose.

Even as our great wise Empress that now reigns
By sovereign title over sundry lands
Borrows in mean affairs her subjects' pains,
Sees by their eyes, and writeth by their hands,

But things of weight and consequence, indeed,
Herself doth in her chamber them debate,
Where all her counsellers she doth exceed
As far in judgment as she doth in state:

Or as the man whom she doth now advance
Upon her gracious mercy-seat to sit
Doth common things, of course and circumstance,
To the reports of common men commit,

But when the cause itself must be decreed,
Himself in person, in his proper Court,
To grave and solemn hearing doth proceed
Of every proof and every by-report:

Then like God's angel he pronounceth right,
And milk and honey from his tongue doth flow;
Happy are they that still are in his sight,
To reap the wisdom which his lips do sow:

Right so the Soul, which is a lady free,
And doth the justice of her State maintain,
Because the senses ready servants be,
Attending nigh about her Court, the brain,

By them the forms of outward things she learns,
For they return into the fantasy,
Whatever each of them abroad discerns,
And there enroll it for the Mind to see.

But when she sits to judge the good and ill,
And to discern betwixt the false and true,
She is not guided by the Senses' skill,
But doth each thing in her own mirror view.

Then she the Senses checks, which oft do err,
And even against their false reports decrees;
And oft she doth condemn what they prefer,
For with a power above the Sense, she sees.

Therefore no Sense the precious joys conceives
Which in her private contemplations be,
For then the ravish't spirit the Senses leaves,
Hath her own powers and proper actions free.

Her harmonies are sweet and full of skill
When on the Body's instrument she plays,
But the proportions of the wit and will,
Those sweet accords, are even the angels' lays.

These tunes of Reason are Amphion's lyre
Wherewith he did the Theban city found,
These are the notes wherewith the heavenly quire
The praise of Him which made the heaven doth sound.

Then her self-being nature shines in this,
That she performs her noblest works alone:
'The work the touchstone of the nature is,
And by their operations things are known.'

That the Soul is More than a Perfection or Reflection of the S

ARE they not senseless then, that think the Soul
Nought but a fine perfection of the Sense,
Or of the forms which fancy doth enroll
A quick resulting and a consequence?

What is it then that doth the Sense accuse
Both of false judgments and fond appetites?
What makes us do what Sense doth most refuse?
Which oft in torment of the Sense delights?

Sense thinks the planets spheres not much asunder;
What tells us then their distance is so far?
Sense thinks the lightning born before the thunder;
What tells us then they both together are?

When men seem crows far off upon a tower,
Sense saith they 're crows: what makes us think them men?
When we in agues think all sweet things sour,
What makes us know our tongue's false judgment then?

What power was that whereby Medea saw,
And well approv'd and prais'd, the better course,
When her rebellious Sense did so withdraw
Her feeble powers as she pursu'd the worse?

Did Sense persuade Ulysses not to hear
The mermaids' songs which so his men did please
As they were all persuaded, through the ear,
To quit the ship and leap into the seas?

Could any power of Sense the Roman move
To burn his own right hand with courage stout?
Could Sense make Marius sit unbound and prove
The cruel lancing of the knotty gout?

Doubtless in Man there is a nature found
Beside the Senses and above them far;
'Though most men being in sensual pleasures drown'd,
It seems their Souls but in their Senses are.'

If we had nought but Sense, then only they
Should have sound minds which have their Senses sound;
But Wisdom grows when Senses do decay,
And Folly most in quickest Sense is found.

If we had nought but Sense, each living wight
Which we call *brute* would be more sharp than we,
As having Sense's apprehensive might
In a more clear and excellent degree.

But they do want that quick discoursing power
Which doth in us the erring Sense correct;
Therefore the bee did suck the painted flower,
And birds, of grapes, the cunning shadow, peckt.

Sense outsides knows: the Soul through all things sees.
Sense, circumstance: she doth the substance view.
Sense sees the bark, but she the life of trees.
Sense hears the sounds, but she the concords true.

But why do I the Soul and Sense divide?
When Sense is but a power which she extends,
Which, being in divers parts diversified,
The divers forms of objects apprehends?

This power spreads outward, but the root doth grow
In the inward Soul which only doth perceive;
For the eyes and ears no more their objects know
Than glasses know what faces they receive.

For if we chance to fix our thoughts elsewhere,
Although our eyes be ope we cannot see,
And if one power did not both see and hear,
Our sights and sounds would always double be.

Then is the Soul a nature which contains
The power of Sense within a greater power,
Which doth employ and use the Senses' pains,
But sits and rules within her private bower.

That the Soul springs not from the blend of the Body's Humours

IF she doth then the subtle Sense excel,
How gross are they that drown her in the blood,
Or in the body's humours tempered well,
As if in them such high perfection stood!

As if most skill in that musician were,
Which had the best and best-tuned instrument!
As if the pencil neat and colours clear
Had power to make the painter excellent!

Why doth not beauty then refine the wit,
And good complexion rectify the will?
Why doth not health bring wisdom still with it?
Why doth not sickness make men brutish still?

Who can, in memory, or wit or will,
Or air or fire or earth or water find?
What alchemist can draw, with all his skill,
The quintessence of these out of the mind?

If the elements, which have nor life nor sense,
Can breed in us so great a power as this,
Why give they not themselves like excellence,
Or other things wherein their mixture is?

If she were but the body's quality
Then would she be with it sick, maim'd, and blind;
But we perceive, where these privations be,
A healthy, perfect, and sharp-sighted mind.

If she the body's nature did partake,
Her strength would with the body's strength decay;
But when the body's strongest sinews slake,
Then is the Soul most active, quick, and gay.

If she were but the body's accident,
And her sole being did in it subsist—
As white in snow—she might herself absent,
And in the body's substance not be miss'd.

But it on her, not she on it, depends;
For she the body doth sustain and cherish;
Such secret powers of life to it she lends
That when they fail then doth the body perish.

Since then the Soul works by herself alone,
Springs not from Sense nor humours well agreeing,
Her nature is peculiar, and her own:
She is a substance and a perfect being.

That the Soul is a Spirit

BUT though this substance be the root of Sense,
Sense knows her not, which doth but bodies know:
She is a spirit and heavenly influence
Which from the fountain of God's Spirit doth flow.

She is a Spirit, yet not like air, or wind,
Nor like the spirits about the heart or brain;
Nor like those spirits which alchemists do find
When they in everything seek gold in vain.

For she all natures under heaven doth pass,
Being like those spirits which God's bright face do see;
Or like Himself whose image once she was,
Though now (alas!) she scarce His shadow be.

Yet of the forms she holds the first degree
That are to gross material 'bodies knit,
Yet she herself is bodiless and free,
And though confined is almost infinite.

That it cannot be a Body

WERE she a body, how could she remain
Within this body, which is less than she?
Or how could she the world's great shape contain
And in our narrow breasts containèd be?

All bodies are confined within some place,
But she all place within herself confines;
All bodies have their measure and their space,
But who can draw the Soul's dimensive lines?

No *body* can at once two forms admit,
Except the one the other do deface;
But in the Soul ten thousand forms do sit,
And none intrudes into her neighbour's place.

All bodies are with other bodies fill'd,
But she receives both heaven and earth together;
Nor are their forms by rash encounter spill'd,
For there they stand, and neither toucheth either.

Nor can her wide embracements fillèd be;
For they that most and greatest things embrace
Enlarge thereby their minds' capacity,
As streams enlarged enlarge the channel's space.

All things receiv'd do such proportion take
As those things have wherein they are receiv'd:
So little glasses little faces make,
And narrow webs on narrow frames be weav'd;

Then what vast body must we make the *mind*,
Wherein are men, beasts, trees, towns, seas, and lands,
And yet each thing a proper place doth find,
And each thing in the true proportion stands?

Doubtless this could not be but that she turns
Bodies to spirits by sublimation strange,
As fire converts to fire the things it burns,
As we our meats into our nature change.

From their gross matter she abstracts the forms
And draws a kind of quintessence from things
Which to her proper nature she transforms,
To bear them light on her celestial wings:

This doth she when from things particular
She doth abstract the universal kinds
Which bodiless and immaterial are
And can be lodg'd but only in our minds:

And thus, from divers accidents and acts
Which do within her observation fall,
She goddesses and powers divine abstracts:
As Nature, Fortune, and the Virtues all.

Again, how can she several bodies know
If in herself a body's form she bear?
How can a mirror sundry faces show
If from all shapes and forms it be not clear?

Nor could we by our eyes all colours learn
Except our eyes were of all colours void,
Nor sundry tastes can any tongue discern
Which is with gross and bitter humours cloy'd.

Nor may a man of passions judge aright
Except his mind be from all passions free,
Nor can a judge his office well acquite
If he possest of either party be.

If, lastly, this quick power a body were,
Were it as swift as is the wind or fire
(Whose atomies do the one down sideways bear,
And make the other in pyramids aspire),

Her nimble body yet in time must move,
And not in instants through all places slide;
But *she* is nigh and far, beneath, above,
In point of time which thought cannot divide:

She is sent as soon to China as to Spain,
And thence returns as soon as she is sent;
She measures with one time, and with one pain,
An ell of silk and heaven's wide-spreading tent.

As then the Soul a substance hath alone,
Besides the Body in which she is confined;
So hath she not a body of her own,
But is a spirit, and immaterial mind.

That the Soul is created immediately by God

SINCE Body and Soul have such diversities,
Well might we muse how first their match began,
But that we learn that He that spread the skies
And fixt the Earth first form'd the soul in man.

This true Prometheus first made Man of earth
And shed in him a beam of heavenly fire,
Now in their mothers' wombs, before their birth,
Doth in all sons of men their souls inspire.

And as Minerva is in fables said
From Jove without a mother to proceed,
So our true Jove, without a mother's aid,
Doth daily millions of Minervas breed.

Erroneous Opinions of the Creation of Souls

THEN neither from eternity before,
Nor from the time when Time's first point begun,
Made He all souls, which now He keeps in store,
Some in the moon and others in the sun:

Nor in a secret cloister doth He keep
These virgin spirits until their marriage-day,
Nor locks them up in chambers where they sleep
Till they awake within these beds of clay:

Nor did He first a certain number make,
Infusing part in beasts, and part in men,
And, as unwilling further pains to take,
Would make no more than those He framèd then:

So that the widow Soul, her body dying,
Unto the next-born body married was,
And so, by often changing and supplying,
Men's souls to beasts and beasts' to men did pass.

(These thoughts are fond; for since the bodies born
Be more in number far than those that die,
Thousands must be abortive, and forlorn,
Ere others' deaths to them their souls supply.)

But as God's handmaid, Nature, doth create
Bodies in time distinct and order due,
So God gives souls the like successive date,
Which Himself makes, in bodies formèd new:

Which Himself makes of no material thing,
For unto angels He no power hath given
Either to form the shape or stuff to bring
From air or fire or substance of the heaven.

Nor He in this doth Nature's service use,
For though from bodies she can bodies bring,
Yet could she never souls from souls traduce,
As fire from fire, or light from light doth spring.

Objection : That the Soul is ex traduce

ALAS that some, that were great lights of old
And in their hands the lamp of God did bear,
Some reverend Fathers did this error hold,
Having their eyes dimm'd with religious fear!

For when (say they) by Rule of Faith we find
That every soul unto her body knit
Brings from the mother's womb the sin of kind,
The root of all the ill she doth commit,

How can we say that God the Soul doth make
But we must make Him author of her sin?
Then from man's soul she doth beginning take,
Since in man's soul corruption did begin.

For if God make her, first He makes her ill
(Which God forbid our thoughts should yield unto!)
Or makes the body her fair form to spill,
Which of itself it had no power to do.

Not Adam's body but his soul did sin
And so herself unto corruption brought,
But the poor soul corrupted is within
Ere she had sinn'd, either in act or thought:

And yet we see in her such powers divine,
As we could gladly think from God she came;
Fain would we make Him author of the wine,
If for the dregs we could some other blame.

The Answer to the Objection

THUS these good men with holy zeal were blind,
When on the other part the truth did shine;
Whereof we do clear demonstrations find,
By light of Nature, and by light Divine.

None are so gross as to contend for this,
That souls from bodies may traducèd be
Between whose natures no proportion is,
When root and branch in nature still agree.

But many subtle wits have justified
That souls from souls spiritually may spring:
Which, if the nature of the soul be tried,
Will even in nature prove as gross a thing.

Reasons drawn from Nature

FOR all things made are either made of nought,
Or made of stuff that ready-made doth stand:
Of nought no creature ever formèd ought,
For that is proper to the Almighty's hand.

If then the Soul another soul do make,
Because her power is kept within a bound
She must some former stuff or matter take;
But in the Soul there is no matter found.

Then if her heavenly Form do not agree
With any matter which the world contains,
Then she of nothing must created be,
And to create to God alone pertains.

Again, if souls do other souls beget,
'Tis by themselves, or by the body's power:
If by themselves, what doth their working lett,
But they might souls engender every hour?

If by the Body, how can wit and will
Join with the Body only in this act?
Sith, when they do their other works fulfill,
They from the Body do themselves abstract?

Again, if souls of souls begotten were,
Into each other they should change and move;
And change and motion still corruption bear
How shall we then the Soul immortal prove?

If, lastly, souls do generation use,
Then should they spread incorruptible seed;
What then becomes of that which they do lose
When the acts of generation do not speed?

And though the Soul could cast spiritual seed,
Yet would she not, because she never dies;
For mortal things desire their like to breed,
That so they may their kind immortalize.

Therefore the angels sons of God are nam'd,
And marry not nor are in marriage given;
Their spirits and ours are of one substance framed,
And have one Father, even the Lord of heaven,

Who would at first, that in each other thing,
The earth and water living souls should breed;
But that man's soul, whom He would make their king,
Should from Himself immediately proceed.

And when He took the woman from man's side
Doubtless Himself inspired her soul alone;
For 'tis not said He did man's soul divide,
But took flesh of his flesh, bone of his bone.

Lastly, God being made Man for man's own sake,
And being like Man in all, except in sin,
His body from the virgin's womb did take;
But all agree God form'd His soul within.

Then is the Soul from God; so Pagans say,
Which saw by Nature's light her heavenly kind;
Naming her kin to God, and God's bright ray,
A citizen of Heaven to Earth confined.

But now, I feel, they pluck me by the ear
Whom my young Muse so boldly termèd blind,
And crave more heavenly light, that cloud to clear
Which makes them think God doth not make the mind.

Reasons drawn from Divinity

GOD doubtless makes her, and doth make her good,
And graffs her in the body, there to spring;
Which, though it be corrupted, flesh and blood
Can no way to the Soul corruption bring:

And yet this Soul (made good by God at first,
And not corrupted by the body's ill)
Even in the womb is sinful, and accurst,
Ere she can judge by wit or choose by will.

Yet is not God the Author of her sin,
Though Author of her being and being there,
And, if we dare to judge our Judge herein,
He can condemn us and Himself can clear.

First, God from infinite eternity
Decreed what hath been, is, or shall be done;
And was resolv'd that every man should be,
And in his turn his race of life should run:

And so did purpose all the souls to make
That ever have been made or ever shall,
And that their being they should only take
In human bodies, or not be at all.

Was it then fit that such a weak event
(Weakness itself, the sin and fall of Man)
His counsel's execution should prevent,
Decreed and fixt before the World began?

Or that one penal law by Adam broke
Should make God break His own eternal Law,
The settled order of the World revoke,
And change all forms of things which He foresaw?

Could Eve's weak hand, extended to the tree,
In sunder rend that adamantine chain
Whose golden links effects and causes be,
And which to God's own chair doth fixt remain?

Oh could we see, how cause from cause doth spring,
How mutually they linkt and folded are,
And hear how oft one disagreeing string
The harmony doth rather make than mar,

And view at once how death by sin is brought,
And how from death a better life doth rise,
How this God's justice and His mercy taught,
We this decree would praise, as right and wise.

But we that measure times by first and last
The sight of things successively do take,
When God on all at once His view doth cast,
And of all times doth but one instant make.

All in Himself as in a glass He sees,
For from Him, by Him, through Him, all things be:
His sight is not discursive, by degrees,
But, seeing the whole, each single part doth see.

He looks on Adam as a root or well,
And on his heirs as branches and as streams;
He sees all men as one Man, though they dwell
In sundry cities and in sundry realms.

And as the root and branch are but one tree,
And well and stream do but one river make,
So, if the root and well corrupted be,
The stream and branch the same corruption take.

So, when the root and fountain of mankind
Did draw corruption, and God's curse, by sin,
This was a charge that all his heirs did bind,
And all his offspring grew corrupt therein.

And as when the hand doth strike, the Man offends
—For part from whole Law severs not, in this—
So Adam's sin to the whole kind extends,
For all their natures are but part of his.

Therefore this sin of kind, not personal,
But reall and hereditary was,
The guilt whereof, and punishment, to all
By course of Nature and of Law doth pass.

For as that easy Law was given to all,
To ancestor and heir, to first and last,
So was the first transgression general,
And all did pluck the fruit and all did taste.

Of this we find some footsteps in our Law,
Which doth her root from God and Nature take;
Ten thousand men she doth together draw,
And of them all one corporation make:

Yet these and their successors are but one,
And if they gain or lose their liberties
They harm or profit, not themselves alone,
But such as in succeeding times shall rise.

And so the ancestor and all his heirs,
Though they in number pass the stars of heaven,
Are still but one; his forfeitures are theirs,
And unto them are his advancements given.

His civil acts do bind and bar them all,
And as from Adam all corruption take,
So, if the father's crime be capital,
In all the blood Law doth corruption make.

Is it then just with us, to disinherit
The unborn nephews for the father's fault?
And to advance again for one man's merit,
A thousand heirs that have deservèd naught?

And is not God's decree as just as ours,
If He, for Adam's sin, his sons deprive
Of all those native virtues and those powers
Which He to him and to his race did give?

For what is this contagious sin of kind
But a privation of that grace within,
And of that great rich dowry of the mind
Which all had had but for the first man's sin?

If then a man on light conditions gain
A great estate, to him and his for ever,
If wilfully he forfeit it again
Who doth bemoan his heir or blame the giver?

So, though God make the Soul good, rich, and fair,
Yet when her form is to the body knit
Which makes the Man, which man is Adam's heir
Justly forthwith He takes His grace from it:

And then the Soul, being first from nothing brought,
When God's grace fails her doth to nothing fall;
And this declining proneness unto naught,
Is even that sin that we are born withal.

Yet not alone the first good qualities,
Which in the first soul were, deprivèd are:
But in their place the contrary do rise,
And reall spots of sin her beauty mar.

Nor is it strange that Adam's ill desart
Should be transferr'd unto his guilty Race,
When Christ His grace and justice doth impart
To men unjust and such as have no grace.

Lastly, the Soul were better so to be
Born slave to sin than not to be at all,
Since (if she do believe) One sets her free,
That makes her mount the higher for her fall.

Yet this the curious wits will not content;
They yet will know: sith God foresaw this ill,
Why His high Providence did not prevent
The declination of the first man's will.

If by His Word He had the current stay'd
Of Adam's will, which was by nature free,
It had been one as if His Word had said:
'I will henceforth that Man no man shall be.'

For what is Man without a moving mind
Which hath a judging wit and choosing will?
Now, if God's power should her election bind,
Her motions then would cease and stand all still

And why did God in man this soul infuse
But that he should his Maker know and love?
Now, if love be compell'd and cannot choose,
How can it grateful or thankworthy prove?

Love must free-hearted be, and voluntary,
And not enchanted, or by Fate constrain'd;
Nor like that love which did Ulysses carry
To Circe's isle, with mighty charms enchain'd.

Besides, were we unchangeable in will,
And of a wit that nothing could misdeem,
Equal to God, whose wisdom shineth still,
And never errs, we might ourselves esteem.

So that if Man would be unvariable,
He must be God, or like a rock or tree;
For even the perfect Angels were not stable,
But had a fall, more desperate than we.

Then let us praise that Power which makes us be
Men as we are, and rest contented so;
And knowing Man's fall was curiosity,
Admire God's counsels, which we cannot know.

And let us know that God the Maker is
Of all the souls in all the men that be:
Yet their corruption is no fault of His,
But the first man's that broke God's first decree.

Why the Soul is united to the Body

THIS substance, and this spirit of God's own making,
Is in the body placed, and planted here:
'That both of God, and of the world partaking,
Of all that is, Man might the image bear.'

God first made angels bodiless pure minds,
Then other things, which mindless bodies be;
Last, He made Man, the horizon 'twixt both kinds,
In whom we do the World's abridgement see.

Besides, this World below did need one wight
Which might thereof distinguish every part,
Make use thereof, and take therein delight,
And order things with industry and art:

Which also God might in His works admire,
And here, beneath, yield Him both prayer and praise,
As there, above, the holy angels' quire
Doth spread His glory with spiritual lays.

Lastly, the brute unreasonable wights
Did want a visible king on them to reign:
And God Himself thus to the World unites,
That so the World might endless bliss obtain.

In what manner the Soul is united to the Body

BUT how shall we this union well express?
Naught ties the Soul: her subtilty is such,
She moves the Body, which she doth possess,
Yet no part toucheth but by Virtue's touch.

Then dwells she not therein as in a tent,
Nor as a pilot in his ship doth sit,
Nor as the spider in her web is pent,
Nor as the wax retains the print in it,

Nor as a vessel water doth contain,
Nor as one liquor in another shed,
Nor as the heat doth in the fire remain,
Nor as a voice throughout the air is spread:

But as the fair and cheerful morning light
Doth here and there her silver beams impart,
And in an instant doth herself unite
To the transparent air, in all and part:

Still resting whole when blows the air divide,
Abiding pure when the air is most corrupted,
Throughout the air, her beams dispersing wide,
And when the air is tost, not interrupted:

So doth the piercing Soul the body fill,
Being all in all, and all in part diffused;
Indivisible, incorruptible still,
Not forced, encountered, troubled, or confused.

And as the sun above the light doth bring,
Though we behold it in the air below,
So from the Eternal Light the Soul doth spring,
Though in the body she her powers do show.

How the Soul doth exercise her Powers in the Body

BUT as the world's sun doth effects beget,
Divers, in divers places every day,
Here Autumn's temperature, there Summer's heat,
Here flowery Spring-tide, and there Winter grey:

Here Even, there Morn, here Noon, there Day, there Night;
Melts wax, dries clay, makes flowers, some quick, some dead;
Makes the Moor black and the European white,
The American tawny, and the East-Indian red—

So in our little World. This soul of ours,
Being only one, and to one body tied,
Doth use on divers objects divers powers,
And so are her effects diversified.

The Vegetative or Quickening Power

HER quick'ning power in every living par
Doth as a nurse or as a mother serve,
And doth employ her economick art
And busy care her household to preserve.

Here she attracts and there she doth retain;
There she decocts and doth the food prepare;
There she distributes it to every vein;
There she expels what she may fitly spare.

This power to Martha may comparèd be,
Which busy was, the household things to do
Or to a Dryas, living in a tree,
For even to trees this power is proper too.

And though the Soul may not this power extend
Out of the body, but still use it there,
She hath a power which she abroad doth send,
Which views and searcheth all things everywhere.

The Power of Sense

THIS power is Sense, which from abroad doth bring
The colour, taste, and touch, and scent, and sound,
The quantity and shape of every thing
Within the Earth's centre or Heaven's circle found.

This power, in parts made fit, fit objects takes,
Yet not the things but forms of things receives;
As when a seal in wax impression makes,
The print therein, but not itself, it leaves.

And, though things sensible be numberless,
But only five the Sense's organs be,
And in those five all things their forms express
Which we can touch, taste, feel, or hear, or see.

These are the windows through the which she views
The light of knowledge, which is life's loadstar:
'And yet while she these spectacles doth use,
Oft worldly things seem greater than they are.'

Sight

FIRST the two eyes, that have the seeing power,
Stand as one watchman, spy, or sentinel,
Being placed aloft within the head's high tower;
And though both see, yet both but one thing tell.

These mirrors take into their little space
The forms of moon and sun, and every star;
Of every body and of every place
Which with the World's wide arms embracèd are:

Yet their best object and their noblest use
Hereafter in another World will be,
When God in them shall heavenly light infuse,
That face to face they may their Maker see.

Here are they guides, which do the body lead
Which else would stumble in eternal night;
Here in this world they do much knowledge read,
And are the casements which admit most light:

They are her farthest-reaching instrument,
Yet they no beams unto their objects send;
But all the rays are from their objects sent,
And in the eyes with pointed angles end:

If the objects be far off the rays do meet
In a sharp point, and so things seem but small;
If they be near, their rays do spread and fleet
And make broad points, that things seem great withal.

Lastly, nine things to Sight requirèd are;
The power to see, the light, the visible thing,
Being not too small, too thin, too nigh, too far,
Clear space, and time, the form distinct to bring.

Thus we see how the Soul doth use the eyes
As instruments of her quick power of sight;
Hence do the arts optic and fair painting rise:
Painting, which doth all gentle minds delight.

Hearing

NOW let us hear how she the Ears employs:
Their office is the troubled air to take,
Which in their mazes forms a sound or noise
Whereof herself doth true distinction make.

These wickets of the Soul are placed on high
Because all sounds do lightly mount aloft;
And, that they may not pierce too violently,
They are delay'd with turns and windings oft.

For should the voice directly strike the brain,
It would astonish and confuse it much;
Therefore these plaits and folds the sound restrain,
That it the organ may more gently touch.

As streams which with their winding banks do play,
Stopt by their creeks, run softly through the plain,
So in th' Ears' labyrinth the voice doth stray,
And doth with easy motion touch the brain.

It is the slowest yet the daintiest sense;
For even the Ears of such as have no skill
Perceive a discord and conceive offence,
And, knowing not what is good, yet find the ill.

And though this sense first gentle Music found,
Her proper object is the speech of men;
But that speech chiefly which God's heralds sound
When their tongues utter what His Spirit did pen.

Our Eyes have lids, our Ears still ope we see,
Quickly to hear how every tale is provèd;
Our Eyes still move, our Ears unmovèd be,
That though we hear quick we be not quickly movèd.

Thus by the organs of the Eye and Ear
The Soul with knowledge doth herself endue:
'Thus she her prison may with pleasure bear,
Having such prospects, all the world to view.'

These conduit-pipes of knowledge feed the Mind,
But the other three attend the Body still;
For by their services the Soul doth find
What things are to the body, good or ill.

Taste

THE body's life with meats and air is fed,
Therefore the soul doth use the tasting power,
In veins which, through the tongue and palate spread,
Distinguish every relish, sweet and sour.

This is the body's nurse; but since man's wit
Found the art of cookery, to delight his sense,
More bodies are consumed and kill'd with it
Than with the sword, famine, or pestilence.

Smelling

NEXT, in the nostrils she doth use the smell:
As God the breath of life in them did give,
So makes He now this power in them to dwell,
To judge all airs whereby we breathe and live.

This sense is also mistress of an art
Which to soft people sweet perfumes doth sell,
Though this dear art doth little good impart,
'Sith they smell best that do of nothing smell.'

And yet good scents do purify the brain,
Awake the fancy and the wits refine;
Hence old devotion incense did ordain
To make men's spirits apt for thoughts divine.

Feeling

LASTLY, the feeling power, which is Life's root,
Through every living part itself doth shed,
By sinews which extend from head to foot
And like a net all o'er the body spread.

Much like a subtle spider which doth sit
In middle of her web, which spreadeth wide,
If aught do touch the utmost thread of it
She feels it instantly on every side.

By Touch the first pure qualities we learn
Which quicken all things: hot, cold, moist and dry.
By Touch, hard soft rough smooth we do discern;
By Touch, sweet pleasure and sharp pain we try.

These are the outward instruments of Sense,
These are the guards which everything must pass
Ere it approach the mind's intelligence,
Or touch the Fantasy, Wit's looking-glass.

Apprehension: Fantasy: Memory

AND yet these porters, which all things admit,
Themselves perceive not, nor discern the things;
One common power doth in the forehead sit
Which all their proper forms together brings.

For all those nerves which spirits of Sense do bear,
And to those outward organs spreading go,
United are as in a centre there,
And there this power those sundry forms doth know.

Those outward organs present things receive,
This inward Sense doth absent things retain,
Yet straight transmits all forms she doth perceive
Unto a higher region of the brain:

Where Fantasy, near handmaid to the mind,
Sits and beholds, and doth discern them all;
Compounds in one thing divers in their kind;
Compares the black and white, the great and small.

Besides, those single forms she doth esteem,
And in her balance doth their values try;
Where some things good and some things ill do seem,
And neutral some, in her fantastic eye.

This busy power is working day and night;
For when the outward senses rest do take,
A thousand dreams, fantastical and light,
With fluttering wings do keep her still awake.

Yet always all may not afore her be;
Successively, she this and that intends;
Therefore such forms as she doth cease to see,
To Memory's large volume she commends.

The ledger-book lies in the brain behind,
Like Janus' eye, which in his poll was set;
The layman's tables, storehouse of the mind,
Which doth remember much, and much forget.

Here Sense's apprehension end doth take;
As when a stone is into water cast,
One circle doth another circle make,
Till the last circle touch the bank at last.

The Passions of Sense

BUT though the apprehensive power do pause,
The motive virtue then begins to move
Which in the heart below doth Passions cause,
Joy, grief, and fear, and hope, and hate, and love.

These passions have a free commanding might,
And divers actions in our life do breed;
For all acts done without true Reason's light
Do from the passion of the Sense proceed.

But sith the brain doth lodge the powers of Sense,
How makes it in the heart those passions spring?
The mutual love, the kind intelligence
'Twixt heart and brain, this sympathy doth bring.

From the kind heat which in the heart doth reign
The spirits of life do their beginning take;
These spirits of life ascending to the brain,
When they come there, the spirits of Sense do make.

These spirits of Sense, in Fantasy's high court,
Judge of the forms of objects, ill or well;
And so they send a good or ill report
Down to the heart, where all affections dwell.

If the report be good it causeth love,
And longing hope and well-assurèd joy:
If it be ill, then doth it hatred move,
And trembling fear, and vexing grief's annoy.

Yet were these natural affections good
(For they which want them, blocks or devils be)
If Reason in her first perfection stood,
That she might Nature's passions rectify.

Besides, another motive power doth rise
Out of the heart, from whose pure blood do spring
The vital spirits which, born in arteries,
Continual motion to all parts do bring.

This makes the pulses beat, and lungs respire,
This holds the sinews like a bridle's reins;
And makes the Body to advance, retire,
To turn or stop, as she them slacks or strains.

Thus the soul tunes the body's instrument;
These harmonies she makes with life and sense;
The organs fit are by the body lent,
But the actions flow from the Soul's influence.

The Intellectual Powers of the Soul

BUT now I have a will, yet want a wit,
To express the working of the wit and will;
Which, though their root be to the body knit,
Use not the body when they use their skill.

These powers the nature of the Soul declare,
For to man's soul these only proper be;
For on the Earth no other wights there are
That have these heavenly powers, but only we.

The Wit the pupil of the Soul's clear eye,
And in man's world the only shining star,
Looks in the mirror of the Fantasy,
Where all the gatherings of the Senses are.

From thence this power the shapes of things abstracts,
And them within her passive part receives,
Which are enlightned by that part which acts,
And so the forms of single things perceives.

But after, by discoursing to and fro,
Anticipating, and comparing things,
She doth all universal natures know,
And all effects into their causes brings.

When she rates things and moves from ground to ground,
The name of Reason she obtains by this;
But when by Reason she the truth hath found
And standeth fixt, she Understanding is.

When her assent she lightly doth incline
To either part, she is Opinion light:
But when she doth by principles define
A certain truth, she hath true Judgment's sight.

And as from Senses Reason's work doth spring,
So many reasons understanding gain;
And many understandings knowledge bring;
And by much knowledge wisdom we obtain.

So, many stairs we must ascend upright
Ere we attain to Wisdom's high degree:
So doth this Earth eclipse our Reason's light,
Which else (in instants) would like angels see.

Yet hath the Soul a dowry natural,
And sparks of light some common things to see;
Not being a blank where naught is writ at all,
But what the writer will, may written be.

For Nature in man's heart her laws doth pen,
Prescribing truth to wit, and good to will,
Which do accuse, or else excuse all men,
For every thought or practice, good or ill:

And yet these sparks grow almost infinite,
Making the World and all therein their food;
As fire so spreads, as no place holdeth it,
Being nourisht still with new supplies of wood.

And though these sparks were almost quencht with sin,
Yet they whom that Just One hath justified
Have them increas'd with heavenly light within,
And like the widow's oil still multiplied.

And as this wit should goodness truly know,
We have a Will, which that true good should choose;
Though Will do oft (when wit false forms doth show)
Take ill for good, and good for ill refuse.

Will puts in practice what the Wit deviseth:
Will ever acts, and Wit contemplates still;
And as from Wit the power of wisdom riseth,
All other virtues daughters are of Will.

Will is the prince, and Wit the counsellor,
Which doth for common good in Counsel sit;
And when Wit is resolv'd, Will lends her power
To execute what is advis'd by Wit.

Wit is the mind's chief judge, which doth control
Of Fancy's court the judgments false and vain;
Will holds the royal sceptre in the soul
And on the passions of the heart doth reign.

Will is as free as any emperor;
Naught can restrain her gentle liberty;
No tyrant nor no torment hath the power
To make us will when we unwilling be.

The Intellectual Memory

TO these high powers a storehouse doth pertain,
Where they all arts and general reasons lay,
Which in the Soul even after death remain
And no Lethean flood can wash away.

This is the Soul, and these her virtues be,
Which, though they have their sundry proper ends,
And one exceeds another in degree,
Yet each on other mutually depends.

Our Wit is given Almighty God to know;
Our Will is given to love Him, being known;
But God could not be known to us below
But by His works which through the sense are shown.

And as the Wit doth reap the fruits of Sense,
So doth the quickening power the senses feed;
Thus while they do their sundry gifts dispense,
'The best, the service of the least doth need.'

Even so the King his magistrates do serve,
Yet Commons feed both magistrate and king;
The Commons' peace the magistrates preserve
By borrow'd power which from the Prince doth spring.

The quickening power would be, and so would rest;
The Sense would not be only, but be well;
But Wit's ambition longeth to be best,
For it desires in endless bliss to dwell.

And these three powers three sorts of men do make:
For some, like plants, their veins do only fill;
And some, like beasts, their senses' pleasure take;
And some, like angels, do contemplate still.

Therefore the fables turn'd some men to flowers,
And others did with brutish forms invest;
And did of others make celestial powers,
Like angels, which still travel yet still rest.

Yet these three powers are not three souls, but one,
As one and two are both contain'd in three,
Three being one number by itself alone:
A shadow of the blessed Trinity.

An Acclamation

OH what is Man, great Maker of mankind,
That Thou to him so great respect dost bear,
That Thou adornst him with so bright a mind,
Mak'st him a king, and even an angel's peer!

Oh what a lively life, what heavenly power,
What spreading virtue, what a sparkling fire!
How great, how plentiful, how rich a dower
Dost Thou within this dying flesh inspire!

Thou leav'st Thy print in other works of Thine,
But Thy whole image Thou in Man hast writ;
There cannot be a creature more divine
Except, like Thee, it should be infinit.

But it exceeds man's thought to think how high
God hath rais'd Man since God a man became:
The angels do admire this mystery,
And are astonisht when they view the same.

That the Soul is immortal, and cannot die

NOR hath He given these blessings for a day,
Nor made them on the body's life depend;
The Soul, though made in time, survives for aye,
And, though it hath beginning, sees no end.

Her only end is never-ending bliss,
Which is the eternal face of God to see
Who Last of Ends and First of Causes is:
And, to do this, she must eternal be.

How senseless then and dead a soul hath he
Which thinks his soul doth with his body die!
Or thinks not so, but so would have it be,
That he might sin with more security.

For though these light and vicious persons say
Our Soul is but a smoke or airy blast
Which during life doth in our nostrils play,
And when we die doth turn to wind at last:

Although they say 'Come let us eat and drink:
Our life is but a spark which quickly dies!'
Though thus they say, they know not what to think,
But in their minds ten thousand doubts arise.

Therefore no heretics desire to spread
Their light opinions, like these Epicures:
For so the staggering thoughts are comforted,
And other men's assent their doubt assures.

Yet though these men against their conscience strive,
There are some sparkles in their flinty breasts
Which cannot be extinct, but still revive,
That though they would, they cannot quite, be beasts.

But whoso makes a mirror of his mind,
And doth with patience view himself therein,
His Soul's eternity shall clearly find,
Though the other beauties be defaced with sin.

REASON I

Drawn from the Desire of Knowledge

FIRST in Man's mind we find an appetite
To learn and know the truth of everything,
Which is co-natural, and born with it,
And from the essence of the soul doth spring.

With this desire she hath a native might
To find out every truth, if she had time;
Th' innumerable effects to sort aright,
And by degrees from cause to cause to climb.

But—sith our life so fast away doth slide
As doth a hungry eagle through the wind,
Or as a ship transported with the tide,
Which in their passage leave no print behind:

Of which swift little time so much we spend
While some few things we through the sense do strain
That our short race of life is at an end
Ere we the principles of skill attain—

Or God (which to vain ends hath nothing done)
In vain this appetite and power hath given,
Or else our knowledge, which is here begun,
Hereafter must be perfected in heaven.

God never gave a power to one whole kind
But most part of that kind did use the same;
Most eyes have perfect sight, though some be blind;
Most legs can nimbly run, though some be lame:

But in this life no soul the truth can know
So perfectly as it hath power to do:
If then perfection be not found below,
An higher place must make her mount thereto.

REASON II

Drawn from the Motion of the Soul

AGAIN how can she but immortal be?
When with the motions of both Will and Wit
She still aspireth to eternity,
And never rests till she attain to it?

Water in conduit pipes can rise no higher
Than the well-head from whence it first doth spring:
Then sith to eternal God she doth aspire,
She cannot be but an eternal thing.

'All moving things to other things do move
Of the same kind, which shows their nature such.'
So earth falls down and fire doth mount above,
Till both their proper elements do touch.

The Soul compared to a River

And as the moisture, which the thirsty earth
Sucks from the sea to fill her empty veins,
From out her womb at last doth take a birth,
And runs a Nymph along the grassy plains:

Long doth she stay, as loth to leave the land
From whose soft side she first did issue make;
She tastes all places, turns to every hand,
Her flowery banks unwilling to forsake:

Yet Nature so her streams doth lead and carry
As that her course doth make no final stay
Till she herself into the Ocean marry,
Within whose watery bosom first she lay:

Even so the Soul which in this earthly mould
The Spirit of God doth secretly infuse,
Because at first she doth the earth behold,
And only this material world she views,

At first her mother-earth she holdeth dear,
And doth embrace the world and worldly things:
She flies close by the ground, and hovers here,
And mounts not up with her celestial wings.

Yet under heaven she cannot light on aught
That with her heavenly nature doth agree;
She cannot rest, she cannot fix her thought,
She cannot in this world contented be:

For who did ever yet, in honour, wealth,
Or pleasure of the sense, contentment find?
Who ever ceas'd to wish, when he had health?
Or having wisdom was not vext in mind?

Then as a bee which among weeds doth fall,
Which seem sweet flowers, with lustre fresh and gay,
She lights on that, and this, and tasteth all,
But pleas'd with none doth rise and soar away,

So, when the Soul finds here no true content,
And, like Noah's dove, can no sure footing take,
She doth return from whence she first was sent,
And flies to Him that first her wings did make.

Wit, seeking Truth, from cause to cause ascends,
And never rests till it the first attain:
Will, seeking Good, finds many middle ends,
But never stays till it the last do gain.

Now God the Truth and First of Causes is;
God is the Last Good End, which lasteth still;
Being Alpha and Omega named for this;
Alpha to Wit, Omega to the Will.

Sith then her heavenly kind she doth bewray,
In that to God she doth directly move
And on no mortal thing can make her stay,
She cannot be from hence, but from above.

And yet this First True Cause and Last Good End
She cannot here so well and truly see:
For this perfection she must yet attend
Till to her Maker she espousèd be.

As a king's daughter, being in person sought
Of divers princes who do neighbour near,
On none of them can fix a constant thought,
Though she to all do lend a gentle ear,

Yet she can love a foreign emperor,
Whom of great worth and power she hears to be,
If she be woo'd but by ambassador,
Or but his letters or his pictures see,

For well she knows that when she shall be brought
Into the kingdom where her spouse doth reign
Her eyes shall see what she conceiv'd in thought,
Himself, his state, his glory, and his train:

So, while the virgin Soul on earth doth stay,
She woo'd and tempted is ten thousand ways
By these great powers which on the Earth bear sway,
The wisdom of the World, wealth, pleasure, praise.

With these sometime she doth her time beguile,
These do by fits her Fantasy possess;
But she distastes them all within a while,
And in the sweetest finds a tediousness.

But if upon the World's Almighty King
She once do fix her humble loving thought,
Who by His picture, drawn in everything,
And sacred messages her love hath sought,

Of Him she thinks she cannot think too much;
This honey, tasted still, is ever sweet;
The pleasure of her ravisht thought is such
As almost here she with her bliss doth meet:

But when in heaven she shall His Essence see,
This is her sovereign good and perfect bliss:
Her longings, wishings, hopes all finisht be,
Her joys are full, her motions rest in this:

There is she crown'd with garlands of content,
There doth she manna eat, and nectar drink;
That Presence doth such high delights present
As never tongue could speak nor heart could think.

REASON III

From Contempt of Death in the Better Sort of Spirits

FOR this the better Souls do oft despise
The body's death, and do it oft desire;
For when on ground the burden'd balance lies,
The empty part is lifted up the higher:

But if the body's death the soul should kill,
Then death must needs against her nature be;
And were it so all souls would fly it still,
'For Nature hates and shuns her contrary.'

For all things else which Nature makes to be
Their being to preserve are chiefly taught,
And though some things desire a change to see,
Yet never thing did long to turn to naught.

If then by death the soul were quenchèd quite,
She could not thus against her nature run;
Since every senseless thing by Nature's light
Doth preservation seek, destruction shun.

Nor could the World's best spirits so much err
(If death took all) that they should all agree,
Before this life their honour to prefer;
For what is praise to things that nothing be?

Again, if by the body's prop she stand,
If on the body's life her life depend,
As Meleager's on the fatal brand—
The body's good she only would intend:

We should not find her half so brave and bold,
To lead it to the wars and to the seas;
To make it suffer watchings, hunger, cold,
When it might feed with plenty, rest with ease.

Doubtless all souls have a surviving thought,
Therefore of death we think with quiet mind;
But if we think of being turn'd to naught,
A trembling horror in our souls we find.

REASON IV

From the Fear of Death in the Wicked Souls

AND as the better spirit, when she doth bear
A scorn of death, doth show she cannot die,
So when the wicked soul Death's face doth fear,
Even then she proves her own eternity.

For when Death's form appears she feareth not
An utter quenching or extinguishment:
She would be glad to meet with such a lot,
That so she might all future ill prevent:

But she doth doubt what after may befall,
For Nature's law accuseth her within,
And saith, 'tis true that is affirm'd by all,
That after death there is a pain for sin.

Then she which hath been hoodwinkt from her birth
Doth first herself within Death's mirror see,
And when her body doth return to earth
She first takes care how she alone shall be.

Who ever sees these irreligious men
With burthen of a sickness weak and faint
But hears them talking of Religion then,
And vowing of their souls to every saint?

When was there ever cursèd atheist brought
Unto the gibbet but he did adore
That blessèd Power which he had set at naught,
Scorn'd and blasphemèd all his life before?

These light vain persons still are drunk and mad
With surfeitings and pleasures of their youth,
But at their deaths they are fresh, sober, sad:
Then they discern, and then they speak, the truth.

If then all souls, both good and bad, do teach
With general voice that souls can never die,
'Tis not man's flattering gloss, but Nature's speech,
Which, like God's Oracle, can never lie.

REASON V

From the General Desire of Immortality

HENCE springs that universal strong desire
Which all men have of immortality.
Not some few spirits unto this thought aspire,
But all men's minds in this united be.

Then this desire of Nature is not vain,
'She covets not impossibilities;
Fond thoughts may fall into some idle brain,
But one assent of all is ever wise.'

From hence that general care and study springs,
That launching and progression of the mind,
Which all men have so much, of future things,
That they no joy do in the present find.

From this desire that main desire proceeds
Which all men have surviving Fame to gain,
By tombs, by books, by memorable deeds:
For she that this desires doth still remain.

Hence, lastly, springs care of posterities,
For things their kind would everlasting make;
Hence is it that old men do plant young trees,
The fruit whereof another age shall take.

If we these rules unto ourselves apply,
And view them by reflection of the mind,
All these true notes of immortality
In our hearts' tables we shall written find.

From the very Doubt and Disputation of Immortality

AND though some impious wits do questions move,
And doubt if souls immortal be or no,
That doubt their immortality doth prove,
Because they seem immortal things to know.

For he which reasons on both parts doth bring,
Doth some things mortal, some immortal call;
Now, if himself were but a mortal thing,
He could not judge immortal things at all.

For when we judge, our minds we mirrors make:
And as those glasses which material be
Forms of material things do only take,
For thoughts or minds in them we cannot see,

So, when we God and angels do conceive,
And think of truth, which is eternal too,
Then do our minds immortal forms receive,
Which, if they mortal were, they could not do.

And as, if beasts conceiv'd what Reason were,
And that conception should distinctly show,
They should the name of *reasonable* bear,
For without reason, none could reason know:

So, when the Soul mounts with so high a wing
As of eternal things she doubts can move,
She proofs of her eternity doth bring,
Even when she strives the contrary to prove.

For even the thought of immortality,
Being an act done without the body's aid,
Shows that herself alone could move and be
Although the body in the grave were laid.

That the Soul cannot be destroyed

AND if herself she can so lively move,
And never need a foreign help to take,
Then must her motion everlasting prove,
'Because herself she never can forsake.'

But though corruption cannot touch the mind
By any cause that from itself may spring,
Some outward cause Fate hath perhaps design'd
Which to the Soul may utter quenching bring?

Perhaps her cause may cease and she may die?
God is her cause, His Word her maker was,
Which shall stand fixt for all eternity
When Heaven and Earth shall like a shadow pass.

Perhaps some thing repugnant to her kind
By strong antipathy the Soul may kill?
But what can be contrary to the mind,
Which holds all contraries in concord still?

She lodgeth heat, and cold, and moist, and dry,
And life, and death, and peace, and war together:
Ten thousand fighting things in her do lie,
Yet neither troubleth or disturbeth either.

Perhaps for want of food the soul may pine?
But that were strange, sith all things bad and good,
Sith all God's creatures mortal and divine,
Sith God Himself is her eternal food.

Bodies are fed with things of mortal kind,
And so are subject to mortality,
But Truth, which is eternal, feeds the mind;
The Tree of Life, which will not let her die.

Yet violence perhaps the Soul destroys,
As lightning or the sunbeams dim the sight,
Or as a thunder-clap or cannons' noise
The power of hearing doth astonish quite?

But high perfection to the Soul it brings
To encounter things most excellent and high;
For, when she views the best and greatest things
They do not hurt, but rather clear her eye,

Besides—as Homer's gods gainst armies stand—
Her subtle form can through all dangers slide;
Bodies are captive, minds endure no band,
'And Will is free, and can no force abide.'

But, lastly, Time perhaps at last hath power
To spend her lively powers and quench her light?
But old god Saturn, which doth all devour,
Doth cherish her and still augment her might.

Heaven waxeth old, and all the spheres above
Shall one day faint, and their swift motion stay:
And Time itself in time shall cease to move:
Only the Soul survives, and lives for aye.

'Our Bodies, every footstep that they make,
March towards death, until at last they die;
Whether we work, or play, or sleep, or wake,
Our life doth pass, and with Time's wings doth fly.'

But to the Soul Time doth perfection give,
And adds fresh lustre to her beauty still,
And makes her in eternal youth to live,
Like her which nectar to the gods doth fill.

The more she lives, the more she feeds on Truth:
The more she feeds, her strength doth more increase:
And what is strength but an effect of youth?
Which if Time nurse, how can it ever cease?

Objections against the Immortality of the Soul

BUT now these Epicures begin to smile,
And say my doctrine is more false than true,
And that I fondly do myself beguile,
While these receiv'd opinions I ensue.

Objection I

FOR what, say they, doth not the Soul wax old?
How comes it then that aged men do dote,
And that their brains grow sottish, dull and cold,
Which were in youth the only spirits of note?

What? are not souls within themselves corrupted?
How can there idiots then by nature be?
How is it that some wits are interrupted,
That now they dazzled are, now clearly see?

Answer

THESE questions make a subtle argument
To such as think both sense and reason one;
To whom nor agent, from the instrument,
Nor power of working, from the work, is known.

But they that know that wit can show no skill
But when she things in Sense's glass doth view
Do know, if accident this glass do spill,
It nothing sees, or sees the false for true.

For, if that region of the tender brain
Where the inward sense of Fantasy should sit
And the outward senses gatherings should retain
By Nature or by chance become unfit,

Either at first uncapable it is,
And so few things, or none at all, receives;
Or marr'd by accident, which haps amiss,
And so amiss it everything perceives.

Then, as a cunning prince that useth spies,
If they return no news doth nothing know;
But if they make advertisement of lies,
The Prince's counsel all awry do go.

Even so the Soul to such a body knit,
Whose inward senses undisposèd be,
And, to receive the forms of things, unfit,
Where nothing is brought in, can nothing see.

This makes the idiot, which hath yet a mind
Able to know the truth and choose the good
If she such figures in the brain did find,
As might be found if it in temper stood.

But if a frenzy do possess the brain,
It so disturbs and blots the forms of things
As Fantasy proves altogether vain,
And to the Wit no true relation brings.

Then doth the Wit, admitting all for true,
Build fond conclusions on those idle grounds;
Then doth it fly the good, and ill pursue,
Believing all that this false spy propounds.

But purge the humours, and the rage appease
Which this distemper in the fancy wrought,
Then shall the Wit, which never had disease,
Discourse and judge discreetly, as it ought.

So, though the clouds eclipse the sun's fair light,
Yet from his face they do not take one beam;
So have our eyes their perfect power of sight
Even when they look into a troubled stream.

Then these defects in Senses' organs be
Not in the soul or in her working might:
She cannot lose her perfect power to see,
Though mists and clouds do choke her window light.

These imperfections then we must impute
Not to the agent but the instrument:
We must not blame Apollo, but his lute,
If false accords from her false strings be sent.

The Soul in all hath one intelligence,
Though too much moisture in an infant's brain,
And too much dryness in an old man's sense,
Cannot the prints of outward things retain:

Then doth the Soul want work, and idle sit,
And this we childishness and dotage call;
Yet hath she then a quick and active Wit,
If she had stuff and tools to work withal:

For, give her organs fit and objects fair,
Give but the aged man the young man's sense,
Let but Medea Aeson's youth repair,
And straight she shows her wonted excellence.

As a good harper stricken far in years,
Into whose cunning hand the gout is fall,
All his old crotchets in his brain he bears,
But on his harp plays ill, or not at all.

But if Apollo takes his gout away,
That he his nimble fingers may apply,
Apollo's self will envy at his play,
And all the world applaud his minstrelsy.

Then dotage is no weakness of the mind,
But of the Sense; for if the mind did waste,
In all old men we should this wasting find,
When they some certain term of years had past:

But most of them, even to their dying hour,
Retain a mind more lively, quick, and strong,
And better use their understanding power,
Than when their brains were warm, and limbs were youn;

For, though the body wasted be and weak,
And though the leaden form of earth it bears,
Yet when we hear that half-dead body speak,
We oft are ravisht to the heavenly spheres.

Objection II

YET say these men: If all her organs die,
Then hath the Soul no power her powers to use;
So, in a sort, her powers extinct do lie
When unto act she cannot them reduce.

And if her powers be dead, then what is she?
For sith from everything some powers do spring,
And from those powers some acts proceeding be,
Then kill both power and act, and kill the thing.

Answer

DOUBTLESS the body's death, when once it dies,
The instruments of sense and life doth kill,
So that she cannot use those faculties,
Although their root rest in her substance still.

But (as the body living) Wit and Will
Can judge and choose without the body's aid,
Though on such objects they are working still
As through the body's organs are convey'd,

So, when the body serves her turn no more,
And all her Senses are extinct and gone,
She can discourse of what she learn'd before,
In heavenly contemplations, all alone.

So, if one man well on a lute doth play,
And have good horsemanship, and learning's skill,
Though both his lute and horse we take away,
Doth he not keep his former learning still?

He keeps it doubtless, and can use it too,
And doth both the other skills in power retain,
And can of both the proper actions do
If with his lute or horse he meet again.

So, though the instruments (by which we live
And view the world) the body's death do kill,
Yet with the body they shall all revive,
And all their wonted offices fulfill.

Objection III

BUT how, till then, shall she herself employ?
Her spies are dead which brought home news before;
What she hath got and keeps she may enjoy,
But she hath means to understand no more.

Then what do those poor souls, which nothing get?
Or what do those which get, and cannot keep?
Like buckets bottomless, which all out-let,
Those souls, for want of exercise, must sleep.

Answer

SEE how man's Soul against itself doth strive!
Why should we not have other means to know?
As children while within the womb they live
Feed by the navel: here they feed not so.

These children, if they had some use of sense,
And should by chance their mothers' talking hear
That in short time they shall come forth from thence,
Would fear their birth more than our death we fear.

They would cry out: 'If we this place shall leave,
Then shall we break our tender navel strings;
How shall we then our nourishment receive,
Sith our sweet food no other conduit brings?'

And if a man should to these babes reply
That into this fair world they shall be brought
Where they shall see the Earth, the Sea, the Sky,
The glorious Sun, and all that God hath wrought:

That there ten thousand dainties they shall meet,
Which by their mouths they shall with pleasure take,
Which shall be cordial too, as well as sweet,
And of their little limbs tall bodies make:

This would they think a fable, even as we
Do think the story of the Golden Age;
Or as some sensual spirits amongst us be,
Which hold the world to come a feignèd stage:

Yet shall these infants after find all true,
Though then thereof they nothing could conceive;
As soon as they are born the world they view,
And with their mouths the nurses' milk receive.

So, when the Soul is born (for Death is naught
But the Soul's birth, and so we should it call),
Ten thousand things she sees beyond her thought,
And in an unknown manner knows them all.

Then doth she see by spectacles no more,
She hears not by report of double spies;
Herself in instants doth all things explore,
For each thing present and before her lies.

Objection IV

BUT still this crew with questions me pursues:
If souls deceas'd (say they) still living be,
Why do they not return, to bring us news
Of that strange world where they such wonders see?

Answer

FOND men! If we believe that men do live
Under the Zenith of both frozen Polès,
Though none come thence advertisement to give,
Why bear we not the like faith of our souls?

The Soul hath here on Earth no more to do
Than we have business in our mother's womb.
What child doth covet to return thereto,
Although all children first from thence do come?

But as Noah's pigeon, which return'd no more,
Did show she footing found, for all the Flood,
So when good souls departed through Death's door
Come not again, it shows their dwelling good.

And doubtless such a soul as up doth mount,
And doth appear before her Maker's face,
Holds this vile world in such a base account
As she looks down and scorns this wretched place.

But such as are detruded down to Hell,
Either for shame they still themselves retire,
Or, tied in chains, they in close prison dwell,
And cannot come, although they much desire.

Objection V

WELL, well, say these vain spirits, though vain it is
To think our souls to Heaven or Hell do go,
Politic men have thought it not amiss
To spread this lie, to make men virtuous so.

Answer

DO you then think this moral virtue good?
I think you do, even for your private gain;
For commonwealths by virtue ever stood,
And common good the private doth contain.

If then this virtue you do love so well,
Have you no means her practice to maintain
But you this lie must to the people tell,
That good souls live in joy, and ill in pain?

Must virtue be preservèd by a lie?
Virtue and Truth do ever best agree;
By this it seems to be a verity
Sith the effects so good and virtuous be.

For, as the devil father is of lies,
So vice and mischief do his lies ensue;
Then this good doctrine did not be devise,
But made this lie which saith it is not true.

The General Consent of All

FOR how can that be false which every tongue
Of every mortal man affirms for true?
Which truth hath in all ages been so strong
As, lodestone-like, all hearts it ever drew.

For, not the Christian, or the Jew alone,
The Persian, or the Turk, acknowledge this:
This mystery to the wild Indian known,
And to the Cannibal and Tartar is.

This rich Assyrian drug grows everywhere,
As common in the North as in the East;
This doctrine does not enter by the ear,
But of itself is native in the breast.

None that acknowledge God, or Providence,
Their soul's eternity did ever doubt;
For all Religion takes her root from hence,
Which no poor naked nation lives without.

For sith the World for man created was
(For only Man the use thereof doth know),
If man do perish like a withered grass
How doth God's Wisdom order things below?

And, if that Wisdom still wise ends propound,
Why made He man of other creatures king,
When (if he perish here) there is not found
In all the world so poor and vile a thing?

If death do quench us quite we have great wrong,
Sith for our service all things else were wrought,
That daws, and trees, and rocks, should last so long,
When we must in an instant pass to naught.

But blest be that great Power that hath us blest
With longer life than heaven or earth can have,
Which hath infused into our mortal breast
Immortal powers not subject to the grave.

For though the Soul do seem her grave to bear,
And in this world is almost buried quick,
We have no cause the body's death to fear,
For when the shell is broke, out comes a chick.

Three Kinds of Life answerable to the Three Powers of the Soul

FOR as the Soul's essential powers are three
The quickening power, the power of sense and reason—
Three kinds of life to her designèd be
Which perfect these three powers in their due season.

The first life in the mother's womb is spent,
Where she her nursing power doth only use;
Where, when she finds defect of nourishment,
She expels her body, and this world she views.

This we call *birth*; but if the child could speak
He *death* would call it, and of Nature plain
That she would thrust him out naked and weak
And in his passage pinch him with such pain.

Yet, out he comes, and in this world is placed
Where all his Senses in perfection be,
Where he finds flowers to smell, and fruits to taste,
And sounds to hear and sundry forms to see.

When he hath past some time upon this stage,
His Reason then a little seems to wake,
Which, though she spring, when sense doth fade with age,
Yet can she here no perfect practice make.

Then doth the aspiring Soul the body leave:
Which we call death, but, were it known to all
What life our souls do by this death receive,
Men would it birth or jail-delivery call.

In this third life, Reason will be so bright
As that her spark will like the sunbeams shine,
And shall of God enjoy the reall sight,
Being still increast by influence divine.

An Acclamation

O IGNORANT poor man, what dost thou bear
Lockt up within the casket of thy breast?
What jewels and what riches hast thou there!
What heavenly treasure in so weak a chest!

Look in thy soul, and thou shalt beauties find
Like those which drown'd Narcissus in the flood:
Honour and Pleasure both are in thy mind,
And all that in the world is counted good.

Think of her worth, and think that God did mean
This worthy mind should worthy things embrace;
Blot not her beauties with thy thoughts unclean,
Nor her dishonour with thy passions base;

Kill not her quickening power with surfeitings,
Mar not her Sense with sensuality;
Cast not her serious wit on idle things;
Make not her free-will slave to vanity.

And when thou think'st of her eternity,
Think not that Death against her nature is:
Think it a *birth*, and, when thou goest to die,
Sing like a swan, as if thou went'st to bliss.

And if thou, like a child, didst fear before,
Being in the dark, where thou didst nothing see,
Now I have brought thee torchlight, fear no more;
Now when thou diest thou canst not hoodwinkt be.

And thou my Soul, which turn'st thy curious eye
To view the beams of thine own form divine,
Know that thou canst know nothing perfectly
While thou art clouded with this flesh of mine.

Take heed of overweening, and compare
Thy peacock's feet with thy gay peacock's train;
Study the best and highest things that are,
But of thyself an humble thought retain.

Cast down thyself, and only strive to raise
The glory of thy Maker's sacred Name;
Use all thy powers that Blessed Power to praise
Which gives thee power to be and use the same.

SONNETS AND OTHER POEMS

Sonnets to Philomel

i

OFT did I hear our eyes the passage were
By which Love entered to assail our hearts
Therefore I guarded them, and, void of fear,
Neglected the defence of other parts.
Love, knowing this, the usual way forsook,
And seeking found a byway by mine ear,
At which he, entering, my heart prisoner took
And unto thee, sweet Philomel, did bear.
Yet let my heart thy heart to pity move,
Whose pain is great, although small fault appear.
First it lies bound in fettering chains of love,
Then each day it is rackt with hope and fear,
And with love's flames 'tis evermore consumed,
Only because to live thee it presumed.

ii

SICKNESS, intending my love to betray
Before I should sight of my Dear obtain,
Did his pale colours in my face display,
Lest that my favour might her favours gain.
Yet, not content herewith, like means it wrought
My Philomel's bright beauty to deface:
And nature's glory to disgrace it sought,
That my conceivèd love it might displace.
But my firm love could this assault well bear,
Which virtue had, not beauty, for his ground.
And yet bright beams of beauty did appear,
Through sickness' veil, which made my love abound.
If sick (thought I) her beauty so excel,
How matchless would it be if she were well!

iii

ONCE did my Philomel reflect on me
Her crystal pointed eyes as I pass'd by;
Thinking not to be seen, yet would me see:
But soon my hungry eyes their food did spy.

Alas, my dear, couldst thou suppose that face
Which needs not envy Phoebus' chiefest pride
Could secret be, although in secret place,
And that transparent glass such beams could hide?
But if I had been blind, yet Love's hot flame
Kindled in my poor heart by thy bright eye
Did plainly show, when it so near thee came,
By more than usual heat the cause was nigh.
So, though thou hidden wert, my heart and eye
Did turn to thee by mutual sympathy.

iv

IF you would know the love which I you bear,
Compare it to the Ring which your fair hand
Shall make more precious when you shall it wear:
So my love's nature you shall understand.
Is it of metal pure? so you shall prove
My love, which ne'er disloyal thought did stain.
Hath it no end? so endless is my love,
Unless you it destroy with your disdain.
Doth it the purer wax the more 'tis tried?
So doth my love: yet herein they dissent,
That whereas gold, the more 'tis purified,
By waxing less doth show some part is spent,
My love doth wax more pure by your more trying,
And yet increaseth in the purifying.

On a Pair of Garters

GO, loving woodbine, clip with lovely grace
Those two sweet plants which bear the flowers of love;
Go, silken vines, those tender elms embrace
Which flourish still although their roots do move.
As soon as you possess your blessed places
You are advancèd and ennobled more
Than diadems, which were white silken laces
That ancient kings about their forehead wore.
Sweet bands, take heed lest you ungently bind,
Or with your strictness make too deep a print:
Was never tree had such a tender rind,
Although her inward heart be hard as flint.
And let your knots be fast and loose at will:
She must be free, though I stand bounden still.

The Muse Reviving

LIKE as the divers-fretchled Butterfly,
When winter's frost is fall'n upon his wing,
Hath only left life's possibility,
And lies half dead until the cheerful Spring:

But then the Sun from his all-quick'ning eye
Darts forth a sparkle of the living fire
Which with kind heat doth warm the frozen fly
And with new spirit his little breast inspire:

Then doth he lightly rise and spread his wings
And with the beams that gave him life doth play:
Tastes every flower that on the earth's bosom springs,
And is in busy motion all the day:

So my gay Muse, which did my heart possess,
And in my youthful fantasy doth reign,
Which clear'd my forehead with her cheerfulness
And gave a lively warmth unto my brain,

With sadder study, and with grave conceit
Which late my imagination entertain'd,
Began to shrink and lose her active heat,
And dead as in a lethargy remain'd.

Long in that senseless sleep congeal'd she lay,
Until even now another heavenly eye,
And clear as that which doth beget the day,
And of a like reviving sympathy,

Did cast into my eyes a subtle beam
Which piercing deep into my fancy went,
And did awake my Muse out of her dream,
And unto her new life and virtue lent:

So that she now begins to raise her eyes,
Which yet are dazzled with her beauty's ray,
And to record her wonted melodies:
Although at first she be not full so gay.

To his Lady

IN this sweet book, the treasury of wit,
All virtues, beauties, passions, written be:
And with such life they are set forth in it
As still methinks that which I read I see.
But this book's mistress is a living book
Which hath indeed those virtues in her mind,
And in whose face, though envy's self do look,
Even envy's eye shall all those beauties find.
Only the passions that are printed here
In her calm thoughts can no impression make:
She will not love, nor hate, nor hope, nor fear,
Though others seek these passions for her sake.
So in the sun, some say, there is no heat,
Though his reflecting beams do fire beget.

A Contention betwixt a Wife, a Widow, and a Maid

Wife.   Widow, well met; whither go you today?
Will you not to this solemn offering go?
You know it is Astraea's holy day,
The Saint to whom all hearts devotion owe.

Widow.   Marry, what else? I purpos'd so to do:
Do you not mark how all the wives are fine,
And how they have sent presents ready too,
To make their offering at Astraea's shrine?

See, then, the shrine and tapers burning bright.
Come, friend, and let us first ourselves advance.
We know our place, and if we have our right,
To all the parish we must lead the dance.

But soft, what means this bold presumptuous maid
To go before without respect of us?
Your forwardness (proud girl) must now be stay'd.
Where learn'd you to neglect your betters thus?

Maid.   Elder you are, but not my betters here,
This place to maids a privilege must give:
The Goddess, being a maid, holds maidens dear,
And grants to them her own prerogative.

Besides, on all true virgins, at their birth,
Nature hath set a crown of excellence,
That all the wives and widows of the earth
Should give them place and do them reverence?

Wife. If to be born a maid be such a grace,
So was I born and graced by nature too,
But seeking more perfection to embrace
I did become a wife, as others do.

Widow. And if the maid and wife such honour have,
I have been both, and hold a third degree.
Most maids are wards, and every wife a slave,
I have my livery sued and I am free.

Maid. That is the fault, that you have maidens been
And were not constant to continue so:
The falls of angels did increase their sin,
In that they did so pure a state forgo.

But Wife and Widow, if your wits can make
Your state and persons of more worth than mine,
Advantage to this place I will not take;
I will both place and privilege resign.

Wife. Why marriage is an honourable state.
Widow. And widowhood is a reverend degree.
Maid. But maidenhead, that will admit no mate,
Like majesty itself must sacred be.

Wife. The wife is mistress of her family.
Widow. Much more the widow, for she rules alone.
Maid. But mistress of mine own desires am I,
When you rule others' wills and not your own.

Wife. Only the wife enjoys the virtuous pleasure.
Widow. The widow can abstain from pleasures known.
Maid. But the uncorrupted maid preserves such measure
As being by pleasures wooed she cares for none.

Wife. The wife is like a fair supported vine.
Widow. So was the widow, but now stands alone:
For being grown strong, she needs not to incline.
Maid. Maids, like the earth, supported are of none.

Wife. The wife is as a diamond richly set.
Maid. The maid unset doth yet more rich appear.
Widow. The widow a jewel in the cabinet,
Which though not worn is still esteem'd as dear.

Wife. The wife doth love, and is belov'd again.
Widow. The widow is awaked out of that dream.
Maid. The maid's white mind had never such a stain:
No passion troubles her clear virtue's stream.

Yet if I would be loved, loved would I be,
Like her whose virtue in the bay is seen:
Love to wife fadeth with satiety,
Where love never enjoy'd is ever green.

Widow. Then what's a virgin but a fruitless bay?
Maid. And what's a widow but a roseless briar?
And what are wives, but woodbines which decay
The stately oaks by which themselves aspire?

And what is marriage but a tedious yoke?
Widow. And what virginity but sweet self-love?
Wife. And what's a widow but an axle broke,
Whose one part failing, neither part can move?

Widow. Wives are as birds in golden cages kept.
Wife. Yet in those cages cheerfully they sing.
Widow. Widows are birds out of these cages leapt,
Whose joyful notes make all the forest ring.

Maid. But maids are birds amidst the woods secure,
Which never hand could touch, nor net could take,
Nor whistle could deceive, nor bait allure,
But free unto themselves do music make.

Wife. The wife is as the turtle with her mate.
Widow. The widow as the widow dove alone,
Whose truth shines most in her forsaken state.
Maid. The maid a phoenix, and is still but one.

Wife. The wife's a soul unto her body tied.
Widow. The widow a soul departed into bliss.
Maid. The maid an angel which was stellified,
And now to as fair a house descended is.

Wife.   Wives are fair houses kept and furnisht well.
Widow. Widows old castles, void but full of state.
Maid.   But maids are temples where the gods do dwell,
         To whom alone themselves they dedicate.

         But marriage is a prison during life,
         Where one way out, but many entries be.
Wife.   The nun is kept in cloister, not the wife:
         Wedlock alone doth make the virgin free.

Maid.   The maid is ever fresh, like morn in May.
Wife.   The wife with all her beams is beautified
         Like to high noon, the glory of the day.
Widow. The widow, like a mild sweet eventide.

Wife.   An office well supplied is like the wife.
Widow. The widow, like a gainful office void.
Maid.   But maids are like contentment in this life,
         Which all the world have sought, but none enjoy'd.

         Go, wife, to Dunmow, and demand your flitch.
Widow. Go, gentle maid, go lead the apes in hell.
Wife.   Go, widow, make some younger brother rich,
         And then take thought and die, and all is well.

         Alas, poor maid, that hast no help nor stay!
Widow. Alas, poor wife, that nothing dost possess!
Maid.   Alas, poor widow! (charity doth say)
         Pity the widow and the fatherless!

Widow. But happy widows have the world at will.
Wife.   But happier wives, whose joys are ever double.
Maid.   But happiest maids whose hearts are calm and still,
         Whom fear, nor hope, nor love, nor hate doth trouble.

Wife.   Every true wife hath an indented heart,
         Wherein the covenants of love are writ,
         Whereof her husband keeps the counterpart,
         And reads his comforts and his joys in it.

Widow. But every widow's heart is like a book,
         Where her joys past imprinted do remain;
         But when her judgment's eye therein doth look,
         She doth not wish they were to come again.

Maid.   But the maid's heart a fair white table is,
           Spotless and pure, where no impressions be
           But the immortal characters of bliss,
           Which only God doth write and angels see.

Wife.   But wives have children; what a joy is this!
Widow. Widows have children too, but maids have none.
Maid.   No more have angels, yet they have more bliss
           Than ever yet to mortal man was known.

Wife.   The wife is like a fair manurèd field.
Widow. The widow once was such, but now doth rest.
Maid.   The maid, like Paradise, undrest, untill'd,
           Bears crops of native virtue in her breast.

Wife.   Who would not die a wife, as Lucrece died?
Widow. Or live a widow, as Penelope?
Maid.   Or be a maid, and so be stellified,
           As all the virtues and the graces be.

Wife.   Wives are warm climates well inhabited,
           But maids are frozen zones where none may dwell.
Maid.   But fairest people in the north are bred,
           Where Africa breeds monsters black as hell.

Wife.   I have my husband's honour and his place.
Widow. My husband's fortunes all survive to me.
Maid.   The moon doth borrow light, you borrow grace,
           When maids by their own virtues gracèd be.

           White is my colour, and no hue but this
           It will receive, no tincture can it stain.
Wife.   My white hath took one colour, but it is
           My honourable purple dyed in grain.

Widow. But it hath been my fortune to renew
           My colour twice from that it was before.
           But now my black will take no other hue,
           And therefore now I mean to change no more.

Wife.   Wives are fair apples serv'd in golden dishes.
Widow. Widows good wine, which time makes better much.
Maid.   But maids are grapes desired by many wishes,
           But that they grow so high as none can touch.

Wife. I have a daughter equals you, my girl.
Maid. The daughter doth excel the mother then,
As pearls are better than the mother of pearl.
Maids lose their value when they match with men.

Widow. The man with whom I matcht, his worth was such
As now I scorn a maid should be my peer.
Maid. But I will scorn the man you praise so much,
For maids are matchless, and no mate can bear.

Hence is it that the virgin never loves,
Because her like she finds not anywhere;
For likeness evermore affection moves;
Therefore the maid hath neither love nor peer.

Wife. Yet many virgins married wives would be.
Widow. And many a wife would be a widow fain.
Maid. There is no widow but desires to see,
If so she might, her maiden days again.

Widow. There never was a wife that liked her lot.
Wife. Nor widow but was clad in mourning weeds.
Maid. Do what you will, marry, or marry not,
Both this estate and that, repentance breeds.

Wife. But she that this estate and that hath seen,
Doth find great odds between the wife and girl.
Maid. Indeed she doth, as much as is between
The melting hailstone and the solid pearl.

Wife. If I were widow, my merry days were past.
Widow. Nay, then you first become sweet pleasure's guest.
For maidenhead is a continual fast,
And marriage is a continual feast.

Maid. Wedlock indeed hath oft comparèd bin
To public feasts, where meet a public rout;
Where they that are without would fain go in,
And they that are within would fain go out.

Or to the jewel which this virtue had,
That men were mad till they might it obtain,
But when they had it, they were twice as mad,
Till they were dispossest of it again.

Wife.   Maids cannot judge, because they cannot tell,
      What comforts and what joys in marriage be.
Maid.   Yes, yes, though blessed saints in heaven do dwell
      They do the souls in purgatory see.

Widow.   If every wife do live in purgatory,
      Then sure it is, that widows live in bliss,
      And are translated to a state of glory.
      But maids as yet have not attain'd to this.

Maid.   Not maids?   To spotless maids this gift is given,
      To live in incorruption from their birth.
      And what is that but to inherit heaven
      Even while they dwell upon the spotted earth?

      The perfectest of all created things,
      The purest gold that suffers no allay;
      The sweetest flower that on the earth's bosom springs;
      The pearl unbored, whose price no price can pay;

      The crystal glass that will no venom hold;
      The mirror wherein angels love to look;
      Diana's bathing fountain clear and cold;
      Beauty's fresh rose, and virtue's living book;

      Of love and fortune both, the mistress born;
      The sovereign spirit that will be thrall to none;
      The spotless garment that was never worn;
      The princely eagle that still flies alone.

      She sees the world, yet her clear thought doth take
      No such deep print as to be changed thereby;
      As when we see the burning fire doth make
      No such impression as doth burn the eye.

Wife.   No more, sweet maid, our strife is at an end;
      Cease now, I fear we shall transformèd be
      To chattering pies, as they that did contend
      To match the Muses in their harmony.

Widow.   Then let us yield the honour and the place,
      And let us both be suitors to the maid,
      That since the goddess gives her special grace,
      By her clear hands the offering be convey'd.

Maid.   Your speech I doubt hath some displeasure moved,
          Yet let me have the offering, I will see;
          I know she hath both wives and widows loved,
          Though she would neither wife nor widow be.

*Contention between Four Maids concerning that which addeth most
                        Perfection to that Sex*

THE FIRST FOR BEAUTY

OUR fairest garland, made of Beauty's flowers,
Doth of itself supply all other dowers.
Women excel the perfect'st men in this,
And therefore herein their perfection is.
For beauty we the glorious heavens admire;
Fair fields, fair houses, gold and pearl, desire.
Beauty doth always health and youth employ
And doth delight the noblest sense, the eye.

THE SECOND FOR WIT

Beauty delights the soul, but wit the reason:
Wit lasts an age, and beauty but a season.
The sense is quickly cloy'd with beauty's taste,
When wit's delight still quick and fresh doth last
Beauty weak eyes with her illusion blinds:
Wit conquers spirits and triumphs over minds.
Dead things have beauty, only man hath wit,
And man's perfection doth consist in it.

THE THIRD FOR WEALTH

Wealth is a power that passeth nature far,
Makes every goose a swan, and spark a star.
Queen Money brings and gives with royal hands
Friends, kindred, honour, husband, house and lands.
Not a fair face, but fortune fair, I crave:
Let me want wit so I fools' fortune have.

THE FOURTH FOR VIRTUE

Yet those perfections most imperfect be
If there be wanting virtuous modesty.
Virtue's aspect would have the sweetest grace
If we could see as we conceive her face.
Virtue guides wit with well-affected will,
Which if wit want, it proves a dangerous ill.
Virtue gains wealth with her good government:
If not, she 's rich because she is content.

GLOSSARY

accoll: embrace [the neck]

babery: grotesque ornamentation
bateful: full of strife
blast: blare forth
blive: quickly
bolne: swollen
bourd: jest
brawl: a dance
brenning: burning
Bullen: Boulogne

carefull: full of care [sorrow]
chase: chose
chere, cheer: countenance, behaviour
clive: cliff
corse: body
cure: care

dere: hurt, injury
despoiled: stripped [for the game]
dooms: judgments
do way: cease, give over
drencheth: drowns
dribb'd shot: shot falling short or wide

eft: again, often

favel: duplicity
feres: mates, companions
fet: fetch
fine: end
flyne: fly
fremd: unfriendly

gait: way
geason: rare, scarce
gests: exploits
gin: engine
girasol: sunflower
gledes: hot coals
glimsing: glimmering

glome: look gloomily
grame: sorrow

halse: embrace
hay: country dance
hent: seized, taken
hire: desert [reward or punishment]

incontinent: immediately

keels: kayles, ninepins or skittles
kest: cast
kind: nature

laied neck: *colla subjecta*
Laundersey: Landrecy
lese: lose
lett: hinder, prevent
levening: lightning
livelood: livelihood
lopen: leapt

make: mate
micher: truant
Muttral: Montreuil

narre: nearer

overthwartes: cross-currents [of fortune]

palme-play: tennis
peason: peas
percase: perhaps
persant: piercing
pight: pitched
preve: prove

rakel: rash, reckless
rathe: soon, early
raught: reached
rebell: rebellion
rede: counsel

415

seeled: blinded
shene: bright
shope: shaped
sith: since
soote: sweet
stale: bait
sterve: starve
stithe: stithy
strait: *v.* tighten, *adj.* narrow

targe: target, shield
than: then
tho: then
tickle: uncertain
tine: perish
to year: this year
trains: snares, wiles

ugsome: frightful
unegal: unequal
unnethe: hardly
unwroken: unrevenged

Ver: Spring
vild: vile

waltring: wallowing
wanhope: despair
wanton: playful
whereas: where
whist: become silent
wonning-place: dwelling-place
woode: mad, furious
woxe: waxed
wry (to): to turn aside

NOTES

WYATT. Sonnets I, II, and V are adapted from Petrarch. Sonnet VI is traced by Miss Foxwell to Serafino's *Lasso oimè*. Epigram V was written during Wyatt's imprisonment (on a false charge) in the early months of 1541. It is addressed to his friend Sir Francis Brian, who was in favour at Court. The Rondeau, *Help me to seek*, uses an old theme, which others were to use again: e.g. Michael Drayton (1563–1631). Page 93: *private*, deprived of. Page 98: *at a point*, resolved. The Satires, their metre borrowed (and adapted) from Alamanni, provide the earliest examples of *terza rima* in English. The First Satire is largely a translation. *An Epitaph of Sir Thomas Gravener*: Miss Foxwell aptly remarks that Wyatt's estimate of his friend might well be applied to the poet himself.

SURREY. Several of Surrey's sonnets are adapted from Petrarch. Page 138, sixth line from foot: *death*, emendation of *breath*, which must be a transcriber's error. *The Happy Life* is translated from Martial. *A Satire on London*: Surrey had been in trouble for behaving riotously in the streets at night, with two other young men. *Translation from Virgil*: The eighteenth line is virtually the same as Gawin Douglas's "The Grekis chiftanis irkit of the were'. It is one of many borrowings. It was presumably Douglas's example, too, that betrayed Surrey into mistranslating *amor* as delight (instead of as desire or longing) in the fourteenth line: *But since so great is thy delight to hear*. The Latin runs: *sed si tantus amor casus cognoscere nostros*. Aeneas would hardly wish to imply that Dido took 'delight' in hearing of Troy's fall. Page 159: *common trade*, thoroughfare (*pervius usus*).

SIDNEY. *Astrophel and Stella*. Sonnets XXIV, XXXV, XXXVII: Stella, by her marriage, had become Lady Rich. LXXXIII: Philip was a traditional name for the sparrow. Skelton (died 1529) had so used it in his *Boke of Phyllyp Sparowe*. Third line: according to O.E.D. 'to keep one's cut' means to keep one's distance, be reserved. So also in Skelton.

Page 232: I retain the early spelling of *barly-brake*, because it seems improbable that this old English game has any connexion with barley. The origin of the name is obscure.

Page 252: *Another Version*. From Puttenham's *Arte of English Poesie*, 1589.

Page 272: *The Nightingale*: 'To the tune of *Non credo già che più infelice amante*.'

Page 274: *O fair, O sweet:* 'To the tune of *Se tu señora no dueles de mi.*'

Page 276: *Who hath his fancy pleasèd:* 'To the tune of *Wilhemus van Nassaw.*'

Page 277: *No, no, no, no:* 'To the tune of a Neapolitan song which beginneth *No, no, no, no.*'

Page 278: Misled by a pious imagination, Grosart regards these two sonnets as ending, and crowning with contrition, the *Astrophel and Stella* sequence. There is no warrant for such an idea.
Leave me, O love which reachest but to dust. This new reading of a famous line first appeared in the present editor's *The English Galaxy of Shorter Poems* (1933). All previous editions have: 'Leave me, O Love, which reachest but to dust.' By omitting the comma after 'love', and spelling that word with a small initial letter, we make 'which reachest but to dust' a defining clause, and point the contrast—which is the whole burden of the poem—between the earthly love the poet is repudiating in the first line and the Eternal Love to which he aspires in the last.

RALEGH. *Epitaph on Sir Philip Sidney:* Attributed to Ralegh by Sir John Harington in 1591, and afterwards by Drummond of Hawthornden. It appears anonymously in the Elizabethan anthology *The Phoenix Nest*, 1593, and with Spenser's *Astrophel* elegy in 1595. *The Wood, the Weed, the Wag:* Given in the Malone MS under title 'Sir Walter Ralegh to his Son'. *The Pilgrimage:* Said, in one MS, to be 'verses made by Sir W. R. the night before he was beheaded'. This may or may not be true. Possibly the poem was written, in expectation of death, during the interval between his sentence and the last-minute reprieve. Sentence of death was carried out many years afterwards. *The Ocean's Love to Cynthia:* With all its confusion, obscurity, and manifest lack of finish, this strange poem has Ralegh's own quality. Whether it was written with the idea of melting the Queen's heart, or merely as a private distraction, is a matter for conjecture.

DAVIES.
Page 326: *respecting,* looking at (L. *specere*, to look).

Page 329: *jump,* exactly. Cf. Hamlet I (i): 'Thus twice before, and jump at this dead hour.'

Page 330: *crown.* Dr Tillyard, in his edition (1945) of this poem, notes: 'Grosart and E. K. Chambers wrongly emend to *crowd*. Love has got his audience in a ring. Davies knew that the Latin *corona* often means a collection of men.'

Page 341: The five stanzas enclosed between square brackets appeared in the first edition (1596) but were omitted in the second (1622). *Geoffrey* is Chaucer; *Colin*, Spenser; *Delia's servant*, Samuel Daniel, whose sonnets are addressed to Delia. *Salve's* remains unexplained.

Page 358: The cross-heading, mid-page, is a translation into modern terms of: *That the Soul is more than the Temperature of the Humours of the Body.* The mediaeval 'humours'—four in number—were liquid substances supposed to exist in the human body: blood, phlegm, choler, and black bile. Each played its part in determining mood, disposition, and temperament: hence sanguine, phlegmatic, choleric, and melancholy.

Page 359: *the body's accident.* In mediaeval philosophy, *accident*, as opposed to *substance*, means a contingent attribute of a thing, not part of its essential nature.

Page 363: *Tradux* is properly a vine-branch 'layered' or trained to the ground for propagation. Hence *ex traduce*, of the belief that the soul is begotten as the flesh is. Cf. *Faery Queen* IV, iii, 13, where the 'weary ghost' of Priamond 'through traduction was eftsoones derived . . . Into his other brethren that survived.' This note is kindly contributed by Mr Charles Lee, of the Temple Press, whose vigilance nothing escapes.

Page 376: The cross-heading *Apprehension* is here substituted for: *The Imagination or Common Sense*, terms which do not, in Elizabethan usage, mean what we usually mean by them to-day.

Page 405: *Astraea :* Queen Elizabeth.

INDEX TO FIRST LINES